D0592986

This is Neil Chayet

Looking at the Law

Everything that ever could have been said
has been said—but since no one was listening,
it all has to be said again.

Neil Chayet's
Looking at the Law

Illustrations by Bill Nilsen

THE RUTLEDGE PRESS

New York, New York

A FRIENDLY WARNING

This book is based on the premise that the law is a living and changing entity. Justice Holmes once said that the law is a "seamless web," and as true and reassuring as this is, it must be realized that any given piece of the fabric can be altered or overruled by subsequent legislative or judicial action. The cases that have become the stories in this book are no exception, and the reader should exercise great caution before assuming that any of the following represents the present law. There is a listing of case citations at the back of the book, and accuracy has been strived for to the utmost extent. Nevertheless, we strongly advise that before relying on any of the following materials to guide your behavior, you contact a lawyer in your own state and ask him or her for advice.

Copyright © 1981 by The Rutledge Press

All rights reserved. No part of this book may be reproduced or transmitted in any form or by any means, electronic or mechanical, including photocopying, recording or by any information retrieval system, without permission in writing from the Publisher.

"Looking at the Law" is a registered trademark of Neil Chayet. All scripts © copyright Neil Chayet.

Published by The Rutledge Press, A Division of W.H. Smith Publishers Inc., 112 Madison Avenue, New York, New York 10016

First Printing 1981. Printed in the United States of America.

Library of Congress Cataloging in Publication Data
Chayet, Neil L.
Looking at the law.
Includes index.
1. Law—United States. I. Title.
KF385.A4C47   349.73   81-1024
                    347.3   AACR2
ISBN 0-8317-5623-3

CONTENTS

To my wife, Martha, who helped me get it all together—at last.

ACKNOWLEDGMENTS

Looking at *Looking at the Law,* it is hard to believe that it has all happened, and it would never have, but for many people with whom I have worked through the years and who have become my friends and colleagues along the way. First, my thanks to all at WEEI in Boston and throughout CBS who inspired me, taught me, and above all told me that I could do it and helped me do it well. These include Les Woodruff, now of CBS in Washington, who planted the seed; Mike Ludlam, former News Director at WEEI, who encouraged me; Lou Adler of WCBS in New York, who taught me that briefer *is* better; Mike Wheeler, my first editor, and Nance Guilmartin, my first research assistant; and Gene Lothery, Vice President and General Manager of WEEI, who watches over it all and was always there when it counted. And there are the people who every week make it happen: Mel Miller, News Director at WEEI; Neil Ungerleider, Assistant News Director, who calmly listens to every word; Technical Supervisor Charles "Buddy" Giordana; and all the other techs who perform big and little miracles every day. And I would like to especially thank Ann Hathaway, who week after week for more than five years has produced, directed, and suffered through it all —but always with dignity, grace, and patience.

I would also like to thank Anna Mae Sokusky and Joe Durso, Jr., of CBS in Washington who encouraged me from the very beginning and who, week after week, edit and process "Looking at the Law" and see to it that it reaches the millions of listeners around the country. Their high standards and careful attention are very much appreciated.

But "Looking at the Law" might never have appeared in print if it weren't for John Sammis of The Rutledge Press, whose middle-of-the-night perambulation resulted in the telephone call that launched this project just one year ago. And my special thanks go to my editor, Jay Hyams, whose quiet perseverance, thoroughness, and style come through on every page.

I would also like to thank all the judges who have written the opinions in the cases that form much of the substance of this book. Judges are under siege nowadays, and we often forget the day-after-day effort they put into very difficult decisions. I would also like to thank the legislators and administrators who write the laws and regulations and the many unsung heroes of the law, such as court clerks, reporters of decisions, and all those who make sure the word gets out.

My thanks also to all those people whose stories these are, people from all walks of life, whose lives have become part of the law. Some have won, some have lost, some have come out even, but all have been part of the story.

Lastly, I would like to thank my wife, Martha, to whom this book is dedicated, who listened, looked, and encouraged, all along the way.

INTRODUCTION

This is a book of real-life short stories. For the most part they are stories of ordinary people who, for one reason or another, have met the law. "Looking at the Law" began more than five years ago when Les Woodruff of WEEI/CBS in Boston suggested that I prepare a radio feature on the law. My reply was, "What's a feature?" and his answer was, "Two minutes on the air—start to finish." I decided that two minutes a week wasn't all that difficult; you can imagine my surprise at learning that what he meant was two minutes every single day, five days a week, fifty-two weeks a year. My initial reaction was that nobody could prepare and broadcast two minutes every single day on any subject, least of all the law. But my friends at WEEI persisted, and "Looking at the Law" began.

The first thing I noticed was how much faster the weeks went by—it would seem that I had just taped a series of five when suddenly the next week was upon me. I take my hat off to the working press, for few know of the constant deadlines and the incessant demands of the people, who just flick a dial or pick up a paper and find us there, day after day.

My biggest fear was that I would quickly run out of material. I had forgotten that there are so many sources spewing out the law. In fact, I soon didn't have any more room to store the hundreds of cases, statutes, rules, and regulations that found their way to me from every corner of the country and, indeed, from around the globe.

In fact, it appears that as a nation we are drowning in laws, rules, and regulations, and after telling nearly 1,500 stories (more than 400 of which appear in the following pages) one cannot but wonder if it is all worth it and whether the law is achieving its objective. Sometimes it seems that the more laws we have, the less order and justice we achieve. One cannot help but be struck by the inverse result of so many laws that seek one result but achieve another, making things worse instead of better.

Most books about the law are put together based on the kind of law they deal with, i.e., contracts, torts (wrongs), and the like, and in many the sheer weight of the jargon quickly wears you down. (My wife, Martha, is convinced that law school is nothing more than a cleverly disguised school of foreign language.) And far too often the law is boring, confusing, or both—instead of coming alive and reflecting the human behavior that brought the case about. The stories in this book are not organized by the kind of law they represent but, rather, by the kind of people they are about: a wife who has walked out on her husband, a criminal who has gone free because the police have erred, an unwanted child beaten by his mother's boy friend, or any number of other human situations that somehow end up in conflict and sooner or later (mostly later) are resolved. At the root of the law lie the common everyday experiences of 230 million people, and just as their stories go on and on without end, so does the law that governs our behavior and by which we live.

There is, however, something very disturbing about the stories that follow—there aren't many happy endings. The question of why this is so is a complicated one and at the root of it is the question of just what is the task or role of the law and whether the law is doing its job. When I was at law school and for a short while thereafter, I thought that I was entering a profession that always aspired to the search for truth. As the years have passed, I have come to the reluctant conclusion that, alas, there may be no truth and that much of life, particularly as reflected in the court room, is the account of differing recollections. I have found remarkably little perjury in my years as a lawyer; rather, most people are able to convince themselves that the recollection that aids their case the most is, in fact, the truth. Well, even if the search for truth has fallen short, at least, I once thought, we lawyers end dispute. One case in which I am involved (the question of whether oral hypoglycemic drugs for diabetes do or do not increase the risk of heart disease) is entering its thirteenth year, and many cases of even the most ordinary sort consume more than five years before they are ended. One cannot help but ask, if we cannot seek truth, and if we do not end dispute with dispatch, what then do we do?

Perhaps a more productive question is what is the purpose of the law and what should we who control the law be doing to improve the lot of the law and the people it represents. It seems to me that the law should exist to protect people's basic and fundamental rights and to end dispute in a fair and just manner with a minimum of delay. The law must also hold out, and deliver, to all, the opportunity to seek and obtain a just result at the bar of justice. And, most important, the law should be the means by which a society tells right from wrong and strives to do that which is right. And we who create, practice, and judge the law should make sure, each in our own way, that the law achieves its true objectives.

There is little question that, while the vast majority of lawyers, legislators, and judges struggle to achieve these ends, the system in which they function has become more and more encumbered and mired in delay, frustration, and uncertainty. This has led to deep dissatisfaction at every level. Far too often it appears that there are no winners at all, and the only question is who has lost more. Many have used these difficulties as fodder to demean the profession of law and those who practice it, and, indeed, former President Jimmy Carter reserved some of his bitterest venom for lawyers and the law. And yet, as the law, like many of our institutions, is under siege, we might ask the question: When we tear down the law and these institutions and reduce them to rubble, what will be left other than rubble? Perhaps instead we might realize that the law, like the people and their stories that comprise it, is fallible and in need of all our help; if we work together to make the law more accessible, more understandable, and demand of it a high standard of fairness and performance, perhaps together we can once again make it a system of which we can be proud.

It was written in 1779 that we are a government of laws and not of men; it is doubtful that this was ever true, and it is certainly not true today. We are a government of men and women, and it is the interpretation and implementation of the law by men and women that really counts.

With all the laws, rules, and regulations that may be put on the books, they will stand for naught if we do not have people of humanity, integrity, and competence to interpret, implement, and enforce them. And it may be that as we have placed our emphasis on court decisions, legislative acts, and administrative regulations, we have forgotten the most important source of the law—the individual and his innate desire to do that which is right.

As a profession, we may well have to reexamine the very basis of the adversary system, with its emphasis on the killer instinct, and the belief that out of the presentation of two disparate stories the best result will always be forged. We will also have to reexamine, in this age of rapid technological development, the relationship of law and science, and, perhaps most important, the relationship of law and morality, and review once again the meaning of right and wrong, justice and injustice, and the relationship of the law to these basic concepts.

And perhaps we can then look, in law and in life, to a better tomorrow, and to real-life short stories with happier endings, just, in time.

1

IN THE FIRST PERSON:

Speaking for myself, I

I don't like to use the word "I" very much, but its use seems unavoidable in this first chapter, for the things that are reported here have happened to, or around, me. This chapter should be very reassuring to those who think that things always happen only to them, and it is dedicated to all those people who thought they were the only ones—and weren't.

All around all of us, every day, things are happening that involve us with some aspect of the law. And they have happened to me, too. The following pages deal with my own personal mugging, my being told that I could not take a hamburger out of an airport restaurant, because it's "against the law," and the rather frightening result of my insatiable desire to ask taxi drivers about their most exciting experience.

I have found life—and the law—to be filled with humanity, humility, and humor. And a good healthy look and—on occasion —laugh at ourselves as we travel through life is essential.

Many of the stories in this chapter and throughout the book may seem rather strange, and at first blush you might think they could never happen to anybody else and that the person involved was the first person—and the last person—to run into such a situation. Quite often, however, no matter how strange the story, I will be told repeatedly, "That's just what happened to me." While we are all very different as individuals, so are we very much the same, and perhaps we would do well to remember that "there but for the grace of God go I," and sometimes, despite God's grace, we do go there after all.

Protecting the unborn

One of the most difficult situations that I ever faced as a lawyer began with a call from the clerk of the Supreme Judicial Court of Massachusetts, asking if I would accept an appointment as guardian for an unborn fetus. At first, I couldn't believe the request, but it was true. A woman had entered a hospital in Western Massachusetts, and her husband, from whom she had been separated, had gone to court and secured a temporary restraining order preventing the abortion.

His claims were most interesting. He said that since he was now separated, this might be his last opportunity to have a child in lawful wedlock. He also asked that a guardian be named to speak for the right to life of the fetus.

I reluctantly accepted the appointment and adjourned to the law library in an attempt to define my responsibilities. What I found was somewhat disturbing to one who has just been named guardian of a fetus. I found that according to the law, I did not have a client. What I represented was rather an interest called the "potential of developing human life," something which regardless of its potential for being had no legal or constitutional rights. The Supreme Court case of *Roe* v. *Wade* held that this interest of potential life is outweighed by the constitutional right of privacy that a woman has, and that the state cannot by law interfere with the decision of her and her physician if she wishes to have an abortion. This right outweighs the interest even during the second trimester, but in this context the state can pass laws relating to maternal health and safety and closely regulate the circumstances under which the abortion is performed. It is not until the last trimester of pregnancy that the state can pass laws giving supremacy to the interest of developing human life, due to the viability and advanced stage of development of the fetus.

One might wonder how a conservative Supreme Court came up with a decision that was so pleasing to so many liberals. The reason is that the concepts in the *Roe* case are based on a fundamental precept of conservative thinking—the right to be left alone and free from the interference of the state except when there is a compelling reason for that interference. I was so concerned about the legal aspects of the situation that I even invited a colleague to enter the case who believed that the law as stated by the Supreme Court was wrong and that constitutional rights should attach to the fetus from the moment of conception. He was permitted by the court to share my time in oral argument and to file a brief statement before the court.

The case was argued and the abortion was allowed, but somehow the issue of abortion will never be the same for me again.

Getting mugged

It was about 1:00 in the morning and misty as I walked across the parking lot in Boston's South End. I had a camera slung over my shoulder and a bright yellow rain slicker on, and I felt danger in the air. As I approached my apartment, I heard footsteps along the pavement and knew instinctively that those footsteps were headed for me. I started to run, and the footsteps started to run too. I got to the apartment, took out my keys, and in the darkness started to unlock the first of three locks that had always made me feel so secure when I was on the other side of them.

I got one open, and then the second—I heard the footsteps stop, and I could hear breathing. Then I felt it coming. I moved slightly left and took the blow on my shoulder rather than the back of my head. As I waited for the next one, I realized I had to do something. I decided I would turn around and face him, and if I was going to get it, I might as well watch. He looked surprised that I was no longer crouching in the doorway. I yelled at him as loud as I could, and the combination of turning and yelling threw him just enough off balance so that when I pushed him, he fell backward down the stairs.

I finished unlocking the third lock, walked in, slammed the door, and dialed 911. Only then did I realize I was shaking.

The police arrived in about ten minutes; first they chastised me for walking across a parking lot in a bright yellow slicker at 1:00 in the morning. Then they said that if they got the mugger, chances were that nothing would happen to him. Finally, they said he was probably sick or on drugs anyway. Well, let me tell you how I feel about this. Why shouldn't I be able to walk anywhere I want to day or night? And why is it true that the mugger is often out of jail before his victim is out of the hospital? And as far as being sick is concerned, since when does sickness mean a license to beat and rob?

I learned a lot that night. I learned that the police couldn't prevent it before it happened and couldn't do much about it afterward. I learned that once a mugging is underway, your best weapon is surprise. And I learned firsthand that our cities have become jungles and that those of us who refuse to become prisoners in our own homes have got to be able to do something about it.

The trials of the good citizen

A few weeks ago I was standing at the window of my office looking out on a deserted street. I had been working late, and it was 2:00 A.M. I saw three young men, obviously intoxicated, staggering across the street, each holding a can of beer. They were talking loudly, enjoying themselves, and looking for something to do before going home. Then I heard one of them say, "Let's get that Mercedes." As I watched transfixed, they approached a Mercedes parked below me and with surprising rapidity that showed great experience, they ripped off the hood emblem, doused the car with beer, and bounced the half-empty cans off the roof.

I decided that as a law-abiding citizen, I would call the police. My motives were many. First, I realized that it was acts like this that were driving insurance rates through the roof, since vandalism is not deductible; second, I felt that since I talk about the law all the time, all of you out there would expect me to take some action; and third, I figured there but for the grace of God went *my* Mercedes!

So I dialed 911, figuring that by the time my call was answered and responded to, the perpetrators would be long gone. Not so, to my amazement. Within three minutes, while the culprits decided to polish off another beer for the road in their own car, a uniformed foot patrolman was on the scene. I went over to the uniformed man and told him in a calm voice that I had seen one of the kids in that car rip off the hood emblem of that Mercedes and throw beer cans at it. He responded by asking me my name and address, what I did for a living, and why I was in the area at this time of the night—and he wrote down all my answers.

When he heard I was a lawyer, he asked me if I knew the case of *Commonwealth* v. *Lehan.* When I said it sounded familiar but I couldn't recall it in detail since it was now 2:30 A.M., he said, "You're no lawyer, because if you were you'd know that *Commonwealth* v. *Lehan* prevents me from stopping and frisking people." I began patiently to explain that I was giving him reasonable cause to feel that a crime had been committed.

When we approached the kids' car and walked around the

other side, we saw three beer cans, a Mercedes emblem lying in the gutter, and three perfect gentlemen sitting in the car, hands folded and looking straight ahead. He then said, "Which kid?" and I said, "The one in the striped jersey," and he said, "There are two in striped jerseys, and you don't know which one, do you?" As I started to ask him if I could take another look, a man approached, got into the Mercedes, and started it up. The officer stopped him and asked if it was his Mercedes emblem; the man took it and said, "Yeah, I guess so, did he take it?" He then put the emblem in his pocket, said thanks, and when I asked him if he would stay and help out in a possible prosecution, his response was, "Are you kidding?" He drove off.

By this time there were a lot of people standing around wondering what I had done, and I decided sadly that this had become an exercise in futility. As I walked slowly to the doorway, another uniformed man who had arrived came over and said, with his arm around my shoulder, "Don't worry, kid; the judge probably wouldn't have done anything even if we did."

When eating out is against the law

Is it against the law to eat at the airport? Lest you think this question is ridiculous, let me tell you what happened to me recently at Boston's Logan International. I arrived at the airport and asked the agent if the 1:00 P.M. flight I was headed for was a lunch flight. He answered that no food at all was served on the flight. I had eaten at 6:00 in the morning and decided that I would go to the cafeteria at the airport and get a sandwich to take on the plane.

I ordered a hamburger and then asked the short-order cook to wrap it. He looked at me as if I had just suggested he join me in an international smuggling ring. He explained that no food could be taken out of the restaurant and that if he put the hamburger on anything but a plate, he would be in big trouble.

So I took the hamburger on a plate, paid $1.50 for it, then took it off the plate and started to wrap it up in napkins. As I was doing this, a young woman obviously in authority approached me and asked what I was doing. I replied that I was wrapping my hamburger up in a napkin. She said that I could not take it out of the restaurant. I said that I had only ten minutes until my plane took off; and she said that that was plenty of time for me to sit down and eat my hamburger. I said, "I am walking out of here with my hamburger." She said, "You can't." I asked why, and then she said it: "It's against the law." Now, I haven't read all the FAA regulations, but I found it difficult to believe that there was a law forbidding me to eat a hamburger on the plane. I know you can't take your own alcoholic beverages to drink on the plane, but this was only a hamburger.

I decided to chance it. I slowly backed away from her, holding my hamburger, and headed for the gate, hoping my hamburger, which by this time had become rather cold and heavy, wouldn't set off the metal detector. As I ate it on the plane during takeoff, I wondered if it had all been worth it.

When I got back to Boston, I called the port authority and was referred to a helpful gentleman who informed me that the reason for my difficulties was that if people could take food out of the restaurant, they would mess up the new carpets that had been recently installed. It was related, he said, to the reason you can't buy gum in the terminal, even though you might like to have it for when your ears get blocked up. Thanks to his efforts, though, the policy on food at least has changed. Although you are not encouraged to take food out, it *will* be wrapped up for you if you request it, and you *can* take it with you—without breaking the law.

Getting a passport is a tough passage

Have you tried to get a passport lately? I hope you have better luck than I did when I tried recently. I went to the John F. Kennedy building in Boston and found the passport office without much trouble. When I got inside, there was a large group of people standing around some pink and white forms in a plastic rack on the wall. The people were confused, because instead of a sign saying which form to take, there was a little decal stuck on the plastic rack which read: "The completed pink mail-in form may be submitted to the agent at the counter." Did it mean that the white form had now been superceded by the pink form, or that, by implication, you should take the white form home and mail it in, since you were now allowed by law to bring the pink mail-in form to the counter.

I decided that although the sign said that I *could* bring the pink mail-in form to the counter, it didn't say that I *had* to. Just to play it safe, I decided to use the white form which, by the way, turned out to be the wrong one.

A fellow in the line next to me finally got to the counter after about a twenty-minute wait and presented his completed form. He was asked for his thirteen dollars and plunked down a twenty-dollar bill. He was then told by the clerk that he had to have the exact change. Then it was almost my turn; I say almost because little did I know that I was never going to make it.

You see, there was a little old lady in front of me who couldn't speak English very well and who was being cross-examined by the clerk. Someone else had helped her fill out the form and had put down her birth date as December 9 instead of December 6, a fact that was brought out by five minutes of careful questioning. The lady became very upset, and when the clerk asked her if she knew she was going to be held responsible for any misstatements on her application, I asked him if perhaps he might not consider leaving the woman alone.

Well, that did it! He glared at me and picked up his brass "closed" sign, slammed it down on the counter, and left. And there we were: the little old lady, me, and four more people behind me. As I was wondering what to do next, someone opened a door, and I was ushered into a spacious office and invited to discuss the problems of the passport office.

I've always wondered why passports were only given out every five years. Now I know.

Selling one seat to two people

What happens when an airline sells one seat to two people? Well, like Ralph Nader, I'm unhappy to report that I found out firsthand that the one who gets strapped into the seat first wins.

If you've been flying lately, you've probably noticed some changes around airports. First of all, it seems that there are a lot more people flying; second, you may have noticed a little sign that tells you, "The airline reserves the right to sell more seats than there are on the plane."

Well, I never really believed that could happen until a few weeks ago when I was trying to get from New York's LaGuardia Airport to Cincinnati on a Friday afternoon. I have since decided never to try to get anywhere from New York on a Friday afternoon—ever again.

I did everything I was supposed to—made a reservation, had my ticket, and even confirmed my reservation on the day of departure. I got to the airport in plenty of time, just in time to find the longest line at a ticket counter that I'd ever seen. I waited patiently, feeling there was no way that all of these people could possibly get on one airplane. But I was wrong; there *was* room for all the people in line, except me. The airline had oversold the flight.

I explained to the young woman at the counter that I had to be in Cincinnati, and she patiently explained that there was nothing she could do, because all the seats were taken. I still believed I'd get on the plane, even as the jet-way pulled away and the plane was pushed toward the runway and finally took off, headed nonstop for Cincinnati.

Then came the Passenger Service Agent who courteously acknowledged that my ticket was valid, my reservation was valid, and that I'd gotten to the airport on time. He explained that ordinarily I would have had no trouble, because a certain predictable number of people with confirmed reservations simply don't show up for their flight. He then handed me a piece of paper entitled, "Compensation for Denied Boarding." It said that first airline personnel must ask for volunteers on the airplane who will give up their seats. If there aren't any volunteers, the airline must then pay you, on the spot, the amount of your fare and fly you to your destination without charge. If you arrive more than two hours after you're supposed to, you're entitled to double fare. You can refuse the money and bring a lawsuit, or try to "collect in some other manner," but I decided to accept the $152 the agent offered.

As I sat on the plane on my expected stopover in Dayton, I wasn't sure how I felt about all this, except that I did find out what happens when there's not room for one more.

Talking to taxi drivers

You'd be amazed what you can learn about the law by talking to taxi drivers. It may be a bad habit, but I've been talking to taxi drivers for a long time, although talking to taxi drivers isn't what it used to be because now you have to shout through the shield that's supposed to protect the driver from being shot or stabbed. The reason I talk to taxi drivers is that you can find out more about a city from a taxi driver than just about anybody else.

I particularly like to talk to taxi drivers in New York. On a recent visit I began to talk to a taxi driver in the Big Apple and had a conversation that says a lot about taxi drivers, crime and violence, and the law. I began the conversation with my favorite taxi-driver question: "What's the most interesting or exciting thing that's happened to you since you've been driving?" This driver, kind of a burly fellow, answered immediately. "That's easy, buddy," he said. "It was the night I got me a mugger." I urged him on, although I had the feeling that nothing would stop him from telling the story.

He said, "I had this fare in the car. Me and him came around a corner, and we see this old man pushed down by this punk and he's taking out the old man's wallet, and he gets the wallet and he starts to run across the street. I turned to my fare and I said, 'What do you think, should we get him?' and my fare said, 'Let's get him.' And so I stepped on the gas and got to him just before he got to the sidewalk. When I hit him I must have been going about sixty, and he went fifty feet into the air and landed with the old man's wallet in the street right next to him. He was awake; and he just lay there swearing at me. He couldn't move because both his legs were broken. Then the police came and took the old man and the punk to the hospital.

"The police asked me what happened and I told them, and I never heard anything more from them." Then the taxi driver stopped talking; and you know when a New York taxi driver stops talking, he's got something else to say. He said, "You know what happened next? The punk sued me for running him over, and my insurance company settled. What do you think of that?" I'm not sure what I think of that, but I know what I think about punks mugging old men, and I know one more thing: You sure can learn a lot about life from a taxi driver.

Criminal justice without the justice

It was about 8:30 in the morning when I came around the front of my house in Boston's Bay Village section. An old man was lying half on the sidewalk and half on the road, his head in a pool of blood. On the scene was a police car with two young men looking sullen and bored sitting in the back of the cruiser. I helped one of the officers stop the bleeding, and a few minutes later an ambulance came and took the old man to Boston City Hospital.

There it was, an open-and-shut case of robbery, assault, and battery. The police officers actually saw the two men throw the older man to the ground and then begin rifling through his pockets. In addition, there was a third witness who, while he was deaf, saw it all and was ready and willing to testify.

On the same day the two men were arraigned in court, and thus began a chronology that speaks for itself. Although the record of one of the men included murder, assault and battery with a dangerous weapon, and armed robbery, and the record of the other included assault and battery with a dangerous weapon, both men were released on the same day they were arrested. They were released on personal recognizance; that means no bail was set and they were let go because they promised to come back for trial.

The trial date was set for about three weeks later, May 11, 1979. On that day the witness showed up and the police showed up, but one of the defendants didn't show up and was defaulted. The other man's case was continued. On May 31, the date of the continuance, the man whose case was continued didn't show up either, and at this point both men were at large and unaccounted for.

A default warrant was issued, and on June 12 one of the men was arrested and brought to court; but he was again let go, and he defaulted again when he was to appear before the grand jury. He was finally indicted on September 10, but on September 24, when he was supposed to appear, he was again nowhere to be found. He turned up again, when he was arrested on a new charge of larceny. He was held, briefly, and—you guessed it—he was let go again and his case continued for three months. On January 11, 1980, the case was called. The defendant was again nowhere to be found; he had defaulted for the third time and to this day has never been found.

On April 17, 1980, almost a year to the day after the crime, the other codefendant was finally arrested on a default warrant. His case was continued on April 18 and April 25. On May 8, 1980, he was finally indicted and is now held awaiting trial.

Two more facts: The witness appeared in court eight times for nothing before he got discouraged and didn't want to go back again, and on June 30, 1980, the victim of the assault died. And that's just one example of the American criminal justice system at work.

Giving away your body

A few years back, I participated in the drafting of a statute that would allow a person to leave his or her body to a medical school for anatomical study, or kidneys, eyes, or any other organ for use by other living persons. This was the year that the Uniform Commercial Code had sailed through the legislature, a law consisting of hundreds of pages, the full implications of which wouldn't be understood for years. I looked forward to the easy passage of a law that took up just a few paragraphs and had as its goal something we were certain no one could argue with.

But we were sadly mistaken, and year after year the law went down to defeat. The committee hearing the bill would listen to people who were alive only because each one had received a kidney transplant from a dead person. The committee would approve the bill, and it would be defeated, each year.

You might wonder from where the opposition came. It did not come from the sources we anticipated; in fact, all religions either actively supported or entered no objection to the law. The opposition came from *undertakers,* who opposed the law with a vengeance. I remember one particular hearing when the bill was branded a communist plot, and I along with the other drafters and supporters of the legislation were branded pseudo-intellectuals (pronounced swaydo-intellectuals). Finally, after a great deal of very bad publicity, the bill did pass, prompting the comment that the opposition had at last gone underground.

We've come a long way from those days, however, for now virtually every state has passed the Uniform Anatomical Gift law, which provides clearly that any person of sound mind who is eighteen years or older can make a gift of all or part of his or her body. The law even allows next of kin to give away the body of a deceased relative in the absence of a contrary indication by the person prior to death. So if you take the point of view that you don't want to be given away, you should perhaps have imprinted on you the words "do not tear, spindle, or mutilate."

It has recently been found that there is an acute shortage of teaching and transplantation material, and your physician or hospital can assist you on request with the details on how this gift of life can be effectuated.

Crimes of violence

I recently studied crimes of violence around the world and found that crimes against persons have dropped precipitously in Denmark and are practically nonexistent in Israel. In the course of my study, I interviewed leading criminologists from Denmark, Israel, and Australia. Some of the comments made by the Australians are reported here.

The Australians said they were very worried, not so much over their present crime rate (although it is much higher than in Israel or Denmark), but because, as they put it, whatever happens in the United States happens in Australia—just about exactly *five* years later. So it was with more than passing interest that Drs. Johnston and Waller from Melbourne were observing the American scene. They were particularly interested in the recent phenomenon in the United States of attacks by gangs—not on other gangs, which used to be the pattern, but on innocent bystanders.

They discussed in particular the rape and assault in broad daylight of innocent persons in Detroit, and they expressed the opinion that these attacks were on the increase both in their nation and in ours. The Australians were outspoken about the causes of the increased violence; Dr. Johnston felt that it was the natural response to the violence and lack of order within government itself. He claimed that Watergate has taught lawlessness and that until there is both integrity within governments and some kind of enforceable world order, personal violence will continue to escalate.

Dr. Waller felt two things were at fault. In his opinion, there is simply too much law, and the police are so busy enforcing the thousands of laws we've put on the books, they don't have time to deal with all the major crimes any more. He also said that the greatest preventer of trouble is the foot-patrol officer, who has now largely disappeared in most cities, replaced by a kind of cavalry that spends most of its time rushing around after the trouble has begun. He issued a clear call for less law and more visible police presence.

Trained in ESP

Although there has never been a lawsuit against a good Samaritan, the fear of suit and the myths surrounding the good Samaritan have become a really serious problem. These myths have prevented those who are most capable of responding quickly and properly from actually responding. How many times have you heard the announcement, "Is there a doctor in the house?"— only to be left with a stunned silence?

Doctors are particularly prone to the myth, despite the fact that no doctor has ever been sued for playing a role of the good Samaritan. In a survey taken a few years back, more than 50 percent of the doctors questioned admitted that they would not stop at an automobile accident for fear of legal liability.

Fear of legal liability, while it is most often cited, may not be the only reason that doctors don't stop. After a recent speech on the subject, one doctor approached me and asked if he could see me out of the hearing of the others in the group. When we were outside in the corridor, he said, "You know why I don't stop?" I asked why, and he said, "Because I don't know what to do." When I looked into the curriculum of most medical schools, I could understand why physicians as well as too many of the rest of us are not proficient in the handling of trauma.

Even if the doctor does decide to help out, he or she often runs into some serious resistance. I remember being in a conference room in the city of Atlanta, working with a group of the finest emergency-medicine physicians in the world, when there was a terrific crash outside. I heard it immediately and jumped to the window. (It's interesting that none of the doctors seemed to hear it, and I've wondered ever since this incident what the difference in the training of lawyers is that makes them hear accidents much more quickly.)

When I looked out the window, I saw that a bus had hit a car and the car had overturned, spilling both its occupants onto the roadway, both obviously seriously injured. A policeman was already on the scene, talking on his walkie-talkie and directing traffic. I called to one of the physicians; he grabbed his bag and we raced down to the street.

The doctor approached the injured man and began to work with him; the policeman came over, grabbed the doctor by the shoulder, and said, "What do you think you're doing?" The doctor replied, "I'm trying to help this man," and the policeman said, "Get back on the sidewalk. We have a special squad on the way, trained in ESP." He meant, of course, EMT (Emergency Medical Technicians).

I decided it was time for the profession of law to help out the profession of medicine. I said to the police officer, "I am an attorney, and if you interfere one more moment with the physician-patient relationship that has just been established there on the roadway, you are going to be in more trouble than you have ever been in your life." So he left the scene and I ended up directing traffic—but the good Samaritan was able to complete his work.

CHAPTER

2

THAT OLD FAMILIAR THEME:

Husbands and Wives, Friends and Lovers, and All Their Children

Happy families are all alike;
every unhappy family is unhappy in its own way.
—Tolstoy, *Anna Karenina*

The American family has lost its way, and the repercussions of its troubled wanderings are felt around us every day. This year more than 2 million people will be divorced, and the disintegration of the traditional family has brought about much loneliness and despair for all family members, but for the children and the elderly in particular. Unmarried couples living together, abortion, unwanted or battered children, and mothers, fathers, and children just plain running away from home have all become epidemic. Although the problems of depression and other kinds of mental illness as well as crime and deliquency have not been definitively tied to the collapse of the family, there can be little doubt that the lack of strong family relationships is itself related to the rise in grim statistics of all kinds.

But despite the changes in family life, people still need people, and living, loving, and leaving, and holding, having, and hating still go on day after day and night after night. And the law reflects it all.

It has been said that the law is perpetually twenty years behind the times when it comes to family and related matters, such as sexual morality and the way people conduct themselves and their affairs. And perhaps that's a good thing, particularly in the area of intimate relationships. The law has grudgingly finally accepted the fact that it cannot keep a marriage together or force one to occur.

It is a fact that it is easier to get a divorce in 1981 than it was in 1950, and the parties involved are more likely to get a fair shake in the settlement, although complete fairness in this area has not yet been achieved. There is also little question but that abortions are becoming harder to come by, particularly for the poor, and many of the children who are brought into the world are having a very tough time. The foster-home picture verges on scandal in many areas of the country, and despite the stiffening of penalties for battered children the problem of where to put the battered child once he or she is taken away remains extraordinarily difficult.

Although there are many storm clouds over intimate relationships, there have been some positive developments as well. The most striking of these is the liberation of women from the home and the entry of women as partners in the business of living. Also, we may unexpectedly find that children of broken but more honest families may grow up to become stronger and healthier adults.

A lot of attention has been focused on unmarried couples living together, and the way they are treated—legally at least—depends on the state they're in. In California live-ins are sometimes treated better by the law than true spouses, but in New York when unmarried couples split, they're on their own.

And so is born this chapter on intimate relationships, the stories of marriage and divorce, children suing parents for malpractice and other wrongs, battered children, abortion, and much else. These are the stories of those who keep trying to put it together—any way they can. Some of the stories are heartrending, some are humorous, and some are violent, but they have all happened to someone, and their humanity touches us all.

Lee and Betty Marvin

If you're living together, you should be aware of a recent decision of the California Supreme Court. The case awarded alimony even though there was no marriage.

In October 1964, actor Lee Marvin began living with a woman, although he was still married at the time. According to the woman, they made an oral agreement that they would hold themselves out to the public as husband and wife, and that she would serve as a companion, homemaker, housekeeper, and cook. She even took Marvin's last name and claimed she agreed to give up her lucrative career as an entertainer and singer in order to devote her full time to keeping her part of the bargain. In return, she says that Marvin agreed to provide for all of her needs and financial support for the rest of her life. Seven years and $1 million later, Marvin allegedly forced the woman to leave. He continued to support her for about a year longer and then refused to make any more payments.

The judges noted the long-recognized principle that unmarried partners can lawfully contract concerning the ownership of property acquired during their relationship. They refused to accept any of Marvin's reasons as to why this rule shouldn't hold in this case.

Marvin argued first that the whole arrangement was immoral, and therefore any contract based on it had to be against public policy. The court said that this wasn't quite the law, and for such a contract to be void, it had to be explicitly for illicit sexual services.

Marvin next claimed that the contract had to be unlawful because to enforce it would impair the community property rights of Betty Marvin, his real wife. But the court said that since he was now divorced from Betty and all her rights had been granted to her, there was no longer any reason to void the contract.

He next claimed that the contract violated the California Civil Code, which provides that all contracts for marriage settlements must be in writing, but the court said that this contention "is noteworthy for the lack of authority advanced in its support," and besides, no marriage was involved.

In concluding, the court cited Toffler's book *Future Shock* and noted that many young couples live together for a trial period in order to make sure that they can later successfully undertake marriage. The court added that "the mores of society have changed so radically in regard to cohabitation that we cannot impose a standard based on alleged moral considerations that have apparently been so widely abandoned by so many." So, in California at least, if you are living together to avoid the marriage and divorce law, you'd better find another reason.

Living together in Illinois

Living together in Illinois is a lot different from living together in California. That's the message of a recent case decided by the Illinois Supreme Court. The case showed that the *Marvin* case decided in California may not be sweeping the country after all.

The *Marvin* case, as you remember, held that if you live together and make certain promises to one another those promises may end up causing you to divide your property just as if you were married.

Well, when the same kind of case was brought in Illinois, the Illinois Supreme Court simply didn't accept the reasoning of the *Marvin* case. The *Marvin* case used a kind of contract theory which holds that as long as the deal was based on something more than sex, the deal could be enforced by the courts. The Illinois Supreme Court, on the other hand, said that when we talk about people living together, we're dealing with a lot more than the law of contracts. What's really at stake, said the court, is the impact on society and the institution of marriage.

The court asked, "Will such arrangements weaken marriage as a foundation for our family-based society? What happens in the event of death? And most important, what about the children? Who has the duty of supporting them? And what are their inheritance rights, and by what standards will their support, inheritance, and custody be determined?"

The court said that changing a law in this area involves fact-finding and reevaluation of sociological data best done in the halls of legislature, not in courtrooms. The court noted that common-law marriage had been abolished in Illinois back in 1905, and recent laws had tried to preserve the integrity of marriage and safeguard family relationships. The *Marvin* case has received a lot of publicity, said the court, and if the Illinois legislature wanted to follow it, it would have said so.

So you can live together in Illinois, but as far as getting hold of your roommate's property, forget it.

She rode in on a set of wheels

She rode in on a set of wheels, and that's how she's going to leave. That's the result of the most recent palimony case, this one decided by a Tennessee court.

The case involved a woman who, along with her fifteen-year-old daughter, moved in with her boy friend. Fifteen months later the boy friend asked the woman and her daughter to leave, and the woman went to court claiming that the court should order relief based on the time she spent living in. She claimed that when she moved in she sold all her furniture and used the seventeen hundred dollars worth of proceeds for her boy friend's benefit.

She also claimed she had some medical bills which had been brought about by "contact" with him. Lastly, and most painful of all, she said she'd sold her 1973 Monte Carlo for twenty-three hundred dollars and used the money for a down payment on a Cadillac Seville which he registered in his name.

The boy friend, on the other hand, claimed that he made all the house payments (where she lived rent-free), paid for the utilities, clothing, and food, and even provided spending money. He also claimed he wasn't legally responsible for her medical bills.

The court said that if the woman had married her boyfriend these rights and benefits might well have been hers. But she had voluntarily entered into a relationship that was not sanctioned by natural or divine law. The court added that any contract that there may have been between the two was void because it was for an immoral purpose, since they were living together without the benefit of marriage. The court said that this case was a modified and less publicized version of the West Coast palimony cases between the Hollywood stars. While each case must be decided on an individual basis, the court wanted all to know that even though a live-in relationship may be the thing to do, it is nevertheless illegal and immoral, and courts won't help out either party, at least in Tennessee.

But the last paragraph of the opinion showed that the judge, while writing and talking tough, had a soft spot. He added, "Plaintiff came in on wheels and she left walking, and therefore the court feels that compassion—not justice or equity, mind you, but simple compassion—dictates she receive three thousand dollars to purchase a set of wheels for herself." So she rode in, stayed a while, and then rode out again.

If your sex life's an open book

How much trouble can you get into if your sex life's an open book? A lot, found two library workers who were living together under circumstances one community considered unbecoming for librarians. The library was located in a small Pennsylvania town. The problem started when a librarian requested a leave of absence because she was pregnant. It turned out that the father-to-be was the library's custodian, who promptly left his wife and moved in with his pregnant co-worker.

The board of trustees of the library began receiving comments about the couple and tried to get them to stop living together. When they refused, they were fired. The couple brought suit in the U.S. District Court for Western Pennsylvania, claiming that their constitutional rights to equal protection and privacy were violated.

In reviewing what would have to be considered a novel case, the court noted that the couple was not discharged for having an affair, or even for having an illegitimate child, but rather for living together in what the community considered open adultery. The board of trustees claimed that the living arrangements affected the ability of the couple to perform their functions; if they retained their jobs the library would be unable to perform its function in the community. The librarian and the janitor claimed that these issues were not rationally related to any legitimate governmental interest.

The court said that even though the couple hadn't tried to force its life-style on the community, the whole community was aware of their living arrangements, that the plaintiffs were called upon daily to deal with that community, and that their right to live together had to be balanced against the state's interest in the library being able to serve the community properly.

As for their right of privacy, the court agreed that people have a right to privacy, but that that right does not include the right of two people, one of whom is married, to live together under the circumstances of this case.

The couple appealed to the U.S. Supreme Court, and that court denied certiorari, which means it will not hear the case and the lower court opinions will hold. Justice Marshall dissented, writing that what this couple did was not against the law, since laws against adultery and fornication were repealed by the Pennsylvania legislature back in 1972 and that what the trustees had done was to deprive the couple of their jobs unless they "normalized their relationship."

The judge said the right to pursue an open, rather than a clandestine, personal relationship and to rear their child together should be a protected and fundamental right and that certiorari should have been granted.

But the majority ruled, so if you want to live life as an open book, you can't work in the library.

When a woman wants a baby

What happens when a woman who desperately wants a baby promises the father that she'll take care of it? That was the question recently decided by the California Court of Appeals for the First District. The case involved a man and a woman who, according to the court, carried on a love affair for approximately three years. The woman involved had a history of medical problems with her reproductive organs and was told by her physician that within a year or two she would have to have surgery that would prevent her from ever being able to have a child.

She discussed this with her boy friend and asked him if he would father a child for her. He said he couldn't possibly afford the financial responsibility of caring for a child, but she replied that if he would father the child, she would in turn raise it and assume all financial responsibility.

A year later the child was born—and a few months after that the woman brought a paternity case against the father to obtain child support. The man defended the case on the grounds of an oral contract, which he claimed should fully exonerate him. In fact, he countersued for damages for breach of contract.

The woman admitted the oral contract, but claimed it was invalid since, she said, it was based on an illicit sexual relationship. She cited recent cases, including the *Marvin* case, that held that if it can be proved that illicit sexual activity was the basis of a contract, that contract is void as against public policy. The court said that there was no question but that the agreement not to hold the father responsible was given in exchange for his sexual services; therefore it was clear that the contract was based on "illicit consideration of meretricious sexual services."

One judge filed a strong dissent, saying this was not a contract in aid of prostitution but rather one in aid of procreation, and therefore it should not be held against public policy. But the majority ruled, and if a woman asks you to father her child and promises to take care of it, that contract will hold unless she changes her mind.

I'll marry you if you fix up my house

What happens when a woman says to a man, I'll marry you if you'll fix up my house, and then she changes her mind? That was the question recently decided by the Connecticut Supreme Court. The case involved a lawsuit by a man who claimed he sunk forty thousand dollars into his fiancee's home based on the promise that she would marry him right afterward. The home was renovated, refurnished, and refurbished, and then came the bad news that she had decided not to marry him after all. He went to court to get his money back.

The lower court found for the woman on the basis of the Connecticut Heart Balm Act. Heart Balm acts are laws that are present in many states and that provide that suits based on a breach of promise to marry are void. Connecticut law specifically provides that no suit shall be brought upon any cause arising from alienation of affections or from breach of promise to marry.

The jilted suitor, however, claimed the Heart Balm Act should not prevent his getting his money back. He said the law should prevent suits and damages based on a broken heart, but not on a broken pocketbook. And he appealed to the Connecticut Supreme Court.

That court agreed with the man and said that Heart Balm laws were designed to do away with excessive claims for damages based on confused feelings, wounded pride, mental anguish, and social humiliation. But, said the court, sinking forty thousand dollars into your intended's home based on a promise to marry —that's a different story, and the Heart Balm law should not prevent an action for restitution of specific money transferred in reliance on a fraudulent representation.

One judge dissented, saying the purpose of the act was to ban vexatious litigation arising out of aborted plans to marry. But the majority ruled, and while you won't be able to get damages for a broken heart, you might be able to get your money back.

"What's in a name?"

William Shakespeare once asked the question, "What's in a name?" According to a recent opinion of the Maryland attorney general, the answer is, "Not much." The opinion was issued recently as a result of a question from the state registrar of vital records. The question was whether or not the registrar could legally require that the last name of a newborn child placed on a birth certificate be the same as one of its parent's.

The Maryland attorney general noted that this question is on people's minds all over the country. With women no longer automatically taking on the last name of their husband, and with people living together unmarried, it was predictable that a father's last name, a mother's last name, a hyphenated name, or a completely new name would be placed on a birth certificate, to the dismay of the keepers of the records. The recordkeepers are worried as to how future generations will ever find their roots if the names are not the same.

The attorney general reviewed recent cases in the area. In one, a woman who remarried wanted to change the last names of her children by her first marriage because she claimed the children were being teased at school because their last names weren't the same as hers. The natural father protested, and the court refused to allow the change of name in the long-term best interest of the children. Also reviewed was a recent case decided by the Supreme Judicial Court of Massachusetts holding that town clerks simply did not have authority to tell people what their names could or could not be. That court added that freedom of personal choice in family life is one of the liberties protected by the due process clause of the Fourteenth Amendment, and there is a private realm of family life that the state cannot enter. As for administrative confusion, the Maryland attorney general noted that that can be solved by cross-indexing.

As for the question, "What's in a name?" Shakespeare's answer may still be the best: "That which we call a rose by any other name would smell as sweet."

Can you change your name?

Can you change your name just because you feel like it? Well, at the moment, the answer appears to be yes in Virginia and no in New York. The Virginia case involved two women who wanted to take their maiden names back, even though they were still married. The lower court in Virginia denied the petitions for change of name on the ground that Virginia law, like that of many states, allowed a married woman to resume her maiden name *after* she was divorced. But the Virginia Supreme Court reversed the lower court, saying that there was nothing in the law that indicated that a name could *only* be changed after divorce.

The court then pointed out that under the common law, a person is free to adopt any name as long as it's not for a fraudulent purpose or to cheat creditors.

If you live in New York, however, you may well have a more difficult time changing your name. A woman named Cooperman went to court to have her name changed to Cooperperson. She went to court, she said, because she believed in the feminist cause and because she felt that the name Cooperperson "more properly reflects her sense of human equality than does the name Cooperman." But New York Supreme Court Justice John Scileppi did not agree with Miss Cooperman's reasoning and refused to grant the change-of-name request. The judge gave a number of examples of what could happen if he granted the request, stating that he would next encounter someone named Jackson trying to change that name to Jackchild, or Manning wanting to be known as Peopleing, or a woman named Carmen wanting to be called Carperson. Judge Scileppi wrote that "the possibilities are virtually endless and increasingly inane, and this would truly be in the realm of nonsense." So Miss Cooperman will remain Miss Cooperman, unless she gets married . . . or moves to Virginia.

The name's the same, but everything else isn't

The name's the same, but there are differences as to almost everything else. That's about all that can be said of the relationship between Irma Kozlowski and Thaddeus Kozlowski and the decision involving the couple recently handed down by the New Jersey Supreme Court.

The case got started back in 1962 when a woman named Irma Kozlowski, who was married, was approached by Thaddeus Kozlowski, who was also married. The problem was that although the Kozlowskis were married, they were not married to each other. Thaddeus convinced Irma to leave her husband and establish a new life with him, and they lived together for fifteen years and raised three of the four children of their prior marriages. During those fifteen years Thaddeus's business prospered, and he supported Irma and the three children. Irma, in turn, provided substantial services, including housekeeping, shopping, acting as a mother, and escorting and accompanying Thaddeus when necessary for his business activities.

The couple separated twice during the fifteen years. After the second separation, Thaddeus made it clear he had no intention of marrying Irma, but promised that he'd take care of her for the rest of her life if she'd only come back. But then in 1977 Thaddeus demanded Irma leave the house, which she did, and Thaddeus promptly married a woman thirty years younger.

Irma filed suit claiming breach of the contract based on Thaddeus's promise to support her for the rest of her life. The trial judge believed Irma and found damages for her in the amount of fifty-five thousand dollars. Thaddeus appealed to the New Jersey Supreme Court. That court found that agreements, oral or written, made by adult non-marital partners that are explicit and not founded on sexual services are enforceable.

The court was quick to point out that it was not revising common-law marriage, which had been done away with back in 1939, and added, "We do no more than recognize that society's morals have changed and that an agreement between adult parties is enforceable to the extent that it is not based on a relationship prohibited by law."

As for the damages, Irma's now headed back to the Supreme Court claiming fifty-five thousand dollars just isn't enough.

Just what is a family, anyway?

Just what is a family nowadays, anyway? That question was recently decided by the New Jersey Supreme Court. This case was different from the ones involving six elderly women (page 38) and six retarded children (page 39) because those cases concerned restrictive covenants while this case challenged a zoning law. The New Jersey case raised the question of just what zoning boards can do when they don't like communes, halfway houses, or groups of people who want to live together in nice neighborhoods.

The case involved a New Jersey town ordinance that sought to preserve the family character of a neighborhood by prohibiting more than four unrelated individuals from sharing a single-family house. The law said that more than four persons not related by blood, marriage, or adoption would not be considered to constitute a family.

The ordinance was challenged in this case by a Presbyterian minister who was charged with violating the law. He lived in a house with his own wife and their three daughters. He let another woman and her three children, who weren't related to him, live in the house as well. The nine people lived together in what the minister called an extended family and ate together, shared common areas, and held communal prayer sessions.

The court expressed sympathy with the goals of the ordinance and the attempt to preserve certain areas as exclusively residential and said that communities could be free to preserve a family style of living.

But, said the court, there's a fatal flaw in the ordinance as written—it uses biological or legal relationships to prohibit property use that would never be a threat to a family way of life. For example, said the court, the ordinance would prohibit a group of five unrelated widows or even five unrelated judges from living in a single-family unit while, on the other hand, a noisy group of ten distant cousins could live in a single-family home without violating the law.

The New Jersey court said it did not choose to follow the Village of Beltare case in which the U.S. Supreme Court had upheld a similar statute. As for how to maintain a family residential character, the court suggested the town draft a law that concerned itself more with how people lived in a single-family home rather than who lived there. One judge dissented, saying that a group of unrelated persons should not be elevated to the status of a family. But the majority ruled, and blood may not be thicker than water after all.

Getting along alone

If you can't get along by yourself, then you can't live in Jayno Heights. That's the result of a case decided by a Michigan Court of Appeals. The case held that a housing subdivision that's for residential purposes exclusively is just that—exclusive. The case involved six elderly women who wanted to live together in a single-family home quietly and with dignity, but the case equally applies to the mentally or physically disabled, the poor, and all those who want to team up with somebody else if for no other reason than that they can't afford the rent.

The problem was that the house in which the six elderly women lived had a restrictive covenant. That meant that only single-family homes and single families could be present in Jayno Heights.

One resident of the subdivision brought a lawsuit seeking to force the six elderly women from their home. The lawsuit claimed that there was no way that six women could be considered a single family.

The women, in defending their claim, said they were a family, and while there was no blood tie between them, they got along better and were a lot closer than a lot of blood relatives. But the court said there was no way that this group of six elderly women could measure up to a family. It said they were nothing more than a group of unrelated individuals sharing a common roof.

The women also claimed that public policy was on their side. But the court said it did not believe that the policy which favored foster homes for adults outweighed the public policy which favored the right of property owners to restrict their property.

One judge dissented, saying that the word *family* should merely mean a distinct domestic or social body, and that the women lived up to that definition. But the majority ruled, and the six elderly women will have to move along.

But on the other hand . . .

We just looked at a case in which six elderly women were held not to be a family and so had to leave their single-family home in an exclusive subdivision. That case was decided by a Michigan Court of Appeals. Just a few months before, another case was decided by a Michigan Court of Appeals dealing with a similar question and coming to exactly the opposite result. This case involved six retarded children living with a resident foster parent.

The plaintiff in this case was also a landowner, who claimed that the six mentally retarded children did not constitute a family as that term was used in the restrictive covenant in the deed.

The court said that on the one hand, it wished to promote the development of quality programs and facilities for the care and treatment of the mentally and physically handicapped. And on the other, it recognized that restrictive covenants may constitute a valuable property right. The court then turned to the question of what constitutes a single family and said its examination of cases and authorities shows that there's no specific definition of the term *family*. Rather, a family is a concept that depends on the group being analyzed and the public policies involved.

Here, said the court, these retarded children have been afforded treatment in a household instead of an institution, and that is very different from a group of college students or a commune. The court said the group had developed a family image and occupied a favored position in the state's public policy. And, said the court, we conclude they do constitute a family as perceived in the eyes of the law.

So six elderly women are out, but six retarded children are in. And if there's one question that's undecided in the state of Michigan and across the nation, it is: just what does "all in the family" really mean?

Check out your intended for the record

Before you get married, make sure your intended isn't a criminal because you may end up paying for his or her lawyer. That's the message of the case recently decided by the U.S. District Court for Eastern Pennsylvania. A man was indicted for mail fraud just before he was married. Since he was indigent at the time the offense was committed, he was represented by a court appointed lawyer under the Criminal Justice Act, which requires that a person accused of crime be provided with an attorney at government expense if the accused cannot afford one.

Then the man got married, and the government moved to get the legal fees back from his wife. The wife claimed she should not have to pay her husband's legal fees in any case, and particularly in a case where the whole incident had taken place before the marriage.

The Criminal Justice Act specifically provides that the government does have a right to recover costs for court-appointed counsel, if it is found that funds are available to, or on behalf of, a person furnished representation.

Since there have been no cases on this point, the court had to look to the common law, which holds that the husband has a legal duty to support his wife and children. And under the Equal Rights Amendment to the Pennsylvania Constitution, the obligation of a husband to a wife is now made reciprocal, so the wife has the same obligation to her husband and children. As for the definition of support, it used to include only food, drink, and a place to live, but now it includes a lot more. For example, said the court, it is clear that spouses are liable for medical expenses, and legal expenses are just as important.

The wife argued that even if all this were true, the crime was committed before the marriage. The court answered that, although the act was committed before the marriage, the debt was incurred after the marriage. So before you accept his ring, ask to see his record.

For richer or poorer

When you take your wife or husband for richer or poorer there isn't much doubt about which one it's going to be. That's the result of a recent case decided by the U.S. Court of Claims that upheld the provisions of the Internal Revenue Code making it more expensive to be married.

When there is a great difference in what the husband and wife are earning, there are still some benefits to be gained by filing a joint return because of the possibilities for income splitting. But when the husband and wife are earning close to the same thing —that's when the difficulty starts. For example, the deduction that a married couple can take is less than if two single people making the same amount file separate returns. Another area of discrimination was the general tax credit. When that was in effect, individual taxpayers were allowed to take an annual credit against their incomes of up to one hundred eighty dollars. Married tax-payers together got the same one hundred eighty dollars instead of one hundred eighty dollars each.

The plaintiffs in this case were a husband and wife earning roughly the same amount. They claimed that these laws and regulations were marriage penalties and as such were unconstitutional. They said the laws and regulations violated the equal protection clause of the Constitution and, because they involved the fundamental right to marry, strict scrutiny had to be applied to the law. In support of their argument they cited a case that held unconstitutional a Wisconsin law preventing people from marrying a second time unless they could prove they could financially support the children of the first marriage. But here, said the Court of Claims, strict scrutiny was not appropriate, since the tax laws complained of did not prevent marriage—they just made it more expensive. And besides, said the court, marriage wasn't more expensive in all cases, just in those in which the husband and wife were earning approximately the same amount.

As for the argument that the laws discriminated against women by lumping women's salaries in with higher earnings, the court said that didn't happen because of the law but rather because it's a fact of life that husbands usually earn more than wives. If a wife did earn more than her husband, he would have the same gripe.

So, said the court, since fundamental rights and sex discrimination were not involved, the only thing left to see was if the law was rationally related to its purpose. And the court said that even though it may be unfair that married people sometimes pay more than two single people, that's just the way it is.

And you thought your first marriage was over

What happens when you think your first marriage is over and you get married again, but it all turns out to be a terrible mistake? That was the question in a case recently decided by the Maryland Court of Appeals. What happened was that a man got divorced and then he got married again, not realizing that the divorce from his first wife had not yet become final. He found out about this about one month after his new marriage, but he decided not to tell his wife.

Twenty years later he decided to leave his second wife for another woman. The wife, thinking she was his wife, went to court seeking alimony and support for the couple's two children. The husband defended his case by arguing that he was never really legally married to the woman to begin with because he had gotten married before his first marriage had legally come to an end; the marriage was void, and therefore no alimony or child support was due.

The wife learned about this and became extremely upset. Instead of just turning the other cheek, she withdrew her request for alimony and child support and changed her case to a lawsuit for damages and emotional distress caused by finding out that she had spent twenty years in a marriage that wasn't.

The court said that, although recovery for emotional distress is difficult to prove, in this case the damage the woman had suffered was clearly sufficient to permit the lawsuit and in fact mandate victory. The court said that the disclosure of a void twenty-year marriage was devastating and that she had gone into a state of shock, engaging in spontaneous crying, and for a long period of time seemed detached and unaware of her own presence. According to the court, she was unable to function normally, unable to sleep, and too embarrassed to socialize. She underwent a marked deterioration in her physical appearance, including unkempt hair, sunken cheeks, and dark eyes. The husband argued that no doctors had come forward supporting her claim, but the court held that there are some situations in which a person can prove injury without a doctor saying so.

So, if your ace in the hole is a void marriage, you'd better think twice before you play it.

Have you bought your divorce insurance yet?

This could become a very common question in the next few years if Diana Dubroff has her way. For several years she has been attempting to convince the American public that divorce insurance is the way of the future and that, like all the other risks that are insured nowadays, the risk of divorce shouldn't be different.

She cites as evidence for her case the fact that there were more than 1 million divorces last year, many of which resulted in financial ruin because the about-to-be-dissolved family could barely make it economically as a single unit, much less as two households needing support.

The way it would work is that before or just after a marriage takes place, a couple would purchase divorce insurance. The insurance would be for a specific amount which would be payable upon the occurrence of a divorce. If the marriage succeeded and the divorce never occurred, the policy would be convertible to pay for college tuition, additional life insurance, or retirement benefits. If the divorce did occur, the policy would be used to provide for basic family support.

Ms. Dubroff has founded an organization known as N.O.I.S.E., or National Organization to Improve Support Enforcement. It has caught the attention of a number of insurance executives and state legislators, and at least one state is reported to have formed a special study commission to look into the matter. Ms. Dubroff, who is a sixty-five-year-old widowed lawyer, has made a careful analysis of the arguments for and against such insurance, paying particular attention to the argument that to have a paid-up insurance policy would encourage divorce. She argues that the fact that divorce is so prevalent is proof that economics aren't keeping people together anyway, and the fact that people might get divorced just to get the money is unlikely and besides is fraud and should be treated as such.

Well, we'll just have to wait and see what happens, but don't be surprised if divorce insurance someday becomes a very popular wedding present.

"Until death do us part"

It looks like the time-honored phrase "until death do us part" may be on the way out. That's the message of a recent case that dealt with something that has become very popular, the antenuptial agreement. Antenuptial agreements are contracts entered into before a marriage takes place, so that if the marriage doesn't last, there will be a way of dividing property without a major court battle. Antenuptial agreements have for the most part been upheld by the courts and are being used more and more as people are beginning to realize that many marriages don't last forever.

In the particular case before the California Supreme Court, the couple, James and Betty, began living together and were about to break up when Betty suddenly discovered she was pregnant. Being a teacher, she was afraid that if she had a child out of wedlock, she would lose her job. So she asked James to marry her. When he refused, she threatened him with a paternity suit. And so, based on her fear of losing her job and his fear of a lawsuit, they decided the only thing to do was get married. But before they did, they went to a lawyer, who drew up an antenuptial agreement because James was concerned that once he got married his property would become community property and when the time came to dissolve what was intended to be a temporary situation, he'd lose half of everything he owned. They signed this agreement, which said that their separate property would remain their own.

The marriage took place, the baby was born, and although the whole arrangement was only intended to last fourteen months, the couple apparently decided that being married wasn't so bad, because they stayed together another seven years. Then James filed for dissolution of the marriage, and his wife claimed that the antenuptial agreement was invalid because it related to a marriage which wasn't intended to last until death.

There are some old cases that have held that agreements contemplating a temporary marriage are illegal because it is the policy of the state to foster and protect marriage. But the California Supreme Court said what is meant is that as long as the contract itself did not contemplate or provoke the dissolution of the marriage, it didn't matter what the parties themselves may have had in mind. The wife also claimed that the agreement was invalid because she was forced to sign it under undue influence because of her fear of losing her job; but the court held that, because James signed under fear of a paternity suit, there was a rough equivalent of bargaining power.

So agreements entered into in contemplation of marriage are valid even if something other than death do them part.

She put her husband through medical school

She put her husband through medical school, and then he divorced her. This all-too-frequent scenario was the subject of a recent case decided by the Minnesota courts. What happened was that a couple got married, the husband entered medical school, and the wife went to work, making seventy-two hundred dollars a year to support them. She expected when he finally got out of medical school she'd be able to take it a little easier, since he'd be making about fifty thousand dollars a year right after graduation. But he had different ideas in mind and divorced her instead, and she went to court asking for her money back.

The court reviewed the cases from around the country on this subject. The Kentucky Court of Appeals, for example, held that a professional license to practice law, medicine, or dentistry should be treated as a marital asset, just like real estate. An Ohio court went even further, holding that not only is the license to practice an asset, but the education itself is a marital asset, the value of which should be figured in a divorce.

In this case, the court said there was nothing else; there was no house, no land, no accumulated capital, because everything the wife had earned had gone into supporting her husband. And the court said it was unfair to allow the husband to leave the marriage with all the benefits of additional education without compensating the spouse for much of the burden and sacrifice incident to procuring that education. The court ordered restitution in the amount of twenty-four thousand dollars. (By the way, *restitution* is a term usually reserved for repayment ordered to the victim of a crime.) The court also ordered another eight thousand dollars paid to the wife because she wanted to go to graduate school.

And so it's fine to get your wife to put you through medical school, but if you decide to divorce her afterward, it may be a loan for you in more ways than one.

When a wife turns her husband in

What happens when a husband is arrested on the basis of evidence uncovered by his wife? That was the question recently answered by the California Court of Appeal for the First District. The marriage was a recent one, with the wife and her four children by her first marriage moving in with her new husband to a house that was in both their names. Some time after they moved in, the husband built a darkroom in the garage. He routinely kept it padlocked, keeping the single key with him at all times and saying he wanted to keep the children away from some expensive camera equipment.

One day one of the wife's sons told his mother he discovered an electronic recording device in a tree house where the children routinely played and that the device led to the darkroom. The mother and son searched the house and found another electronic recording device in her daughter's bedroom which also led to the darkroom. A few days later she and her son broke into the darkroom and found tape recordings plus a scrapbook filled with lewd pictures of her partially clothed daughter.

The woman immediately called the sheriff's department, and when two deputies arrived she told them she was the co-owner of the house and had broken into her husband's darkroom. She gave the deputies permission to enter the darkroom, and they found even more pictures involving the husband and the other children in a variety of lewd poses. The husband was arrested and pleaded guilty to eleven counts of lewd conduct with a child, but now claimed on appeal that the whole case against him should be thrown out because the search of his private place, the darkroom, without a warrant was invalid.

The court reviewed cases in which a third person has given the police permission to search another person's private property. In one case, the U.S. Supreme Court threw out evidence seized in a hotel room opened by a hotel clerk who told police he thought he was authorized to open the room. The Supreme Court said, "Our decisions make clear that the rights protected by the Fourth Amendment are not to be eroded by strained applications of the law or unrealistic doctrines of apparent authority." But in this case, said the California court, the woman was a part owner of the house and had been in the darkroom before with her husband. Therefore, the court held, she was authorized to allow the police to enter.

As for her marriage, she tells me divorce proceedings are

pending, and the lady thinks she'll wait until her children are all grown up before she marries again.

A new approach to wife beating

A new approach to wife beating is being tried by a judge in Hammond City, Indiana. Alarmed by an increase in the incidence of wife beating, Judge Crawford has decided to try something new. He puts a husband who has been found guilty of wife beating on probation—to his wife. The judge brings the woman into court, swears her in, and appoints her an officer of the court— a deputy probation officer—for a period of six months to a year. The husband is instructed that if he hits his wife again, he will, in effect, be striking an officer of the court, and probation will be immediately revoked and he will be sent to jail.

The judge noted in a recent interview that a surprising number of battered wives don't want divorces but, on the contrary, are often both financially and psychologically dependent on their husbands. They merely don't want to be beaten any more and seek the help of the court to stop the beating. The judge also said that alcoholism is frequently a major part of the problem. He sees one or two wife-beating cases every week and feels that increasing domestic violence is an educational and psychological problem for both the husband and the wife, as well as a problem for the law. He says that the husbands view their wives more as property than persons and feel that they have a right of privacy to do what they want with their wives, even if a beating is what they have in mind.

The judge said that the way these cases are handled by the law is also a problem, with the wife having to seek a criminal complaint against the husband and the husband being prosecuted for the crime of assault and battery. What should happen, said Judge Crawford, is for the court to arrange for a visit with a marriage counselor and/or a psychiatrist to discuss the situation.

But until that happens the judge intends to keep trying his new program, which eliminates a lot of red tape and gives the wife immediate relief. In theory, husbands will think twice before they hit an officer of the court. If the husband does hit his wife, he will be held in contempt of court and will serve ten to twenty days in jail, which time will be served on weekends, when the husband is least likely to lose his job and most likely to beat his wife. In the two and one-half months the program has been in effect, no wife beating has recurred, proving that deputizing the wife may in fact keep the husband under control.

When the battering order is reversed

Should an expert on battered women be able to testify when one battered woman goes on trial for murder? That was the question in a case recently decided by the District of Columbia Court of Appeals. The case involved a woman who was married to a doctor and whose marriage was marred by recurring violent episodes in which she was repeatedly beaten. The woman became pregnant, but despite her pregnancy, her husband continued to beat her.

One morning the husband hit her, threatened her with a gun, ordered her to leave the house, and then left himself. When he came back a short time later, he was shot and killed by his wife. The wife claimed that he had come back to renew the attack and that she had shot him while trying to get out of the house. The government claimed that what really happened was that the woman had lured her husband back to the house and ambushed him when he returned.

At the trial, the defense introduced the testimony of an expert in wife battering. The trial judge refused to allow the expert to testify, stating that the expert would have preempted the jury's function by speaking too directly to the issue of guilt or innocence, and would have had too great an impact on the jury's ultimate decision. The case went to the Court of Appeals.

That court first looked at what the expert would have testified had she been permitted to take the stand. The expert would have told the jury that there is a class of battered women, that this wife clearly fell within that class, and that a battered woman might well have thought her husband was returning to kill her even if he wasn't. This particular expert also had studied in detail 110 women who had been severely beaten by their husbands and found three distinct periods in the battery relationship. In the first, there are small incidents of battering. The second is called the acute battering-incident stage, where the battering is prolonged and severe. The third is the loving and contrite stage, and then the whole thing starts over again. The expert would have told the jury that battered women are powerless and low in self-esteem and sometimes feel there is no way out.

The court held that the expert should have been able to testify to enhance the wife's credibility and undermine the government's arguments. So the woman will be tried again, this time with an expert on her side.

Can a man be convicted of raping his wife?

Can a man be convicted of rape—if the woman he raped is his wife? A New Jersey court has recently taken a close look at this question. The decision shows us that the law has a tough time breaking away from tradition even if it wants to. The case involved a woman who claimed she was brutally raped by her husband. The man was brought to court and prosecuted. He raised as his defense the common-law principle that a husband cannot be found guilty of raping his wife.

New Jersey law provides that any person who has carnal knowledge of a woman against her will is guilty of a high misdemeanor and can be punished by a fine of up to five thousand dollars or thirty years in prison. Since nothing was said in the law about husbands and wives, the state argued that the husband should be convicted of the crime.

The judge traced the history of the principle that a husband cannot be convicted of raping his wife back to Lord Hale's pleas of the crown, where in 1847 it was stated, "A husband cannot be guilty of a rape committed by himself upon his lawful wife, for by their matrimonial consent and contract, the wife hath given up herself in this kind unto her husband which she cannot retract." So according to Lord Hale, when a woman marries a man she enters into an irrevocable contract to give him her sexual favors, whether she wants to or not. The only exception at common law is when marriage is ended by an act of Parliament. This exception has come over into our law and has been slightly enlarged upon, so the rule does not apply if there is either a divorce or a court-approved separation.

The judge who wrote the decision was disturbed by the common-law rule. He wrote that women who are raped, whether they are married to the rapist or not, may suffer grave psychological consequences. But despite a lot of language calling for respect for woman's rights, the judge threw out the charge of rape and allowed the husband to go free. He felt that courts have to follow settled legal principles regardless of their lack of logic. He called upon the legislature to change the law, but in the meantime felt he could not impose criminal responsibility where none existed before. So unless there has been a court decree of separation, the common law continues in force.

A wife lets her husband die

What happens when a husband is dying and his wife doesn't call a doctor? That was the question in a recent Pennsylvania case that resulted in a man's wife and a friend being convicted of involuntary manslaughter because they let him die.

The man was a college chaplain and a severe diabetic who had administered insulin to himself on a daily basis for seventeen years. One night he listened to an evangelist tell him he should turn his care and treatment over to God, and he publicly proclaimed that he would withdraw himself from insulin and would turn to God to be healed. He and his wife and a friend made a pact together to enable him to "resist the temptation" to take the insulin. But things did not go well, and the man grew progressively worse. His wife and friend did not seek medical assistance and instead began to pack the man in crushed ice. To make sure he didn't take his insulin, they hid it from him. When he tried to leave the house, his wife blocked the driveway, and when he finally tried to call the police, his wife and friend ripped the telephone wires from the wall and he died.

The wife and friend were indicted on a charge of involuntary manslaughter. The court pointed out there were no other cases like this in Pennsylvania, and very few in the entire country. And the court reminded us that in the United States, which still has a strong frontier spirit, there is usually no legal duty to help other people who are in trouble. But the court did find a Montana case in which a husband was held to have the duty to seek medical aid for his wife, who died of exposure. The Pennsylvania court came to a similar conclusion, holding that the husband-and-wife situation was one of the few situations where one can be held criminally liable for failing to help.

One judge concurred in the result because he felt that hiding the insulin, blocking the driveway, and pulling the telephone wires was a bit more than merely failing to help.

There was one dissent, with a judge saying that the majority opinion would frustrate the wishes of a spouse who might choose to die rather than seek medical attention. But the majority ruled, and if your spouse dies for want of medical attention, the law may hold you responsible.

Dollars and divorce

Many people who think about getting divorced don't think hard enough about the financial ramifications of that decision. While it is relatively rare that this would be the deciding factor in whether or not the divorce should take place, thinking through the financial aspects might prove somewhat surprising to the more than 2 million people who will get divorced this year.

Again, we're seeing basic changes in concepts that have regulated alimony payments for decades. The typical scene down through the years was the bread-earning husband getting divorced from the bread-baking wife; the standard always cited was that the wife should be supported in the manner to which she had become accustomed. The trouble is, nobody knew exactly what this amounted to in dollars and cents, but it very often amounted to as much as 50 percent of the husband's earnings. This factor loomed larger and larger as it became more and more difficult to keep both husband and wife going in the standard to which they had become accustomed and by which they still wanted to live. Courts also became more responsive to the movement towards women's independence and have begun to consider the question of the woman's earning capacity in arriving at the final figure. Some courts have even taken the step of requiring women to pay alimony to their husbands, with a Florida court recently ordering a divorced wife to pay her ex-husband eight hundred dollars per month until his death or remarriage—but husbands should not become overly excited at hearing this, as such orders are very rare.

The more common situation is still represented by the South Dakota Supreme Court, which upheld an order that a physician earning forty thousand dollars per year pay to his wife fifteen hundred dollars of the husband's first twenty-three hundred dollars earned each month and 50 percent of anything over twenty-three hundred. The court, in upholding the agreement which the husband now terms blackmail, took note of the fact that the husband did talk his wife into obtaining a no-contest divorce so that he could marry his paramour, and that the husband is getting "exactly what he bargained for."

The only consolation to this bleak situation is the fact that a well-drafted divorce agreement can be structured to take advantage of the tax laws allowing alimony payments to be deducted by the party making the monthly payments. Some people actually pay less taxes after their divorce than when they were married.

One factor that should be kept in mind is that divorce agreements—or at least the parts relating to child support—are not cast in cement and can be modified if there is what is known as a substantial, serious change in circumstances. The modification can, by the way, go in either direction. Although it is usually upward during today's inflationary spiral, it can sometimes go the other way, as in the case of the Pennsylvania court which lowered a support order from one hundred to fifty dollars per week for an ex-husband who changed jobs from a salaried construction worker to being a lawyer. His income had been cut exactly in half.

Unchained melody

I read recently about the case of a man who was really upset when his wife divorced him in a New Jersey court. It seems that the main bone of contention in the case was who was going to end up with the house, which was worth about eighty-thousand dollars. Apparently he couldn't stand it anymore, because he went out, got himself a chainsaw, and began cutting his house in half.

If you don't pay your alimony

If you don't pay your alimony or child support, it may be taken right out of your paycheck. That's the message of a case recently decided by the New York Supreme Court, Appellate Division. The case involved the constitutionality of a New York law that allowed a judge to order without further hearing that alimony or child support be deducted by an employer as a payroll deduction and sent directly to where the court ordered.

A New York Supreme Court judge who first heard the case decided that the law was unconstitutional because an employer might decide he didn't want a deadbeat around any more and fire the person. Also, said the lower court judge, a person who gets a payroll check should not be treated differently from one who is self-employed.

But the case was appealed, and the appellate court reversed the lower court's finding and reinstated the law allowing the payroll deduction. The court stated that there were no due process rights lost since the affected persons already had a fair hearing on whether they should have to pay alimony or child support, and how much. If people didn't pay when they should, all the law did was to see to it that it would come out of paychecks.

The court also said an employee got fifteen days notice before the employer was notified, so if a person was worried about being fired, all the person had to do was pay up. The court said the law was reasonable because many people were on state aid for the simple reason that they weren't getting their alimony and child support payments.

So the law is back on the books. Automatic deductions for social security, state and federal withholding taxes, pension plans, and health insurance may soon be joined by deductions for alimony and child support.

No, you can't pay your alimony in pennies

No, you cannot pay your alimony in pennies. That's the message of a recent decision by the Georgia Supreme Court holding a husband in contempt of court because of the way he wanted to pay his alimony.

The case got started when the Jeff Davis County Superior Court decided a divorce case and ordered the husband to pay his wife a lump sum of five thousand dollars of alimony plus one hundred twenty-five dollars in attorneys' fees to her lawyer. Lump-sum alimony payments and attorneys' fees are often ordered by the courts, and up to this point the case was routine. The problem came when the husband informed his wife that he intended to pay the ordered amounts in combinations of pennies and dollar bills. He told her he'd be delivering the pennies and dollar bills to her lawyer's office, that he wanted it all counted in front of him, and that he wanted a receipt.

The wife and her attorney didn't think much of the husband's idea and went back to court asking that the husband be restrained from paying his alimony in pennies and dollar bills, and asking that he be held in contempt of the earlier court order. The lower court judge found the husband in contempt and ordered that he pay the alimony by certified or cashier's check, along with an extra two hundred dollars as additional legal fees. The husband appealed this order to the Georgia Supreme Court, claiming to the last that he could pay the alimony any way he pleased and that the order forcing him to pay by certified check was an improper modification of the original order.

The Georgia Supreme Court with great patience reviewed the facts of the case. The court noted that the husband had not offered to pay the expenses for the time that would be consumed in counting five thousand dollars in pennies and one-dollar bills, and that it was clear that the wife and her attorney would have been tied up for several hours counting all the money. The Supreme Court went on to say that the lower-court judge had the power to see to it that there was compliance with the intent and the spirit of its decrees and that no party should be permitted to take unfair advantage of the other.

Thus ended the case of the man who couldn't change a court order and wanted to pay it off in change instead.

Living together may cost you your alimony

That is the result of a case recently decided by the New York Supreme Court. The case involved a woman who divorced her husband and was awarded sixty-five dollars a week alimony. Then she moved in with a man named Castillano and, according to claims made by her ex-husband, began living with him as his wife.

A lot of states have nothing specific in their laws as to what happens when a divorced spouse begins living with someone while still collecting alimony. Unless there's something specifically in an agreement of the parties about the subject or something in the court order, living together ordinarily would not affect alimony, which is usually payable until death or remarriage. But in New York, the law is very specific on the subject, and Section 248 of the New York Domestic Relations Law provides that an award of alimony may be annulled upon proof that the wife is habitually living with another man and holding herself out as his wife. In this case the former husband went to court to have the alimony stopped. The woman claimed she was merely a boarder in Mr. Castillano's home and there was nothing to her former husband's claims.

The court reviewed the evidence, which showed that, first of all, Carmine Castillano had died on December 7, 1977, and his death certificate listed the woman's name under the line entitled "surviving spouse's maiden name." Shortly after Carmine's death, the woman was admitted to a hospital, signing in under the name Castillano and claiming benefits under Carmine's Blue Cross policy. Benefits of thirty-six hundred dollars were paid on her behalf.

And so the court was faced with a dilemma: if the woman had *not* been holding herself out as the deceased's wife, she was in the position of having defrauded Blue Cross. And if she *was* to be considered his wife, she would lose her alimony. The court said since a strong presumption exists that people are innocent of criminal acts, she must have considered herself married to the decedent and the alimony would have to stop.

So if you really are just a boarder, don't go by your landlord's last name, list yourself as a surviving spouse on his death certificate, or try to use his Blue Cross benefits.

Can a court force you to part with your body?

Can a court force you to give up part of your body to a relative if you don't want to? That was the question recently brought before the court of common pleas in Allegheny County, Pennsylvania. The case involved a thirty-nine-year-old man who suffered from aplastic anemia, a rare disease of the bone marrow. The only chance the man had was to receive a bone marrow transplant from a compatible donor, and usually only close relatives can be compatible donors.

It turned out that the man had a cousin who could be a compatible donor. There was only one hitch: The cousin didn't want to give up any of his bone marrow—even though there was virtually no risk to him, and the chances of his cousin recovering would be raised from near zero to 50 percent. The man with aplastic anemia pleaded with his cousin to let him have the transplant, but to no avail. As a last-ditch measure he went to court asking the court to grant a preliminary injunction ordering his cousin to give up twenty-one ounces of bone marrow.

The court began its opinion noting it could find no authority for such an order to be made. The plaintiff said there was a precedent in an ancient statute of King Edward I, a law that was more than seven hundred years old. That law said that an individual has a moral and legal obligation to secure the well-being of other members of society. But unfortunately for the plaintiff, since the thirteenth century not a single case could be found where such an obligation was enforced. In fact, to the contrary, the common law has consistently held that one human being is under no legal obligation to give aid or take action to save another human being or to rescue one.

The court said that such a rule, although revolting in a moral sense, is founded upon the very essence of a free society, and while other societies may view things differently, our society has as its first principle respect for the individual—and society and government exist to protect that individual from being invaded and hurt by another.

The court did say that the refusal of the defendant was morally indefensible, but a society that respects the right of one individual must not sink its teeth into the jugular vein or neck of another —that would be revolting to our concepts of jurisprudence.

The plaintiff is dead now, but the common law remains intact.

Changing sex instead of partners

Does changing your sex violate your marriage contract? That was the question in a case recently decided by a Pennsylvania court of common pleas. What happened was that a husband, after several years of an apparently normal marriage, announced to his wife that he had been regularly receiving female hormone treatments and intended to undergo a sex-change operation. After learning this, the wife moved out. The husband began making harassing telephone calls demanding that she pay all the bills because he was "sick" and threatened to kill her if she refused. He also punched holes in the walls of the house, smashed his wedding pictures, and gouged his wife's face from all of the wedding photographs.

The case finally ended up in the divorce court with the husband petitioning the court for support from his wife, who he claimed deserted him. The court reviewed the facts of the case and found that the wife intended to be married to a male person in a traditional heterosexual marriage relationship for the remainder of her life. The husband, on the other hand, said he had taken hormones and undergone surgery "because he felt throughout his life he should have been born female." The court said it was apparent that the husband never conveyed these feelings to the wife before or during the marriage.

The court then turned to the reason the husband claimed he should be supported by his wife. The husband claimed that the transition from male to female was compelled by an obsession. And just as a husband has to care for a wife who suffers from a mental or physical disorder, so should a wife have to support a husband who has a similar problem.

The court turned down the husband's claim, stating the prevailing viewpoint to be that transsexuals are psychologically healthy individuals. The court decided after observing the husband during the hearing that the sex-change operation and the later behavior were the product of a rational, competent, and intelligent mind.

So you can change your sex from male to female, but don't expect your wife to hang around and take care of you after you've done it.

Lucy from Skunktown and the $5 million

For those of you who think the Howard Hughes will contest is complicated, it doesn't hold a candle to the case of the O'Dea estate. So far, the Hughes case has seen the filing of thirty-three wills and twenty agreements by both sides of the Hughes family, seeking to divide the $2.5 billion estate. That may seem like a lot, but it's simple compared to the O'Dea case, which was recently written up in the California State Bar Journal by retired judge Frank Mackin.

The O'Dea case involved $5 million left by a ninety-year-old recluse who died in 1938 without a will, or intestate, as lawyers call it. There were five hundred claimants who got themselves two hundred lawyers. The case was heard by five judges and two juries, who listened to the testimony of five hundred witnesses and reviewed more than two thousand exhibits, resulting in forty volumes of testimony, seven appeals, and eight appellate court decisions, all of which consumed more than eleven years. The first judge succeeded in reducing the number of claimants from five hundred to forty-two, but he was disqualified shortly thereafter and a mistrial declared because it was proven that he favored one set of claimants over another.

At about the same time, all parties were astounded by the entry of Lucy Fay, who claimed to be Mr. O'Dea's daughter, saying Mr. O'Dea was not a bachelor after all, but was married to her circus-performer mother, who deposited Lucy with relatives in Skunktown, Oklahoma.

The next judge on the scene denied Lucy's claim to fame, but he was reversed for this error. He then disqualified himself. The next judge heard evidence for several years before falling ill and disqualifying himself on the grounds of his illness. The fourth judge did the same.

Finally, in January 1944, Judge Frank Swain took over and commenced trial of the case. This time the judge stayed healthy, but two of the jurors died. Attorneys for all sides decided the case should go forward anyway, and the jury returned after only five hours' deliberation—after a trial that lasted for sixteen months, with the closing argument alone lasting ten days. Lucy lost, and the remaining heirs won. And at long last the case of O'Dea's estate was over.

If you're pregnant, you don't have to tell

If you're pregnant, you don't have to tell your parents you're having an abortion, and you don't have to wait forty-eight hours to have it. That's the result of a case recently decided by the U.S. District Court of Maine. The case involved Maine's new abortion law, two sections of which were under attack in this case. The law, as passed by the Maine legislature, required that before performing an abortion on a minor less than seventeen years old, the physician who was going to perform the abortion had to notify one of the girl's parents. The actual consent of the parents was not required, because the Maine legislature was aware of the fact that the parental-consent requirement had been ruled unconstitutional by the U.S. Supreme Court.

But the Maine District Court held that the parental-notification requirement was also unconstitutional. The court said that notification could prove just as burdensome as consent to some of the minors involved. It added that parents might pressure the minor not to have the abortion, and this would cause great emotional stress and disruption of the family relationship. The court said that notifying parents could create physical and psychological risks to the woman involved and could even cause some minors to refuse competent professional advice concerning pregnancy or to seek out doctors or others who would illegally agree not to notify their parents.

The Maine law also required that a doctor secure the informed consent of the woman having the abortion by informing her of the particular risks associated with pregnancy and abortion and providing her information concerning public and private agencies that would assist her in carrying the fetus to full term. Then the physician had to wait forty-eight hours before performing the abortion to give the woman the time to think things over and perhaps change her mind.

The court said that the forty-eight-hours requirement was unconstitutional also. The court said the evidence showed that the forty-eight-hours waiting period may increase the medical risks, the emotional stress, and the financial cost of the abortion, and the vast majority of women have no doubt about the abortion decision after talking with the doctor the first time.

Minors and contraceptives

Should a fifteen-year-old be able to buy contraceptives? Well, if New York State has its way, the answer to its teenagers will once again be no. The state of New York has appealed to the U.S. Supreme Court a lower federal court decision holding unconstitutional the New York law. The law made it illegal for a person under sixteen to buy contraceptives. It also said a person over sixteen could buy contraceptives only from a licensed pharmacist, adding that all advertising or display of contraceptives was illegal.

According to the Center for Disease Control in Atlanta, teenage pregnancy has reached epidemic proportions in the United States. The CDC says that in 1974 there were more than two-hundred twenty-one thousand illegitimate births to women under age twenty, including eleven thousand babies born to women under fifteen years of age. With the lowering in most states of the age of majority to eighteen, women eighteen years old or more are not usually prohibited access to contraceptives. But for those under eighteen, access to contraceptives, while improved, is still a problem for teenagers in most states. As of 1976, twenty-six states and the District of Columbia had affirmed the right of teenagers under eighteen to get contraceptive services. Most of the rest of the the states had no position either way, although many legal commentators say that if a state does not specifically prohibit minors from getting contraceptive services, it is not necessarily illegal to provide them.

A lower federal court said that New York's prohibition was an unconstitutional limitation on the right of access to contraceptives. As far as prohibiting all advertising of contraceptives, the court said that the state could not ban all such advertising without violating first amendment rights relating to free speech. The state appealed the ruling to the Supreme Court and the case was argued before the justices. A decision will be handed down in the near future. In the meantime, New York teenagers can't be told when or where to buy their contraceptives.

Family planning and the whole family

If your children want to use contraceptives, do you have the right to know about it? More and more courts are being asked to decide just how much authority parents can exercise over their minor children.

The latest decision on the subject comes out of the U.S. District Court for Western Michigan. The case started when a group of concerned parents went to court to protest the fact that a state-run family-planning center was distributing contraceptives to their minor children without their prior knowledge. The parents claimed that this deprived them of their family privacy and right to care for and control their own children. The family-planning center's defense was that parents have no constitutional right to keep their children from getting contraceptives. They also argued that minors who are capable of giving informed consent have a right to receive contraceptives without their parents finding out.

The court was faced with three choices. It could stay out of the whole controversy, in which case the parents would continue to be kept in the dark; it could intervene and give the parents a veto over the question of whether their children can get contraceptives; or it could merely require that the parents be notified each time their children showed up at a family-planning center.

The court realized that, in light of the *Danforth* case, it would not be able to provide parents with an absolute veto. (The *Danforth* case was a Supreme Court case that struck down a Missouri law giving parents the right to veto their children's abortions.) In this case, the court did what it considered to be the next best thing: It required that the family-planning center notify the parents when their child came to the center seeking contraceptives. The court did not say what should happen next, nor did it com-

ment on what the children might do when they find out that their
parents would be notified of a visit.

This case is likely to be appealed, but until it is, the state can't
stop the parents from trying to stop their children.

Roe v. Wade

In 1973, the U.S. Supreme Court handed down the landmark
case of *Roe* v. *Wade,* which ignited the current controversy on the
subject of abortion. While that case answered many questions
about the rights of women and state regulation of abortion, it left
many more unanswered; when the Supreme Court decided the
Danforth case, it put to rest some of the issues unresolved in *Roe*
v. *Wade.*

Roe v. *Wade* held that a woman is free to secure an abortion
during the first three months of pregnancy and that the states
cannot interfere in any way with the constitutional right of privacy. After the first three months and before the fetus is viable,
the state can interfere, but only by promulgating laws that relate
to the safeguarding of maternal health. After viability of the fetus,
the state may intervene and even prevent abortions, except in
those cases where it is necessary as a medical judgment to preserve the life or health of the mother.

What *Roe* v. *Wade* did not tell us was whether a state could
require that the consent of the woman for the abortion had to be
in writing, whether the state could require that the woman's
parents give consent for the abortion, whether it could tell doctors what kinds of abortions they could perform, and whether it
could convict doctors for manslaughter if they failed to safeguard
the life of the fetus when they aborted it.

The *Danforth* case answered all of these questions and struck
down portions of the Missouri law that had been passed shortly
after *Roe* v. *Wade.* Section 3 (3) of that law required that the
consent of the woman's husband had to be secured before any
abortion could be obtained. The court, which had specifically
reserved judgment on this issue in *Roe* v. *Wade,* held that a state
may not constitutionally require a spouse's consent during the
first twelve weeks of pregnancy on the grounds that a state cannot
delegate to a spouse a veto power which the state itself is absolutely prohibited from exercising. The court also struck down
that portion of the law that gave the veto power to parents of an
unmarried minor, but upheld the right of the state to require the

woman herself to consent in writing and certify that the consent is freely given and not the result of coercion.

Sensitive and earnestly contested

Another landmark abortion case has just been decided by the U.S. Supreme Court. Just a few days before the sixth anniversary of its decision in *Roe* v. *Wade,* the court decided the case of *Colautti* v. *Franklin.* At issue were certain controversial sections of the Pennsylvania Abortion Control Act, which was passed over the governor's veto the year following the historic decisions.

The section of the law that caused this case to get to the Supreme Court was Section 5A, which said that in every abortion a doctor has to decide whether or not the fetus is viable, and if it is viable or may be viable, he has to do everything he can to preserve its life and health.

The court first reviewed the key cases in what it called the "sensitive and earnestly contested abortion area." In *Roe* v. *Wade,* the court held that there was a right of privacy broad enough to encompass a woman's decision whether or not to terminate her pregnancy, but that the state's interest in the potential life of the fetus reached a compelling point at the stage of viability. The court said a fetus is viable if it is able to live outside the mother's womb, even with artificial aid. That time, said the court, usually occurs at about the end of the second trimester, between twenty-four and twenty-eight weeks into the pregnancy.

The plaintiffs argued that the law should be held unconstitutional because it fails to inform the doctor just when his duty to the fetus arises, and it does not make the doctor's good-faith determination of viability conclusive. Furthermore, it could prevent a couple from aborting a fetus determined to be defective through means of genetic testing, testing that often cannot be completed until after twenty weeks of pregnancy.

The court dodged the genetic testing issue, but it did agree with the plaintiffs that the viability section of the law was void for vagueness and therefore unconstitutional.

The chief justice, joined by justices White and Rehnquist, dissented on the grounds that the wording was clear enough and did protect the doctor's individual professional opinion. But the majority ruled; the viability section was aborted. Only one thing is certain: The earnestly contested and sensitive area of abortion will be back on the U.S. Supreme Court's docket for a long time to come.

Saving saline abortions

We have already looked at the *Danforth* case, the Supreme Court's most recent statement on the subject of abortion. Now, I'd like to look at the impact of this case on women, and in particular on their physicians, who have the responsibility of performing the abortion and safeguarding the life and health of their patients.

The Missouri law that was before the Supreme Court and that gave rise to the opinion in the *Danforth* case provided as follows: "The general assembly finds that the method of abortion known as saline amniocentesis is deleterious to maternal health and is hereby prohibited after the first twelve weeks of pregnancy." The doctors who were trying to have this law declared unconstitutional claimed that if it were upheld, it would preclude virtually all abortions after the first twelve weeks of pregnancy, since saline is the method used in nearly all such abortions.

The lower court had upheld this section of the law on the basis that there were safer alternative methods of abortion such as the new drugs known as prostoglandins. The Supreme Court, however, reversed the lower court on the basis that it did not feel that the lower court was aware of just how prevalent the saline procedure was, and also because there was no evidence presented that there were any physicians in the state of Missouri who were proficient in the use of prostoglandins.

The Missouri law also provided that the physician performing the abortion had to use the same standard of case and do as much to preserve the life and health of the fetus being aborted as he would do to preserve the life and health of any fetus which was not going to be aborted but was going to be born. And then the law made a sudden leap, providing that anyone who failed to sustain the life of the "child" ". . . shall be guilty of manslaughter and liable in an action for civil damages." The Supreme Court read this portion of the statute as requiring the preservation of life of the fetus at all stages of pregnancy, not just after viability. Since this would prevent abortion at any time, this portion of the law was also declared unconstitutional.

And so, as constitutional amendments await action, and as the candidates for the presidency debate the merits of the issue, the

Supreme Court has reaffirmed and clarified its earlier statements on the subject. One can be sure, however, that this will not be the last case to deal with this subject.

"Three generations of imbeciles are enough"

"The principle that sustains compulsory vaccination is broad enough to cover cutting the Fallopian tubes. Three generations of imbeciles are enough." So wrote Justice Holmes in the case of *Buck* v. *Bell,* which upheld the compulsory sterilization of an eighteen-year-old who was the daughter of a feeble-minded woman. Mother and daughter were in the same mental institution, and the daughter had given birth to an illegitimate feeble-minded child.

This case was handed down in 1927, but lest you think it is a legal anachronism, the case of *Buck* v. *Bell* was cited recently by the North Carolina Supreme Court. It upheld compulsory sterilization of mentally ill or retarded individuals who were found by the court to be unable to care for children.

In examining the law which allowed sterilization of the mentally ill, the North Carolina Supreme Court had to consider several issues involving a person's constitutional rights. The court examined the growing body of cases that pay great heed to the right of privacy of the individual. That right exists within the Fourteenth Amendment's concept of personal liberty. These cases specifically recognized the right of the individual to be free from governmental intrusion in the decision to bear children.

But the North Carolina court cited the *abortion* case of *Roe* v. *Wade* for the proposition that the right to bear children is not unqualified, and that the interest of the unborn child is sufficient to warrant sterilization of a retarded individual. The court also stated that the U.S. Supreme Court has held that the welfare of all citizens should take precedence over the rights of individuals to procreate. The court concluded that the person involved may not be able to cope with children, may not even be able to know he or she can't cope with children, and may be incapable of using other methods of birth control, and thus require sterilization.

And so, citing cases that stand *against* governmental intrusion, the court upheld the right of the government to take away irrevocably the ability of a person to have a child.

Hiring someone to have your children

If you can't have children of your own, can you hire someone to have them for you? That was the question in a case recently decided by the circuit court for Wayne County, Michigan. What happened was that a couple was unable to have children of their own and decided to enter into a contract with a woman identified as Mary Row. Sperm from the husband would be implanted into Mary Row by artificial insemination. Mary Row would conceive the child, carry it to full term, and after it was born deliver it to the couple, who would raise it as their own. Mary Row was to be paid five thousand dollars plus medical expenses. The problem with all of this was that there is a law in Michigan, as in most states, that makes it illegal for a person to offer, give, or receive money in connection with placing a child for adoption.

The couple claimed the law was too vague and also violated their constitutional right to privacy. The court responded that there was nothing vague at all about the law. The law says that private parties can't exchange money for babies, which is about as specific as you can get.

As for the question of the constitutional right to privacy, the court had a little more trouble with that one, admitting the existence of such a right. But, said the court, only fundamental rights are protected by the right of privacy, and while protection has been extended to marriage, conception, and family relationships, that's not what this case was about. The court said it was not dealing with the question of who was having the child, but rather with the right to swap a child for five thousand dollars. The court said that the right of privacy is not absolute and must be balanced against important state interests, such as preventing commercialism in adoptions.

So you might be able to find someone to have your child for you, but they'll have to do it for nothing.

The best interests of the child

By far the most serious and tragic side of divorce is the pain and trauma that is visited on the children. Often the most bitter cases found anywhere in the system by which we resolve disputes are found where one parent battles the other for the custody of their children. The tragedies of these cases are sometimes spectacular, as in the widely publicized *Mellon* case, in which the concept of self-help was invoked to get the children. Most of the cases receive no public notice. The factor that makes them all virtually the same is the harm that they do to the parents and children involved.

The standard most often quoted is, "What's in the best interests of the child?" The only problem is that *both* parties claim to know exactly what is in the best interests of their children. Sometimes one parent is right, sometimes the other, and, tragically, sometimes neither. It often seems that everyone has a different theory. Some say that the children's relationship with both parents should continue; some say that there should be finality and that the relationship with the parent with whom the child does not live should be minimized. Some say that there should be a lawyer for the husband, a lawyer for the wife, and a lawyer for the child—leaving unresolved for the moment how these lawyers are to be selected or paid.

Some stress leaving some of the decisions to the children themselves. The difficulty with this approach was pointed out by a recent New York case in which two of the children, custody of whom had been given to the mother, decided they wanted to live with their father, one of their reasons being that he had a nicer house. The court denied the change, stating that the best interests of the child, particularly over the long term, often require the overbalancing of subjective desires by more dependable objective criteria. But perhaps the most meaningful language of all is found in the same case, where it was stated, "Most crucial is a gentle, wise, and forebearing attitude on the part of the parents, when a mother and father continue to be devoted to their youngsters."

In recent years, many divorcing couples have sought to avoid this trauma, with custody resting in one parent and reasonable visitation in the other, or even with the developing concept of joint custody. Most important, many people are hoping that some day the disciplines of law, psychiatry, psychology, and sociology will be able to tell us what *really* is in the best interests of the child.

"Black is black"

"Black is black, I want my baby back"—that's the way the song goes, and it's also the way a New York court recently ruled. The court was faced with the question of whether a black child should be left with its white foster mother or returned to its natural parents.

The foster mother argued that she could give the child much more than his natural mother—a more affluent life, better education, and more attention, since he would be her only child.

The court was influenced by the fact that the natural parents wanted all their children who had been placed in foster homes returned. If the court allowed this child to remain with the foster mother, then the children would remain separated. But the court was even more concerned over the fact that the foster mother was white and the child was black. The court cited a recent study published by the Child Welfare League of America entitled "Black Children, White Parents." The study noted that any child who is more than eleven months old and is placed in a white adoptive or foster home is likely to have developed negative feelings about his or her own race. The study also made the rather discouraging point that it doesn't matter that the white adopting or foster parent isn't prejudiced against blacks. In fact, the study said that the more pro-black the white parent is, the more uncomfortable the child is likely to be. The court also noted that the child involved was a little boy and that the problems of interracial adoption are much worse for the black male than for the black female. Lastly, the court noted that the white foster mother was living alone and that the poor chances of success were made even poorer with a single parent.

So the court concluded that the child's best interests lay in coming to terms with who he really is. In short, said the court, the boy is entitled to his black pride and to be raised by his black parents. As for the foster mother, the court added, "She was there when needed, and her place in the boy's life can never be taken from her."

Sexual morality and child custody

What does sexual morality have to do with child custody? That was part of the question that came before a New York court in a recent case. What happened was that a husband and wife were divorced, with the husband getting custody of the three children, ages fourteen, thirteen, and five. A short time later, the husband decided to remarry. His second choice was a woman who was what was termed by the court as bisexual, meaning that she enjoyed sexual relationships with both men and women. After

the marriage, things got a little complicated, since the new husband and wife, along with the ex-wife, engaged in a *ménage à trois*,
which is French for a sexual relationship engaged in by three
parties—in this case, the husband, his present new wife, and his
ex-wife.

Afterward, the ex-wife apparently had second thoughts about
the second wife, claiming that it was not in the best interests of
the children to be living with their father and his new wife, and
she sought a court order to change custody.

The law is that once there is a decree of divorce, that decree
stands unless the entire divorce is attacked as having for some
reason been illegal. The only way that a decree can be changed
is to show there is a material change of circumstances affecting
the welfare of the children. The court said that the evidence
showed the husband had not changed, nor had the ex-wife who
was seeking custody changed. The only thing that had changed
was the husband's new wife. The court noted that the ex-wife
presented evidence about some of the activities of the new wife,
but that her own involvement in those activities made such evidence a two- or even three-edged sword.

The court went on to state that no evidence was presented that
the past interrelationships of the three parties, complicated
though they may be, had affected the children in any way or
spilled over into any area of the children's lives. And so, said the
judge, "On the basis of all the credible evidence presented, I am
satisfied that the father and stepmother are fit and capable in all
respects to be custodians of the children."

Kidnapping your own child

Kidnapping one's own child can be very costly. That's the
result of a landmark case recently decided by the U.S. District
Court for the Eastern District of New York. The case dealt with
a problem that is becoming more frequent—fathers and mothers
who kidnap their own children when they don't like the way the
court ruled in a custody battle.

The case involved a child who was kidnapped by his father and
his relatives and taken to Yugoslavia, where he remains. The case
started when the wife began an action for divorce and won custody of the child in a California court. A few days later, while the
wife was talking on the telephone with her attorney, the father
kidnapped the child and took him to his relatives' home in New

York City. At the time of the abduction the child was in need of surgery to correct a neurological condition.

The wife immediately went to New York in search of the child, sure that he was with her husband's relatives. Her New York lawyer served a writ of habeas corpus on the father and his relatives, ordering the child brought before the court. The relatives appeared in court and said they didn't know where the child was, but a week later one of them was back in court admitting that he had lied and that during the intervening week the father and child had flown to Yugoslavia.

The mother decided to bring a lawsuit against the husband and his relatives claiming damages on behalf of herself and her kidnapped child. The court found that the child is entitled to twenty dollars per day for each day he's been held, five thousand dollars more for the false imprisonment itself, and fifty thousand dollars in punitive damages, and that the mother is entitled to fifty dollars a day, five thousand dollars for legal expenses, and one hundred thousand dollars more in punitive damages because of the intentional and malicious abduction. Efforts are now underway to collect the nearly quarter of a million dollars from the relatives who are alive and well and still living in New York.

After divorce, where do all the children go?

After a divorce, how much choice should a child have in deciding where to live? That was the question decided by the Court of Appeals for the state of Oregon. A couple was divorced a number of years back, and the wife received custody of two daughters aged five and three. A few years after the divorce, the mother's emotional and physical health began to deteriorate, and she voluntarily turned her children over to her former husband, who by this time had remarried and had two more children by his second wife.

Two years later, after the mother had fully recovered, she asked that the daughters be returned. When her husband refused, she went to court seeking to have custody of the children, who were now nine and eleven, restored.

The court family counselor recommended that the children stay with their father, and the doctor who'd taken care of them since birth recommended the same thing. In addition, the children's schoolteacher joined in the recommendation, saying that the girls got along very well with their stepmother and were doing very well in their school work. The only problem was that the father was getting ready to move to Seattle, and the children would have to leave Portland and go with him.

At this point the judges decided to interview the girls themselves in their chambers. The older daughter said she would rather stay in Portland with her mother than move to Seattle with her father. The younger child said it wasn't that she loved one of her parents more than the other, but she would rather not move to a new community, and she added, "In a way, I should live with my mother because she is my real mother."

After hearing from the children, the judges decided a material change in circumstances had occurred, since the mother was now physically and mentally recovered, and they had the right to order a change in custody if they wanted to. And because the daughters said they wanted to go with their mother, the court decided to let that fact override all of the other opinions. The court said in determining what's in the best interest of the children, we must give weight to the girls' preferences, and the court joined the growing trend around the nation to allow children to decide with which parent they want to live. One judge dissented, saying that the wishes of the children should not override all of the other opinions, but the majority ruled. When it comes to deciding where to live, children do have a choice after all.

A grandmother's rights to her grandchildren

Vietnam is at war again, but cases spawned by the last conflict are still rolling in. One of the most recent was decided by the Sixth Circuit Court of Appeals. The case involved baby-lifting, and it's the story of a grandmother's attempt to get back her grandchildren who were baby-lifted out of Vietnam toward the end of the last conflict. The dispute was between the American foster parents who had custody of the children and the grand-mother, who claims the baby-lift was just temporary and now wants her grandsons back.

The case began in 1975 when the grandmother, who was car-ing for her four grandsons in South Vietnam, turned them over to an orphanage as a way of getting them out of the country. The orphanage arranged for the transfer of the children to the United States, where they were placed in two foster homes in the state of Michigan. The director of the orphanage signed papers releas-ing the children for adoption, saying the children were orphans and had no living relatives. The children were taken to Michigan even though the Michigan authorities were told orally that the grandmother was coming to the United States and that the re-leases were probably invalid. In fact, the grandmother was in the country, but couldn't seem to catch up with the children. By the time she learned of their location, they had already been placed in Michigan foster homes with people who refused to give them up, claiming they had relied on the releases that said the children were orphans.

The grandmother went to federal court claiming that in the absence of the natural parents, who were lost in the war, she had parental rights. She claimed the refusal to return her grandchil-dren was a violation of international law and asked the federal court to intervene.

She claimed the Geneva Convention required that children separated from their parents by war be entrusted to persons of a similar cultural tradition and that other treaties granted to refugees the right to teach their religion to their children and guarantee the integrity of the family.

But the court held that none of these treaties applied and that the federal court was the wrong place to try out these issues. The court said that once the children were placed in foster homes in the state of Michigan it was the law and the courts of the state of Michigan which would have to hear the case and make the judg-ment, hopefully in the best interest of the children. The federal court dismissed the case, and the next battle for these children will be fought near their new hometown.

Adoption: Can a mother change her mind?

Can a mother who gives up her baby for adoption change her mind later on? That was the question recently decided by the Pennsylvania Supreme Court. The case involved a mother who'd arranged to have her six-week-old son adopted by a Pennsylvania couple. Shortly after the adoption the woman traveled to Pennsylvania and consented in writing to the adoption, signing a consent form in the office of the adopting couple's lawyer. But six months later the woman changed her mind and informed the couple she wanted her baby back.

The lower court that first heard the case held that on the basis of Pennsylvania law, the mother could not reclaim her baby, since she had "evidenced a settled purpose" to reliquish parental claims. The mother appealed to the Pennsylvania Supreme Court.

That court reversed the lower court decision and ordered the baby returned to its natural mother. The court said the reason it was allowing the consent to be revoked was that the natural mother was physically ill and emotionally upset at the time she made her decision to give up her child. She had been harassed by her estranged husband and his girl friend, and her house had been shot at and set on fire. Based on these problems, said the court, she decided the baby would be safer and happier with someone else, but claimed that she reserved the right to change her mind. As for the consent form, she said she didn't read it before she signed it and was told it was just an agreement transferring custody, not actually giving the child up for adoption.

The Pennsylvania court said the record in the case revealed a mother who was under stress and, therefore, the court could not sustain an involuntary termination based on failure to perform parental duties.

One judge dissented, saying the adoption should not be disturbed and that parents have an affirmative duty to provide love, protection, guidance, and support and that temporary hardship does not justify a parent's failure to fulfill that affirmative obligation. But the majority ruled, and a woman, in Pennsylvania at least, who gives up her baby for adoption can change her mind for the right reason.

When a foster child is deliberately scalded

When a foster child is deliberately scalded in boiling water, can the agency that chose the foster home be sued? That was the question recently decided by the New York Supreme Court. The case began when a two-year-old girl was placed in a foster home by a Westchester County social service agency. According to papers filed in the lawsuit, she began to show bruises and abrasions that could not be accounted for. Although the agency was aware of these injuries, it did not remove her from the foster home; a few months later the foster parents placed the child in scalding water, resulting in second- and third-degree burns over 40 percent of the child's body.

The social service agency raised many defenses to the lawsuit. First, it said that intra-family immunity should apply and that the county could not be held responsible for the acts of foster parents because those parents were independent contractors, not agents of the county. The county also claimed that the social workers employed by the agency were exercising governmental functions traditionally immune from liability. And lastly, the county said if it were to be held responsible, it would add a new and heavy burden which could destroy the foster-placement program.

The court did not accept any of the defenses put forth by the county. As for the claim that such a suit should be barred because of intra-family immunity, the court said the doctrine of intra-family immunity is on the decline anyway, and it does not apply to foster parents. As for the parents being independent contractors, the court said it was not all that clear just what the relationship was, and foster parents could very well turn out to be agents of the county. As for governmental immunity, the court said there is nothing uniquely governmental about the care and supervision of children.

The court concluded that the county has to be held to have a special duty toward every infant that is placed, and parents who surrender their children and the court that transfers custody of them have the right to expect that the county will act with reasonable care—reasonable care that was missing in this case. And so the blanket of immunity for those who place children in foster homes may not cover any more.

When adopted children dig for their roots

Adopted children—what's going to happen when they begin digging for their roots? That was the question recently decided by the Superior Court of the District of Columbia, which has joined a growing number of states in allowing adopted children to know from where and from whom they have come.

Like many jurisdictions, the law of the District of Columbia requires that unless there's sufficient reason, adoption records must remain sealed forever. The young woman involved in this particular case was twenty-two years old, married, and a mother of two young children of her own. She was only three-and-a-half years old at the time of her adoption and wanted to examine the sealed records to find out who her parents were and as much as possible about the circumstances surrounding her birth and adoption. She claimed she had desired to know the identity of her biological parents since her early teenage years, and the lack of knowledge left her with feelings of emptiness and confusion concerning her identity. She was also concerned, she said, about possible hereditary diseases or conditions that could affect her children.

The court reviewed the various reasons behind the laws encouraging secrecy of adoption records, including the intention to protect the child and the adoptive parents from a stigma of illegitimacy and also to encourage biological parents to surrender their children for adoption secure in the knowledge that they could pick up the threads of their lives without adverse notoriety.

The court held that the need for privacy of the biological parents must bow to the interest of the adopted child and that any conflict between the interests of the biological parents or the adoptive parents and the child must be resolved in favor of the child. The court ordered the Department of Human Resources to begin an immediate investigation at the woman's expense to ascertain the whereabouts of her biological parents and to contact them in as unintrusive and sensitive a manner as possible. So mother and daughter may well be meeting once again after twenty-two years, and if adoptive children want to find their roots, it looks like the law will be there to help uncover them.

Lord Mansfield's Rule

Lord Mansfield's Rule may be on the way out! Your initial reaction may be, so what? But I think that when we look at just what Lord Mansfield's Rule is, you will agree with me that this is a very significant development. Lord Mansfield's Rule, directly quoted is, "Neither husband nor wife will be permitted, as a witness, to bastardize the issue of the wife after marriage by testifying to the nonaccess of the husband." What this says is that the common law, as quoted in Lord Mansfield's Rule, means that once you are married, neither the husband nor the wife can claim that the child is illegitimate. Legitimacy is presumed, even if the husband could show, for example, that he was out of the country and had no access to his wife during the months when the child must have been conceived.

In a Michigan case, a husband claimed that when the child born to his wife must have been conceived, he was at a "duty station on base" and had received no three-day passes or any other passes and, therefore, the child could not possibly be his. The lower court, adhering to Lord Mansfield's Rule, did not allow such testimony into evidence and, in granting him a divorce, also ordered him to pay child support.

The appeals court set aside this case, holding that the rationale for Lord Mansfield's Rule no longer exists. The court pointed out that at the time Lord Mansfield's Rule was imposed, there was no way that an illegitimate child could be legitimized, and the stigma of illegitimacy was so great that extraordinary steps had to be taken to prevent the label of illegitimacy from being placed on a child. Now, said the court, state laws and decisions of the U.S. Supreme Court have removed much of the social stigma and done away with many of the legal disabilities of illegitimacy. The court, perhaps out of deference to the memory of Lord Mansfield, concluded by saying, "We are not overturning Lord Mansfield's Rule. Rather, we are rejecting its application where that application works injustice far beyond the purpose of the rule." In other words, Lord Mansfield's Rule still rules, except it just doesn't mean quite as much any more.

The right to name an illegitimate child

Who has the right to name an illegitimate child? That was the question recently raised in a case before the New York Supreme Court. The case involved a child born out of wedlock. Usually, the mother's last name is placed on such a baby's birth certificate and that's all right with the father, since he'd rather not have his name attached to a child with whom he does not live and whose mother he never married. This case was different. The father of the child wanted the child's last name to be the same as his; the mother refused, and the case ended up in court.

The court first noted that there were no previous cases, at least in the state of New York, which had raised this question. The court also said that recent legislation and court decisions involving illegitimate children have given greater rights to the fathers of those children. However, those cases, said the court, have been based on giving the father the same rights as a mother, not more rights, and if the court were to order that the father had a right to insist his name be on the birth certificate, this would actually be giving more rights to the father.

So the court decided that neither unwed parent has a right superior to the other to determine the last name of the child. The real question is whether the child's best interest will be served by having the mother's or father's name.

Under the facts of this case, the court found that it was in the child's interest to retain her mother's name on the birth certificate. The court said that although there was a great deal of proof that the father and his family wanted to maintain a warm relationship with this child, the mother had custody of the child and would make the major decisions during the child's early years. And lastly, said the court, it recognized that children as they grow older generally prefer to use the name of the parent with whom they live. And so fathers of illegitimate children do have rights, but choosing their child's name is not one of them.

"Tommy hits hard"—battered to death

Beaten and battered children are on the increase. Throughout the country thousands of child-abuse reports are being filed monthly by doctors, teachers, friends, and relatives, but the reports are only the beginning. What happens next is the real problem.

A case just decided by the Fourth Circuit Court of Appeals shows us how much trouble the law has in dealing with those who batter children or allow them to be battered, even in cases where the children are battered to death. The case involved a three-year-old child who lived with her mother in the home of a married couple. One night when the mother returned home, she found the child had some bruises and complained of cramps and seemed to have a fever. The mother gave her child some bicarbonate of soda and put her to bed, not knowing that the child had been punched in the stomach by the man of the house. The blow had ruptured the duodenum, and the little girl was dying from peritonitis.

Her mother called a neighbor, and together they bathed the now-comatose child in alcohol and put her back to bed. When the neighbor asked about the bruises on the child's body, the mother said, "Tommy hits hard." A short time later the mother found her child wasn't breathing, and she was dead on arrival after being rushed to a local hospital. Tommy was acquitted of any connection with the child's death, but the child's mother was indicted and convicted and imprisoned under a Maryland law that makes it a crime to delay needed medical attention for a child.

The Maryland Court of Appeals upheld the woman's conviction on the basis that she did not promptly seek medical attention for her child and that her failure to do so was cruel and inhumane and was the cause of the child's death. The mother appealed to the federal courts, and the Fourth Circuit Court of Appeals reversed her conviction on the grounds that while the law may have been constitutional, it was unconstitutionally applied because one key element to the case was missing. There was no proof that the mother knew she was risking the child's life when she didn't call the doctor. To convict this woman would, said the court, "be a radical overthrow of the universal understanding of motherly devotion."

There was a strong dissent, with one judge saying that anybody would have known that bruises and a comatose condition were not symptoms of the flu, but that the child was dying. He also added that the fact that she had told her neighbor that Tommy hits hard showed that she suspected serious injury, and the fact that Tommy was also the woman's lover proved that she consciously did not seek help to protect him and cover her own shame.

But the majority ruled, and when it comes to convicting those involved in child beating, it's going to be an uphill battle.

What happens when a bystander stands by?

What happens when a bystander stands by while a child is beaten to death? That was the question that had to be answered recently by the Maryland Court of Appeals. The case involved a three-month-old baby boy who was beaten to death by his mother.

The tragedy unfolded one weekend when the child's mother returned from church and began acting strangely. According to a bystander, who was later to become the defendant, one moment the mother seemed entirely normal and the next she began acting in a religious frenzy, declaring she was God. On the morning in question she prepared a tub of water to bathe the baby and suddenly cried out that Satan had hidden in the body of her son. She began to verbally exorcise the spirit, and then began to beat the child mercilessly, finally, according to the bystander, shaking the child like a rag doll. The bystander did nothing, although she later admitted she knew the baby was being seriously injured.

Then the baby's mother became lucid again and, with the bystander, took the limp child to church, passing several hospitals, police stations, and rescue squads along the way. When an ambulance finally was called, it was too late because the child was dead.

The woman in whose house the beating took place was indicted and convicted of the crime of child abuse under a recently expanded Maryland Child Abuse Law. That law was recently changed to allow either an act of commission or an act of omission to be the foundation of a charge of child abuse. That is, if a person responsible for a child beats that child, that's a crime, and if a person responsible for a child does nothing to help a child being beaten, that too is a crime. The court reviewed recent cases in the area and agreed that under certain circumstances a person who did nothing could be held responsible for just that —doing nothing.

But, said the court, to be a crime, it must be the act or non-act of a person responsible for the child, and the woman in this case, despite the fact that the exorcism and beating took place in her home and in front of her, had no legal responsibility for the child. One judge dissented on the ground that an irreparable damage was being done to the Child Abuse Law, but the majority ruled, and it looks like a bystander can stand by with impunity.

Protecting the battered child

The *Washington Post* recently reported the story of a twenty-seven-year-old mother who was sentenced to prison for from two to ten years for having beaten her ten-month-old son to death. Why is it that the professions of law and medicine are so helpless in preventing such tragedies and in dealing effectively with those who commit them after they occur?

Although there has been much heated debate over the years, relatively little light has been generated on the subject. The most common situation is the mother's boy friend administering a beating to her son or daughter, but fathers, mothers, aunts, baby-sitters, and strangers of all kinds are by no means immune from the child-beating syndrome.

The attempts of the law to deal with this problem can best be characterized as thoroughly impotent. The first thrust was to provide protection from libel or slander suits to doctors, who have always been worried about reporting such incidents because they were afraid they would be sued by the parents for making the allegations. This fear is unfortunately realistic because no matter how telltale are the burns, bruises, and poorly healed long-bone fractures, the problem of proving that the injuries actually occurred because of child beating is extremely difficult. Much depends on circumstantial evidence. In addition, courts have traditionally been reluctant to interfere in intra-family con-duct or to limit parents' rights to discipline their children—and some people have rather strict means of making their children toe the line.

To get around the circumstantial-evidence problem, some states are contemplating a fundamental change in the time-hon-ored concept that a person is innocent until proven guilty. Once the medical facts are presented, the burden of proof would shift to the person accused of child beating, and he or she would have to prove that the injuries were *not* caused by a beating.

An example of that problem is a case reported to me by a medical examiner from Boston that involved a baby who died of massive skull fractures. An autopsy revealed all the indications of child beating—but what in fact happened was that the infant was catapulted into the air and onto a marble coffee table by its mother when she slipped on a highly polished floor. Because she spoke very little English, it was a long and difficult time before the truth finally emerged.

Many lawyers feel the answer may be to move away from criminal law altogether in these cases, and to intervene in some way before it's too late. When we learn of a child-abuse case that does not end in death, we should remove the child from the environment in which these beatings are occurring, instead of using traditional punishments meted out by the system, which some feel do little more than seek vengeance on some very sick people.

Parental malpractice

Can you be sued for malpractice because of the way you brought up your children? That was the question recently decided by the Oregon Supreme Court. And it looks as if parents have joined the ranks of doctors, dentists, lawyers, and engineers in being sued because someone didn't think they did their job correctly.

The Oregon high-court decision dealt with three cases, which were consolidated for purposes of appeal. In each case guardians had been appointed for the children, ranging in age from two to eight. The guardians sued the mothers of the children for emotional and psychological injury caused by their failure to properly perform parental duties.

The court said these cases were very different from cases in which children have successfully sued their parents for beating them, raping them, or injuring them in an automobile accident. But the court said there was no previous case that permitted children to recover from their parents for solely emotional or psychological damage resulting from failure to properly care for a child. The court went on to point out that the Oregon legislature, like legislatures of many states, has passed many laws dealing with parental neglect and abuse, some of which even allow children to be taken away from the parents. But one thing that legislatures have not yet done is give children the right to sue their parents for malpractice. And the Oregon high court refused to read such a right into the common law—saying it might destroy whatever relationship was left.

There was a strong dissent, with one judge saying that since the legislature had made child neglect a crime, there is no reason why that law should not serve as the basis for a lawsuit by a child against a parent, and that to worry about seriously impaired family units may sacrifice children's legal rights and turn them into nothing more than a pious hope.

But the majority ruled, and suits for parental malpractice have not yet arrived—but maybe you'd better give your insurance agent a call just in case.

If your child is kicked in the head

If your child is kicked in the head by a horse, can you be sued? That was the question recently decided by the Delaware Supreme Court in a case that deals once more with the sensitive issue of lawsuits within families.

The case got started when a parent didn't keep a close enough eye on a toddler who wandered up to pat a pony tethered in a field. As the child approached the pony, he was kicked and severely injured. The parents brought suit against the owner of the land where the pony was tethered, and also sued the person who leased the land and owned the horse. The owner of the horse filed what is known as a third-party action against the parents, seeking compensation from them for the injury because they had been careless in letting the boy get too near the horse to begin with.

The court began by stating that a third-party action such as this has to be treated as though it were a lawsuit by the child directly against his parents. The horse owner argued that since courts in Delaware and a number of other states have abolished parental immunity in automobile accidents, they ought to abolish it across the board and allow children to sue parents in any situation where they are injured because of their parents' negligence.

But the Delaware Supreme Court refused to abolish totally the doctrine of parental immunity. The court said there is a great difference between auto accidents and other situations, such as this one. The reason the auto accident is so different, said the court, is that domestic tranquility is ordinarily not disturbed by childrens' suits against parents arising out of auto accidents; almost always there is an insurance company, and while the parents and children may be suing each other, it's really a friendly suit, with the real enemy being the insurance company. But situations such as this, said the court, involve issues of parental control, authority, and discretion. And the court said that parents must have the right to supervise their children as they see fit, and anything that interferes with their authority, discretion, or control is repugnant to the institution of the family and against public policy.

And so, in Delaware at least, children who want to sue their parents will have a very hard time indeed.

Payment for injured parents

Which is more important, husband and wife, or parent and child? This was the question put to the New Jersey Supreme Court in a case that raised for the first time in that state the question of whether children have a right to be compensated for the loss of services of a parent injured in an automobile accident.

Suits for loss of services of a husband or wife are very common. If a wife is injured in an automobile accident, for example, she of course has the right to recover damages for her own injuries; but her husband also has the right to recover for the value of the loss of her services, or loss of consortium, as it is known in the law. The measure of such damages has been held to take into account his having to hire a housekeeper to take care of his household and can include compensation for the loss of his wife's companionship, sexual and otherwise.

A New Jersey couple was involved in an automobile accident in which the husband was killed and the wife severely injured. Suit was brought not only on the dead husband's behalf, but also by the children, who claimed that they had lost the aid, comfort, and companionship of their mother and as such should be entitled to damages. Approximately ten other U.S. courts have faced this issue in this decade and none appears to have recognized such a cause of action.

The children's attorney argued that if a husband or wife is entitled to damages for the loss of services of the other, why shouldn't the children be similarly compensated for the loss of services of a parent? The court said, "The law has always been most solicitous of the husband-and-wife relationship, perhaps more so than the parent-and-child relationship. In any event, policy rather than logic is the determinative factor."

The court added that there is only one husband or wife, while there may be many children, each one of whom would have a claim, and this would greatly enlarge the damages that would have to be paid by insurance companies or individuals. Lastly, the court noted, changing the law might lead to an increase in family squabbling over who is entitled to what part of the proceeds. So the court turned down the children—until another day.

Getting sued by your daughter

How would you feel if you were sued by your daughter in an action brought by your wife? Not only might you be pretty upset, you might even lose the case. The Supreme Judicial Court of Massachusetts recently dealt with such a case when a daughter brought suit through her mother against her father alleging that he had been grossly negligent in causing the automobile accident in which she had been injured.

In earlier cases, this court, along with many courts throughout the country, held that such intra-family suits were against public policy and barred by the doctrine of parental immunity. The roots of this doctrine are unclear, since children could always sue parents and vice versa for actions arising out of contracts or property. The first known application of the doctrine of parental immunity was in 1891 when a daughter sued a father for "willfully, illegally, and maliciously securing her imprisonment in an 'insane asylum' in order to obtain her property." The court said in that early case that the peace of society and of the families composing it forbid to the minor child the right to assert a claim for civil redress for personal injuries suffered at the hands of the parent.

The Massachusetts court has become one of the first to discard the immunity doctrine, stating that the "primary disruption to harmonious filial relations is not the lawsuit brought for damages after the injury, but the injury itself, and when a wrong has been committed, the harm to the basic fabric of the family has already been done and the source of rancor and discord already introduced into family relations." The court added further "that people living together in conditions of mutual love and respect are not likely to initiate suit against one another. There is something finer and deeper than artificial legal compulsions that makes the family relationship [as] strong and causes it to be zealously maintained as in [an] ancient age." By the way, this last quote is itself a quote from a 1939 case, apparently the most recent case of record in which such language could be found.

While the court devoted a great deal of attention to the family harmony question, perhaps the clue to what is really going on is the pursuit of money rather than the pursuit of family harmony. As the court pointed out, the daughter alleged that the amount of money she was seeking did not exceed her father's insurance policy and that the real defendant was not her father but her father's insurance company. The apparent implication is that more money in the family will perhaps be the best protection of family harmony that could be found.

Bribing a child to turn in his mother

What happens when the police bribe a five-year-old child to get him to turn in his mother? That was the unusual question recently decided by the Ninth Circuit Court of Appeals. The case involved the Seattle police and a two-year investigation of a woman who, the police suspected, used her family in a heroin distribution scheme. The police suspected that the woman was having her young children purchase items used in the packaging and sale of the drugs and having them regularly retrieve the drugs, which were buried in underground locations around their home.

One day the police decided to make their move and secured warrants to search the house and the yard. The officers were continually taunted by the entire family, which followed them everywhere as they searched in vain for the large supply of heroin they knew was hidden on the property. They uncovered a small amount of cocaine, but were completely unsuccessful in finding the large amount of heroin for which they were searching.

As the search was underway, the woman's five-year-old son asked if he could go to the bathroom; one of the police officers offered to take him. When the officer got the boy alone, he asked the boy if he knew where the heroin was hidden and offered him five dollars if he'd tell him where it was. The boy took the five-dollar bill, took the officers to the back yard, and pointed out the exact location of the drugs.

The district court that first heard the case refused to allow the seized drugs into evidence, saying that bribery of a child of tender age by a policeman in order to obtain evidence represents police conduct which is shocking to the conscience and so violates civilized conduct as to be a deprivation of due process of law.

The case was appealed to the court of appeals, which reversed the lower court, saying that the offer of money simply removed the boy's reluctance to cooperate and, after all, police lawfully pay for information and evidence all the time. The court said we must refuse to reward a mother for using her minor children in crime, even though the police activity did not show much concern for family life.

So the police can bribe a five-year-old and get him to tell where his mother hid the heroin.

When children confess to their parents

When children talk to their parents, is the law listening in? That was the question recently asked in a case decided by the New York Supreme Court. The case got started when a twenty-three-year-old driver struck two women pedestrians, leaving them lying on the roadway seriously injured. Although he knew that he had caused the accident, he panicked and left the scene without making himself known and without trying to help the injured women.

He would have been indicted on the basis of the testimony of one witness, his father. Two days after the accident occurred, the man told his father all about it. The driver could not be compelled to testify because of the Fifth Amendment, but his father did not have that protection and was forced to testify before the grand jury. Then the father and the son went to court, seeking to have the father's testimony struck from the record on the basis that what a son tells his father is confidential, even if it is the story of a hit-and-run accident. The court first noted that there is no legislated parent-child privilege in the state of New York. Unlike priest and penitent, lawyer and client, physician and patient, social worker and client, there is no confidentiality given to the parent-child relationship by law.

But the court decided that even in the absence of a specific act of the legislature, the parent-child privilege does exist. The court said there must be certain relationships in which the court simply cannot enter or intrude. And the court held that parent-child privilege exists in New York, flowing directly from the right of privacy guaranteed by the federal and state constitutions. The state argued that in this case the driver was twenty-three years old, and even if there is to be a parent-child privilege, it should not hold if the child is an adult.

The court answered that while it's true that the fostering of a confidential parent-child relationship is necessary to a child's development, it does not follow that this fundamental relationship ceases at the stroke of midnight on the last day of the child's eighteenth year.

So what a son tells a father is privileged, even if what he tells him is that he ran down two people in the dead of night.

Privacy in the bedroom

How much privacy is there in a teenager's bedroom? Quite a bit, according to a recent decision by the California Supreme Court.

The case got started when the police arrived at the home of a seventeen-year-old boy and arrested him without a warrant on the basis of information supplied by his mother. His father then gave the police permission to search the boy's bedroom, and the police came across a locked toolbox. When the boy was asked for the key, he first said he lost it, but he turned it over when his father gave permission to the police to open the box by force. Inside the toolbox—in addition to some tools—were, according to the court, nine plastic bags filled with marijuana.

The trial judge ruled that the arrest on the basis of information provided by the boy's mother was invalid, but that the search of the box with the permission of the boy's father was legal and could form the basis of a valid conviction on marijuana charges. The court reasoned that because the father owned the house in which the toolbox was found, and because he had a duty to control his son's activities, he could permit the search.

The boy appealed his conviction to the California Supreme Court. The state claimed the conviction should be upheld because a father must have the authority to inspect his child's belongings in order to promote the child's health and welfare, and that what this case was all about was a father who was merely using the police to assist him in complying with his parental duties. But the California Supreme Court did not agree and reversed the boy's conviction on the basis of improper search and seizure. The court said the argument of the state was misleading, and what this case was all about was not the relationship between parent and child but between people and their government. In this case, the minor's rights were violated by the police. Juveniles enjoy the right to be free from unreasonable search and seizure.

One judge dissented, saying the majority's decision violates parents' Fourteenth Amendment right to care for, discipline, and control their minor children. But the majority ruled, and teenagers do have some privacy in their bedrooms after all.

A child's cancer—who calls the shots?

Can you be convicted of child neglect because of how your child's disease was treated? That was the question recently answered by the New York Court of Appeals. The case involved a seven-year-old child who had Hodgkin's disease, a form of cancer. The parents took the child to a physician who recommended radiation treatment and chemotherapy, but the parents didn't follow this advice and instead took the child to a clinic for laetrile and nutritional therapy.

The county commissioner of social services found out about the case and, being against laetrile as a treatment for Hodgkin's disease, filed a child-neglect petition against the parents. The petition alleged that the parents neglected their child by failing to follow the recommended conventional course of treatment. The child was removed from the parents as the court procedures got under way, but was returned to them after they agreed to have the child monitored by town-licensed physicians, one of whom believed in laetrile therapy and the other of whom did not.

The case finally ended up before the New York Court of Appeals. That court stated "that the testimony revealed a sharp conflict in medical opinion as to the effectiveness of the treatment being administered to the child." Several doctors testified that radiation with chemotherapy was the only acceptable method of treating Hodgkin's disease. But the parents produced two physicians who said that laetrile therapy was beneficial and effective.

The court said that to find child neglect, a court must find that a child's physical condition has been impaired because of the parents' failure to supply the child with adequate medical assistance. As for what constitutes adequate medical assistance, that has to be decided on the facts of each case and, said the court, right or wrong is not the question, for the present state of the practice of medicine does not permit definitive conclusions.

And so while laetrile may or may not save a child, its use will not convict the parents.

If a child commits a crime

If a child commits a crime, can his parents be held responsible? That was the question raised before an Ohio court. The case involved a sixteen-year-old boy who decided he'd had enough of his parents. He moved out, got married, and got a job. A short time later, he raped a woman, and she brought a lawsuit against his father for failing to exercise proper control over his son.

There was no question as to the harm inflicted upon the woman by the boy, but there was a real question for the court as to whether or not his parents could be held responsible. Ohio law, like the law in several states, provides that a person can recover damages from parents having custody and control of a minor under the age of eighteen years who willfully and maliciously assaults another person. The boy's father claimed that he could not possibly control the actions of his son, particularly since he didn't live with him any more, was married and had a job, and should be considered fully emancipated or freed from parental control and guidance.

The court realized that this was an extreme example of what the legislature had in mind when they passed the law, but said that the law did not include only those situations where the father or mother was in physical control of the child. The court stated, "It is unrealistic to believe when the members of the General Assembly used the word *control* that they meant having such physical control over him or her so that the parent would be able at all times to deter the minor from actually committing the assault."

The court pointed out that under the common law, parents were liable for their children's actions only if they had notice of the child's likelihood of committing the type of wrong involved and if they failed to take any steps to control the child. But the statute changed all this and did away with the prior-notice requirement. The court said that the only way a parent would not be responsible would be if, in a divorce action, for example, custody and control had been taken from one parent and given to another.

So the court upheld two thousand dollars in damages from the father of the boy who raped the woman, and the question, "Do you know where your children are tonight?" becomes even more important.

Giving kin your kidneys

What happens when a seven-year-old child wants to give one
of her kidneys to her twin sister? That was the question that had
to be answered by the Connecticut courts in a landmark case that
was one of the first to determine how life-and-death decisions are
made when young children are involved. Although the twins were
not incompetent, they were only seven years old, and therefore
there was a serious question as to whether they had the legal right
to consent to a kidney transplant operation. And if they did not
have the legal right to consent, who did?

The case involved Kathleen Hart, who was seven years old and
was suffering from a serious kidney disorder. As a result of the
progression of the disease, Kathleen had lost virtually all kidney
function and was on dialysis, requiring treatment twice weekly.
Her life expectancy unless she received a kidney transplant was
less than five years, but if her twin sister, Margaret, were allowed
to give Kathleen one of her kidneys, according to the court, the
chance that both girls would live out their normal expected life
span was nearly 100 percent. The court looked at a variety of
factors, including the much-reduced chance of success of a kidney transplant from one of Kathleen's parents, with long-range
survival of a parent transplant at the time the case was brought
being only about 50 percent.

The court placed great emphasis on the report of Margaret's
psychiatric evaluation. The doctor testified that she had an extremely strong identification with her sister and that it would be
of great psychological benefit to Margaret if she were permitted
to give the gift of life to Kathleen. The court had to balance that
benefit with the risk to Margaret of having the operation and of
having to live the balance of her life with one kidney.

The court concluded after opinions from clergy, psychiatrists,
and guardians for each of the children that it would grant Margaret's wish. She was permitted to save the life of her twin sister.

3

THE STATE OF THE PEOPLE:

*The People versus the State (civil rights), the State versus
the People (criminal law), and For Your Own Good
(government regulation)*

The relationship of a people to its government has never been
an easy one. In dealing with the state we constantly confront the
conflict between the individual and the government, which, although it draws its power and being from the people, all too often
becomes an entity existing in its own right, for its own purposes,
removed from the people it is supposed to represent. In the early
days, a person who worked for the state was likely to say he or
she worked for the people, a statement you don't hear much
anymore. The relationship we bear to our government, perhaps
more than any other single human element, determines the quality of our lives. Our government to a large extent determines how
much personal freedom and protection we have, whether our
businesses will thrive, how much money we will have for our own
personal use at the end of the month, and whether we will spend
our days at war or at peace. The stories that follow are the stories
of a people dealing with its government.

State v. People

The criminal law is based on what happens when a person
turns against his fellow man and commits a crime. Although the
crime is against an individual, it is seen as an act against the state,
and it is the state that finds guilt and hands out punishment.

The problem is that the criminal justice system of the United
States is on the rocks and is in need of a major overhaul from top
to bottom. Vicious criminals are returned to society because the
police officer erred, cases are continued to death, prisoners are
bailed out, don't show up when they're supposed to, and when

they do turn up (often in the course of committing another crime) they are bailed again. And when someone is finally found guilty and sentenced, there is often no place to put him or her. Probation and parole are out of favor, mandatory sentencing and removal of judicial discretion is the trend, and crime prevention is thought of in terms of burglar alarms rather than finding out why people do what they do. It is perhaps no coincidence that the mental hospital system is also in complete disarray and mental health services for those who act out violently against themselves or others are either grossly inadequate or completely non-existent. We must consider some radical restructuring, such as deciding within thirty days the initial question of whether the individual did that with which he is charged. And instead of immediately branding the first offender a criminal or mentally ill, we might pause and try to find out why he did what he did and how he might best be persuaded not to do it again. There must be places for those who can be helped, just as there must be places for those who cannot or will not be helped. The criminal justice system has lost its discipline, and we are all victims.

People v. State

The mandate of the law in the area of civil rights is to protect and to give a fair shake to the disadvantaged. That sounds simple, but an untold number of words and hours has been consumed in an effort that has had mixed results. The tragedy is that it remains necessary to legislate or command fairness, and the key question is whether the gains that have been made are real or illusory. Civil rights laws are intended to help those who were discriminated against get to the starting gate. What occurs all too often is that a lot of hardworking people are still nowhere near the starting gate; instead they've been passed by those who have merely learned how to manipulate and intimidate the system. Unfortunately all too often civil rights legislation has had an inverse effect, and has actually made more difficult the pursuit of equal opportunity. What is needed is to make larger the pie from which we all partake, and think more about our long-term self-interest than our short-term greed. We must professionalize many more pursuits, and we will find that there can be dignity, pride, and money for all our people. We need to provide a head start for those we have failed, and we need less rhetoric and more action in this most critical field. Someone once said, "Throw a man a fish and you will feed him for a day; teach him how to fish and he will feed himself for the rest of his life."

For your own good

One of the themes that fueled victory for Ronald Reagan was the fact that regulation in the United States has lost sight of just what the goal of regulation is. A virtual army of nonproductive bureaucrats have forgotten that they are supposed to be working for the people, not against them, and that they are not supposed to exercise power for its own sake or for their own ends. We have lost sight of the fact that the government should be a catalyst and a monitor, not owner, manager, subsidizer, and regulator of everything under the sun. Regulatory agencies that are supposed to protect us are protecting us to death, and others are suffocating us with the weight of paper and pettyness. Even worse, in many cases the regulations themselves are only a veneer that masks the true motivation of all too many bureaucrats—to attack, confront, tear down, and destroy rather than to constructively criticize, help to lead, and see to it that those who know the score are playing the game.

All of these areas have encountered unexpected difficulties in recent years, and while the interaction of the American people with their government may still be preferable to that of any other country in the world, there is a great deal left to be desired, and it is critical that over the next several years we realign the balance and lessen the growing frustration of the people of the United States when they come in contact with their own government.

"You have the right to remain silent"

"You have the right to remain silent. Anything you say may be used against you in a court of law. You have the right to an attorney, and one will be appointed for you if you cannot afford it."

If you've ever been arrested or watched an arrest, even on television, you have probably heard the *Miranda* warning, taken from the case of *Miranda* v. *Arizona* handed down by the United States Supreme Court in 1966. That case has been accused of placing handcuffs on the police instead of on the criminal, and many were certain that the *Miranda* case would not survive a frontal assault before the present Supreme Court. In one case, however, *Miranda* survived by the narrowest of margins. The case of *Brewer* v. *Williams,* which some felt sure was *Miranda*'s death knell, did not strike down or cut back on the *Miranda* case; in fact, it very nearly ignored it altogether.

To fully understand the impact of the court's ruling in the *Williams* case, it is necessary to look at the *Miranda* decision. On March 3, 1963, an eighteen-year-old girl was kidnapped and raped near Phoenix, Arizona. Ten days later, Miranda was arrested by the police. After a line-up, at which he was identified by the victim, he was taken into a room and interrogated. After a brief period, he admitted his guilt, described the crime, and signed a confession.

The basis of the *Miranda* decision was the portion of the Fifth Amendment to the Constitution that states that no person shall be compelled in any criminal case to be a witness against himself.

The court quoted at length from various police manuals and texts that called for the police always to be alone with the person under interrogation, to interrogate with perserverence, to offer the accused excuses for what he did, or to use a friend-foe or Mutt-and-Jeff routine to bring about confession. The Supreme Court extended the protection against self-incrimination from the courtroom, where it had been present since ancient times, to the stage of arrest and custody.

Because of the police error, the confession was stricken and a new trial ordered. That new trial resulted in Miranda's conviction for a second time.

Now let's look at the *Williams* case and what it didn't do to the *Miranda* decision.

The *Williams* case began the day before Christmas in 1968, when a ten-year-old girl went to a wrestling match at a YMCA in Des Moines to watch her brother compete. She went to the washroom and was never seen alive again. A short time later, Williams, who had recently escaped from an Iowa mental hospital and was living at the Y, asked a fourteen-year-old boy for help in putting a bundle in his car. When the youth looked at the bundle, he saw "two legs in it, and they were skinny and white." A warrant was later issued for Williams's arrest.

On December 26, the Des Moines police were called by a lawyer who said Williams would soon turn himself in to the Davenport police. The Des Moines police went to pick up Williams in Davenport after promising lawyers in both cities who were representing Williams that no questions would be asked during the 160-mile trip. Despite the agreement, the detective in the car convinced Williams to tell him where the body was hidden.

The Iowa courts upheld Williams's conviction, holding that Williams had knowingly waived his right to remain silent. When the case reached the federal district and appeals courts, they reversed and held that Williams had been denied his constitutional right to the assistance of counsel and that his self-incriminating statements were not made voluntarily.

The Supreme Court affirmed the reversal, but in doing so did not use the Fifth Amendment, which protects against self-incrimination and was the basis of *Miranda.* They relied solely on the Sixth Amendment, which guarantees a person the right to the assistance of counsel.

Four justices, however, dissented, with Chief Justice Burger calling the result intolerable and complaining that the court continues punishing the public for the mistakes and misdeeds of law enforcement officers instead of punishing the officer directly. But the majority ruled, and the guilty may still be freed if their constitutional rights are denied.

When you're not quite under arrest

What are your rights when you're not quite under arrest? That was the question recently decided by the U.S. Supreme Court in a case that dealt with the issue of a person's rights during the time he or she is held by the police but not placed under arrest.

The case began back in 1971 when the owner of a pizza parlor in Rochester, New York, was killed during an attempted robbery. Shortly after the murder a detective investigating the crime received some information from another officer who heard from an informant that a particular man might have been involved in the crime. The detective learned nothing about the man that would have caused an arrest warrant to be issued, but nevertheless gave an order to "pick him up and bring him in."

The next morning three police officers appeared at the man's home and took him into custody. He was told he was not under arrest, but the officers admitted later on that if he had refused to come along or tried to get away, he would have been physically restrained. At the station the man was placed in an interrogation room and given his *Miranda* warnings, including his right to remain silent and to have a lawyer. After he said he didn't want a lawyer, he was interrogated and made incriminating statements and drew sketches that led to his conviction for murder.

He appealed his conviction on the ground that since there was no probable cause for taking him into custody, it was illegal—and calling it custody rather than an arrest did not make it any less illegal. The New York courts had affirmed the man's conviction on the grounds that since the *Miranda* warning had been given, the causal connection between the initial illegal detention and the giving of the incriminating statements was broken. But the U.S. Supreme Court reversed the man's conviction, saying the Fourth Amendment requires that a citizen's privacy not be compromised in this fashion, and one of the reasons for the adoption of the Fourth Amendment was that rumor or suspicion is not deemed adequate to support a warrant for arrest.

The chief justice and Justice Rehnquist dissented on the basis that this man was not under arrest, and that this decision would greatly hinder police investigating crime. But the majority ruled, and one more convicted killer may be coming back on the streets.

When the police start talking

When the police start talking, there's no question about what happens next. That's the message of a case recently decided by the U.S. Supreme Court. The case involved a man who was accused of killing a taxi driver by firing a shotgun blast into the back of his head and then burying him in a shallow grave. A suspect was arrested when the police responded to a telephone call from another taxi driver who said he had just been robbed by a man wielding a sawed-off shotgun. The man was arrested a few hours later.

Within minutes, a sergeant arrived on the scene and gave the defendant the *Miranda* warning, which in effect says a person cannot be interrogated without having seen an attorney. The man was then placed in a police car with a wire-mesh screen to be driven to the station. On the way to the station, the police officers began talking with each other about the fact that the missing shotgun was probably in an area near a school for handicapped children. One officer said to the other, "God forbid one of them might find the weapon—what if a little girl picked up the gun and killed herself?" The suspect then interrupted the police and told them to turn the police car around so he could show them where the gun was located. They returned to the scene and the *Miranda* warning was repeated, but the defendant said he didn't care, he wanted to get the gun out of the way because of the kids.

He was brought to trial and convicted. The Rhode Island Supreme Court set aside the conviction on the ground that when the police talked in front of the suspect, it was an improper interrogation and the conviction had to be overturned.

The case was appealed to the U.S. Supreme Court, which reversed the Rhode Island high court. The court said that talking in front of a suspect was not interrogation unless it could be shown the officers' discussion was a ploy to trick the defendant into speaking.

Justices Marshall and Brennan dissented, pointing out that the appeal to common decency is the oldest trick in the book when it comes to police interrogation. But the majority ruled, and when it comes to the question of talking, it's okay as long as the talking isn't a question.

If a lawyer's left in the dark

If a lawyer's left in the dark at a line-up, that could be the end of the case against a killer. That's the message of a case recently decided by the New York Supreme Court, a case that reminds the police once again just how careful they must be when they use the line-up as an evidence-gathering device.

The case involved an all-too-common situation on the streets of New York—a shooting of a man who said he didn't have any money. One night three young men approached a man and his fourteen-year-old girl companion and asked him if he had any money. When he said no, one of the men told the young girl to run away because her friend was going to die. She ran away and heard the fatal shot. Later that day the young girl and another witness identified a photograph of the man who pulled the trigger. The police decided to confirm the identification by assembling a line-up.

Attending the line-up was a lawyer for one of the defendants. The identifying witnesses pleaded that they not be seen by anyone, especially a lawyer for the suspected killer. So what the police did was to allow the lawyer to attend the line-up, but they put up a sheet preventing the lawyer from seeing the people who were about to make the identification. The sheet also prevented the lawyer from watching his client. The lawyer protested he couldn't represent his client's interest at a line-up if there was a sheet preventing him from seeing what was going on. But the police persisted, identification was made, and the man was then convicted.

The court decided that a lawyer's presence at a line-up is necessary to insure fairness and added that in this case, where much of the evidence rested on the testimony of a fourteen-year-old girl's nighttime encounter with the defendant, the need for care was particularly important. The lawyer, said the court, was prevented from seeing the moment of confrontation, and therefore his effectiveness was ended. The court said if the police feared for the safety of the witnesses, they could have masked them or covered their faces in some way, rather than separating the lawyer from the line-up procedure.

So the police lost this line-up, and another convicted killer may go free because of it.

Two Sams and pretrial publicity

After a judge was assigned to the Son of Sam case, a serious question arose. If David Berkowitz were found mentally competent to stand trial, where and under what circumstances could he get a fair trial, given the pretrial publicity that had already occurred?

To answer that question, we have to go back to 1966 and a case that involved another Sam. It was the case of Sam Sheppard, whose lawyer, F. Lee Bailey, brought a successful habeas corpus proceeding against a prison warden asking for Sheppard's release because of the massive and inherently prejudicial pretrial publicity.

Marilyn Sheppard was Sam Sheppard's pregnant wife, who was bludgeoned to death in the upstairs bedroom of their lakeshore house in Bay Village, Ohio. Sam's story was that in the early morning hours, he heard his wife cry out, ran upstairs, and saw a "form" standing next to his wife's bed. He struggled with it and was knocked unconscious.

From the beginning the press attention was enormous. Headlines beginning the day of Marilyn's funeral read "Testify Now in Death"; "Dr. Balks at Lie Test"; "Why No Inquest?"; "Do It Now." When the inquest was held by the coroner, it was broadcast live. The trial was held two weeks before the November election at which the chief prosecutor was a candidate for election as a judge and the trial judge himself was up for re-election. Reporters were permitted access to the Sheppard house even though it was placed under protective custody, and the scene at the courthouse was constant bedlam. Pictures of the jurors, who were allowed to go home each night, appeared over forty times in the Cleveland papers, and every juror but one testified to having read about the case in the newspapers or having heard about it on the radio.

The court said that while trial precautions alone might not have violated due process, that plus the carnival aspect of the trial caused Sheppard to be deprived of the judicial calm and serenity to which he was entitled.

As for Son of Sam—the press conference in the middle of the night, the press getting into his apartment, the psychiatrist who was to examine him going on television, and the alleged attempted sale of tapes by one of his lawyers—whether these things denied David Berkowitz due process of law, only time will tell.

Knowing right from wrong

The cases of Sara Jane Moore, Squeaky Fromme, and Patty Hearst all raised an interesting legal question which up till recently has had very little attention paid to it. Were they mentally competent to stand trial? This question has caused great confusion for doctors and lawyers alike and has been responsible for many persons being kept illegally in mental hospitals and prisons throughout the country.

The question of competency to stand trial raises the fundamental issue of when a person is so mentally defective that he or she cannot even be brought to trial for what was done. I recall the case of the man at an institution for the criminally insane who was there because he painted his horse. He was a fruit peddler who had a white horse and who thought business might improve if he turned the horse into a zebra, so he painted black stripes on it. He was arrested for the crime of disfiguring an animal, which

carried the penalty of a year in jail. However, after he was arrested, he was taken to a hospital for the criminally insane for
observation. That was in 1920. He died there in 1968, never
having had a lawyer, never having been tried, and never having
even been in a courtroom. The doctors who examined him probably never even understood the question they were supposed to
answer: Was he competent to stand trial? Instead, they kept him
awaiting trial until his death because they had decided he was ill
and in need of some kind of psychiatric or custodial care.

The test for competency to stand trial is a simple one: Does the
person understand the crime with which he is charged; does he
understand the seriousness of his position relative to those
charges; and is he able to cooperate with his attorney in preparing his defense? If the answer to these questions is yes, the
person must be returned to court for trial. This does not mean
that he or she was not insane at the time the crime was committed
(therefore leaving open the question of criminal responsibility),
and it does not mean that the person is not ill or dangerous and
in need of continuing psychiatric care. What it does mean is that
the person must be brought to trial for what he or she did. Recent
cases have made it clear that a person who is found incompetent
to stand trial ought never to be held for longer than that person
could have been sentenced if found guilty.

Let's say a person has been found competent to stand trial.
When is that person not able to be convicted because he or she
is mentally ill and thus not responsible for his or her actions?

One of the most recent cases that changed the law in this area
involved a man who strolled away from a state mental hospital to
a woman's apartment. He raped her, leaving his pants in her
apartment, and returned to the hospital. On the way, he walked
by several policemen, one of whom even stopped traffic for him,
apparently rather used to seeing patients from the nearby institution in various stages of undress. Only when a nurse inquired
several hours later as to the location of his pants did the story
emerge.

The man was brought to trial and found guilty because he
failed to meet the test of nonresponsibility known as the
McNaughton rule. (The rule developed in 1840 when a man tried
to kill Sir Robert Peel, hitting his private secretary instead. The
man suffered from delusions of being hounded by his enemies,
of whom he thought Peel was one.) This test allows a person to
be found not guilty only if the person did not know the quality
of his or her act or that the act was wrong. The McNaughton rule,
or right-from-wrong test, is the most difficult for a defendant

pleading insanity to fall under because it means that the person must be so ill that he or she does not even know that killing or raping is wrong.

At the other extreme is the Durham rule, which requires that one be found not guilty if one's act is the product of mental illness. When this test was first introduced into the District of Columbia, the jails began to empty and the hospitals filled to overflowing. Many complained that psychopaths and repeated offenders were being found not guilty merely because of the repetition of their antisocial behavior.

The conviction of the rapist in this case was reversed because the McNaughton rule was too rigid. The appeals court adopted the American Law Institute rule, which requires a not-guilty finding if the person did know right from wrong but could not stop himself or herself from doing wrong because of mental illness—and repeated criminal conduct alone is not evidence of mental illness.

The real question, of course, is what happens to a person who is found not guilty by reason of insanity. Many find themselves worse off in the system by which we deal with the mentally ill than if they had gone to prison.

Drunk driving and implied consent

Can you lose your license for holding your breath? That was the question recently decided by the U.S. Supreme Court. The case involved the Massachusetts Implied Consent Law, which says that a person who operates a motor vehicle is deemed to have consented in advance to a chemical test of his or her breath if arrested for operating a motor vehicle while under the influence. A person can refuse to submit to the test, but if so, his or her driver's license is lost for ninety days just for refusing. Like a number of other states, the loss of a license takes place without a hearing being given first.

This case began when the car in which a man was riding was struck in the rear by a motorcycle. The man was arrested for driving under the influence and taken to police headquarters, where he initially refused to take the breathalyzer test. He changed his mind later on, but then the police refused to give it to him. His license was suspended for ninety days in accordance with the law.

The man went to court claiming the Implied Consent Law was unconstitutional on its face because it allowed a license to be lifted without first holding a hearing. A three-judge federal court agreed. The Commonwealth of Massachusetts appealed to the U.S. Supreme Court.

That court reversed, reinstating the Implied Consent Law. The Court agreed that the license to operate a motor vehicle is an important interest, but said that a person who loses a license can request a hearing right afterward, so there is a quick chance to cure error. As for error, the court said the risk is very slight because the officer whose report of refusal triggers a driver's suspension is a trained observer and investigator.

As for the government's interest, the court noted in a footnote that more people were killed in alcohol-related traffic accidents in one year in Massachusetts alone than were killed in the recent DC-10 crash at O'Hare airport, and approximately one-half of the fifty thousand vehicle deaths annually are alcohol related.

Four justices dissented, saying that people in Massachusetts are offered no forum to tell their stories other than at the police station and that the police version of a disputed encounter between the police and a private citizen is not inevitably accurate and reliable. But the majority ruled, and the court has breathed new life into implied consent laws around the nation.

Watergate matters

The caption reads, "United States Court of Appeals, No. 75–1381, *The United States of America* v. *Harry R. Haldeman, John D. Ehrlichman, and John N. Mitchell.*" Then follow 303 pages of opinion, the end result of which is to uphold the conviction of the three men closest to former President Nixon. The opinion reviews in depth the twelve grounds that counsel for the defendants cited as errors in the lower court trial.

The Court of Appeals turned down claims by the defendants of prejudicial pretrial publicity. It also upheld the denial of the motion made by John Ehrlichman that his trial be severed from the others, and held that it was proper to admit evidence of the illegal break-in at the office of Daniel Ellsberg's psychiatrist. The opinion also turned down the appeal of John Mitchell who, despite his having been Attorney General of the United States, claimed he hadn't been given his *Miranda* warning prior to his testimony before the grand jury. Lastly, the court approved the denial of the defense motion to disqualify Judge John Sirica on the ground that he had been so involved in earlier Watergate matters that he could not help but be biased.

One of the major issues in the case involved the tape recordings. The defendants objected to the introduction of the tapes on three grounds. First, they said the tapes could be introduced in evidence only if one of the parties to the conversation consented to this, and that Judge Sirica made no specific finding of such consent. The appeals court said that although the judge did not make a specific point of finding consent, it is clear that the judge felt Mr. Nixon consented by directing the installation of the recording equipment.

Second, the defense challenged the authenticity of the tape recordings. But the court found that the Secret Service did a very careful job of doing the taping, noting and numbering the tapes, each of which coincided with the president's daily diaries, revealing the time, sequence, duration, and participants of every presidential telephone call and conference. And last, the defense claimed that since there was a tape with an eighteen-and-one-half-minute gap on it, this showed that all the tapes may have been tampered with. The appeals court refused to accept this position.

So the lower court verdicts of guilty were confirmed, and the defendants went on to serve time.

Your eyes are getting heavy

Your eyes are getting heavy; you're beginning to fall asleep. These words used to be used mostly at suburban house parties when an amateur hypnotist did his or her thing. But hypnosis has become deadly serious and has proved to be an extremely useful aid to police investigation. The question now coming to the courts is whether the recollections produced under hypnosis are reliable enough to be considered evidence.

Two courts have recently spoken out on this issue. The Minnesota Supreme Court has rejected hypnosis and held that a previously hypnotized witness may not testify at trial about evidence that was produced at a pretrial hypnotic session. The case involved a man who was charged with criminal sexual conduct and aggravated assault on a woman who couldn't remember a single thing about the episode until she was hypnotized, at which time she remembered everything in complete detail. The defendant claimed that hypnosis-prompted recollection is so unreliable it should not be admitted.

The Minnesota high court agreed, saying the case had to be governed by *Fry* v. *United States,* which held that the results of mechanical or scientific testing are not admissible unless the testing has developed or improved to the point where experts in the field widely agree that the results are reliable and accurate. The court cited expert testimony indicating that a hypnotized subject is highly susceptible to suggestion even when that suggestion is unintended, that the hypnotized subject is influenced by a need to fill in gaps, and that there's no way to determine from the content of memory which parts of the memory are historically accurate, which are entirely fanciful, and which are lies.

A New Jersey court, however, came out the other way. The question for that court was whether a citizen who was unable to recognize her attacker until she was hypnotized could testify in court that he was in fact the man who committed the crime. The New Jersey court agreed that hypnosis in general has not progressed to the state where it's universally accepted. But, said the court, hypnosis can be used for limited purposes—for example, to aid a person in making an identification or remembering a specific incident.

So one thing is clear. The final verdict is not in on hypnosis, and all that can safely be said is the admission of evidence gained under hypnosis depends on the state you're in.

Sifting through the ashes

Investigating arson has never been easy, and a recent decision of the U.S. Supreme Court hasn't made it any easier. The question in the case recently handed down by the High Court was whether the Fourth Amendment to the Constitution, which prohibits unreasonable searches and seizures, applied to fire fighters and arson investigators, as well as to police investigating typical crimes.

The facts of the case were that a fire broke out in a furniture store shortly before midnight. When the fire chief arrived at the scene about two hours later, he was told that the remains of some plastic containers full of flammable liquid had been found, and he called in the police detectives to investigate possible arson. The detectives arrived and took some pictures, but left because there was so much smoke and steam. After the fire, the fire chief and the police returned several times and removed materials that would later be used and introduced into evidence against the persons arrested and charged with burning down the building.

At the trial, the attorney representing the defendants claimed that because none of the officials had obtained a search warrant, introducing the evidence against his clients violated their Fourth Amendment rights. The trial judge refused to exclude the evidence, and the men were convicted. They appealed to the Michigan Supreme Court. That court reversed the conviction and ordered a new trial, this time without most of the evidence.

The Michigan high court stated that once the blaze has been extinguished and the fire fighters have left the premises, a warrant is required to reenter and search the premises, unless there is consent or the premises have already been abandoned. The State of Michigan appealed to the U.S. Supreme Court.

The Supreme Court pointed out that the Fourth Amendment is not limited to typical police activities, but rather extends to safeguard the privacy and security of individuals against arbitrary invasions by government officials. This includes health, fire, or even routine building code violations. The State of Michigan argued that there was no right to privacy in a burned-out building. But the Supreme Court replied that many people go on living in their homes or working in their offices after a fire, and even if they don't, private effects often remain on the fire-damaged premises.

The court held that the evidence gathered during the fire and even early the next morning while the fire fighters were still there was admissible, and the rest was not. So in the future, arson investigators may have to gather their evidence even before the fire is out.

The scene of a murder

Did you know that the scene of a murder is just like any place else? That's the result of a recent decision of the U.S. Supreme Court. The question before the court was whether or not the police had to get a warrant to search an apartment where a police officer had been shot to death while making an arrest.

The case started on the afternoon of October 28, 1974, when a plain-clothes member of the metropolitan narcotics squad knocked on the door of an apartment in Tucson, Arizona. He was admitted, but the door was then slammed shut, keeping out the nine other officers who had accompanied him. There was a volley of shots, and the officer staggered out mortally wounded. The other officers then found the man who had killed the officer and a woman, both of whom were wounded. The officers were joined by homicide detectives, and the dead officer and the wounded subjects were removed. The homicide detectives remained and conducted a search of the apartment that lasted for four days. The officers opened drawers, closets, and cupboards, pulled up carpeting, and in all seized an inventory of three hundred objects including bullets, shell casings, guns, narcotics, and narcotics paraphernalia.

The Arizona Supreme Court held that a search of the scene of the homicide without a warrant is constitutionally permissible. But the Supreme Court did not agree and reversed the convictions based on the seized evidence. The court said the Fourth Amendment prohibits all unreasonable searches and seizures, and it is a cardinal principle that searches conducted outside the judicial process without prior approval by a magistrate or judge are illegal, with very few exceptions. The scene of a homicide is not one of them.

The court rejected the State of Arizona argument that those who lived in the apartment forfeited their right of privacy after they killed the police officer. As for the search incident to a lawful arrest, the court said that it is one thing to say that a person who is legally taken into custody has a lessened right of privacy in his person, but quite another thing to say he has a lessened right of privacy in his entire house.

The state also claimed that a homicide is an emergency situation, and it has been held that evidence that is in plain view while the police are carrying out their emergency functions can be seized. The court said that while it did not question the right of police to respond to emergency situations, in this case all of the victims were removed and the emergency was over before the four-day search was begun. The court concluded, "The mere fact that law enforcement may be made more efficient can never by itself justify disregard for the Fourth Amendment."

If the police don't like your looks

If the police don't like your looks, you're in for a lot of trouble. That's the message of a recent case decided by the Minnesota Supreme Court. The case began when a police officer stopped a car for speeding on an interstate highway. While the officer was still seated in his cruiser, he saw the driver get out of his car and walk back toward him. As the man approached, the officer noticed his eyes were fixed in a wide stare and were also watery.

The officer walked up to the stopped car and shined a light into the front seat. He saw a woman crouched down with a brown paper bag lying on the floor tucked in between her legs and the front seat. He testified he asked her to get out, and she did so in a very strange manner, opening the door just enough to get out of the car, sliding around the door, and standing directly in front of the window very awkwardly. The officer noticed her eyes were also fixed in a wide stare. He asked what was in the bag. The reply was that the couple was on the way to Mexico for a vacation and the bag contained their lunch. The officer then reached in, opened the bag, and found that it contained four plastic packages of marijuana.

The driver was arrested for possession of a controlled substance and sentenced to a maximum term of three years in the state penitentiary. He appealed his conviction on the grounds that while the officer had a right to stop the vehicle because of speeding, there had been no arrest and therefore no right to look in the bag.

The court said the fact that the driver immediately got out of his car was characterized by the officer as an unusual maneuver, and the officer could have presumed the person was guilty about something and didn't want the officer to look in the car. Also, wide glassy stares could have indicated recent drug use to an experienced officer. Add to that the furtive gestures of the woman, and the court held the officer did have reasonable cause to believe the bag contained contraband.

One judge dissented, saying that more than hunches must underlie a determination to intrude upon constitutionally guaranteed rights of a private citizen; but the majority ruled, and if you look guilty, that's what you may be found.

A private room

What happens when a hospital visit ends up with the patient being arrested? That was the question recently asked of the California Court of Appeals for the Third District. The case began when a Sacramento, California, police officer stopped a man for questioning. The man was dressed in women's clothing and car-

ried a handbag containing a seven-inch steak knife. The man was
released after a check for outstanding warrants proved negative,
and he walked away in the direction of a nearby park.

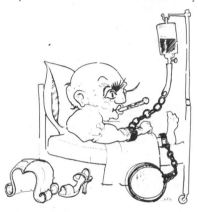

The next morning a man was found stabbed to death in the
park and the police, recalling the man they had stopped the night
before, began to check on his whereabouts. They found that he
had readmitted himself to a psychiatric hospital on the day the
body was discovered, and they decided to pay him a visit. They
were admitted to his room by a ward nurse; as they began to
question him, one of the officers happened to look inside an open
closet in the patient's room and saw a pair of shoes and stockings
with what appeared to be caked blood all over them.

The man was convicted on the basis of the evidence, and he
appealed his conviction to the California Court of Appeals, claiming that the invasion of his hospital room while he was a patient
violated his constitutional rights. He claimed a hospital is a special place, and the officers had no right to be there to question
him in the first place and had no right to look in his closet and
seize his personal possessions, even if they were caked with
blood.

The court said that the question before it turned on whether
the defendant had an expectation of privacy. The defendant asserted a hospital room was always cloaked with such an expectation, and the State of California argued that it never was. The
court said a hospital is in a class by itself, and clearly when a
person checks into a hospital the right to privacy may be waived
as to hospital personnel; but it is obvious that the person hasn't
turned his or her room into a public thoroughfare.

The court did say that when it came to the police, a patient has
the right to refuse to be visited. However, said the court, in this

case the patient accompanied the nurse back to his room voluntarily, knowing that the police were waiting there for him. The court upheld the conviction, proving that a private room in a hospital may not be quite so private after all.

Listening over your shoulder

Breaker 19. What's your 20 and how's it looking over your shoulder? That's CB talk for "Excuse me, where are you located, and have you seen any police cars lately?" The problem with CB is you never know who's listening. A Texas CBer found that out the hard way when his broadcast was monitored by the police and led to his arrest for possessing 285 pounds of marijuana.

What happened was that two Texas police officers were monitoring CB Channel 19 as they sat parked in their patrol car. They suddenly heard someone say, "Look out, red Ford; there's a smokey. Cut off at the next light." The officers decided to find out why a red Ford had been warned to avoid them. A few minutes later they found the red Ford, fully equiped with CB. While questioning the driver, they smelled a familiar odor coming from the car, and when the trunk was opened, 285 pounds of marijuana were found.

The driver of the car claimed the marijuana was improperly seized because the car was stopped illegally. He argued that curiosity raised by an anonymous CB broadcast should not be considered probable cause to stop and search a car. The trial judge let the evidence in and the driver was convicted and sentenced to six years in the penitentiary.

He appealed his conviction to the Texas Court of Criminal Appeals. That court listened to the arguments and decided to reverse the case, holding the marijuana had been improperly seized. The court said that a hunch or suspicion or curiosity is not enough, and there was no proof exactly who sent the message or who received it. And even if there were such proof, the court said the words "There's a smokey" and "Cut off at the next light" are just as consistent with innocent activity as with criminal activity, and therefore cannot justify a stop-and-search procedure.

And so, CBers, keep your ears on, watch out for the bears, and that's a 10–4.

A vigorous search

In recent years the police have had a difficult time securing confessions. Although the impact of the *Miranda* case has been muted in recent months, people arrested for crimes still have the right to remain silent and have to be informed of their right to an attorney who, once arrived on the scene, definitely impedes the ability of the police to secure verbal evidence. Thus the police have become more vigorous than ever in the pursuit of physical evidence.

Just how vigorous they have become was illustrated by the case of the woman who was driving on a suburban street in Fresno, California, when she noticed a car bearing two agents of the California Bureau of Narcotics Enforcement blocking her way. This was of some concern to her, since she had on the floor of the back seat seven balloons filled with heroin which she promptly swallowed as the police approached the car.

The officers arrested her, but instead of taking her to the police station for booking, they took her to the hospital along with a search warrant they had secured five days earlier. This warrant authorized a search of the woman, her husband, their residence, and their persons, and this latter category was about to be utilized to the fullest. The officers showed the search warrant to the attending physician, who prepared to conduct the ultimate search of a human being by ordering the nurse to ready syrup of ipecac, a solution that causes immediate regurgitation. When the woman refused to drink the liquid, she was forcibly strapped to a table and a rubber tube was inserted into her nose. A desperate five-minute struggle ensued, while the nurse, the physician, and the police tried to pour the solution down the tube. The woman finally found the tube too painful and gave up and drank the liquid, immediately producing seven multicolored balloons complete with heroin. The doctor stated that he acted as he did only because of the search warrant, and that he would never cause a person to regurgitate over objection without such a warrant.

The California Supreme Court was thus faced with a difficult dilemma, being cognizant on the one hand of the fact that there is certainly no legal right to conceal or destroy evidence of criminal conduct, and on the other, of the excessive force used in this case. The court made the difficult choice and reversed the conviction for possession of heroin, holding that the use of excessive force shocks the conscience and thus violates due process. The court observed, somewhat wistfully, that it would have been far better if the unfortunate woman had been transported to jail, placed in an isolated cell, and kept under proper serveillance while the natural outcome was awaited.

Getting evidence inside out

What happens when the only proof against a killer is the bullet he's carrying around inside him? That was the question recently decided in a case handed down by the Missouri Court of Appeals for the Eastern District.

The defendant was convicted by a jury of the first-degree murder of a city marshal in the city of Silex, Missouri. In the gun battle that cost the lawman his life, a shot was fired that struck his killer in the right hip, lodging in the man's body beneath the skin. The defendant asked the Missouri Court of Appeals to set aside his conviction on the basis that his constitutional rights were violated when the bullet was removed from him without his consent and then introduced against him as evidence at trial.

The court said there are four requirements to determine whether or not a surgical operation in search of evidence is reasonable: First, a court hearing should be conducted before the surgery has begun in which the defendant is represented by a lawyer and given the opportunity to cross-examine and present witnesses; second, if the court hearing allows the surgery, the individual must be given an opportunity to appeal the case; third, the evidence being looked for must be relevant; fourth, the surgical procedures should be a minor intrusion without risk of harm or injury to the individual involved.

The court pointed out that in this case the defendant was given a court hearing, which found that the operation was necessary to obtain a piece of relevant information—in this case, a bullet. And while the defendant had an opportunity to appeal the lower court's finding, he didn't do so. The court also found that the removal of the bullet did not constitute an unreasonable search and seizure for the reasons that it was not a major operation and there were no vital organs in the particular area where the bullet was lodged. Last, said the court, it would be in the best interests of the defendant health-wise for the bullet to be removed.

So if the police go about it right, it looks as though they can get their evidence even if it takes a surgeon's scalpel to find it.

Right and neighborly

What happens when your neighbor becomes the eyes, ears, and hands of the police? That was the question in a case recently decided by the Montana Supreme Court. The case got started when one Mrs. Arnold observed what she thought was marijuana growing in her neighbor's yard. Being a law-abiding citizen, she notified the sheriff's office, which dispatched a deputy sheriff to the scene of what appeared to be a growing crime. The deputy looked over the fence into the garden and reported back to his superiors that he hadn't seen any marijuana.

But Mrs. Arnold was not to be thrown off the track. One day after making sure her neighbor wasn't home, she entered her neighbor's garden and took a sample of what the court referred to as a leafy material. She took it to the sheriff's office herself, where it was confirmed that it was in fact marijuana. The sheriff got a search warrant and entered the garden for more samples, and then arrested Mrs. Arnold's neighbor.

The question for the court was whether Mrs. Arnold's illegal trespass onto the property of her neighbor constituted an illegal search and seizure. The court decided against the police and Mrs. Arnold, and for the defendant. The court said that a sample obtained by a curious person who trespasses on her neighbor's property is tainted as being the fruit of an illegal invasion of the neighbor's right of privacy.

The state claimed that the Constitution guarantees protection from the wrongful acts of law-enforcement personnel, not from the wrongful acts of private persons like neighbors. But the court said that today we live in an increasingly complex society and there isn't much privacy left. And the court held that in Montana at least, the right of individual privacy is inviolate, and search and seizure provisions apply to private individuals as well as to law-enforcement officers.

Robert Frost wrote that good fences make good neighbors. He might have added that good neighbors stay on their own side.

Minding your own business

What happens when you are sitting in a bar minding your own business and the police come calling? That was the question in a case recently decided by the U.S. Supreme Court. The case got started when a police informant told a special agent of the Illinois Bureau of Investigation that a bartender named Greg was dealing in heroin and that he'd been seen carrying fifteen to twenty-five tin-foil packets. The police secured a search warrant to search the bar.

One spring afternoon eight officers proceeded to the bar and upon arrival told each of the thirteen customers present to stay where they were and be searched for weapons. One customer was standing by the bar in front of a pinball machine, and the police officer who searched him didn't find any weapons, but felt what was like a cigarette pack with objects in it. The officer moved on, searching the other customers, and didn't find any weapons. He then came back and removed the package from the customer. Inside the cigarette package he found six tin-foil packets containing a brown powder that proved to be heroin.

The question for the courts was whether a customer who was in a bar that was being searched and who was a person other than the suspect could be convicted on the basis of evidence taken from him under those conditions. The Illinois Supreme Court said yes, but the Supreme Court in a five-to-four decision said no. The court said that when the police went to the bar they had a warrant to search Greg and to search the bar, but not to search other patrons of the bar.

The court said the customer did nothing to raise the suspicions of the police. It even went so far as to say that there was no right to pat down a patron for weapons, since there was no reason to suspect that because he was in a bar he might have a weapon.

There was a strong dissent, with one judge writing that if a police officer is forced to assume people are unarmed in bars where narcotics are believed to be, it's an assumption that police officers may pay for with their lives. But the majority ruled, and if you're sitting at the bar when the police come calling, you don't even have to turn around.

Strip searches for speeding

If you're stopped for speeding, can you be stripped and searched? That was the question recently decided by the U.S. District Court for Eastern Wisconsin. The case got started when a woman who was a resident of Colorado was driving one night with her four children through Racine County, Wisconsin. She was stopped for speeding by a state trooper. Because she didn't live in Wisconsin, she was told she'd have to post a forty-dollar cash bond on the spot. She didn't have forty dollars and was told to follow the police officer to the Racine County jail.

She was placed in a cell where a female guard told her to remove all her clothing so she could be searched for contraband. The woman refused, saying she was not a common criminal, but was only in jail because she'd been speeding and didn't have forty dollars. Her clothes were removed from her and every part of her body was searched for contraband. She was finally able to reach an uncle, who posted the forty dollars. She was then released.

The woman brought suit against the Racine County officials claiming that strip searches of persons arrested for traffic offenses were unconstitutional and violated the right to due process and the right to be free from unreasonable search and seizure. The woman did not ask for damages, but merely sought to have the court order a halt to the strip-and-search procedures of the Racine County jail.

The court reviewed the facts of the case and agreed that strip searches in cases such as this were unreasonable and did violate a person's constitutional rights under the Fourth and Fourteenth amendments to the Constitution. The court said it realized that people could be searched without a warrant after a valid arrest; but the mere fact of an arrest does not mean that any kind of a search can be carried out. Strip searches, said the court, are only justified if there is reason to believe a person may be concealing a weapon or evidence. The court said there was no reason to believe this woman had a weapon, and the only evidence was what her speedometer and that of the patrol car were reading just before she was stopped.

The court said this type of search was demeaning and dehumanizing, signified degradation and submission, and was unconstitutional. So while speeders can be stopped, strip searches can be as well.

You'd better do it at night

If you're doing something on your boat that you shouldn't be doing, you'd better do it at night. That seems to be the message of a case recently decided by the Ninth Circuit Court of Appeals. The case began in San Francisco Bay when the Coast Guard boarded a boat at night for the purpose of checking safety equipment. When the Coast Guard officer came on board, he saw an open door and what appeared to be bags of marijuana in plain view in a lighted cabin below deck. The officer placed those on board under arrest, and a subsequent search of the vessel showed that all the safety equipment was present, along with two tons of marijuana.

The defendants moved to keep the marijuana out of evidence, claiming it was not legally seized because of the random nature of the stop-and-search.

The court found there was no question but that the Coast Guard has authority to enforce boating safety regulations and also has expressed authority to board vessels in carrying out that enforcement. But, said the court, this boarding took place at night. And it was that point that brought the government's case right up on the rocks.

The court cited cases that have struck down random stops-and-searches of cars because of what is called subjective intrusion, which has to be balanced against governmental need. The court said the stop of an isolated boat after dark followed by a physical intrusion upon the boat has an unsettling effect on the boat owner that is greater than the governmental need. There's no reason why safety inspections cannot take place during the day, said the court, when there is far less intrusion to those involved. The marijuana was kept out of evidence.

One judge dissented, citing a study showing that of three thousand boats boarded in San Francisco Bay in a single year, more than 40 percent were found not to be in compliance with rules and regulations. The judge added that safety violators are far more dangerous at night than during the day. But the majority ruled, and when it comes to random searches at sea, the difference is like day and night.

The police like to be well informed

The police always like to be well informed, so they use informants. Most police intelligence is gathered from police officers who have successfully infiltrated criminal activities, or nonpolice individuals who sell or barter information to the police in return for money or, more frequently, more lenient treatment.

The hazards of relying on informants were illustrated by recent activities in Vermont, where that state's governor had to pardon seventy-one people who were convicted of drug charges on the basis of arrests by a discredited undercover agent. The agent was convicted of perjury and making false reports against people he had arrested on drug charges. He also faced $4 million worth of civil law suits by those who were convicted on the basis of his testimony.

The way it worked was explained by one woman who was walking down a Rutland, Vermont, street when the agent approached her. He reached into her pocketbook and came up with a handful of marijuana, which she claimed was never in the pocketbook to begin with. In all, more than one hundred and seventy-seven people who were "legally innocent," according to a special report on the situation, were arrested as a result of the agent's activities.

Because of the difficulties in the use of informants, the FBI has recently released a set of guidelines for their use. The guidelines state, "While it is proper for the FBI to use informants, it is imperative that individual rights not be infringed upon and that the government itself not become a violator of the law." In using informants, the FBI must now weigh a series of factors, such as the risk that the informant may violate individual rights, and the character and motivation of the informer himself. And if the bureau learns of a commission of a crime by the informant, it must notify the appropriate law-enforcement authorities and see to it that the informant is prosecuted.

The FBI guidelines don't discuss the coercive measures frequently used against informants to get the information, such as charging the informant with crimes more serious than the one actually committed in order to gain bargaining leverage. The guidelines raise some important points; perhaps most important, they serve as a reminder to the public and the police that those who inform as well as those who are informed on have rights too.

Firing at a fleeing felon

When a felon flees, can the force fire? This was the question before the Eighth Circuit Court of Appeals, which became the first court to overturn the time-honored concept that a police officer may use deadly force to prevent the escape of a person who has committed a felony. The landmark case grew out of an incident that took place in Olivette, Missouri, when a police officer found two persons in a golf driving-range office at one o'clock in the morning. He yelled, "Stop, or I'll shoot," and then immediately fired a shot that killed an eighteen-year-old youth.

At issue was a Missouri law that was similar to those of at least twenty-three other states. The law had provided that homicide would be deemed justifiable "when necessarily committed in attempting . . . to apprehend any person for any felony." This law and others like it are based on the common-law principle established back in England, which provides that deadly force can be used to arrest any felony suspect. The court pointed out that this concept goes back to the fifteenth century, when all felonies were punishable by death anyway, so the use of deadly force then was merely seen as accelerating the penal process.

The problem of today is that very few felonies are punishable by death. The court rules that the police officer cannot be constitutionally vested with the power and authority to kill any and all escaping felons, including the thief who steals an ear of corn, as well as one who kills and ravishes at will.

One judge filed a strong dissent, claiming that now the police officer will have to be endowed not only with foresight but also with hindsight. The judge agreed that the right to life is impor-

tant, but he also asked about the interests of effective law enforcement, the apprehension of criminals, the prevention of crime,
and the protection of members of the general populace who, like
fleeing felons, also possess a right to life.

But the majority ruled, and now when a police officer finds a
man in a golf driving-range office at one o'clock in the morning,
the officer may have to assume the man was just getting in some
early morning practice.

Earwitness identification

Earwitness identification—how good is it? Not very good at all,
according to a recent decision handed down by the Montana
Supreme Court. The case depended on a tape recording and a
woman's ability to remember the voice of the man who raped her.

The case began one night as the one woman employee of a
Montana grocery store was preparing to close for the night. A
man entered the store, grabbed her from behind, and told her
not to look at him. To make sure she didn't look, he held a knife
pressed across her right eye. He then raped her, tied her up, took
the night receipts, and fled; the woman didn't look, but she
listened, carefully, to the voice of her assailant. She later claimed
she could positively identify this voice.

After the man left, the woman struggled to a phone and called
the police. She told what happened in a distraught and frightened
voice, and the emotion-filled tape recording was played at the
trial, which resulted in conviction. The man, who was arrested
because someone had written down the registration of his truck
parked outside the store, appealed his conviction on two
grounds: first, that the tape recording was unduly prejudicial and,
second, the woman's identification of his voice was not reliable.

The Montana Supreme Court first took up the issue of the tape.
The court said it contained emotional outpourings of a victim in
the immediate aftermath of a violent crime and that these utter-
ances necessarily induced a feeling of outrage against the defendant and sympathy for the victim, destroying a fair trial climate.

As for the voice identification, the court said to allow it was also
error, since the woman's recollection was not one that could be
depended upon. For example, said the court, because the police
told the woman they had a suspect in custody, when she went to
listen to his voice, she was already prejudiced.

There were some dissenting opinions, with one judge writing

that impressions received through the sense of hearing are facts as to which a witness can testify, and another writing that she described his clothing and the smell of gasoline on him, as well as his voice. But the majority ruled, and when it comes to earwitness identification by a rape victim, the courts, in Montana at least, won't hear of it.

Your telephone may be wired

Your telephone may be wired for trouble. That's what a man found out who was on the receiving end of an opinion by the Fourth Circuit Court of Appeals. That court recently upheld the conviction of a man who was charged with wire fraud based on the use of his telephone. What the man did was to rent an apartment, obtain a business license, and place numerous newspaper ads for the purpose of meeting and seducing young women. He posed as a talent agent and a producer connected with major movie companies.

The man told women who telephoned him in response to the ads that he could place them in legitimate and well-paying modeling and acting jobs. When he met them, however, he also told them there was one more condition for making it big—that they submit to his sexual advances, which a surprising number of young women did. The court said as a result of his activity a large number of women spent time, effort, and money taking leave from their jobs, hiring baby-sitters, traveling to his office, memorizing scripts, and yielding to his advances.

As his defense, the man claimed that to convict him was to extend improperly the federal wire-fraud statute. He claimed that what he did was simply a matter of misrepresentation in order to meet women, the implication being that meeting women is difficult, and so what's a little innovative misrepresentation, anyway? Besides, he said, what did the women really lose?

The court answered that his arguments were unpersuasive and that his scheme was not a simple matter of misrepresentation designed to meet women, but rather an elaborate commercial facade surrounding a completely fraudulent enterprise. The key to an offense under the law, said the court, is the misuse of interstate communication facilities to execute any scheme or artifice to defraud. What the defendant gained or the victim lost is simply not relevant.

The man also claimed that his conviction was unconstitutional in that the law gave him no reasonable notice that his conduct was a violation and in that the law invaded his privacy. The court said the plain language of the law condemns any scheme to defraud in which interstate wires are employed. And as for privacy, the law wasn't being used to punish the man for his sexual activities, but rather for using the telephone to accomplish his fraudulent intentions. So for this man, at least, his number was up.

Checking your bags

If you check your baggage at the airport, you may be home free. That's the message of a recent case decided by the Sixth Circuit Court of Appeals. The case involved an airport arrest by drug enforcement agent Paul Markonni. Markonni has been involved in a number of cases. As the Court of Appeals put it in its opening paragraph, "Markonni has amassed an impressive drug enforcement record in Detroit, resulting in a number of opinions exploring the boundaries of permissible police activity; this opinion adds another dimension to those boundaries."

The case got started when Markonni received a telephone call from another agent in San Francisco informing him that a Detroit resident had been arrested while attempting to clear customs with three pounds of heroin. Markonni checked with the travel agency that had sold the man his round-trip ticket to Bangkok and learned that another Southeast Asia traveler was due in to Detroit later that day. Markonni ordered up a dog specially trained to sniff out the presence of drugs in clothing or luggage.

When the plane arrived, Markonni took the man to an airport security room and relieved him of his tickets and his baggage claim checks. Markonni claimed the luggage and took it back to the airport security room where the soon-to-be defendant was patiently waiting. After finding a small amount of marijuana in the toe of one of the man's socks, Markonni arrested the man, then directed the dog to smell the luggage. The dog sniffed out a quarter-pound of heroin hidden in a talcum powder container.

The lower court allowed the heroin into evidence on the ground that it was a search incident to an arrest. But the Court of Appeals reversed and held that Markonni had once again stepped "over the line." The court said that while a person may be searched after he or she is arrested in order to prevent the destruction of evidence and protect the officer, the luggage wasn't with the defendant until the police officer brought it to him, and a search warrant should have been obtained. And so, while this drug importer will go free, Paul Markonni will probably ask the next suspect to claim his own bags.

Obscenity—contemporary standards

Just who is the people, anyway? That was the question at the heart of a recent case involving obscenity decided by the U.S. Supreme Court. The convicted defendant had been charged with sending obscene brochures and magazines through the mail, which is a violation of federal law. The standard by which things are judged obscene is whether they affront the standards of the community. And just who that community includes was what this case was all about.

The trial judge told the jury, "In determining community standards you are to consider the community as a whole, young and old, educated and uneducated, the religious and the irreligious, men, women, and children, from all walks of life." The defendant claimed that to include children as part of the community when it came to deciding what was and was not obscene was prejudicial to his case.

The Supreme Court agreed that it had not been clear in prior cases whether or not children should be included as part of the community in judging obscenity. The court said that it may well be that a jury conscientiously striving to define the community would reach a much lower average when children were part of the equation than they would if they restricted their consideration to the effect of allegedly obscene materials on adults. Since there was no evidence in the case that children were the intended recipient of the material, or that they had even seen the material, the court said it was error for the judge to include children in his charge.

The trial judge had also included a reference to sensitive persons and deviant groups, implying that sensitive persons and deviant groups also have to be considered when one is viewing the community at large. The defendant claimed that by including the term "sensitive person" or "deviant groups," his case had been unfairly prejudiced. But here the Supreme Court did not agree. It said that the community includes all adults who comprise it, and a jury can consider them all in determining relevant community standards. While it would be improper to focus in on the most susceptible or sensitive members, or on the impact of the material on deviant groups, there is nothing wrong with including them in the community as a consideration.

So, except for children, it looks as though the community includes just about everybody.

A footnote to Gary Gilmore

The following appears in a footnote to the opinion by the U.S. Supreme Court that cleared the way for the execution of Gary Mark Gilmore: "This case may be unique in the annals of the court. Not only does Gary Mark Gilmore request no relief himself; on the contrary, he has expressly and repeatedly stated since his conviction in the Utah courts that he has received a fair trial and has been well-treated by the Utah authorities. Nor does he claim to be innocent of the crime for which he was convicted. Indeed, his only complaint against Utah or its judicial process . . . has been the delay on the part of the state in carrying out the sentence."

The case came to the Supreme Court on December 2 by way of an application for a stay of execution filed by Gilmore's mother, Bessie. She filed as her son's "next friend," which is the language often used when one seeks help in court for a person who is incompetent or at least suspected of being incompetent. The court then received responses to these papers from Gilmore's attorneys and the state, which claimed that Bessie Gilmore had no standing or right to intervene as her son's next friend.

There were two key questions in the case: Was Gary Mark Gilmore mentally competent to waive his rights; and, if he was, could he waive his rights and be executed under a statute that is of questionable constitutionality?

The court, in a five-to-four opinion, held that Gilmore's waiver of rights was knowingly and intelligently made, and it noted that three out of five psychiatrists had found no evidence of mental illness or insanity. The record before the court did not include the findings of the other two psychiatrists. As for the question of the statute's unconstitutionality, the court said simply that that question was not before it because no one other than Gilmore had authority to bring that question to the court; and since he chose not to raise it, it simply wasn't present.

Justice White, dissenting, said, "I believe that the consent of a convicted defendant in a criminal case does not privilege a state to impose a punishment otherwise forbidden by the Eighth Amendment." Justice Marshall added that the suicide attempts, the fact that the psychiatrists were all employed by the state, and the fact that important portions of the record of the case were not before the court should cause a stay to be granted.

But the majority ruled, and Gary Mark Gilmore's battle to be shot at sunrise ended.

How private are your credit cards?

How private are your credit cards? That was the question recently answered by the California Supreme Court. The case involved the question of just how easy it is to get information as to where, when, and how you've been using your credit cards. In this case, a man was convicted of having committed two murders. The evidence that led to his conviction was the fact that he used a Diner's Club card when he checked into a hotel. The police secured his credit-card records just for the asking, and those records led to his arrest and conviction for murder.

The man appealed his conviction to the California Supreme Court, claiming that the evidence based on his credit card should be thrown out because of the manner in which the records were obtained. He claimed that having his credit-card records turned over to the police without a warrant violated his constitutional rights against unreasonable search and seizure.

The State of California claimed that it was proper to have gotten the credit-card information without a warrant in this case because the individual used a false name in applying for his Diner's Club card. The state also claimed that the California right-to-privacy act only prevents banks from releasing information about customers and doesn't cover credit-card companies.

After reviewing the facts, the court held that it was improper for the credit-card information to have been given to the police without a search warrant. As for the argument that the man used a false name, the court noted that Diner's Club didn't consider itself wronged by the use of a false name. In fact, a representative of American Express had testified that if it learned a customer was using a fictitious name on an account, it would not cancel the account.

As for the California privacy act, the court said its decision was based on the Constitution, not on a specific act of the California legislature. So a man may escape being found guilty for murder because he used his credit card.

And how private are your letters?

Do you know when other people can read your mail? If you don't, you should take a look at a whole new set of postal regulations that recently went into effect and that clarify the procedures under which your mail can be detained, opened, and read by somebody other than the person to whom it is addressed.

The regulations start off protecting the privacy of your letters, providing that in general nobody can open or search any sealed letter, even if there is reason to believe that it contains criminal or nonmailable matter, or evidence of a crime. The only exception to this rule is if a postal inspector has gotten the permission of the person who sent the letter and if the inspector has gotten a search warrant. The regulations also give some protection to those who typically send their mail in unsealed envelopes at a much lower rate of postage, like the blind, or schoolchildren. While this mail can still be opened to make sure that those who are sending it really are blind or schoolchildren, the postal inspector who opens it is prohibited under the new regulations from telling anybody else what was in the letter.

The regulations then move into areas where mail can be opened and read without a search warrant. One of the most difficult areas is mail to and from prisoners. In this area the postal service decided not to lay down an ironclad policy, but rather to allow varied practices to continue. The regulations provide that authorized prison officials can open mail addressed to inmates of institutions if the inmate consents to receive his mail through the prison authorities. In case you're wondering why an inmate would give his consent to receive his mail through the prison authorities, the reason probably is that if he doesn't consent, the post office merely returns his mail to the sender marked "refused."

Another area where mail can be opened without a warrant is mail that originates outside the United States sent to somebody inside the United States. Customs and the postal service can continue the practice of opening such mail if they have reasonable suspicion that items on which a customs duty is due are inside.

The only other area where mail may be opened is if it is suspected of containing something dangerous or if there is reason to believe the mail contains plants or pests. As to what constitutes grounds to believe that mail is dangerous or contains plants or pests, that's left up to the postal service.

Next time you write a Russian

Next time you write a Russian, only a Russian will read what you've written. That's the message of a recent decision of the Second Circuit Court of Appeals. The case involved the CIA policy of covertly opening first-class mail going between citizens of the United States and the Soviet Union. This practice went on from 1953 to 1973, and during that time more than 215,000 letters were secretly opened, photocopied, and then returned to postal authorities for delivery. In 1958 the CIA offered to share the project's take with the FBI, with the approval of then-director Hoover.

This particular case involved a lawsuit against the government by three individuals whose mail was opened and copied. They brought suit against the government for invasion of privacy under the federal tort claims act. A federal district court in New York found an invasion of privacy and violation of constitutional rights. The court ordered that the government pay each plaintiff one thousand dollars as damages for mental suffering. The court also ordered that the United States send a letter of apology to each victim.

The government appealed on the basis that the CIA was involved in a "discretionary" act and that the government should not be held liable for mistakes of discretion or judgment. But the court said that a discretionary act has to be within the scope of the agency's authority, and the CIA's legislative charter gave it no authority to gather intelligence on domestic matters. The court also rejected the government's claim that since the letters were going to the USSR, they would have been opened by someone other than the intended reader anyway, sooner or later.

The appeals court did reverse the order of a letter of apology because the federal tort claims act only provides for money damages. While such letters might have value some day as collector's items, said the court, they simply didn't meet the language of the law.

Putting a bounty on a Nazi

What happens when you place a bounty on a Nazi? That was
the question in a case recently decided by the California Court
of Appeals for the Second District. The case occurred just before
the Nazi Party's planned march through Skokie, Illinois. A few
weeks before the march a man who was an official in the Jewish
Defense League called a press conference in Los Angeles to
announce the formation of a counter organization to stop the
march. During the press conference, he held up five $100 bills
and made the following statement: "We are offering five hundred
dollars that I have in my hand to any member of the community
be he Jewish or gentile who kills, maims, or seriously injures a
member of the American Nazi Party. This offer is being made on
the east coast and on the west coast; and if they bring us the ears,
we'll make it one thousand dollars. This is not said in jest, we are
deadly serious." .

The man was charged with the crime of solicitation of murder.
A lower court judge ordered the charges dismissed on the
grounds that while the statements could be interpreted as soliciting the murder of a member of the Nazi Party, those statements
were protected by the First Amendment. This was so, said the
lower court, because the statements were made to attract media
attention and were without the necessary intent to actually have
a murder committed.

The State of California appealed the dismissal and the Court
of Appeals overturned the lower court and ordered the charges
reinstated, deciding that the words did have a murderous intent
and were in no way protected by the First Amendment. The court
said that the crime of solicitation of murder is a simple crime. It
is defined as asking another person to commit murder, and
whether the intent to actually have that murder committed was
present was up to the jury and the case should not have been
dismissed before by the judge prior to the trial.

On the question of the First Amendment, the Court of Appeals
said there was no question but that the man's plain words ad-
vocated violence in the form of murder, mayhem, and serious
bodily injury, and thus were not protected free speech. So even
if you do think that a man has descended to the level of an animal,
you can't place a bounty on his head.

Cancer is the pits

If cancer patients want to be treated with apricot pits, should the government stop them? That's the basic question raised by the laetrile controversy presently sweeping the country. Several state legislatures have approved the drug for manufacture and distribution within state boundaries, and court cases are pending in many jurisdictions concerning the substance, which is made from apricot pits.

One of the most comprehensive looks at the subject has been taken by federal courts in Oklahoma, which have been hearing a case brought by a cancer patient. That patient wanted to prevent the government from interfering with his use of laetrile. He won in the lower court and got that court to issue an injunction keeping the Food and Drug Administration from preventing his getting a supply of laetrile for his own use.

The government appealed the case on the ground that the FDA can't approve a new drug in the first place unless a new-drug application is submitted by the manufacturing company. The government also argued that the lower court exceeded its authority by blocking enforcement of an act of Congress without convening a three-judge court, which the government said was required when such drastic action is taken.

The patient's argument, which was successful in the lower court, was that laetrile was a food, not a drug. Also, if it was a drug, it wasn't a new drug and shouldn't be subject to the rigorous procedures under the Food, Drug, and Cosmetic Act.

The appeals court said that the chances that laetrile was a food and not a drug were slim, because it was admitted that it was a substance intended as a treatment for cancer. But, said the court, the question of whether it is a new drug subject to the act is much more difficult. A new drug is defined in the law as a drug that is not generally recognized as safe and effective for use. But drugs existing before the 1962 amendments to the Food, Drug, and Cosmetics Act are, in essence, grandfathered under the law.

So the court sent the matter back to determine if laetrile was marketed before 1962 for exactly the same uses for which it is now being offered. In the meantime, the injunction allowing the plaintiff to have access to the drug was upheld. So the controversy that pits the public against the FDA goes on.

Looking into *Deep Throat*

If you go after *Deep Throat,* you've got to see it to be believed. That's the message of a recent case decided by the North Dakota Supreme Court. The case dealt with the film *Deep Throat* and an attempt to have the film declared obscene after it was seized at a showing at the University of North Dakota.

The case got started when a student activities programming committee called the Spoke Committee scheduled *Deep Throat* for showing at a university symposium on the subject of obscenity. The film was seized at the symposium and a lower court entered a statewide injunction prohibiting the film from being shown anywhere in the state of North Dakota.

The Spoke Committee appealed to the North Dakota Supreme Court, and that court reversed the lower court on the grounds that the film was unlawfully seized. The Supreme Court said although the prosecutor had a search warrant, the basis of the warrant was what the prosecutor had read or been told by others about the film. The prosecutor claimed in an affidavit that he had read numerous articles about and critiques of the movie. The court said that the affidavit was hearsay and should not have been accepted. The court said that while an affidavit for a search warrant can sometimes be based on hearsay, the information must be shown to be credible or reliable, and newspaper reviews and casual comments just don't do the trick.

The Court cited the *Aruilar* case decided by the U.S. Supreme Court in which that court allowed an affidavit based on hearsay of an unidentified informant, but only because the officer involved swore that the informant was reliable and credible. In this case the prosecutor said that he'd read reviews of the film in *Time* magazine, in a book entitled *Adam Reviews Porno Films,* and in the *Minneapolis Tribune,* but he never submitted the dates and pages of the articles.

The court ordered the film returned to the students. One judge concurred in the result; he filed a separate opinion saying he conceded that the film had to be returned, but expressing disappointment in the rule that excludes evidence because of improper activity on the part of officials. He was disappointed, he said, that it is necessary to exclude the truth from judicial searches for truth.

So *Deep Throat* will return to the University of North Dakota, and you can guess who may be in the audience next time around.

Bare buttocks and church parking lots

Is it legal for a bare buttock to be seen from a church parking lot? Well, believe it or not, the answer to this searching question is yes, according to the U.S. Supreme Court. The case pitted the operators of a drive-in movie theater against an ordinance of the city of Jacksonville, Florida. The ordinance read, "It shall be unlawful for any person to exhibit any motion picture in which the human male or female bare buttocks, human female bare breasts, or human bare pubic areas are shown, if such motion picture is visible from any public street or public place."

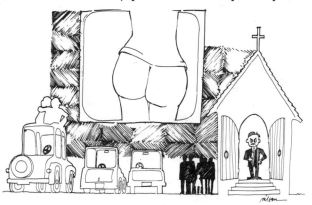

It seems that the drive-in theater was adjacent to two public streets as well as a church parking lot. There was testimony that the movies were visible and were regularly watched by people sitting outside the theater on the grass, in parked cars along the streets, and even in cars parked in the church parking lot. The trial court that initially heard the case held that the ordinance was a legitimate exercise of the city's police power.

The city of Jacksonville argued that there were three reasons its law should be upheld: First, the city had the obligation to protect its citizens against unwilling exposure; second, the ordinance was justified as a traffic ordinance to prevent rear-end collisions that might result when persons drove by the theater and watched the movie at the same time; and, third, it was proper exercise of the power and duty of the state to protect children from improper influences.

The Supreme Court answered these points by saying that the law did not protect citizens from all movies that might offend, but rather singled out films containing nudity, and that "the burden normally falls upon the viewer to avoid further bombardment of his sensibilities simply by averting his eyes." As far as children were concerned, the court said that scenes of a body's buttock, the nude body of a war victim, or a film about a country where nudity is accepted were situations that could not be considered obscene even for children. As for the traffic patterns, the court noted that a fleeting glimpse of nudity might be less distracting than violence or a wide variety of other scenes in the customary screen diet.

While four justices dissented, the majority ruled, and the only way those in the church parking lot can avoid seeing the movie is not to look.

Making living mandatory

Can the city where you live force you to stay alive? This was the question in a recent Michigan case that upheld a city ordinance requiring all motorcyclists to wear helmets within city limits. The motorcyclist who brought the case claimed that the ordinance was an unlawful invasion of his individual rights, including his right to privacy, which he said was protected by the state and federal constitutions. The city attorneys, on the other hand, claimed that the ordinance was a valid exercise of the state police power, which is often cited as a reason for interference with personal or private rights.

The court stated that the question for decision was whether the interest of the public generally requires interference with the motorcyclist's rights to drive without a helmet. The court held that there is a distinction between regulations that solely protect an individual from himself and those that primarily protect the individual while also protecting other members of society.

Now, you may ask, how could a regulation designed to protect a motorcyclist from suffering a fractured skull protect other members of society as well? Well, as the court put it, "more is involved than the unfettered freedom of the cyclist." The court cited as an example the fact that the ordinance also benefits the driver of a car that might be struck by the motorcycle. Since the purpose of the helmet is to prevent the death of the motorcyclist, if the helmet saves the life of the motorcyclist, not only has the cyclist survived, but also the automobile driver hasn't killed anyone; thus the driver can avoid the legal and psychological problems that are inevitable when someone is involved in a fatal traffic accident. The court also waxed poetic about just what the helmet ordinance really is, stating, "It is therefore a creative, relatively non-intrusive response of government to protect the public from detrimental technological change."

The decision presents one perspective on the continuing question of whether the government has the right to pass laws that protect you as well as other people. Another perspective is found in a recent decision of a former Secretary of Transportation. He announced that the government wasn't going to require air bags in cars because people weren't ready yet to be told they had to have them. But in Michigan, at least, cyclists will have to wear a helmet, for the other person's sake.

The toughest handgun law

What has been called the toughest handgun law in the country was upheld by the District of Columbia Superior Court. What the law did was to freeze the number of handguns in the District by providing that handguns couldn't be bought or registered any more. There was a grandfather clause allowing people to keep their guns if the guns were registered at the time the law went into effect, but only in their places of business, not at home. The law also prohibited residents or nonresidents from bringing handguns into the District from someplace else.

The National Rifle Association and others went to court claiming that the law was unconstitutional because it deprived homeowners of the right to self-protection while allowing those running businesses to protect themselves. The court cited a report issued by a legislative committee that, it said, provided the factual basis for the distinction. Arguments for the home/business difference have included the fact that the home is a more dangerous place to have a gun because of children and because of the chance for domestic problems to be permanently settled with a gun. The plaintiffs also claimed that this section of the law violated equal protection by treating business people and homeowners differently; but the court disagreed, saying that everybody was treated just the same, with all homeowners prohibited from having guns and all businesses allowed to keep theirs.

The plaintiffs also claimed that the law violated the constitutional right to travel because gun-toting travelers coming into the District would have to leave their guns at home or check them at the District line. The court answered that prohibiting travel with a handgun was a very different matter from prohibiting travel altogether, and that a handgun, regardless of how some of the plaintiffs may have felt, is not a necessity of life.

The only part of the law that the court did find unconstitutional was that section permitting nonresidents to travel to a recreational shooting event in the District. The court said that it could not see how residents and nonresidents could be treated differently under the law and struck down that part of the law—not exactly the result the NRA was shooting for.

The right to wear a swastika

Does the First Amendment to the Constitution give you the right to wear a swastika? That was the issue raised in a lawsuit brought by the Village of Skokie, Illinois, against the National Socialist Party. The case got started when the members of the party announced plans to assemble and march through the village single file, wearing storm trooper uniforms that included Nazi swastika armbands. The village went to court and got an injunction prohibiting the party members from parading or marching through the village and from displaying the swastika on their arms or anywhere else. The party appealed to the Illinois appeals court, which recently issued its decision.

The first question the appellate court looked at was whether the lower court acted properly in prohibiting the march regardless of what the marchers wore. The village claimed that it acted to prevent violence, because if the march was held, thousands of irate Jewish citizens would attack the marchers. The court held that it was not proper to stop the march, because legal First Amendment activities like assembling and marching can't be restrained because of the possibility of a hostile audience attacking. The court also ruled that a uniform that didn't have any symbols on it could be worn.

Then it came time for the court to consider the displaying of the swastika, and here the court agreed with the village officials that the wearing of the swastika would in fact incite large numbers of the Jewish population of Skokie to violence and retaliation. The court recognized the principle laid down by the U.S. Supreme Court that fighting words are not protected by the Constitution. Fighting words were defined by the Supreme Court as personally abusive epithets which, when addressed to ordinary citizens, are inherently likely to provoke violent reaction. Since there was evidence that thousands of Jewish citizens would be provoked by the swastika, which was the symbol of fighting words, the court said it must follow that the swastika would offend all those who respect the honestly held faith of their fellows, including the ordinary citizen.

So the Nazi swastika will not be on parade in Skokie.

Nazis in the U.S.A.

For the first time in the United States, persons suspected of being Nazi war criminals will face this country's courts. They won't be tried for their war crimes, however, because the United States has no laws on its books to punish what these people are accused of having done. What they will face are deportation proceedings, and they will be deported if it can be proved that they lied when they applied for their visas, or if it can be shown they were persons whose entry would have been barred because such entry was prejudicial to interests of the United States.

The investigation has been plodding along, carried out by the Immigration and Naturalization Service at the urging of a number of members of Congress, and there has been some criticism that the whole matter has taken more than thirty years to reach this point. Not much was done until 1972, when Hermine Brausteiner Ryan, a Queens housewife, was extradited from New York to West Germany, where she was tried for murder because of her role as a guard at the Maidanek concentration camp in Poland.

Recently, orders to show cause and notice of hearing were served on the first sixty-one persons who had been under investigation. The notices were starkly simple. One read as follows: "In your application you falsely stated that you were a bookkeeper, whereas in fact you were employed as a member of the Latvian Police Department and performed, participated in, and acquiesced in activities contrary to civilization and human decency." Another charged a Connecticut man with participating in the shooting of sixty children and selecting a group of four hundred Jews for execution in the Krupas Woods on or about August 1941.

The government must prove by clear and convincing evidence that these people lied upon entering the United States, and all of them, regardless of what they might have done, will be given the right of appeal to the Board of Immigration Appeals, the U.S. Court of Appeals, and the Supreme Court. Then and only then will they be deported, if a country can be found to accept them.

A promise is a promise

A promise is a promise. That's the moral of a case recently decided by the Second Circuit Court of Appeals. The question raised was whether U.S. citizens who are imprisoned in Mexican jails for marijuana offenses and then transferred to U.S. jails under a treaty have to keep their promises.

The case began when hundreds of Americans were arrested and convicted in Mexico because of marijuana and narcotic violations. The courts said there was no question but that these people were tortured by police trying to get confessions, and that while in prison they suffered from unsanitary conditions, were beaten, and were forced to pay for even the basic necessities of life.

In 1974, Congress and a number of American journalists began to investigate the situation. Those investigations led to a treaty between the United States and Mexico. Under the terms of the treaty, a U.S. citizen convicted of a criminal offense in Mexico can transfer to an American prison for the balance of his sentence if he agrees that only the courts of Mexico shall have jurisdiction to modify or set aside the conviction handed down by a Mexican court.

A number of prisoners, however, went to the U.S. courts as soon as they were returned to American soil. They claimed they should be able to challenge the Mexican convictions on the grounds that the Mexican police officers had violated their search-and-seizure rights. A lower court agreed with the petitioners, but the Court of Appeals reversed, saying the promise not to challenge was the very basis of the treaty. If U.S. courts allowed such a challenge, hundreds of Americans still held in Mexican jails and those who might be arrested in the future might never see the light of day.

So a deal is a deal, and the petitioners can always ask to go back to Mexico to argue their cases.

When a county releases a killer

When a county releases a killer, it had better take care. That's the message of a recent case decided by the California Court of Appeals for the First District. The case involved a juvenile delinquent by the name of James who was described as an extremely violent individual with propensities for sexual assault of young children. Although James was diagnosed as having very serious mental disorders that rendered him potentially violent, he was released into the community in the custody of his mother, who had not been able to control his behavior in the first place. Within twenty-four hours of his release, James sexually assaulted and murdered a five-year-old boy who lived in the same neighborhood.

The parents of the dead boy brought suit against Alameda County, claiming the county had acted recklessly in releasing James into the community. They also claimed as a major part of their case that the county failed to warn police and parents of young children that James was coming home.

The county claimed it was completely immune from liability for the release or failure to warn. In its defense the county cited a section of the California code that says a public employee or public entity is not liable for any injury resulting from an act or omission that is the result of the exercise of discretion. The county also pointed to another section of the law that gave immunity for release of prisoners, including wards of the juvenile court.

The court agreed that the decision whether or not to release James was in fact a matter of discretion, and therefore neither the county nor its officials could be held liable for that decision. But, said the court, sounding a warning is a different matter; while the decision to release may have been a matter of discretion, once that decision was made, it was mandatory that a reasonable warning be given to endangered persons or foreseeable victims.

So the case was sent to trial for a jury to decide just what reasonable warning really means and how much a total failure to give it is worth.

A captive audience

A well-orchestrated lobbying effort was conducted not long ago by the Boston Symphony Orchestra against various and sundry Massachusetts politicians who wanted to put a prison near Tanglewood, the symphony's summer home.

All around the country, new prisons are being designed and are ready to be built. Many believe that new prisons are necessary, since many state and federal facilities are antiquated, overpopulated, or both. And the growing disfavor with leniency, suspended sentences, probation, parole, and the entire rehabilitation effort has resulted in an expanded prison population, a trend that seems destined to continue. But while many believe new prisons are necessary, they all want them located in somebody else's town.

So the strings the symphony attempted to pull were symbolic of a nationwide struggle. And who can blame someone who gets a little uncomfortable when hometowns come up in conversation and he has to say he's from Leavenworth, Kansas, or Attica, New York.

The proposal that caused strains different from what Tanglewood is used to was to place a medium-security prison at Shadowbrook, which is about one hundred yards from Tanglewood and, according to the executive director of the Boston Symphony, overlooks Tanglewood and dominates the entire area. Shadowbrook itself was originally an eighty-five-room mansion built in 1893. It was later owned by the Jesuits, who wanted to sell it to the Commonwealth of Massachusetts, which was then playing to a full house, with twenty-seven hundred prisoners and only twenty-six hundred beds, and a long waiting line at the box office. The director of planning for correctional facilities was quoted as saying, "If we don't get these new facilities, we face very grave problems." When asked about waste disposal, he said, "There was no problem for Tanglewood when Shadowbrook was a seminary, and there is no reason to suppose that two hundred prisoners will be more of an environmental problem than two hundred seminarians."

Well, based on all of this, one could say there will be some treble ahead, and we'll just have to wait and see whether the notes will be on the bars or passed between them.

Copping a plea

Not long ago, a man who admitted killing two New York City policemen on New York's Lower East Side was allowed to plead guilty to a lesser charge rather than face the death penalty if convicted. Senator James Buckley of New York said that the deal was "an affront to every policeman, every wife of a policeman, and every widow of an officer slain in the line of duty."

The fact is that this is merely one of the more striking examples of something that goes on in the criminal courts every day throughout the country. It's called plea bargaining or, in street terms, "copping a plea." What it means in most cases is that a person accused of a crime will plead guilty to the same or lesser offense rather than go through a trial, and he does this usually because he's been advised by his lawyer that he'll get a lighter sentence than if he fights the charge all the way and is then found guilty.

There are many problems with plea bargaining, some of which have been lessened by recent changes in the Federal Rules of Criminal Procedure, which set the ground rules for criminal trials in the federal courts. From the point of view of the accused, the biggest problem is the fact that in most cases deals are made with the prosecuting attorney, who agrees to recommend a certain sentence, but there's no guarantee that the judge will accept the deal. A second problem with plea bargaining is that it is overused. Crowded court calendars and a much easier job for the defense attorney lead to plea bargaining in cases where a finding of guilty is by no means assured.

The new federal rules make a basic change in the way plea bargaining is carried on because it provides that if the judge refuses to go along with the recommended sentence, the defendant can change his mind and withdraw his plea of guilty and go on trial. The rules also require that the court try to make sure that the person actually committed the crime he says he committed, since one of the most frequent motives for plea bargaining on the part of the prosecution is something less than an airtight case against the accused.

Striking a bargain

If you're accused of a crime and you want to strike a bargain with the prosecutor, you'd better not do it in Judge Eisel's court. That's the result of a recent decision by Judge Eisel, who's a federal district court judge for the U.S. District Court for Eastern Arkansas. Plea bargaining, as it has been called, has become an integral part of our system of justice. As we just saw, if a person is accused of a crime, the prosecutor can offer a deal asking the person to plead guilty and avoid a trial in return for a lesser charge or a lighter penalty.

While it may sound a little strange that the prosecutor and the defense can enter into a deal without consulting the victim, the practice is fully recognized in the Federal Rules of Criminal Procedure. It is allowed as long as the plea is voluntary, is not made as a result of force or promises, and is approved by a judge. But Judge Eisel does not believe in plea bargaining and wrote an opinion saying why. He began by saying the process of negotiating pleas has a tendency to demean all participants—the attorneys, the defendant, and even the court. He added that some judges, like many lawyers, don't like trials and even fear them. The decision of a judge to accept or reject a plea bargain may make the difference between a hard six-week trial or a chance to relax and clean up his motion calendar.

Further, said Judge Eisel, if a judge has a reputation of throwing the book at people, chances are the defendant will go along with practically any bargain offered by the prosecutor. But if the judge is known as lenient or even fair, defense attorneys will be less likely to go along with the deal. This leads, said the judge, to disparity rather than to uniformity. And the whole process, he said, has a back-room and sinister character. When the object of the deal does go to prison, the opportunity to compare bargains tends to show a system that proclaims justice as its goal, but dispenses deals instead. When a man is accused of a crime, said the judge, he's either guilty or not, and he and the public have a right to know which it is.

As for plea bargaining being voluntary, the judge added, "A bargain taken to avoid the risk of being convicted of a more serious crime is not more voluntary than the choice of the rock to avoid the whirlpool."

Should prosecutor error = free criminal?

Should the criminal be freed because the prosecutor was unethical? That was the question recently faced by the Michigan Supreme Court. The case involved a man who had been convicted of first-degree murder and who nearly succeeded in having his conviction reversed because of an out-of-court error made by the prosecuting attorney.

The case began when the police arrested the defendant after his homosexual lover had implicated him in the murder of a woman. While awaiting trial the man asked detectives to come to the jail three times. Two of those times a prosecuting attorney accompanied the detectives. The prosecutor did not get the permission of the defendant's court-appointed lawyer to pay these visits, and during the last visit the man confessed to the murder.

The defendant tried to have his conviction set aside on the grounds that the prosecutor violated the disciplinary rules of the code of professional responsibility forbidding a lawyer from communicating with another lawyer's client without that other lawyer's permission. Because of the violation, the defendant claimed his conviction should be reversed. The state conceded that the disciplinary rules applied to prosecuting attorneys, but claimed the rules weren't violated in this case because the defendant did not ask his lawyer to be present and because the prosecutor didn't coerce or badger the man. But the court said all that meant was that the violation of ethics wasn't as bad as it could have been and that these factors could be considered mitigating circumstances by the bar association when it punished the offending attorney. It was a violation of the rules, nevertheless.

Then the court turned to the question of whether or not a lawyer's violation of an ethical rule should cause the conviction to be overturned. A majority of the court refused to overturn the conviction, saying the argument for overturning rests on a basic misconception of the code of professional responsibility. The provisions of the code, said the court, are not constitutional or statutory rights guaranteed to individual persons, but instead are self-imposed internal regulations prescribing the standards of conduct for members of the bar.

Several judges dissented, saying the only way to make sure such things didn't happen again was to overturn the conviction. But the majority ruled, and while lawyers who don't go by the rules may find themselves in trouble, criminal defendants won't get off because of it.

Paying back the victim

Is paying back the victim better than going to jail? This was the question looked at in a recent issue of the *Journal of the American Judicature Society.* The society is a group dedicated to improving the administration of justice. The authors of the article surveyed nineteen restitution programs in the United States and Canada and concluded there are some benefits as well as problems that have come from the programs.

Restitution and payment by the offender can be set up as a formal, carefully regulated system, or it can be more free-wheeling and used by judges even without being a formal part of the law, in which case it is usually called alternative sentencing. One example of alternative sentencing involved an embezzlement case, in which a defendant in San Francisco was found guilty of taking about four thousand dollars from the government by falsifying overtime claims. His jail sentence was suspended for five years on the condition that he work four hours a day five days a week in a dining room that served free meals to the poor.

The judge who imposed this alternative sentence argued that it was better than conventional sentencing because it benefitted the poor by providing more free labor to staff the dining room; made the defendant realize there were a lot of people less fortunate than he; saved the cost of imprisonment in the county jail (which cost the county twenty-seven dollars per day); and came closer to attaining real justice, which is the ultimate objective of the judicial system.

Other states have developed service or payment restitution directly to the victim of the crime. The *Judicature* article points out that this full restitution is feasible in many cases, since the average personal loss in burglary or thefts is less than five hundred dollars. Some states have programs where an offender can actually work off the damage by performing services for the victim, but there have been problems determining just when the criminal has done enough work to pay off the debt.

So future victims of crimes may be hearing from the criminal again, but this time he'll be giving instead of taking.

Bailing out Patty Hearst

When Patty Hearst was free on bail, she was the most celebrated of the thousands of state and federal prisoners who had been freed under the bail reform movement of the middle 1960s. Getting bailed out is now the rule rather than the exception, but it wasn't always so.

The subject of bail is covered in the Eighth Amendment to the Constitution, which provides, "Excessive bail shall not be required, nor excessive fines imposed, nor cruel and unusual punishments inflicted." The wording of the amendment was lifted almost verbatim from the English Bill of Rights of 1689, but as has been pointed out in many cases, neither the amendment nor its British predecessor guarantees a person the right to be freed on bail. The wording merely provides that if bail is to be set at all, it cannot be excessive.

There were many cases in which the U.S. Supreme Court upheld the right of judges not to grant bail at all, regardless of the nature of the case. One of the more celebrated cases in which bail was not allowed was that of *Carlson* v. *Landon,* in which aliens who were not even accused of a crime were held without bail while their deportation was considered. Why? Because, in the words of Justice Black, "Some subordinate Washington bureau agent believes they are members of the Communist Party."

Now, however, things are very different. Federal law and the law of many states provide that a person charged with crime not punishable by death must be released on his or her own recognizance, that is, on the promise to return, without the posting of any bail at all, unless the judge believes that the person will not return to court for trial. If the judge feels that the person's promise alone is not sufficient, the judge may place the person in someone else's custody, restrict travel, and require the filing of an appearance bond and the deposit in court of up to 10 percent of the amount of the bond in cash.

All of these conditions were brought to bear in the Hearst case, with the judge ordering that Patty live with her parents, that she not leave California without prior approval of the court, and that a bond of $1 million, with 10 percent or $100,000, being deposited in court in cash.

Bras behind bars

Can a woman wear whatever she wants when she visits a prison? The answer to that question, according to the Hawaii Supreme Court, is no. A woman can't wear what she wants to, even if what she wants to wear is nothing.

The case got started when a woman wanted to pay a visit to an inmate of the all-male Oahu State Prison, the main prison facility for the state of Hawaii. According to the court, the woman consented to a routine search of her person, and during the search it was discovered—and the woman freely admitted—that she was not wearing a bra. She was told that she would not be permitted to enter the prison unless she wore an appropriate undergarment. The matron who searched her said she was only following regulations and pointed to a sign that read: "Visitors will be properly dressed. Women visitors are asked to be fully clothed, including undergarments."

The woman went to court seeking declaratory and injunctive relief and money damages for the deprivation of her constitutional rights and for emotional injury. She lost at the trial court level and appealed her case to the Hawaii Supreme Court.

That court began its opinion noting that the primary thrust of the appellant's argument was that the prison directive, on its face, discriminated on the basis of sex. The court also noted in a footnote that the woman happened to be executive director of the American Civil Liberties Union of Hawaii, which did not entitle her to special consideration.

The court said there were a lot of questions that were unanswered in the record of facts before it. For example, there was no proof that male visitors were admitted without certain undergarments, and no showing of what the requirements were for other women visitors, or exactly what this woman's physical characteristics were.

But the court said that even in the absence of these vital statistics, it had no trouble reaching a decision that maintenance of order and control in a prison is a proper governmental objective, and that dress standards are intimately related to sexual attitudes. And the court said that while it was being careful not to express individual views of propriety, the omission of a bra has been held to be regarded as sexually provocative by some members of society.

The court held that the regulation did indeed withstand strict scrutiny. So liberated women can visit prisons, as long as they're liberated in spirit alone.

Hanging around with the judge

The case of Salvatore Albanese gives us a glimpse into the workings of the criminal justice system in the area of sentencing, probation, and parole. Mr. Albanese was convicted in 1969 along with three other men in the hijacking of a trailer truck loaded with piece goods.

Instead of being jailed, he was placed on probation for five years, with one of the conditions being that he would not associate with known criminals during the five-year probation period. He was subsequently brought into court and found to have violated probation and was sentenced to ten years in prison.

It seems that agents of the Federal Bureau of Investigation kept Mr. Albanese under surveillance constantly and reported to the court that he had been seen at least fifty times in the company of individuals with criminal records. Included were such men as Thomas DiBella, Anthony Abbatemarco, Albert Gallo, and James Napoli, names that aren't exactly unfamiliar to those who know about organized crime in the state of New York.

Mr. Albanese's only defense was that these were his friends and that they were really the only people he knew. He also said that many people who lived in his neighborhood had been in jail at some time or other. To quote Mr. Albanese directly, "It don't make sense, who am I supposed to associate with? Who do I know in my life?" Then he added, "Your Honor, will you hang around with me? Will you associate with me? Will you go to dinner with me?" Mr. Albanese's lawyer added that if Mr. Albanese had been having dinner with Spiro Agnew, "You wouldn't have complained." The judge replied, "I would certainly wonder why Mr. Albanese was having dinner with the one vice-president who had pleaded guilty of a criminal offense, and that would not be a plus on his record."

The case will be appealed on the point of whether associating with known criminals is proper ground for revoking probation, but in the meantime, Salvatore Albanese is back in jail, where he can now associate with all the known criminals he wants to.

Crime in the suites

There's plenty of concern about crime in the streets and the terrible cost of the murders, rapes, and assaults. I'd like to look at another kind of crime, which has been dubbed for want of a better term "crime in the suites." These crimes, frequently called white-collar crimes, are receiving increasing attention by the press, law enforcement officials, and the public. A recent report by the Bureau of National Affairs takes a sobering look at the costs of white-collar crime and the problems it presents for our system of law enforcement.

Just so we can get a handle on what we're talking about, the U.S. Chamber of Commerce estimates that white-collar crime costs this country at least $40 billion each year. That figure is based on about $800 million for bankruptcy fraud, in which people and companies fraudulently go through bankruptcy to bilk their creditors; $3 billion in crimes related to computers and the various means of making the machines kick out money to which somebody is not entitled; and $21 billion lost in consumer fraud schemes. The rest is taken in frauds involving credit cards, checks, embezzlement, insurance, and stocks.

One study showed that corporate fraud and embezzlement have increased 313 percent since 1969. A recent poll showed that three out of five of the corporate executives questioned said that young managers in business would commit unethical acts to exhibit their loyalty to superiors.

You might be wondering what the law has done about all this. Studies have shown that it often has done very little. One study, which was confirmed by another, showed that thirty-seven people who stole or mismanaged an average of $21 million received only suspended sentences, probation, or fines. One judge made legal history by sentencing a group of price fixers to make a dozen speeches each to civic groups about the evils of price fixing.

If you steal what's in the computer

If you steal what's in the computer, is that a crime? That was the novel question recently raised before the U.S. District Court for the District of Columbia. What happened was that an employee of the Drug Enforcement Administration stole some very valuable information stored in a computer data bank. The purloined printouts contained such tidbits as the names of persons who had expressed a willingness to work for the government as informers, plus the status of many major drug investigations. As you can imagine, there would be a number of very willing buyers for such information.

The employee was indicted and charged with violating Section 641 of Title 18 of the U.S. Code, which provides that it is a crime to steal a record, voucher, money, or thing of value from the United States. The defense was that the law only applies to tangible goods, such as the actual documents or records containing information, but not the raw information itself, which exists in intangible form within a department's computer. Since Congress was silent on the subject of computers back in 1875 when the law was passed, the court had to turn to judicial interpretation of the federal statute.

In one case, a defendant claimed that because he had photocopied papers and put back the original documents, he was not guilty of violating a similar statute making it a crime to convey stolen property in interstate commerce. He said the documents weren't the actual property, but merely photocopies. The court held in that case that the physical form of stolen goods is secondary. In an even more recent case, employees of the FBI periodically copied documents and sold them to persons under investigation. In that case, the court held that because the copies were made during regular office hours, on government copy machines,

and with government paper, the copies themselves were government property.

In the computer case, the court said an individual of common
intelligence would probably include the information held in a
government computer in the statutory definition of the word
record, but that even if the word *record* did nót include the stored
data, *thing of value* would do the trick.

The last argument of the defendant was that he shouldn't be
found guilty because there was no clear definition of who was or
was not authorized to remove data from department computers.
But the court said it was clear enough that there was no authority
to remove data and try to make money on it by selling it to the
underworld, so stealing software can lead to hard labor.

On the warpath against ticket scalping

Can a state outlaw ticket scalping? That was the question recently raised before the Georgia Supreme Court. For those of
you not familiar with ticket scalping, that's the practice of selling
tickets to an event at a rate higher than the admission price
printed on the ticket. Scalping takes place regularly, not only at
World Series and Super Bowl games, but at sellout events of all
kinds.

A Georgia law made it a crime for any person to sell or offer
to sell a ticket to a football, basketball, baseball, soccer, or hockey
game at a price that exceeded the price printed on the ticket. The
only exception was for authorized ticket agents, who could
charge an extra dollar as a service charge. The law was quickly
ignored, and one afternoon three persons were arrested and
accused of scalping tickets to a football game between the Atlanta
Falcons and the Minnesota Vikings. They had sold nine-dollar
tickets for twenty dollars each.

The defendants all claimed the law was unconstitutional. The
lower court agreed, stating the law had to fall because it was
against the due process clause of the Constitution and because
"it unduly interfered with the private property right of disposing
of one's property in a nonfraudulent way at one's own price."

The State of Georgia, trying to save its law, appealed the case
to the Georgia Supreme Court, which unanimously reversed the
lower court and held that it was constitutional to outlaw scalping
after all. The court said the issue was whether the state could
regulate the sale of tickets to sporting events under its general

police power. The court reviewed the cases around the country, noting that the U.S. Supreme Court, which had once thrown out a New York law prohibiting scalping of theater tickets, had changed its mind on the issue and upheld a later New York law making it unlawful to sell theater tickets for more than a dollar and a half above the price printed on the ticket.

The court said that prohibiting ticket scalping is a proper legislative objective and that the law had a reasonable relationship to that objective. The court added that there is a legitimate state interest in the regulation of the resale price of tickets to places of entertainment, and this law puts all sports fans on an equal footing in the race to the ticket window. So if states want to declare open season on scalpers, it looks as if the courts won't stand in their way.

Three-time losers are truly lost

Three-time losers are truly lost. That's the message of a case recently decided by the U.S. Supreme Court. The case involved a man convicted of three crimes. In 1964 he pleaded guilty to fraudulently using a credit card to obtain $80 worth of goods and services. He served three years in a penitentiary. In 1969 he pleaded guilty to passing a bad check in the amount $28.36 and was sentenced to four years in prison. Then came a third crime. He was convicted of having fraudulently obtained $120.75, and that may be the last time this man will ever see the light of day as a free man. For Texas law provides that whoever shall have been three times convicted of a felony, shall on the third conviction be imprisoned for life.

The man went to court claiming that to sentence him to life in prison for crimes the total value of which amounted to $229.11 was grossly disproportionate and constituted cruel and unusual punishment in violation of the Eighth Amendment to the Constitution. The defendant depended on an old U.S. Supreme Court case setting aside a sentence on the grounds that it was too harsh. That case involved a Philippine law that said if you committed the crime of putting a single false entry in a public document, you went to jail for twelve years and a day, and during that time you were chained at your wrist and ankle.

While the court had deemed the Philippine punishment too much for too little, the three-time loser statute in Texas was a far different story. The court said to qualify for a life sentence, a person had to have been convicted and imprisoned for felonies on three separate occasions. That, said the court, should be enough to deter future criminal behavior of any kind. The amount of money really isn't the point. The court said different states have different priorities; for example, it's a felony to steal a horned animal in Arizona regardless of its value, and it's also a felony to steal an avocado in California.

Four justices dissented, arguing that disproportionate sentences were outlawed as far back as the Magna Carta in 1215. But the majority rules, and if you have to steal $229.11, you might consider doing it all at once—at least in Texas.

Statutory rape is trouble

If you're charged with statutory rape, you're in deep trouble. That's the result of a recent decision of the California Supreme Court upholding the law that says a man who has sexual intercourse with a woman under age eighteen to whom he is not married may be convicted of rape regardless of how willing a partner the woman was. This case involved a sixteen-year-old girl and a seventeen-and-one-half-year-old boy. The boy was arrested and convicted of the crime of rape and appealed his conviction to the California high court, claiming it was unconstitutional to punish him but not the girl.

The court refused to overturn the law, saying that the challenged statute is supported by the immutable physiological fact that it is the female exclusively who can become pregnant. Since the state has established a valid and compelling interest in preventing pregnancies among unwed teenage girls, the legislature was well within its power in imposing criminal sanctions against males alone, because they are the only ones who can physiologically cause the result the law seeks to avoid.

The defense responded that if the main purpose of the law was to prevent pregnancy, all those who used birth-control devices should be removed from the reach of the law. But the court responded that it would be too difficult for the law to find out whether or not birth-control devices were actually used.

As for not punishing the female, the court said that the female is subjected to all the risks, and therefore it's understandable why she is not to be punished by the criminal law. In addition, said the court, this law isn't very different from laws prohibiting other kinds of behavior, such as preventing minors under sixteen from attending prize fights, participating in bingo games, or buying cigarettes.

One judge dissented, saying he could not subscribe to the majority's opinion that the female of the human species is weak, inferior, and in need of paternalistic protection from the state. When both parties make the decision to engage in the sexual act, said the judge, each must be presumed equally responsible if pregnancy results. But the majority ruled, and when it comes to the crime of statutory rape, the man alone must pay the price.

The wrong question

Can you go to prison for asking a question? The answer, in Oklahoma at least, is yes. That's the message of a case recently decided by the Oklahoma Criminal Court of Appeals. The case involved a man on a white horse and a thirteen-year-old girl. The girl had come to a park with her brother and two friends and had gotten separated for a few minutes from the others. The man rode up to the girl and said, "Do you want to make some money?" She replied no. Then he asked a question, the plain meaning of which was did she want to have sexual relations with him. She said no again and ran off and rejoined her friends.

She told them what had happened to her, and the police were called. The officers located the man on the white horse, and without much difficulty he was arrested and convicted for the offense of making an indecent proposal to a child. He was sentenced to three years in the Oklahoma State Penitentiary.

The man appealed his conviction to the Criminal Court of Appeals, claiming that there was no proof that his actual words were proposals for sexual relations. The court answered, "We find no merit to this argument," as the words used are generally understood as referring to sexual intercourse. The man also claimed that it had to be proved that he actually wanted to have intercourse with the girl, and that the state failed to prove this specific intent. Again the court answered that the contention was wholly without merit. The offense is committed when the proposal alone is made.

The man also argued that his freedom of speech was being abridged. But the court said that a law undertaking to punish speech may be upheld with the showing of a compelling state interest, which was present in this case. The last argument was that the prosecutor acted improperly when, in open court, he threatened to take the defense attorney out in the hall for a fistfight. The court said remarks made by the prosecutor were grossly improper, but that was not reason enough to overturn the decision.

The court did reduce the sentence from three years to one. But the man went to prison, proving that sometimes in law, as in life, the question is more important than the answer.

If you ever run into a stewardess

If you ever run into a stewardess whose nickname is Legs, you'd be best off if you just let her walk on by. That's the message of a recent case handed down by the Fifth Circuit Court of Appeals. The case got started when the manager of a Gulf Coast news agency decided to send some obscene films to a TWA employee in Atlanta whose nickname was Legs. The film was brought to a St. Petersburg Greyhound station for delivery by bus to Atlanta. As a joke the box was addressed to Legs, Incorporated, and sent on a will-call basis to the Greyhound station in Atlanta. There, it was assumed, Legs would pick it up in due course.

But, alas, all did not go as anticipated. The Greyhound baggage department forwarded the box of films to L'eggs, Incorporated, the well-known hosiery manufacturer, which does a lot of business with Greyhound. Greyhound thought someone just left off the apostrophe and so L'eggs was informed a package was waiting for it at the local Greyhound terminal. A L'eggs employee went to get the package and discovered "sexually explicit films" inside. He immediately called his superior, who ordered him to bring the carton to the office. After some quick viewing, the L'eggs employees decided to call in the FBI. The FBI took possession of the films and viewed them on a home movie projector and then traced the films to Gulf Coast News. All involved were convicted of conspiring to use a common carrier to ship obscene materials.

Those convicted appealed their case on the basis that the FBI did not secure a warrant before viewing the films. But the Eighth Circuit Court of Appeals said that once the L'eggs employee opened and looked at the material, the FBI's viewing was not a search but merely a continuation of the search which had been commenced by the L'eggs employees.

One judge dissented, saying it was wrong for the government to take possession of 871 films, look at them, and hold them for four months, all without securing a warrant. But the majority ruled, and you'll just never know where your L'eggs will take you.

Ladies' night

Did you know that ladies' night is unconstitutional? That's the result of a recent decision of the Washington Court of Appeals. What happened was that the Seattle Supersonics had a policy of offering half-price tickets to women in order to attract female fans and make it easier for families to attend basketball games.

Well, a male fan went to court claiming that ladies' nights were discriminatory and violated the Equal Rights Amendment of the State of Washington's constitution. The Equal Rights Amendment provides that "equality of right and responsibility under the law shall not be denied on account of sex." The court said that because the games were played in a publicly owned stadium, that was state action and the state became responsible constitutionally at least for anything that went on in the stadium. The court cited other cases which had been decided under the Equal Rights Amendment, one of which held that a high school's refusal to allow girls to play on the football team was sex discrimination. The court said, "We hold that the ladies' night ticket policy is discriminatory and unconstitutionally favors women over men."

The court held that not only did ladies' night violate the Constitution, but it also violated a specific Washington law which said that everyone had the right to full enjoyment of any accommodation, advantages, or privileges of a place of amusement and none of these privileges could be denied on account of race, creed, or color. The court said although the word sex was missing, it was clear that the legislature had intended to prohibit sex discrimination as well. The law conferred on all men and women alike the right to be admitted to public facilities on equal terms.

And so, in the State of Washington at least, ladies' nights have become a thing of the past.

Dancing in the dark

Can the state stop dancing in a darkened disco? That was the question in a case recently decided by the Kansas Supreme Court. The case involved a local ordinance of the city of Baxter Springs, Kansas, which provided that it was unlawful for dancing of any kind to be permitted in a place where malt beverages were sold and that it was further unlawful for malt beverages to be sold in any room with curtains, screens, or other obstructions across the windows that prevented an unobstructed view from the street. The case came to court when the proprietor of the Sugar Bear Disco was arrested and convicted of the crime of dispensing beer and allowing dancing without permitting an unobstructed view of his premises from the street. The case was appealed to the Kansas Supreme Court, which was asked to declare the statute unconstitutional. The city of Baxter Springs claimed the statutes were proper and necessary to safeguard the health, safety, and morals of the people of Baxter Springs and surrounding communities.

The court defined a disco, saying, a "disco or more properly known as a Discotheque as we are informed is a commercial enterprise where people gather to listen and dance to recorded music formerly recorded on records or discs but now frequently recorded on tapes, and also to partake of food and other refreshment."

The court said the type of dancing going on in this disco was not the kind of dancing that can be prohibited by the state. There was no claim in this case that the dancing in the Sugar Bear Disco was nude, obscene, or sexually explicit, or, said the court, anything other than the rhythmic movements of fully clothed patrons for their own enjoyment. As for the state's argument that if there were no dancing, less people would come to the bar and there would be less drinking, the court said it is unreasonable to control drinking by banning dancing. As for the curtain rule, the court said the law was just too vague and could prevent blocking the sun out of people's eyes just as it could prevent a den of iniquity. And so the Sugar Bear Disco will be able to open its doors, close its windows, and keep the tapes rolling along.

Snorting over cocaine

A recent decision in a Massachusetts lower court has caused a lot of angry snorting among law-enforcement officials throughout the country. The subject was cocaine, and the end result of the decision of Judge Elwood McKenney was to dismiss the charges against a thirty-six-year-old man accused of possession of the drug.

The case started simply enough with the defendant being arrested for possession of about twenty-eight-dollars worth of cocaine, a rather small amount when one considers that the drug sells for about twenty-five hundred dollars per ounce. The next thing that happened was that lawyer Joseph Oteri was appointed to represent the defendant. The Playboy Foundation then came up with thirty-five hundred dollars to pay for expert testimony, and a test case was born.

The defense raised the ultimate issue by filing a motion to dismiss the charges on the grounds that the penalties for cocaine, which ranged up to a year in prison and up to a thousand dollars fine, were unconstitutional. The experts presented evidence that formed the basis of many of the judge's findings of fact. Some of these findings were that alcohol is far more dangerous than cocaine, that it is not possible to control the use of psychoactive substances through criminal sanctions, and that criminalizing a drug makes it more attractive. The judge also found that cocaine was used as the basis for Coca Cola until 1903, and that the drug has many medical uses.

The prosecution said that these arguments should be made in the legislature, not in court. But the judge stated, "A court shamefully shirks its duty if facts are ignored, constitutional infirmities are left uncorrected, and the buck is passed to a legislative committee." At one point during the trial, the judge announced his intention to try the drug, but because of the ensuing publicity, he changed his mind and confined his fact-finding to the evidence presented.

Since in Massachusetts the state does not have the right of appeal when a case is thrown out, it was not exactly clear what the end result of all this would be. The police announced that they intended to go on arresting people, since, they argued, a lower-court judge does not have the authority to strike a state statute from the books.

In the meantime, while Boston's Roxbury section was never known for its safety, for a while it was probably the safest place in the country to try cocaine.

It's normal to lose

When it comes to marijuana, it's the government one and NORML nothing. That's the result of a recent decision of a three-judge federal court in Washington, D.C. The case brings to a close another big push by NORML—the National Organization for the Reform of the Marijuana Laws—which tried to knock out federal criminal laws punishing marijuana use and possession.

Federal law establishes five schedules for classifying controlled substances. Those schedules are based on a drug's potential for abuse and whether or not there's a medical use for the drug. The drafters of the law found a lot of abuse and no medical use for marijuana, despite some recent claims that it helps glaucoma and cancer patients. Marijuana was placed at the top of the list in Schedule 1, carrying a fine of up to five thousand dollars and a sentence of up to a year in jail for use and possession.

NORML claimed that prohibiting private possession and use of marijuana violates the constitutional right to privacy in one's home. NORML cited the case of *Roe* v. *Wade* in which the U.S. Supreme Court struck down state laws prohibiting abortions in the early stages of pregnancy. The judges in this case agreed that the Supreme Court did recognize a right of privacy, but said that right of privacy is not absolute and includes only those personal rights that can be deemed fundamental, such as marriage, use of contraceptives, and child rearing. Smoking marijuana, said the court, does not qualify as a fundamental right. The court said that marijuana's use as a recreational drug undercuts any argument that it's as important, for example, as the use of contraceptives. As for privacy at home, a home only offers a refuge for activities grounded in other protected rights.

NORML also asked how the law can put marijuana in Schedule 1 and leave out alcohol and tobacco. But, said the court, legislatures have wide discretion in attacking social ills. So despite all the arguments of the NORML people, the court decided to keep the lid on; decriminalization of marijuana may be coming, but it isn't here yet.

The paraquat scare

Marijuana smokers now have to worry about something more than the law—paraquat. Paraquat is a deadly poison that has been sprayed on a lot of the marijuana coming into the United States from Mexico. The questions raised by the paraquat scare are tough ones, the key question being whether the U.S. government can be forced to stop contaminating marijuana that is supposed to be illegal in the first place.

The question has now been brought to the courts by a group called NORML, which stands for the National Organization for the Reform of the Marijuana Laws. NORML had been lobbying for the decriminalization of marijuana and naturally became concerned when 21 percent of the marijuana tested near the Mexican border was found to contain paraquat. Developed in the 1950s, the herbicide paraquat is extremely dangerous to human lungs. According to the memorandum filed by NORML, research on laboratory animals has shown that extremely small amounts of paraquat produces lesions in the lungs.

Apparently, the paraquat was sprayed on the marijuana as a result of $50 million given to Mexico by the U.S. government for the purpose of marijuana and poppy control. The State Department supplied forty-one Bell helicopters and thirty-five planes to wipe out poppy and marijuana plants by spraying them with herbicide. But things haven't turned out exactly as planned. Seventeen Mexican and American officials have been killed and twelve persons injured in airplane crashes during spraying. Also, although it has been sprayed with paraquat, a marijuana plant does not die immediately but lives for several days thereafter—just long enough for Mexican farmers to follow the planes around, harvest the contaminated marijuana, and sell it to unsuspecting buyers in the United States.

NORML claims that the spraying program violates the National Environmental Protection Act because no environmental impact statement was filed to evaluate the impact of the spraying program. The court has not yet decided whether to halt the spraying. Meanwhile, private labs are doing a land-office business testing marijuana, demand for Colombian marijuana has skyrocketed, and Mexican marijuana is under a deadly cloud.

Should girls be able to drink beer?

Should girls be able to drink beer at eighteen, but boys have to wait until they're twenty-one? Well, the State of Oklahoma thought so, but the U.S. Supreme Court declared the Oklahoma law unconstitutional as violating the equal protection clause of the Fourteenth Amendment to the Constitution.

Although Oklahoma, like most states, doesn't keep a record of legislative history, which tells why laws are passed in the first place, the state sought to justify the law on the ground that it was related to traffic safety. The state cited three surveys, which showed that in the age-group involved, more males than females were killed in traffic accidents, and that boys were more inclined than girls to drive and drink beer.

The court agreed that protection of the public health and safety was an important role for state and local governments, but that the statistical data given to the court could not support the state's conclusion. The court noted, for example, that the strongest statistical information showed that only 2 percent of males in the suspect age-group were arrested for drinking-related offenses, while less than 1 percent of girls were so arrested. While 2 percent is statistically much greater than 1 percent, the total of 2 percent is still so small, said the court, that it is not enough to enable the law to withstand the equal-protection challenge.

To rely on such flimsy statistics, said the court, might next give rise to drinking statutes favoring Jews and Italian Catholics, since statistics show they have the lowest rate of problem drinking. Or, in the case of adolescents, there might be statutes saying that only black teenagers should drink, followed by Asians and Spanish-

Americans, since the figures show that whites and American Indians have the highest proportion of teenage heavy drinkers, and blacks, Asians, and Spanish-Americans the lowest.

Justice Powell stated that the gender-based classification does not bear a fair and substantial relation to the object of the legislation. He added that the fact that it's so easily circumvented makes it virtually meaningless.

So Oklahoma and all other states that draw a difference between the sexes when it comes to drinking won't be able to draw that difference any more.

Can a taxpayer be taxed?

Can a taxpayer be taxed if his tax return is timely filed? This was the question before the Seventh Circuit Court of Appeals in a recent case that ended in victory for a tired taxpayer who argued with the Internal Revenue Service, the U.S. Tax Court, and finally the Court of Appeals that he should not have to pay a deficiency assessment.

The whole thing started when the taxpayer prepared his tax return on time and mailed it before the deadline for filing. But it was received by the IRS after the filing deadline. The IRS has three years to complain that you didn't pay enough taxes, and sure enough, three years later the IRS decided that more tax should have been paid when the return was originally filed. The problem was that the IRS issued the deficiency notice more than three years after the mailing of the return by the taxpayer, but within three years of the date it was actually received from him.

The law is clear that if you mail your tax return any time up to midnight on April 15, it will be deemed filed with the service as soon as you drop it in the mailbox. The question for the court in this case, however, was, does the three-year statute of limitations start when you drop the return in the mailbox or when it is actually received by the service? The IRS argued that the law that deems mailing the same as filing is for the limited purpose of allowing the taxpayer to avoid paying an additional penalty as long as the return is mailed before the deadline, and that the law has no effect on anything else and does not start the three-year statute of limitations running.

The Court of Appeals disagreed, saying there was nothing in the Internal Revenue Code limiting the definition of "timely filed" to just the mailing of an income tax return. If a return was deemed properly filed when it was dropped in the mailbox, said the court, there was no reason why the statute of limitations didn't start too.

The IRS argued that such a ruling would shorten the time it had to make deficiency assessments; but the court stated that except in very exceptional circumstances, the three-year period which the IRS has to make a deficiency assessment would be shortened only by the time it took the post office to deliver a mailed tax return to the IRS. So the taxpayer's tax return was timely filed, and the deficiency assessment was just a little bit too tardy.

All that glitters is not gold

All that glitters is not gold. That seemed to be the message from the Federal Trade Commission as it implemented new regulations that dramatically changed the marketing of gold.

At issue was just what items could be sold as gold. Until recently, only gold articles that were ten karat or greater could be sold as gold or even carry the karat symbol. The new guidelines allowed an item to be sold as gold even if it were less than ten karats, provided it conspicuously carried a tag carrying the following warning: "Gold alloys of less than ten karats can be expected to tarnish and corrode."

What caused the change in the FTC regulations was a lot of pressure from jewelers who wanted to sell cheaper gold and were able to convince the FTC to change the rules. This was because the price of gold skyrocketed from thirty-five dollars per ounce, where it had been for many years, to more than one hundred and thirty dollars per ounce. Since then, of course, it has gone much higher. Even one hundred thirty dollars per ounce was a price that took gold jewelry out of the reach of many buyers.

The main problem with gold that's less than ten karats is that it tarnishes. When the new regulations were being discussed, a tarnish test was performed on seven-karat gold, ten-karat gold, and fourteen-karat gold. The seven-karat gold turned dark brown, the ten-karat was only slightly tarnished, but the fourteen-karat remained bright yellow. A major problem for consumers is that the tarnish effect can't be seen in the jewelry shop, but begins only after the article has been put to use.

The question for the FTC was how to make gold jewelry items more available to the public, but still protect the buyer from being disappointed or surprised when gold jewelry turned brown. The commission recommended allowing the word "gold" to be used for items less than ten karat because it was possible through the warning to disclose the major disadvantages of the product, allowing each consumer to make an individual decision and balance decreased price against decreased quality. So, thanks to the Federal Trade Commission, gold jewelry may become available to more people, even if it won't stay yellow quite as well.

Banning pay toilets

Can pay toilets be banned? That was the question before New York's courts in a recent case. The question arose because of the passage by the New York State legislature of a law saying that no person who owned or leased real estate could permit pay toilet facilities to be operated on the property. In fact, if you had a pay toilet on your property after September 1, 1975, you violated the law and could be fined well in excess of your pay toilet proceeds.

This statute was naturally quite upsetting to the Nik-o-lok Company and the Advance Pay Toilet Lock Company, who specialize in building and maintaining pay toilets. They claimed that since they were in the business of regulating access to toilets, the law simply destroyed their business and was an unreasonable use of the state's police power. They also claimed that the law violated the equal protection clause of the Constitution because it prohibited pay toilets but did not prohibit toilets that were locked with a key, like those at gas stations.

The court took a close look at the matter and, contrary to what former patrons of pay toilets might think, did not decide the case on the ground that pay toilets constitute cruel and unusual punishment. Rather, the court looked in support of the statute to the legislative history behind the law. That history reads in part, "Pay toilet facilities are essentially a tax on human biological function." The legislative history also stated that the tax was discriminatory because women often have no choice but to use pay facilities while men have access to free toilet facilities.

As for the equal protection claim based on the fact that pay toilets were prohibited while key-locked toilets were allowed, the court rejected the argument with the implication that the equal protection clause was written to insure equal protection for people, not toilets.

The court, whose decision was upheld by the appeals court, said that what must be asked is whether there was a fair and a reasonable connection between the law and the promotion of the health and safety and comfort of the public. Never before has the word *comfort* in that clause played such a role.

Zoning away abortion

Can you get rid of an abortion clinic by zoning it out of existence? Throughout the country, state legislatures are tightening the laws dealing with abortion. Most of the legislation deals with the doctor and the pregnant woman, but the town of Southboro, Massachusetts, tried something different. The board of selectment passed an amendment to its zoning bylaws that prevented abortion clinics from coming to town by simply prohibiting any building in the town from being used as one. Abortion was defined as "the knowing destruction of the life of an unborn child, the intentional expulsion of or removal of an unborn child from the womb other than for the principal purpose of producing a live birth."

The zoning bylaw was challenged by the Framingham Clinic, which wanted to expand its operation into Southboro. The Supreme Judicial Court of Massachusetts held that the zoning bylaw was invalid. The basis of the decision was the Supreme Court case of *Roe* v. *Wade* in which the court held that a woman has a fundamental right of privacy that cannot, at least in the first trimester of pregnancy, be overridden by any other interest, including that of a developing human life.

The Massachusetts court said that while a state could require women to sign consent forms, and could require that the physician performing the abortion be properly licensed, and could even require that the clinic or hospital where the abortion was being performed have the necessary license and equipment, it could not prohibit the clinic altogether.

In its defense, the town cited public opinion and produced a report prepared by its planning board showing that public opinion was on the side of the ban. The court said that the report was not only an irrelevancy, but a dangerous one, since that path points to the extinction of many liberties that are constitutionally guaranteed against invasion by a majority.

The court also dismissed the town's claim that if a town could regulate places where obscene movies were shown, it could prohibit abortion clinics. Also turned down was the argument that the right to an abortion was still available elsewhere in the state —it just wasn't available in Southboro. The court said that you can't deny a fundamental right in one county merely because it continues to exist in another.

Turtles, tortoises, and terrapins

Have you been wondering why you haven't seen those little pet turtles around any more? Well, it's because of a regulation of the Food and Drug Administration entitled "Turtles, Tortoises, and Terrapins." The regulation was prompted by an alarming increase in the number of pet turtles carrying salmonella and Arizona organisms, which are not healthy for children or adults. According to the Atlanta Center for Disease Control a few years back, approximately 54 percent of all pet turtles were contaminated with the organisms, after they had been certified as being organism-free.

Not only did the turtles carry salmonella and Arizona on their backs, but they didn't seem to be doing very well as far as longevity was concerned. The Animal Welfare Institute pointed out that pet turtles are not miniature turtles, but are really baby turtles of the red-eared slider variety, which with proper care can attain a shell length of up to eleven inches and can live more than forty years in captivity. However, 90 percent of all pet turtles don't make it beyond the first six months. The Animal Welfare League joined with the Consumers Union in petitioning for the total prohibition of the sale of pet turtles.

The FDA commissioner reviewed the petitions, but published two rules for public comment out of consideration for the pet turtle industry and all the kids who like to own pet turtles. The first would have simply prohibited the sale of any turtle less than four inches long. There was a lengthy appeal process, presumably for those cases where a claim was made that the turtle was more than four inches long. The second proposal would not have prohibited the sale, but would have resulted in drastically tightened rules for pet turtle transactions.

First, every shipment of turtles would have to carry a warning sign reading, "Handling turtles may result in salmonella infection"—and there had to be one sign for every two hundred turtles or fraction thereof. The sign had to be printed in boldface type in letters not less than a half-inch high, since apparently turtles can't see very well. Also there had to be a leaflet telling children to wash their hands after petting their pet turtles, and there had to be at least twice as many leaflets as there were turtles. Last, there were directions on how you could tell if your turtle had salmonella on it. The directions·said that you should place five turtles in each of twelve sterile glass containers, using a larger container if necessary to avoid overcrowding. Next you added water. From then on the directions appear to be easily convertible to turtle soup.

Well, the proposals were published. The result was overwhelming silence. The prohibition won, and that's why you don't see pet turtles around any more.

Get ready to meet your air bag

Get ready to meet your air bag, but don't hold your breath till it gets here. That's the result of a case recently decided by the Court of Appeals for the District of Columbia. The case involved a challenge to the Department of Transportation's plans to require air bags on all 1982 cars. The air bag is known as a passive restraint system—that means you won't have to do anything like fasten your seat belt, and supposedly you'll be held in place by an air bag that will explode on impact.

The proposal came under attack from both sides; from a group called the Pacific Legal Foundation, which wanted air bags scrapped completely, and from Ralph Nader, who said they weren't coming soon enough. The first argument made by those who wanted to bag the whole project was that the testing of the air bags by DOT was faulty. Since 1969, the Department of Transportation has conducted thousands of tests with air bags and come up with a finding that if air bags were installed in all cars, more than nine thousand deaths and one hundred thousand injuries would be prevented each year. Incidentally, that's about the same number that would be prevented without air bags if everybody used their seat belts. The courts said that although simulated tests using dummies can never duplicate real collisions, the tests could provide the basis for the air bag standard.

The second point made by the anti-air bag forces was that the twelve thousand cars with air bags presently on the road haven't been doing too well as shown by the fact that there have been proportionally more deaths in frontal collisions in cars with air bags than anyone would have suspected. The court said the sample of the actual accidents was too small to be meaningful and of that actual number several of the accidents were so extraordinary they simply couldn't be counted at all.

The last point made was that sometimes the air bag goes off even when you're not involved in an accident; that's called inadvertant air bag deployment, but, said the court, that has only happened three times and therefore the risk that any one person's air bag would inadvertantly deploy is one in two hundred.

As far as Ralph Nader's argument that the air bags aren't coming soon enough, the court said that the four-year lead time would give the auto and air bag industries necessary breathing room to gear up production. Also, said the court, the additional time will give the public time to live with and perhaps love their air bags.

Seat belts do save lives

I hope that you use your seat belts when you drive. My most graphic memory of the use of seat belts came during the early years of a project carried out for the Department of Transportation. The idea of the project was to study automobile accidents ending in fatality just about as carefully as airplane crashes. An immediate-response team was sent to every accident involving a single vehicle that occurred within the Route 128 beltway around Boston.

The calls would usually come on a Friday or Saturday night, and the team was on the scene within a matter of minutes. We found many things; the most routine finding was a high percentage of alcohol in the victims' blood. We also found a suicide automobile. But there was one thing that I never remember seeing—a buckled seat belt around the victim. There was one case in which a car had run off the road and traveled more than three hundred feet before slamming into a solitary tree standing in the middle of a field. We wondered why the driver hadn't turned his wheel just a fraction to either side to avoid the tree; the reason was that when the car left the road, it hit a shallow ditch, and the bump threw the driver against the roof of the car, knocking him out so that he was powerless to change direction. We knew this because we found a dent in the roof of the car that conformed to the shape of the driver's head.

To understand the importance of seat belts, one need only cite several recent cases where people have been in multiple-car accidents and brought a lawsuit for their injuries against the driver they thought was clearly at fault—and lost because the courts have held that the failure to attach a seat belt contributed materially to their injury and thus barred their recovery.

Swine flu swindle

If you're thinking about getting your swine flu shot, you may be interested to hear about the informed-consent form that you have to sign before you can get it. The form was required by the law that brought the government into the malpractice insurance business because it's the government that'll be sued rather than doctors, nurses, or companies if someone thinks they've been injured by the vaccine.

Those who prepared the form ran into the same problems that all preparers of informed-consent forms face: How do you let people know about very serious risks without scaring them to death? The form attempts to avoid panic in the mind of the reader, but there are still some statements made that may prove most upsetting to anyone who takes the time to read the form.

The form is quite reassuring under the heading Possible Vaccine Side Effects, stating that most people will have no side effects from the vaccine. The only risk included in this paragraph is some tenderness at the site of the shot and the possibility of fever or chills that may occur within the first forty-eight hours. But don't stop reading, for the really serious side effects aren't listed in the paragraph entitled Possible Vaccine Side Effects; they are listed in the next paragraph, however, which is entitled Special Precautions.

Here the form states that "As with any vaccine or drug, the possibility of severe or potentially fatal reactions exists. . . . On the other hand," the form continues, "flu vaccine has rarely been associated with severe or fatal reactions." Then comes an authoritative statement of fact. "In some instances," says the form, "people receiving vaccine have had allergic reactions." The form then concludes that children under a certain age shouldn't get the vaccine, although it doesn't say what age that is, and gives a special warning to people who are allergic to eggs, have a fever, or have recently had another vaccine.

At the bottom of those warnings is a line for your signature that appears under the words, "I understand the benefits and risks of the vaccination and request that it be given to me." What does not appear, however, is that according to a report in the *New York Times,* one person has already suffered a heart attack while reading the informed-consent form.

Killing your own tapeworm

What can you do when the law keeps you from killing your tapeworm? That was the dilemma faced by a Boston doctor who returned from a trip to Outer Mongolia. He brought with him an unwanted guest called *Taenia saginata. Taenia saginata* is the name of a tapeworm, and by the time the doctor noticed the symptoms, the tapeworm was about thirty feet long. In thinking back to the trip, he remembered eating rare lamb, which is the favorite habitat of this particular tapeworm.

The doctor thought that he wouldn't have much difficulty getting rid of his tapeworm, and he looked into the best way to do it. He found that there is a painful treatment that purges the tapeworm from the body, but is so uncomfortable that many people have to be admitted to the hospital and given sedatives while the purge is carried out. He also found that there is another drug, called yomasin, four tablets of which immediately kill the tapeworm, and that the drug has no reported serious or even uncomfortable side effects.

There was only one problem: The drug yomasin had not been approved for human use by the Food and Drug Administration. This is often the case with drugs that treat diseases with a low incidence in this country, since drug companies don't want to spend the large amounts of money required to have a drug approved unless there's a very large market for its use. The doctor found that the only way he could get the drug was to contact the Center for Disease Control in Atlanta. But when he got in touch with the CDC, they told him that yomasin was back-ordered, and it would be some time before he could get it.

In the meantime, the doctor was becoming more and more uncomfortable as the tapeworm grew longer and longer. As he was deciding whether to go through the purge, or learn to live with his tapeworm, he heard that there were large amounts of yomasin just a few miles from his home—in a veterinary hospital. Having a dog whom he had always considered his best friend anyway, he decided to write out a prescription for the dog. When no one was looking, he took four of the pills. That was the end of his tapeworm. His battle makes one wonder if our system of drug regulation isn't going to the dogs after all.

Life won't be quite as sweet

Life won't be quite as sweet any more, if the Food and Drug Administration has its way. The FDA announced it was going to propose the banning of saccharin in foods and beverages because it has been found to cause malignant bladder tumors in laboratory animals. Some of the questions raised by the FDA action are: why is the FDA removing the only remaining artificial sweetener from the market? and what are people who can't use sugar for medical reasons, such as diabetics—to say nothing of those millions of us who care about calories—going to do?

A food additive is unsafe unless there is a regulation prescribing conditions when the additive may be used safely. The FDA has set up a list known as GRAS, which stands for "generally recognized as safe," and there are hundreds of things on it, from dandelion root to zinc. But there is a law known as the Delaney amendment to the Food, Drug, and Cosmetic Act. It says that no additive can be called safe if it is found to induce cancer in man *or* animal. The only exception is that the substance can be used in animal feed as long as the animals won't be hurt by it and no residue of the cancer-causing additive will be found in the edible tissues of the animal after it is slaughtered.

The problem is that methods of detecting cancer in animals have become very sophisticated. There is increasing scientific opinion that with the new detection methods many of the natural things in food as well as those added to it will be shown to produce some kind of a tumor in animals. Another problem is that nobody really knows the correlation between bladder tumors in a rat that has been filled with the equivalent of hundreds of cans of diet soda, and a man or woman who uses a teaspoonful in his or her morning coffee.

As for diabetics, the Delaney amendment applies to food additives but not to prescription drugs, so the FDA may allow the diabetic to get a prescription for saccharin. The rest of us will have to persuade our doctors to deem fear of fat a medical problem so we can get a prescription, too—or maybe things are just going to get bitter before they get worse.

Do you like eggs for breakfast?

Do you like to eat eggs for breakfast? If you do, you'll probably be interested in a recent opinion of the Seventh Circuit Court of Appeals. The case involved the question of whether eggs increase the risk of heart disease by causing an increase in cholesterol.

The case got started several years ago after scientists reported evidence of a relationship between the number of eggs consumed and a person's cholesterol level. Those widely reported findings led to a steady decrease in consumption of eggs, so the egg industry decided to form a National Commission on Egg Nutrition which, despite its high-sounding name, was a trade association formed to counter adverse publicity.

The commission, along with its ad agency, mounted an advertising and public-relations campaign to convince the public that eggs were not only needed in human nutrition, but were harmless. One ad said, "There is no scientific evidence that eating eggs increases the risk of heart disease." That ad caught the attention of a lot of people, including the Federal Trade Commission, which found that such statements constituted false and misleading advertising. The FTC ordered that any future statements had to indicate that many medical experts believe that eggs are a culprit when it comes to cholesterol and that cholesterol does play a leading role when it comes to heart disease.

The egg commission appealed, claiming the statements made were commercial free speech and thus protected by the First Amendment of the Constitution. The court reviewed the evidence and found that although it is impossible to prove whether or not consumption of eggs in fact increases the risk of heart disease, there were certainly a lot of reputable scientists who believed it did. The First Amendment, said the court, only protects honest commercial claims.

So it looks as though the egg commission overdid it, and future ads you see won't be quite as reassuring to those who like two over easy every morning.

The battle of the bacon

A bitter battle over bacon has been cooking on the West Coast, and the result will affect not only bacon lovers but consumers throughout the land. The question was, when federal and state laws require different labels, who wins?

The case started when the director of the California Weights and Measures Department ordered a particular brand of bacon off the shelves. He also stopped the sale of certain flour. His reasons weren't the usual ones; the flour and bacon weren't contaminated. But they didn't weigh as much as the packages said they did.

The reason the contents weighed less was due to moisture loss in the processing and storing of the products. Bacon, for example, just sitting in the display case, loses between three-sixteenths and four-sixteenths of an ounce per day. Flour loses *or* gains as much as 3 to 4 percent of its weight, depending on the humidity where it's kept. And if it were in airtight packaging, it would spoil. California law requires the label to state the exact weight of the contents. Federal law allows "reasonable variations" for such things as moisture loss. When there is conflict between state and federal law, federal law usually wins if the state law interferes with the federal purpose.

The manufacturers of the products sued to reverse the director's directive. The court cited congressional legislative history which acknowledged that "it is impossible to make packages exactly the same size and weight." As for the possibility of over-packaging, a packer would have to overpack flour, for example, in states with California-like labeling laws and low humidity, or overpack for everybody, which the court felt it could not require. So it threw out the California law and put the bacon and flour back on the shelves.

One question not addressed by the court's opinion was this: If bacon loses weight just sitting in the display case, why shouldn't it be required to do the same after we eat it?

Taking a dive for fun and profit

Taking a dive for fun and profit is going to get a lot more complicated. That's due to final regulations published by the Occupational Safety and Health Agency, better known as OSHA. The comprehensive set of regulations is designed to improve the safety of deep-sea and surface-controlled diving.

OSHA is required by law to be sure that places where people work are safe. One of the greatest challenges the agency has faced is how to make the ocean floor a safe place in which to work.

The regulations require that employers develop a safe practice manual, that they have operative two-way communication between the diver and the surface, and that they have available a lot of very expensive equipment at the dive site, such as decompression chambers. In addition, the regulations require that those involved in the dive have special experience and training in diving procedures and that every dive team member be trained in cardiopulmonary resuscitation and first aid. The regulations also require frequent medical examinations and detailed reporting of any fatality or injury.

All of this sounds fine until one begins to look at the cost. OSHA is required to file an IIA, or Inflationary Impact Assessment, estimating how much compliance with the regulations would cost. The IIA filed by OSHA in connection with the diving regulations added up to $22 million. The diving industry itself estimated that the costs would run as much as $40 million. That's a lot of money when one realizes the total amount earned in the whole industry in a year is less than $100 million.

Scuba diving for sport has been exempted from the regulation, but scuba diving, as well as surface-air-supplied and mixed-gas diving for any occupational use is included. Implementation of the standards is sure to bring the agency, the companies, and the divers into arguments of great depth.

The Human Fly

George Willig left his mark on history a little while ago; he may also have left his mark on legal history. George Willig, you may remember, is better known as The Human Fly, since he climbed the 110 stories of the World Trade Center—outside the building, not in. The legal aspects of his feat definitely deserve comment.

The law, of course, was quick to respond all along the way. Shortly after the men in blue arrived, they set about to figure out which crimes were in the process of being committed. It seems that to climb up the side of a building without the owner's permission is trespassing, although one apparently does not have to have the owner's permission to walk around inside the building. It also appears that it may be illegal to climb a building without a permit, although it is unclear exactly where one would go to get a building-climbing permit. After the suspected crimes were identified, the police decided to move in with a suicide prevention team, one member of which later said he was afraid of heights.

Now while all this was going on, the New York City corporation counsel's office was drafting a civil suit against Willig for "willfully and wrongfully scaling and climbing the south tower of the World Trade Center." The suit sought two hundred fifty thousand dollars in damages, presumably to discourage other climbers and to cover the costs to the city, including the eighty police officers sent to control the crowd at the scene. So at the top floor of the World Trade Center, George Willig was arrested for criminal trespass, reckless endangerment, and disorderly conduct and was also served a civil suit for two hundred fifty thousand dollars.

Now without the intervention of the mayor, it is difficult to know where things would have gone; it may have been that George would have filed a countersuit for services rendered, since he straightened out the window-washing tracks as he was climbing with a little hammer he had brought with him.

But the mayor intervened and announced the suit had been settled for $1.10, or one cent per floor, a happy end to litigation that could have taken years. The criminal charges—well, that's another story. But one wonders how far they could go, particularly in light of the comment from the Manhattan district attorney, who said, "I don't want to see anyone with Mr. Willig's talents in a position to be talking with the guys at Riker's Island."

The law of reckless flying

What's the law of reckless flying? The plane that ended up seated in the bleachers of Baltimore Memorial stadium fifteen minutes after the game ended, and a large balloon flying low over Manhattan, have made this question rather important.

The first question is, what is an aircraft? And is a balloon, for example, included in the definition? Part 1 of the Federal Aviation Regulations defines an aircraft as "a device that is used or intended to be used for flight in the air." An airplane, by the way, is a "fixed-wing aircraft, heavier than air, that is supported in flight by the dynamic reaction of the air against its wings."

The regulations also state that "no person may operate an aircraft in a careless or reckless manner so as to endanger the life or property of another." The problem is that the definition of just what is careless or reckless is less than clear. There are a lot of other issues to consider, such as whether a waiver has been granted, as in the case of agricultural spraying, or whether emergency conditions prevailed.

As far as penalties are concerned, the law allows a person's airman's certificate, which is the equivalent of a driver's license, to be revoked or suspended. Of course, if the person operating the balloon or airplane doesn't have one, it complicates things, but there is still a civil penalty of up to one thousand dollars per violation. Criminal penalties are possible, although very difficult to invoke unless someone is actually injured or killed.

So the next time you see a balloon coming at you, or are seated in the bleachers watching a football game, you can rest assured that there are laws against reckless flying.

Shooting to kill

When can you shoot to kill? That was the question recently before the Supreme Judicial Court of Massachusetts, which handed down an opinion setting guidelines as to exactly when a civilian can use a firearm or deadly force to prevent a crime or make an arrest. The case involved a dentist who was asleep in the den of his house with a loaded German Luger beside him. He later testified that the reason he was sleeping downstairs with the gun was that there had been a break into the drugstore across the street a few nights earlier, and the police didn't come in time to catch the thieves.

On the particular night involved, he heard a sound of breaking glass, grabbed the Luger, and went outside to make a citizen's arrest. When the burglars refused to surrender, he shot both men, who were arrested by police a short time later. The dentist was then prosecuted for the crime of assault and battery and convicted by a jury. The question for the Supreme Judicial Court was whether his conviction should be upheld.

The court said that most states had no guidelines as to when citizens should be able to use deadly force. So the court turned to the model penal code, which is the product of a lot of thought by lawyers, judges, and legal scholars as to what should be contained in the criminal law.

The sections of the model penal code adopted by the court provide that the use of deadly force by civilians is justifiable under certain carefully defined conditions. The key requirement is that the person being arrested by the civilian must have committed a felony, which is a serious crime punishable by a term of years in the state prison. And it cannot be just any felony; it must be a felony which itself involved conduct that included deadly force against others. This means a civilian cannot use a firearm or other deadly force to apprehend a criminal who has committed a crime that involved property only.

So under the code, if you come across someone stealing your car, or breaking into the drugstore across the street in the middle of the night, you can't shoot him. As for the dentist who did just that, the court reversed his conviction because of the fact that he couldn't have known what the guidelines were, since they hadn't been stated before. Those guidelines are now clear.

Wanting a warning

If a warning is what you want, a warning is what you are going to get. That's the result of a case recently decided by the Third Circuit Court of Appeals. The case arose out of Three Mile Island and was brought by a group of Pennsylvania residents. The case was a class action filed on behalf of all residents within two hundred miles of Three Mile Island. The defendants were President Jimmy Carter and the United States.

The plaintiffs didn't want money—all they wanted was for the government to issue a formal warning to all residents within the two-hundred-mile limit that they now have an increased risk of injury to health and reproductive capabilities because of their exposure to radiation.

The federal district judge who first heard the case blew it right out of court, saying the plaintiffs had no standing to sue in the first place and no right to the warning they were seeking in the second place. The district court said the federal government should be immune from such a suit simply because it was the federal government and that the case involved a political, not a judicial, question; therefore it had no place in the courts.

The case was appealed to the Third Circuit Court of Appeals, which reversed the lower court decision. The appeals court said the government certainly could be sued in such a case and cited the recent *Jaffey* case in which the government was forced by a lawsuit to issue a warning to U.S. servicemen who had participated in an atomic bomb test in the Nevada desert. That warning had to notify the soldiers of potential health dangers that might develop from radiation exposure.

The court said it wasn't deciding whether or not the precise warning as worded was indicated in this case, but the plaintiffs were entitled to a full trial; and it looks as though the government will have to give another warning. As for those who receive the warning, it's not clear what they'll do with it. But one thing is clear. Residents around Three Mile Island and the federal courts have not seen the last of each other.

Can you stop smoking where you work?

Can you stop smoking where you work? Well, according to a recent New Jersey decision, the answer is yes. And not only can you stop yourself from smoking while you work, but you can also stop your co-workers—whether they want to stop smoking or not.

The plaintiff in the case worked for the New Jersey Bell Telephone Company and complained that she was forced to work in an area where other employees of New Jersey Bell smoked regularly. She said that she was forced by the nearness of these smokers to inhale "secondhand" cigarette smoke, which caused her to have a bad allergic reaction. And she added that by refusing to ban smoking, New Jersey Bell Telephone was forcing her to work in an unsafe environment.

The New Jersey court found that it was clearly the law of New

Jersey, as it is the law of virtually all states, that a person has a right to work in a safe environment and that this right was guaranteed by federal and state law. Now, federal law doesn't say anything about smoking being unsafe, but the New Jersey judge said that a nonsmoking employee also has a common-law right to a safe working environment. The common law, you may recall, is that body of case law that governs when there has been no state or federal legislative pronouncement on a matter.

Then the judge made the final leap necessary for the decision in the case and cited the HEW report for 1975 entitled "The Health Consequences of Smoking," which "indicated that the mere presence of cigarette smoke in the air pollutes it, changing carbon dioxide levels and effectively making involuntary smokers of all who breathe the air." The judge noted with some irony that the company has a regulation prohibiting smoking in the immediate vicinity of telephone equipment and that the reason for this rule is that the machines are extremely sensitive and can be damaged by smoke. The judge then added that human beings are also very sensitive and can be damaged by cigarette smoke, and that a company that has demonstrated such concern for its mechanical components should have at least as much for its human beings.

Where there's smoke there's flyer

How do you feel about smoking on airplanes? Thousands of people have made their feelings on the subject known to the Civil Aeronautics Board, which has considered changing the regulations concerning smoking on commercial aircraft.

A few years ago, the board passed a regulation requiring certified air carriers to provide no-smoking areas on all flights and to enforce actively the prohibition on smoking in these areas. Then the CAB issued proposed regulations that would ban the smoking of cigars and pipes anywhere in the airplane, and at the same time the board requested comments on whether it should ban smoking on planes altogether. The board took these actions, which kindled quite a controversy, in response to a petition filed by a group known as Action on Smoking and Health, better known as ASH.

In an explanatory statement, the CAB noted that the Federal Aviation Administration, which is responsible for the health and safety of airline passengers, found no evidence that smoke in concentrations likely to occur in airplanes is injurious to health of nonsmokers. The CAB accepted the FAA position on the safety question but proposed a ban on cigar and pipe smoke anyway, on the basis that it makes passengers more uncomfortable than cigarette smoke. The theory is that the pipe or cigar smoker inhales less of the smoke and thus produces a large quantity of unfiltered mainstream smoke, and that the smoke is more alkaline, thicker, more voluminous, and much more difficult to dissipate. The CAB statement added that pipes and cigars are also not habit-forming like cigarettes, so that banning them would not be as much of a hardship as would a similar ban on cigarettes.

The CAB statement closed with the observation that now might be the time to ban all smoking on flights, due to the fact that public tolerance of smoking has markedly declined in the last few years. It looks like going up in smoke may be going out.

The gasping Gaspers

Does the Constitution prohibit smoking at indoor sporting events? This was the question before the federal district court in Louisiana. The case was that of a couple named Gasper, a rather appropriate name for a plaintiff in a smoking suit, versus the Louisiana Stadium and Exposition District.

The district operates the Superdome in New Orleans, which has hosted many events ranging from concerts to football games to Mardi Gras parades. And the Superdome allows anybody who has paid admission to enjoy whatever is going on at the time in the Superdome and to smoke as they do so.

In their complaint, the Gaspers, individually and as representatives of all other nonsmoking patrons who come to the Superdome, claimed that to allow smoking violated their constitutional rights to breathe smoke-free air while in a state building. They claimed that they were forced to consume hazardous tobacco smoke in the Superdome, causing them physical harm and discomfort, as well as interfering with their enjoyment of events for which they had paid the price of admission. All this, they said, was in violation of the First, Fifth, and Fourteenth amendments to the United States Constitution.

The court didn't have much trouble doing away with the plaintiff's claim that their First Amendment rights were violated by allowing smoking. The plaintiffs' argument was that their right to free speech was interfered with because while watching and listening to what was being done and said in the Superdome, they had to sit in a cloud of smoke. The court said that merely to allow smoking did not interfere with the receipt of information by the plaintiffs.

The court had a little more trouble with the plaintiffs' claim that nonsmoking patrons were deprived of life, liberty, and property without due process of law guaranteed by the Fifth and Fourteenth amendments. The plaintiffs argued that these freedoms included the right to be free from hazardous tobacco smoke while in state buildings. But the court pointed out that the plaintiffs could be free from the smoke by choosing not to go to the Superdome.

So the Gaspers will have to keep gasping—or watch what's happening in the Superdome on television.

Pulling your own plug

Can the law stop you from pulling the plug—on yourself? That was the question that recently came before the Broward County Circuit Court in Florida. The case involved a seventy-three-year-old man who was suffering from amyotrophic lateral sclerosis—also known as "ALS," and perhaps best known as Lou Gehrig's Disease. ALS is a painful disease without any known cure; it attacks the muscles, causing them to deteriorate slowly until death occurs.

This particular patient was taken to a Florida medical center because of difficulty in breathing, due to deterioration of the muscles used in respiration. Upon arrival at the hospital, a tracheotomy was performed to prevent suffocation, and the patient was then hooked up to a mechanical respirator.

The patient immediately objected to the respirator, and on several occasions physically pulled the respirator out of his trachea. But each time, nurses and orderlies, acting on instruction from the doctor in charge, reinserted it. After he'd removed it several more times, they tied down his hands with leather straps. The patient pleaded with his son, his daughter, his grandson, and his doctor that the respirator be removed. Once, using fabricated letters of the alphabet, he spelled out a phrase on his bedspread; the letters read "P-U-L-L—T-H-E—C-O-R-D." The patient was so insistent that a lawyer was brought into the case and, on his behalf, filed a complaint setting forth all the facts, describing the disease and the patient's repeated attempts to die.

The doctor claimed he might be subject to civil or criminal liability if he did not keep the man alive, and the family might be viewed as accessories. The court responded, citing the *Quinlan* case out of New Jersey, that there must be a right of privacy that supercedes all of the legal issues involved. The court said that in this case the facts were even stronger than in the *Quinlan* case, since this man was competent to make the decision and, in fact, had tried several times to "make the awful choice after realizing the ultimate consequences."

And so the court ordered that the patient could stay in the hospital or leave it, free of the mechanical respirator that was not attached to his body, and the court entered an order restraining doctor, family members, and other individuals from interfering with his decision. A short time later, this patient pulled out the respirator one more time. Forty hours later he was dead.

Who decides on death?

Who decides on death? That was the question that recently came before the Supreme Judicial Court of Massachusetts. Like the New Jersey Supreme Court in the *Quinlan* case, the Massachusetts court was faced with the question of who makes the death decision when the patient can't decide on his or her own.

The patient in this case was a sixty-seven-year-old severely retarded man who was stricken with fatal leukemia. The question was whether the man's life should be prolonged by chemotherapy with its violent side effects, or whether he should be allowed to die. Since the man was clearly unable to make the decision on his own, or even understand the nature of the issues involved, a guardian was appointed by a Massachusetts probate court. The guardian decided that since the man was sixty-seven, was unable to cooperate with the treatment, and would probably suffer immediate pain and discomfort from the drugs, he should recommend that the life-saving treatment not be given. The court accepted the recommendation and the man died.

The Massachusetts high court, reviewing the lower-court action, recognized that it had two questions before it: What are the rights of an incompetent when it comes to dying? And how do these rights get implemented? The court said that the current state of medical ethics is that physicians should not use extraordinary means of prolonging life when, after careful consideration, it becomes apparent that there is no hope of recovery for the patient. And the court went on to point out that recovery has to be defined as life without intolerable suffering.

Justice Liacos, writing for the Massachusetts court, grounded his decision on the constitutional right of privacy. He wrote, "As this constitutional guarantee reaches out to protect the freedom of a woman to terminate pregnancy under certain conditions, so it encompasses the right of a patient to preserve his or her right to privacy against unwanted infringements." He added that if the person in question is incompetent, his or her right of privacy may be asserted by a guardian.

As for who actually makes the final decision, here the Massachusetts court parted company with the New Jersey Supreme Court. The New Jersey court said that the final decision could be made by the hospital ethics committee acting in conjunction with the physicians. The Massachusetts court said it's the courts who must make the final decision.

So we've gone from doctors, who've made the decision for

centuries, to hospital ethics committees, and now to the courts. But we still probably haven't seen the last decision on the subject of which human being should decide when another human being should cease to exist.

Mrs. Green and the Supreme Court

Mother's Day this year was not a happy one for Mrs. Marie Green, for her son wasn't with her any more. The reason he wasn't with her was that he died in a federal prison cell in Indiana. But she did have something else this past Mother's Day: a decision of the U.S. Supreme Court in her favor in the lawsuit she brought against the Federal Bureau of Prisons because of her son's death. While the decision won't bring her son back, it may have the result of making prison officials take better care of those in their charge.

The case got started when Mrs. Green's son, who was a chronic asthmatic, asked to be transferred because of his asthma. The prison officials ignored his plea even though they were aware of the seriousness of his condition. When he suffered what was to be his fatal asthma attack, no competent medical advice was summoned until eight hours later. Drugs were given to him that were later found to be contraindicated in cases of serious asthma attacks. The prison officials attempted to use a respirator that they knew was inoperative and which further impeded the man's breathing. By the time he was transferred to a hospital outside the prison, it was too late.

Mrs. Green brought suit against the director of the Federal Bureau of Prisons, only to have the suit dismissed. The federal district court found that Indiana law provides that if the deceased leaves a spouse or children, substantial damages can be found; but if the deceased does not leave a spouse or children but only a mother, as in this case, damages are limited under Indiana law to the cost of funeral expenses.

Mrs. Green was not to be deterred and appealed the case to the U.S. Supreme Court. That court decided that the lower court had made an error when it dismissed the case and that the federal common law on the question of death claims should have been applied rather than the state law of Indiana.

The court said it is now established case law that victims of a constitutional violation by a federal agent have the right to recover damages in federal court, whether there's any specific state law on the question or not. The case was sent back for a new trial on the question of damages. So if you're a prison official, take care—you may be dealing with a mother as well as a son.

Police brutality in Philadelphia

If there is police brutality in Philadelphia, the federal government isn't going to be able to stop it. That's the message of a case recently decided by the U.S. District Court for Eastern Pennsylvania. The case was brought by the U.S. Department of Justice, which sued the City of Philadelphia. The federal government claimed that there existed in Philadelphia a pervasive pattern of police abuse, the effect of which was to deny basic federal constitutional rights to persons of all races, colors, and nationalities.

The complaint filed by the government claimed that members of the Philadelphia police department used deadly force when it was not necessary, that they physically abused persons under arrest, that they extracted confessions by the use of physical brutality, and that they apprehended persons for crimes without probable cause. The federal government also claimed that the police department maintained policies and procedures that got in the way of investigations of citizen complaints and shielded the officers involved from any kind of discipline or scrutiny.

Before the case was tried, the city moved to dismiss it on the grounds that the federal government had no standing or legal right to bring the case at all.

The court began by noting that Congress had never specifically given the power to the federal government to protect civil rights in general. In fact, when the 1957 Civil Rights Act was introduced into Congress, there was a specific passage in the law that would have allowed the U.S. Attorney General to bring lawsuits to protect civil rights, but that passage was struck before the bill became law. And while the 1964 Civil Rights Act allowed the U.S. Attorney General to bring lawsuits to protect some specific rights such as voting or employment, general authority to protect people's civil rights was not granted.

The government argued that specific legislative history was irrelevant and that the power to sue to halt police brutality is implied. But the court answered, "The Government's argument, though artfully expressed, is unpersuasive." So the case of the federal government against the city of brotherly love is over.

Sleeping off a drunk

When you tell a man you think is drunk to go sleep it off, make sure he isn't dying. That's the message of a recent case decided by the U.S. District Court for Montana. The case involved a man who wandered the streets in what appeared to be a drunken stupor, but who wasn't drunk and instead was suffering from pancreatitis, a disease that if untreated can be fatal.

The case got started when a motorist driving through Great Falls, Montana, told a Great Falls police officer that he had seen an intoxicated blind man walking down the center lane of the roadway. The officer found the man and took him to his squad car, where he tried to find out the man's name and address. When he couldn't, he took the man to the station and told his lieutenant that he had a drunken man with him and asked if he could keep the man in protective custody. The lieutenant responded that department procedure didn't authorize the taking into custody of a man in this condition, and the lieutenant told the officer to take him to a park near the station house. It rained all night, and in the early afternoon of the next day the same officer went to check the man and discovered that he had died.

The man's estate sued, claiming that the officers had an affirmative duty under law to ensure the treatment, safe custody, and shelter of the man. The suit was brought under Section 1983 of Title 42 of the U.S. Code, which provides for damages if it can be proved that someone acted under color of state law to deprive an individual of rights, privileges, and immunities secured by the Constitution of the United States.

The court said there was no question that the officers acted under color of state law and that they were under a clear duty either to take the man into protective custody or to take him to a place of shelter or a hospital. They failed to live up to their duty, said the court, resulting in the deprivation of the man's life without due process of law.

The case was sent back for a new trial to determine damages against the police officers and the City of Great Falls. And so if you are a police officer, you might think twice when you're dealing with someone who's dead drunk.

Dropping off a drunk—to death

Dropping off a drunk can be dangerous. That's the moral of a recent case decided by New York's highest court. The case began when the police received a call that some people were acting in a boisterous manner. When they arrived, they found a rather typical situation—two men fighting with a third who was trying to play peacemaker—all of whom appeared to the police to be very drunk. The police then carried out what they described as a standard procedure, which was to place the men in the patrol car and take them to an abandoned golf course where they would be dropped off to dry out.

The golf course was dark, unlit, and the men stumbled about until they heard the sounds of passing cars, which they took to mean a road that would take them back to town. Unfortunately, the road turned out to be the New York State thruway. They were struck by a car and one of the men was killed and another seriously injured.

Suit was brought against the city for false imprisonment and negligence. The Court of Appeals reversed a lower court decision that had thrown the case out of court. On the question of false imprisonment, the court held that once the men were forced to enter the patrol car, they were confined against their will, and when they were improperly released, that was false imprisonment. The court was not impressed by the city's argument on behalf of the police that a police officer doesn't have to arrest for drunkenness, but can use his discretion and take a person to his home or a safe place to dry out. In this case, the court said, confinement was for the purpose of simply running the person out of town.

As for the question of negligence, the court said the police owed a duty of care to persons in custody who are under the influence of alcohol. The court pointed out that even a stranger who volunteers to help another person has a duty not to place that person in a worse situation than when he found him.

There was a strong dissent in the case, with that judge stating that this was an unfortunate and tragic case, but not one that should result in liability for the city. But the majority ruled, and if you run people out of town, you may run into trouble.

Can you picket on private property?

Can you picket on private property? That was the question recently decided by the California Supreme Court. The answer to that question depends pretty much on the state you live in. As

far as California is concerned, the answer is, you can picket on
private property just about any time you want.

The case involved a Sears store that was in the middle of a
large, privately owned parking lot. The store was surrounded by
privately owned sidewalks, and it was on those sidewalks that the
pickets wanted to picket. But Sears refused to allow them to
picket there, requiring that instead they picket on public sidewalks, which were located four hundred feet away from the store.
The picketing workers complained that was ridiculous because
no one going into the store would be able to read the signs. The
question for the courts was whether the right to picket overrides
the right to control private property.

The first battle was won by Sears, which got a California trial
court to grant a temporary injunction preventing picketing on the
private property. For a while it looked very good for Sears, because the U.S. Supreme Court has held that the Constitution
does not protect picketing on private property.

But while Sears won the battle, it lost the war because of a new
law passed by the California legislature. That law, known as the
Moscone Law, said simply that the courts would no longer have
jurisdiction to prevent people from picketing on any public street
or any place where persons may lawfully be. The California Supreme Court said that since people had a right lawfully to be on
the sidewalk outside the Sears store, that law applied, and the
courts could not stop people from being there, whether they
were customers or pickets.

Besides, said the court, sidewalks outside stores have long
been a traditional place to picket. Whether a store is located on
Main Street, U.S.A., or in a privately owned suburban parking lot
doesn't make any difference.

There was a strong dissent, with one judge saying that private
property is private property, but the majority ruled, and picket
signs on California sidewalks are here to stay.

Testing Renée Richards

Renée Richards won't have a chromosome test after all. That
was the result of a decision by the New York Supreme Court in a
lawsuit brought by Dr. Renée Richards against the Tennis Association, the U.S. Open Tennis Championship Committee, and the
Women's Tennis Association. You may remember that the fields
of tennis and opthamology were somewhat shocked when Dr.

Richard Raskind, who was a New York opthamologist and third-ranked male tennis player, underwent a sex-change operation. Dr. Richards said, "I underwent this operation after many years of being a transsexual, a woman trapped inside the body of a man."

Well, the court opinion doesn't indicate what the impact of the sex change was on the practice of opthamology, but it certainly had a lot of impact on the tennis court. Dr. Raskind, now known as Renée Richards, entered nine women's tennis tournaments, won two, and finished as runner-up in three. The problem came when Renee was headed for the U.S. Open at Forest Hills and was ordered to take the Barr body test. That test determines the presence of a second X chromosome, which is present in the normal female, while a male has a Y chromosome instead. Renée Richards sued for a temporary injunction, claiming a violation of New York State's human rights law.

The defendants said that the Barr test was the only test that would insure fairness, claiming that there would be a competitive advantage for a person who had physical training and development as a male and then switched over to female competition after an operation. They were also apparently worried about an epidemic, because they made the point that there were as many as ten thousand transsexuals in the United States and an even greater number of female impersonators.

The court cited the declaration of the human rights law that the state has the responsibility to assure that every individual in New York State is afforded an equal opportunity to enjoy a full and productive life, and that the proposed test was an unlawful, discriminatory practice on the basis of sex. The court accepted testimony from Renée's surgeon, gynecologist, and psychologist that she was in all respects a woman.

So there is much more to life than a chromosome after all.

"Live Free or Die"

Have you ever thought about the relationship between your license plate and the religious freedom guaranteed by the First Amendment? Well, there is a relationship, according to a recent case in a federal district court. The case involved New Hampshire license plates for passenger cars, all of which carried the slogan "Live Free or Die." George and Maxine Maynard were New Hampshire residents who were Jehovah's Witnesses; they covered up the slogan with red reflector tape because they had a deeply held belief that death is not a reality for a follower of Christ, and that it may be wrong to give up one's earthly life for the state, even if the choice is to live in bondage.

Unfortunately for the Maynards, however, there was a law in the state of New Hampshire making it a crime to cover up the words "Live Free or Die" on your license plates. Beginning in late 1974, Mr. Maynard was arrested three times for violating the law. At first he was merely fined twenty-five dollars, and the fine was suspended if he would only be on good behavior, which presumably meant that he wouldn't tape up his license plates any more. But, alas, the problem with deeply held religious beliefs is that they are not easily discouraged, and Mr. Maynard ended up being ordered committed to the Grafton County House of Correction for fifteen days.

At that point, Mr. Maynard decided to go to federal court, seeking a declaration that the New Hampshire law was unconstitutional as it abridged his religious freedom guaranteed by the First Amendment. The state defended its law on the ground that the slogan fostered appreciation of the state's history and tradition, created state pride, identity, and individualism, and promoted tourism. It also aided, the state said, in identifying New Hampshire vehicles, an argument made rather difficult by the fact that the slogan did not appear on license plates for New Hampshire trucks and buses.

The court declared the law unconstitutional and held that the act of covering it was a clear attempt of the plaintiffs to disagree with the slogan; thus it was symbolic speech and protected by the First Amendment.

And so in New Hampshire the red tape will continue, and while New Hampshire officials may want you to live free or die, they can no longer say so on your license plate if you don't want them to.

A moment of silence

Can a moment of silence in the school day violate the Constitution? This was the question put recently before a three-judge federal court. The case grew out of a Massachusetts law that was passed in 1968, just a few years after the U.S. Supreme Court struck down as unconstitutional the forced recitation of the Lord's Prayer in public school.

The Massachusetts law read as follows: "At the commence-

ment of the first class of each day . . . the teacher in charge
. . . shall announce that a period of silence not to exceed one
minute . . . shall be observed for meditation or prayer." Twelve
students and their parents then sued, asking the court to strike
down the law as violating their constitutional rights. They complained that the law established a religious exercise in the public
schools in violation of the First Amendment, in addition to interfering with the parents' right exclusively to supervise the religious upbringing of their children. They also argued that the
passage of the law just a few years after the invalidation of school
prayer showed that the Massachusetts legislature intended to
violate the spirit and the letter of the earlier court decision.

The federal court decided that the enforced moment of silence
was not unconstitutional and that the legislative history of the
particular law showed that the Massachusetts legislature intended to further secular, not religious, purposes. The court
looked at the fact that the bill as originally introduced by the
legislature contained only the word "prayer," but that the words
"or meditation" were subsequently added to the bill. This
proved, to the court at least, that the Massachusetts legislature
had secular rather than religious thoughts in mind.

As the court noted, the law didn't require the kids to do anything; it just required them to be silent, and "a quiet moment at
the beginning of the day would tend to still the tumult of the
playground and start a day of study." The court noted that meditation is the act of meditating and connotes serious reflection or
contemplation on a subject that may be religious, irreligious, or
nonreligious.

As for the right of parents to exclusively direct the upbringing
of their children, the court noted that the parents were free to
instruct their children that while other children may be praying
silently, they should not engage in prayer during the moment of
silence, but merely remain silent.

The great wall of Memphis

What happens when a city tries to put a wall around a black
neighborhood? That was the question recently decided by the
Sixth Circuit Court of Appeals. The case involved the city of
Memphis, Tennessee, which in its wisdom decided to erect a
barrier that would close off completely a main street that ran
along the edge of a white neighborhood. On the other side of the

street that was to become a wall was a predominantly black neighborhood.

Several residents of the black neighborhood went to court claiming that for a city to close off the street and wall them off violated their constitutional rights under the Fourteenth Amendment, which guarantees due process, and under the Thirteenth Amendment, which supposedly abolished slavery. They also claimed a violation of federal law, which provides that all citizens of the United States shall have the same right as is enjoyed by white citizens to sell, hold, and convey real and personal property. Specifically, the black residents argued that closing them off would enhance the property values in the all-white neighborhood and decrease them in the predominantly black neighborhood.

After noting that the U.S. Supreme Court requires a sensitive inquiry into the evidence in discrimination cases, the appeals court stated, "We are convinced that the erection of the physical barrier between a historically all-white residential neighborhood and a predominantly black neighborhood constitutes a 'badge of slavery' which was the target of the Thirteenth Amendment."

There was no question, said the court, but that the community benefited by the closing was all white. The barrier, said the court, was not a response to a city planning effort, but was a unique step to protect one neighborhood from outside influences that its residents considered to be undesirable.

There was a dissent, with one judge saying that the blacks hadn't shown that the whites intended to discriminate against them by erecting the wall. But the majority ruled, and there may be a lot of things that separate blacks and whites in Memphis, but the Memphis wall won't be one of them.

Records and the private I

Should an ex-con be able to become a private eye? That was the question recently raised before a three-judge federal court in Connecticut. At issue was a Connecticut law that barred all convicted felons from ever being able to become private detectives or security guards, regardless of how rehabilitated a felon might have become. The ex-con who sued claimed that the law was unconstitutional because it denied a person rights without a hearing and because it violated the equal protection clause of the Fourteenth Amendment.

Apparently this man's situation was not an isolated case, for in

Connecticut in one year alone there were 103 rejections of felons who wanted to become private detectives or security guards. All were automatically rejected because of prior felony records. The felons were all the more upset by the fact that a drug addict or an alcoholic who had not been convicted of a felony could become a detective or security guard if found to be fit after a hearing. The felons wanted at least the same rights as the alcoholics and drug addicts.

The U.S. Supreme Court has held that the area of applications for such things as private detectives or security guards isn't one of those equal protection areas where strict scrutiny is required, so the federal court had to judge only if there was a rational connection between the law and its purpose. The court found there was not, and held that it was a denial of equal protection for all persons with felony convictions to be disqualified.

The State of Connecticut claimed that the across-the-board disqualification was designed to keep the criminal element out of the business that affected public welfare, morals, and safety. The court disagreed, stating that the legislation failed to recognize the obvious differences in the fitness and character of people with felony records. For example, said the court, a felony conviction for bigamy or income-tax evasion would have virtually no relevance to an individual's performance as a private detective or security guard. The court also pointed out that if a person was convicted of inciting a riot, which may relate to fitness as a security guard, he or she could get the job, because inciting a riot is only a misdemeanor, not a felony.

So just because you've been to prison, it doesn't mean you can't show other people the way.

Victory for veterans, woe for women

A victory for veterans and another resounding defeat for women. That's the message of a case recently decided by the U.S. Supreme Court. The case reversed an earlier decision that had declared unconstitutional a Massachusetts law giving a preference to veterans who applied for state civil-service positions. A three-judge federal panel had declared that law unconstitutional on the grounds that while the goals of the preference were legitimate to help veterans, and the statute had not been enacted for the purpose of discriminating against women, the exclusionary impact on women was so severe that the law could not stand.

The Supreme Court began its opinion by agreeing that the preference operated overwhelmingly to the advantage of males. But despite this stark fact, the court reversed the lower court ruling and upheld the preference law. The court pointed out that the case was important not only for the Commonwealth of Massachusetts and for the woman who brought the suit, but also for the whole country, because the federal government and virtually all the states grant some sort of hiring preference to veterans.

The woman in this case had taken a number of civil-service examinations, receiving the second highest score on one and the third highest on another, but despite her ability and test scores, she never got the jobs. In one case she was ranked sixth behind five lower-scoring male veterans and in another behind twelve male veterans, eleven of whom had lower scores. She began to realize that competition for civil-service positions in which veterans were interested was futile, so she commenced a lawsuit.

The court said that despite its impact on women, the law was neutral on its face, drawing a difference between veterans and nonveterans, not a difference between men and women. As for discrimination, the court said that to be actionable, discrimination has to be shown to be purposeful, and here the intent of the Massachusetts legislature was to help veterans, not to hurt women.

Justices Marshall and Brennan dissented on the grounds that the Massachusetts choice of an absolute veterans-preference system did indicate a purposeful gender-based discrimination against women. But the majority ruled, and whether you feel veterans won or women lost depends on your preference.

Gay rights at school

The subject of gay rights has been getting a lot of attention at the ballot box and in the courtroom, with mixed results. At the polls, gay rights have gone down to defeat. With the help of Anita Bryant's "Save Our Children" campaign, the Dade County, Florida, ordinance that prohibited bias in jobs, housing, and public accommodations on the basis of sexual preference was repealed. A few years back, Boulder, Colorado, the only other community to vote on a similar question, also repealed a gay rights ordinance.

But in the courts, things have been a little bit different. The most recent decision on the subject has come out of the U.S.

Court of Appeals for the Eighth Circuit. The suit was brought by a group called Gay Lib Against the University of Missouri. University officials had refused to register the group as a student organization because they felt that recognition of the organization would probably result in the commission of felonies, since sodomy is a felony.

The district court upheld the refusal of the university officials to register the group after it heard testimony from a number of psychiatrists. They testified that, in addition to imminent violations of the sodomy law, recognition of the organization would tend to perpetrate or expand homosexual behavior. One psychiatrist made the statement that wherever you have a convocation of homosexuals, you are going to have increased homosexual activity.

But the Court of Appeals reversed the lower court. The judge who wrote the opinion was unimpressed by the psychiatric testimony and said that, even accepting such opinions at face value, they are insufficient to justify a prior governmental restraint on the right of the group of students to associate. The judge also said that there was no evidence that the organization would do things like interrupt classes or substantially interfere with the educational process.

There was strong dissent, with one judge stating that the credible testimony of highly qualified psychiatrists persuasively demonstrated that homosexual behavior is compulsive, an illness, and clearly abnormal. But the majority ruled, and gay lib will be free to take its lawful place at the university.

If your club is private enough

If your club is private enough, you can keep people out because you don't like their color. That's the message of a case recently decided by the U.S. District Court for Eastern Virginia. The case involved a country club which admitted that it rejected black applicants for membership solely because they were black, and claimed that it had the right to do so. One of those rejected for membership brought suit claiming that federal law prohibited such discrimination.

The court agreed that the U.S. Supreme Court has indeed held in some situations that the law does prohibit discrimination by private clubs and individuals as well as public entities. But those situations only involve places that really are open to the public, even though they pretend not to be. One of the cases involved a neighborhood swimming pool, which was open to just about anybody who wanted to join, as long as they were white, and the court held that in such a case private discrimination can be prohibited.

But, said the court, that is a very different case. Here we do in fact have a very exclusive private country club which wants to keep people out on the basis of their race. Membership is not tied to a given geographic area. Second, there have to be two recommendations before a person can even be considered for membership in the club, and to actually get in, 95 percent of the entire membership has to vote yes, and then the persons pay very expensive membership dues.

And the court said that since this country club is a truly private club and not in fact open to the public, the membership policies and practices of the club are beyond the law. The court quoted Mr. Justice Brandeis who said that the Constitution confers the right to be let alone. And, said the court, even an exclusive country club has a constitutionally protected right of privacy. The court did say that it neither endorses nor approves of racially discriminatory membership policies, but the federal government is without the power to change them.

So if you really want to and you're private enough, you can keep people out just because of the color of their skin.

Underground advertising

What happens when a group of homosexuals want to advertise their wares in the subway? That was the question recently decided by the U.S. District Court for the District of Columbia.

The plaintiff in the case was the Gay Activist Alliance of Washington; that group sued the Washington Metropolitan Area Transit Authority because the Authority had rejected proposed advertisements the Gay Alliance wanted to place inside buses and trains operated by the authority.

The Alliance argued that the Authority's rejection violated its First Amendment rights by restricting homosexual's freedom on the subway because selling advertising was more like a private profitmaking function than it was governmental.

The court said the basic First Amendment issue is whether the Authority has created a public forum for speech. The U.S. Supreme Court has held that while a bus is not traditionally a forum for speech, it may be turned into one if the municipality operating it begins to accept advertisements dealing with social or political issues. And, said the court, while the Washington Authority could have rejected all advertising, it did not. In fact, it accepted a broad range of political and social advertisements, including ads from the Edison Electric Institute advocating nuclear power, from the Unification Church, the Church of Scientology, and an antiabortion group. Not only were these ads accepted, said the court, but they were accepted without any clearly defined criteria for determining what could be accepted or rejected.

The court said that while the Authority has a legitimate interest in preventing riders from being exposed to offensive ads concerning homosexuality, that interest must be pursued within the confines of the First Amendment. The court said the Authority has opened up a public forum for political and social advertisements and cannot constitutionally exclude the plaintiffs from access to that forum.

So homosexuals, at least in the nation's capital, will be able to advertise in the subway, for whatever it is they're selling.

Letterhead libel

What happens when a psychiatrist and a police officer do battle —first on the highway and then in the courts? That was the question in a case recently decided by the Maryland Court of Appeals.

The case got started when a psychiatrist was out for a nighttime drive with his wife and child and he was stopped by a police officer. The reason he was stopped wasn't clear, and exactly what happened after he was stopped wasn't clear either, but what was clear was the letter the psychiatrist wrote to the police chief complaining of the police officer's behavior. He wrote that the officer asked for his license without giving a reason and refused to repeat inaudible instructions and kept blinding, high-powered spotlights aimed upon the family. And then the psychiatrist wrote, "I question if this officer is mentally deranged or psychopathic and/or pathologically sadistic."

The police officer involved then decided to sue the psychiatrist for libel, which is what you can sue for if someone's defamed you or held you up to ridicule or disgrace in writing.

The psychiatrist, in defending the case, claimed that a public official cannot recover for libel unless the public official established actual malice or reckless disregard for the truth.

The court noted the fact that the psychiatrist's letter was on his professional letterhead and it was permissible to therefore infer that he wanted his professional knowledge as a psychiatrist to be taken into account when he wrote the officer might have been mentally deranged, psychopathic, or pathologically sadistic. The court said the letter thus goes beyond an ordinary complaint of an outraged citizen, and the psychiatrist was in this situation not an ordinary citizen, but was acting as a psychiatrist. The court added that it did not believe the psychiatrist's statement about the lights and said that the psychiatrist was willfully disregarding the truth and officer's rights when he wrote that the officer may have been crazy.

There was one dissent with one judge saying "subjecting a critic of the police conduct to a full trial and possibly heavy damages even though there was no evidence of actual malice may well have a chilling effect on free speech."

But the majority ruled and next time you write a letter complaining about the conduct of a police officer, maybe you'd only better say nice things.

Who shall we assassinate?

Who shall we assassinate? Is that a harmless political chant or a death threat? That was the question that had to be decided recently by the Supreme Court of Florida.

The case got started when a young black man was shot and killed by a Deputy Sheriff. A grand jury was convened to look into the shooting but decided that the Deputy had fired the fatal shot in self-defense. After that decision, some members of the black community demonstrated in protest of the grand jury's verdict. They demanded the deputy be removed from office, and at one of the demonstrations, one man led the crowd in the chant: "Two, four, six, eight, who shall we assassinate?" And he answered with the words "The whole bunch of you pigs."

The leader of the demonstration was arrested and convicted of the crime of extortion. The theory was that he maliciously threatened injury to the sheriff to force him to fire the deputy. The defendant appealed the conviction, claiming that he was just using the words as part of a political demonstration and to convict him of the crime of extortion because of it was unconstitutional.

The leading case in the area of just what you can say at a political demonstration without getting arrested is that of *Watts* v. *The United States,* in which a person was convicted of threatening the life of the President of the United States. In that case the defendant was a draft resistor who said at a demonstration, "If they ever make me carry a rifle the first person I want in my sights is L.B.J."

The U.S. Supreme Court reversed the conviction saying that while the statement was a crude and offensive way of stating political opposition to the president, it wasn't really a willful threat and we have to be careful to distinguish between real threats and political speech, which must be protected by the First Amendment.

But the Florida Supreme Court, in upholding the conviction, pointed out that there was much more in this case than just the political chanting. The demonstrators had sticks and clubs, and passed a steak knife from one to the other as they chanted. Two justices dissented on the ground that the "Two, four, six, eight" cheer was no worse than what had been said in the *Watts* case, but the majority ruled, and cheerleaders who call for death had better watch their step.

Music in the subway

If you don't like the music in the subway, what can you do about it? Believe it or not, a case involving music on public buses made it all the way to the U.S. Supreme Court. The case got started a few years back when the Capital Transit Company, a privately owned but publicly regulated bus company in Washington, D.C., decided to provide music for its passengers. The bus company contracted with a local radio station to put speakers in its buses and to broadcast music for the riders, the only restriction being that the broadcast had to be 90 percent music and no more than 10 percent weather, commercials, or special announcements.

A short while after the music began, a poll was taken of the riders, who said they liked it, didn't care, or would go along with the majority. Only 3 percent said they were firmly opposed.

But it takes only one person to bring a lawsuit, and some passengers went to court, claiming the music violated their constitutional rights. The Public Utilities Commission found that public comfort, safety, and convenience were not impaired, but that the music actually created more good will between the passengers and improved the conditions of the ride.

The court of appeals set aside the commission's judgment on the basis that the broadcasts deprived the objecting passengers of liberty without due process of law. It added that an important reason for the decision was that it was not dealing just with music alone but with commercials and announcements.

The court of appeals said that compulsory music violated the First Amendment, which prohibits laws abridging freedom of speech. The plaintiffs had contended that the radio programs interfered with their freedom of conversation with other passengers and also claimed that Fifth Amendment guarantees against invasion of privacy were violated.

But the U.S. Supreme Court disagreed with the court of appeals, noting that the music wasn't all that loud and that objectionable propaganda was not being broadcast. As far as invasion of privacy was concerned, the Supreme Court refused to accept the plaintiffs' point of view that one person's privacy was all that counted. So the court of appeals was reversed, and those who don't want to listen will have to wear earmuffs—or walk to work.

4

SERVICES FOR HIGHER:

*Doctor and Patient, Lawyer and Client, Landlord and
Tenant—Give and take when it really matters, or Who can
you trust nowadays?*

Special relationships have not fared well in recent years. Doctor
and patient, lawyer and client, landlord and tenant, and those
who look to one another for help and solace don't seem to be
getting along very well anymore. It reminds me of a sign I saw
in a liquor store some time ago in Boston's north end. You've
probably seen signs like it; one that frequently appears in hardware stores reads, "We have an agreement with the banks: They
don't sell hardware and we don't cash checks." The sign in this
liquor store, a simple hand-lettered sign on an old piece of shirt
cardboard, read simply, "No Trust."

While much of our current lack of trust may be deserved, much
of it is the result of the current syndrome that tries to bring down
to the lowest common denominator virtually every professional
or similar relationship. We have degenerated to an "us against
them" philosophy and have become a nation of vastly polarized
interests, each with vocal spokesmen. Unfortunately, the goal of
the relationship and the spirit of working together toward a common goal have been lost.

Perhaps we should remember that in the long run it is in the
best interest of the lawyer to respect and help his client and in
the best interest of the client to respect and work with his lawyer
—and the same is true with doctor and patient, landlord and
tenant, and all who bear special relationships to one another.
This is not to say that we should return to the days of blind faith
when the M.D.(eity) complex reigned supreme. We need to forge
a new partnership of provider and consumer, a partnership based
on trust, on mutual respect, and on a willingness to work to the
solution of common problems. We may take some momentary
joy from the fact that we place an impossible burden on a psychia-

trist to report a dangerous patient, but in the long run we will be —and all of society will be—the loser, along with the psychiatrist. Some may take pleasure in preventing a landlord from increasing his rent to reflect inflation, but in the long run we will lose because the landlord may simply give up and, like so many landlords, quit because being a landlord simply isn't a very good business anymore.

Somehow we have to reach an accommodation with the provider and the provided. We have already gone too far down the low road, and I have yet to encounter a society that helped itself by pulling down those at the top of the ladder on the false promise that it will help those at the bottom. What happens much more often is that those at the top suffer, and those at the bottom suffer even more.

Medical malpractice in 1767

Lest you think that medical malpractice is a recent phenomenon, I would like to refer you to the case of *Slater* v. *Baker and Stapleton,* which was tried in England before Lord Chief Justice Wilmot in the year 1767.

The case involved a man who had broken both bones in one of his legs and was initially treated by a surgeon who set the leg according to the conventional methods of the time. Mr. Slater was disabled or, as the court put it rather quaintly, "under his hands," for nine weeks. During this time, according to the testimony of an apothecary who treated Mr. Slater, he was doing very well with the bones uniting nicely.

Then came the problem. Two doctors apparently wanted to try out a new machine that they had devised that was described in the court's opinion as a heavy steel thing with teeth and that treated fractures by extending or stretching the leg rather than by the conventional measure of splinting or compression. The court's description of what happened next is rather graphic. Baker took up the plaintiff's foot in both his hands and nodded to Stapleton, and then Stapleton took the plaintiff's leg upon his knee. The leg gave a crack, and the plaintiff cried out to them and said, "You have broke what nature formed." Baker then said, "You have gone through the operation of extension," and Stapleton said, "We have consulted and done for the best," and they left.

The jury found five hundred pounds damages against the doctors. On appeal they sought to have the verdict set aside, raising as their main defense that the wrong form of action was used to bring the case. They said that it should have been an action based on the failure of Mr. Slater to give consent rather than one based on negligence or a failure to act in accordance with the custom of other physicians in the community. The court answered by saying, "We will not look with eagle eyes to see whether the evidence applies exactly. . . . It appears to the court that this was the first experiment made with this new instrument, and if it was, it was a rash action and although the defendants in general may be as skillful in their respective professions as any two gentlemen in England, yet the court cannot help saying that in this particular case they have acted ignorantly and unskillfully contrary to the known rule and usage of surgeons."

And thus appeared in the casebooks for the first time a case of medical malpractice. Lord Chief Justice Wilmot wouldn't have believed that two hundred years later, malpractice insurance premiums alone would exceed $1 billion, doctor protest strikes would be rampant throughout the country, and a major crisis would loom in both research and clinical practice.

The doctor and the X-rated hypnotic trance

What happens when a doctor hypnotizes his patients without their consent and then gives them a prescription that is X-rated? That was the subject matter of a case recently decided by the California Court of Appeals. The case involved a California physician who gave his patients more personal attention than they bargained for. The doctor was appealing the revocation of his license by the California Board of Medical Examiners.

The court carefully reviewed the evidence, which showed that a fifty-five-year-old woman named Florence and her eighty-one-year-old husband had come to the doctor's office, with Florence complaining of a pain in her hip and Harry suffering from a strained back. The doctor took Florence into a treatment room where she put on a hospital gown; he applied heat pads to her and began rubbing her back. He then told her to relax and tried to hypnotize her, engaging in a luridly detailed monologue that described in graphic detail the acts involved in sexual intercourse, rubbing her back the whole time. After treating Florence, the doctor went into a different room, attempted to hypnotize

Harry, and had an equally lurid one-sided conversation with him, prompting Harry's comment on the witness stand, "I lay there dumbfounded and couldn't figure out what the hell was going on."

Although the patients didn't say anything to the doctor about his unusual behavior, they did contact the Board of Medical Examiners, which dispatched two women special agents to pose as patients to find out just what was going on. The doctor covered similar subjects with the agents.

The doctor's defense was that the first patients had come to him for hypnosis and treatment of difficulties they were having with their sexual relationship. As for the agents, he agreed that perhaps he had made an error in professional judgment in diagnosing their problems as sexually related without taking a history. But he claimed that his real purpose was to motivate all his patients to enjoy more happiness and that he had a right of free speech.

The court said that what the doctor had done was unprofessional conduct. As for the free speech, the court said the challenged speech was outside constitutional protection and violated the trust reposed in him by his patients. So this doctor is out, but who knows—perhaps a new career awaits him just around the corner.

Teenage suicide—who's responsible?

Who's responsible when a teenager commits suicide? That was the question recently raised before the California Court of Appeals for the First District. The case involved Tammy, her parents, friends, and doctor, none of whom could stop Tammy from killing herself.

Tammy was what you might call an average teenager until she began running with a close girl friend who was a heroin addict. Her parents got her to go to a psychiatrist in Berkeley, but despite his efforts and those of a lot of people who really loved Tammy, she took an overdose of pills and died.

Tammy's parents decided to bring a lawsuit against the psychiatrist for failing to act when he knew or should have known that Tammy was going to commit suicide. It turned out that the psychiatrist wrote in his notes that he felt Tammy was suicidal. Her parents claimed that he should have hospitalized her or at least warned them of the crisis that had occurred.

The case was brought almost two years to the day after

Tammy's death, which caused an immediate problem, since the statute of limitations in California for wrongful acts of physicians is one year. The parents claimed that the reason they had delayed in bringing the case was that they didn't realize they had a case until the landmark *Tarasott* decision, which held that if a psychiatrist suspects homicidal tendencies on the part of one of his patients, he has a duty to warn foreseeable victims. Tammy's parents claimed that a psychiatrist's duty to warn was not the law until the *Tarasott* case and that the one-year time period should start from the time of the *Tarasott* case rather than from the time of Tammy's death.

The court rejected this reasoning, saying that doctors had had a duty of care for years and that the parents shouldn't have had to wait until *Tarasott* to realize they had a case. The court could have ended its opinion at this point, but it didn't, stating that the *Tarasott* case should not be extended to suicide and that a psychiatrist should only have a duty to warn where the lives of other people are in danger. When one's own life is on the line, the psychiatrist can decide to keep what he knows confidential and the law will not second-guess him. And for the question of who is responsible when a teenager commits suicide, the answer, from the law at least, is no one.

The long arm of the law

Sometimes the long arm of the law is just as close as your telephone. That's the message from a recent case out of the U.S. District Court for Montana. The case got started when a man suffered a detached retina in his right eye. He went to an eye specialist in Butte, Montana, who referred him to a surgeon in Salt Lake City, Utah. The man went to Utah, where he was operated on by the Utah surgeon.

The patient came back to Montana a few weeks later, and then his wife had a telephone conversation with the Utah surgeon. During that telephone conversation, the doctor said it would be all right for the patient to go back to work. But on his first day back the man suffered a massive retinal tear.

The Montana patient brought suit against the Utah doctor in the Montana courts. The doctor tried to have the case dismissed on the ground that he was not subject to the jurisdiction of the Montana courts because he never lived or practiced medicine in Montana.

But the Montana court held that the telephone call was enough to subject the doctor to the jurisdiction of the Montana court. The reason was the Montana "long-arm" statute. That law, like the long-arm statutes of many states, provides that if a person does business in a state or commits a wrong in a state, that's enough to subject the person to jurisdiction even though he or she doesn't live or work in the state or have anything else to do with it.

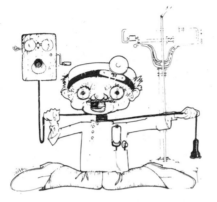

The Montana court held that when the doctor spoke with the patient's wife by telephone and said her husband could go back to work, it was essentially a new diagnosis. And since it may have been wrong, it properly gave rise to an action in the Montana courts. So from this case at least, it really does look as if long distance is just about as good as being there.

M.D.s, Inc.

Does it matter whether or not your doctor is incorporated? The answer is, it certainly does, according to a recent decision out of the Indiana Court of Appeals. The case got started when a patient came to a hospital emergency room needing treatment. The doctor on duty was a member of a corporation that had contracted with the hospital to staff the hospital emergency room on a twenty-four-hour basis.

In the past, emergency rooms had been staffed with either staff physicians who rotated through the emergency room or by residents from large nearby teaching hospitals who moonlighted in their off-duty hours. Many hospitals now prefer full-time emergency-room physicians, many of whom have formed corporations. In fact, many physicians, lawyers, accountants, and other professionals who used to practice as partners or solo practitioners have now incorporated themselves because of tax advantages such as larger pension and profit-sharing plans.

The patient who was injured not only sued the doctor who allegedly injured him, but he sued personally all the other doctors in the corporation. The question for the court was whether the other doctors could be held personally liable even though they weren't in the emergency room when the incident occurred. In the old days when doctors worked as solo practitioners or as partnerships, there was no question but that all of the partners could be held liable for any act of malpractice of any one doctor. The question for the court was whether incorporation changed the rules.

The court first had to decide if a corporation of doctors is just like any other corporation. Internal Revenue Service regulations require that one thing that has to be present before a corporation can be treated as a corporation under the tax laws is limited liability for those in the corporation. The court said that when the legislature let the doctors incorporate, it was careful to prevent the corporate shield from arising between the patient and the doctor. The fear was not only that such a shield would destroy the personal relationship of doctor and patient, but also that the doctor might hide behind the corporate veil if sued.

But the court said that since the doctor himself would be liable and his corporation would be liable, there was no reason to hold the other doctors in the group personally liable as well. So it does matter if your doctor is incorporated, particularly to your doctor.

Who has to pay for a wrongful life?

Who has to pay for a wrongful life? That was the question recently raised before a New York appellate court. The case involved a couple who had had a child with polycystic kidney disease, which is a fatal hereditary illness. There is a high probability that any other children born to the same couple will have the same affliction.

Right after their first baby died, the couple went to a doctor to find out what the risk was of its happening again. They were told that the chances of their having another baby born with the same disease were practically nonexistent. Relying on this advice, they had another child, which also had polycystic kidney disease and died at the age of two.

They brought suit against the doctor, seeking damages for themselves and on behalf of the dead infant. The court reviewed an earlier, similar case which refused to impose upon all obstetricians the duty of becoming forced genetic counselors. But in that case, the parents claimed that the doctors should have told them about the risk of having more defective children even though they didn't ask about it. In *this* case, noted the court, the couple asked the right questions, but got the wrong answers.

On the question of damages, the court said that a doctor who gave the wrong information would be responsible for the medical expenses of the birth and all expenses for the support of the child for as long as it lived.

The court went on to consider the question of whether there could be a lawsuit on behalf of the infant for wrongful life. While virtually every other court has said no to this question, the New York court said that the law must keep pace with expanding technological, economic, and social change; it found for the first time that there is a fundamental right of each child to be born as a whole, functional human being. One judge dissented, saying that a tort action for wrongful life should be created by the legislature, not by the courts. But the majority ruled, and the tort of wrongful life has been born.

Privacy—you, your doctor, and the state

If your doctor gives you a prescription for your migraine headache, does the state have the right to put your name and address into its computers? The U.S. Supreme Court recently decided a case which raised that question. The case was brought about by passage of the New York State Controlled Substances Act of 1972. That law provides that when a patient receives a prescription for certain drugs, the patient's name goes to the New York State Department of Health, where it's plugged into a computer. One hundred thousand patient names and addresses go into the computer every month. The drugs covered are used for pain and treatment of conditions such as epilepsy, narcolepsy, and migraine headaches.

Doctors and patients sued to have the law declared unconstitutional. The federal district court that first heard the case held that the state was unable to demonstrate the necessity for patient identification and that, in fact, in the twenty months that the law has been in effect, only two drug overuse investigations had occurred.

The district court also held that the doctor-patient relationship is one of the zones of privacy accorded constitutional protection and that the patient identification provisions of the act invaded this zone. But the Supreme Court reversed the lower court.

The patients had argued that they were afraid the information would become known and its misuse would affect their reputations. They also argued that some patients would be reluctant to seek the medical help they needed. But the Supreme Court said, simply, that the New York program does not pose a sufficiently grievous threat, and it added that doctors, hospitals, and insurance companies get all the information, anyway, even though those disclosures may affect reputations too. The court also said that just because only two investigations had resulted, it did not mean the law was not a significant deterrent to misuse of drugs. The court did state that it was "not unaware of the threat to privacy implicit in the accumulation of vast amounts of personal information in massive government files," but that was warning for the future. In the meantime, the computers will continue to be fed.

The tragedy of thalidomide

Thalidomide: perhaps the greatest drug tragedy of our time. How did it happen? What have been its results in human and legal terms? And could it happen again?

The scope of the tragedy is enormous. More than eight thousand children were born deformed, many of them without arms or legs, many more suffering from phocomelia, which means that the hands or feet start immediately from the main joint, like the flippers of a seal. Some of these babies were born just as limbless trunks.

The drug was developed as a sedative by a company named Chemie Gruenthal, a small drug company on the German–Belgian border, and was distributed in England by Distillers Company, Limited, which was better known for its manufacture of vodka and Pimms Cup. Thalidomide was billed as a wonder drug that had no toxic dose, no narcotic effect, no influence on breathing or circulation.

There were problems right from the beginning. Gruenthal

tried to interest major drug companies in the compound, but none of these could ever get the results Gruenthal got; one company reported that it couldn't put mice to sleep even with a dose fifty times that recommended by the company. And the drug was never tested on any pregnant animal. Yet, in the early fifties, free samples were sent to British and German physicians, and they gave them to their patients freely. In October 1957 the drug went on sale over the counter, advertised as astonishingly safe and effective. Sales soared, and it was sold to millions. At the same time, doctors were writing from all over that patients were vomiting from the drug and losing sensation in their toes and fingers.

And then it happened. Dr. William McBride, a leading Australian obstetrician, delivered a horribly malformed baby, born without arms or legs. One week later it happened again, and two weeks later, a third time. Dr. McBride discovered that the mothers had all taken Distaval, as thalidomide was known in Australia. He called Distillers. The reply was that it was impossible. It took Dr. McBride five months to get the company to even take a detailed statement from him. And before the nightmare was over, it was repeated more than eight thousand times.

A few months before Dr. McBride notified the Distillers Company about the deformed births, the company had sent a pamphlet to physicians saying that the drug could be given with complete safety to pregnant women and nursing mothers with no adverse effects on mother or child.

In August 1962 the parents of these children were left to the law, which, as the London *Sunday Times* put it, "was to prove a disastrous experience for two reasons." First, Britain's law of contempt prohibited newspapers from printing stories about any matter that was the subject of a legal case, either criminal or civil, and public exchange of information was virtually nonexistent. Second, solicitors and barristers throughout the country became convinced that there was simply no case, that everything that could have been done was done.

According to the *Times,* the lawyers simply never got the facts about the poor or nonexistent testing procedures or the denial by the company for months after the first alarm was given. In the end, it was the actions of Parliament and shareholders of Distillers itself that resulted in a trust fund of 20 million pounds being set up to take care of the special needs of these victims, many of whom are now teenagers.

The editorial comment by the *Times* said that the law, Parliament, and the press all failed in varying degrees, but the law most. "Death, injury, and loss from manufacture is a common-place of our society, but compensation for it is pure roulette, only with lower rewards."

The *Times* seems to be reminding us that we do not live in a risk-free society; that tragedies like thalidomide could happen again, even under the strictest rules and regulations; and that we perhaps might spend our energies devising more effective monitoring and response systems and better ways to take care of the victims.

It's common knowledge and a rough age

Medical malpractice has become a problem of major proportions. In California an orthopedic surgeon has to pay thirty-six thousand dollars per year—that's three thousand dollars a month —just for a single item, malpractice insurance. What has happened to cause the development of such deep-seated problems?

Contrary to popular opinion, the basic rules of proving a medical malpractice case haven't changed; in fact, they are quite similar to proving any other tort case—*tort,* by the way, is the term meaning "wrong" that we lawyers use for describing a case in which one person seeks money damages for a wrong allegedly done to him or her.

In order to recover damages, the plaintiff—or person suing— has to prove first that he or she was actually injured, and then that the defendant—in this case a physician or dentist—owed a duty of care, that there was a breach of this duty, and that what the doctor did actually caused the injury. While the basic rules haven't changed, it has become tougher to defend these cases because of the evolution of certain legal doctrines that have made proving cases of medical and dental malpractice much easier. Let me give an example.

A woman went to her dentist in a suburban Massachusetts community for a root canal. While he was working on her, he accidently dropped the reamer and she promptly swallowed it. Now it's important from a legal point of view to find out exactly what was said after the incident occurred, so I checked to find out what the dentist said. What he said was, "Whoops, I dropped something—I'll be right back." He left the room and dialed a surgeon friend and told him what happened. The surgeon advised him to send her home and tell her to eat roughage. It's not clear how he got her to go home and eat roughage, but in any event she went home and began eating lots of roughage for several hours. Then she decided to go to a hospital. An X-ray was taken, and the reamer had to be immediately surgically removed. Suit was brought against the dentist; did she win or did she lose? She lost because the plaintiff couldn't find a dentist or physician anywhere in the state to come in and say that what her dentist did was wrong.

She appealed, and the Supreme Judicial Court said that from now on, if a jury can by its own common knowledge decide that something is negligent, we'll let them do so. When the case went back for a new trial, it was settled for fifteen thousand dollars. But many lawyers are of the opinion that the damage was done, for we now have on our books a principle of common knowledge that has been applied in many complicated cases in which many feel expert testimony should have been required.

When your patient may be a killer

What can you do when your patient may be a killer? Not much, according to the U.S. District Court for New Jersey. The case involved a patient who was involuntarily committed to a state mental hospital. The hospital staff felt that the patient's condition was deteriorating and that he was becoming highly homicidal. So they administered drugs to him in an effort to keep him from getting sicker and to keep him from killing someone. The patient got a lawyer and brought suit against the hospital and its staff under Section 1983 of Title 42 of the U.S. Code, seeking damages and seeking to stop the hospital from forcibly administering drugs to him in the absence of a real emergency.

The court found that the patient indeed was suffering side effects from the antipsychotic medication and that these side effects included blurred vision, a dry mouth, and a drop in blood pressure. It also said he suffered from akathisia, which results in uncontrolled tremors and that his senses had been dulled.

The court said, "This court believes that any right to receive medication in the absence of an emergency is best founded on the emerging right of privacy. This right is broad enough to include the right to protect one's mental processes from governmental interference and has been used to establish an individual's autonomy over his own body." And the court held that the right of privacy clearly extended to mental patients in nonemergency situations. The court also said that giving medicine involuntarily lessens the chance that the patient will be treated successfully and added that only the patient can know the discomfort associated with medication. Since the whole area of psychiatric diagnosis and treatment is uncertain anyway, said the court, the final decision must be left to the patient.

The court also said that on occasion a patient's refusal to accept medication can be overridden, but only after a court has considered the patient's threat to staff and other patients, the patient's capacity to decide on a particular treatment, whether or not less restrictive treatment exists, and the risk of permanent side effects. The court said that just because a person is involuntarily committed, the state does not have the right to treat involuntarily. The court did say that in the case of a patient who is confined for endangering others, and yet refuses medication that would curb his dangerous tendencies, it might be possible to override the patient's decision to refuse medication, but only after a hearing.

In this particular case, the court said the hospital should try the patient first on lithium salts before going to Thorazine. So if your patient is homicidal, you can still do something—it just takes a little longer than it used to.

Hospitals, doctors, and child beating

Can hospitals and physicians be held liable for malpractice if they don't report child beating? The answer is a clear yes, according to a recent California case that appears to be the first of its kind. The plaintiff in the case was a six-year-old child who, through a guardian, sued a hospital and doctor she had gone to with her mother when she was less than a year old. The doctor at the hospital found she had bad fractures of the bones of the lower leg, which fractures, according to the records, gave the appearance of having been caused by a twisting force. The little girl also had bruises over her entire back and abrasions over the rest of her body. She also had a fracture of the skull which the doctor didn't find, but later X-rays discovered. The girl's mother could not give any explanation as to how the fractures had occurred.

Four months later, the child was brought to a different hospital where, this time, her battered-child syndrome was immediately diagnosed and reported to the police and juvenile probation authorities. This time the little girl wasn't returned home, but was placed with foster parents. Her mother and the mother's common-law husband, who were responsible for the beatings, fled the state, but were apprehended. They were returned for trial and convicted of the crime of child abuse.

Ordinarily, these tragic cases end at this point. But in this case, the foster parents brought a lawsuit on the child's behalf, claiming that the second beating, which caused the child to permanently lose the use of her left hand, would never have happened if the first doctor had reported the case to the authorities. The lower court threw the case out, saying that it was too speculative as to causation and damages. But the appeals court said that the standard of care to which a doctor is held includes a requirement that the doctor know how to diagnose and treat the battered syndrome. The court also said it was reasonably foreseeable that the child would be beaten again if the case were not reported. The California Supreme Court held that these matters were the subject of proper expert testimony and that the case should not have been dismissed.

The law has tried for a long time to encourage reporting of child beating, by granting immunity for the report to the doctors and hospitals involved. Now the carrot of immunity has been joined by the stick of a lawsuit for malpractice.

Determining the future of the fetus

Amniocentesis is a diagnostic procedure by which it can be foretold whether or not a developing fetus is suffering from certain sometimes fatal genetic diseases. It is a relatively new procedure, and sooner or later the question was bound to be raised in the courts as to what happens if a physician does not use this diagnostic procedure and therefore does not find out that the fetus has a fatal disease. The question is, can the doctor be sued for the failure to use an available scientific procedure which would lead a woman to seek an abortion?

Such a case has recently occurred. It involved a child who was afflicted with Tay-Sachs disease, which is a fatal genetic disease and which caused the death of the child shortly after birth. It is a disease that primarily strikes children born to parents of Eastern European background and is diagnosable in advance by amniocentesis, which involves testing the fluid within the amniotic sac.

The parents alleged that their obstetrician knew that they were of Eastern European background and that they were thus potential carriers of Tay-Sachs, and that the doctor should have seen to it that the tests were performed. They said that they suffered intense mental anguish due to the death of their child, which would have been prevented if the fetus had been aborted.

The court had a good deal of trouble with this case, stating that "in order to determine the parents' compensatory damages . . . a court would have to evaluate the denial to them of the intangible, unmeasurable, and complex human benefits of motherhood and fatherhood and weigh these against the alleged emotional injuries." And so the court denied recovery to the parents on the basis that the damages were too uncertain.

The court also noted that were the parents to prevail, an obstetrician functioning in our "ever-expanding and heterogeneous and pluralistic society" would have an absolute duty to conduct an exhaustive genealogical profile of both parents in order to counsel them as to the wisdom of an abortion. Some feel that this will some day indeed be a legal duty of a doctor—but for the moment it is not.

Have you ever heard of cancerophobia?

Have you ever heard of cancerophobia? Well, it means fear of cancer, and a New York woman not only found out what it meant, but collected fifteen thousand dollars because of it. The woman went to a physician for treatment of her bursitis and received a series of X-ray treatments by a group of doctors who specialized in X-ray therapy. She was administered seven treatments, and after the last one, her shoulder began to itch, turned pink, then red; then severe blistering and scarring occurred. The scars lasted for months, and one lasted for several years, leaving the woman with permanent disfiguring.

The woman kept returning to the doctors when the wounds refused to heal. They prescribed a salve, which the woman used regularly, but which brought very little improvement. Several years later she consulted an attorney, who advised her to go to a dermatologist to secure a definitive diagnosis.

It was at this point that what would have been an ordinary malpractice case took a very unusual turn. The dermatologist told her that she must have her shoulder checked every six months without fail because the area of the X-ray burn might well become cancerous. At the trial, the attorney for the woman said that he wished to make it clear that there was no claim that the woman would develop cancer at the site of the treatment, but that damages were sought because of the neurosis she developed— that is, the pathological fear of cancer.

This appears to be the first case in which damages were allowed against an original doctor for what was told to a patient by a second doctor. The court added, "Under our law, the risk of such advice and its effects . . . must be borne by the wrongdoers who started the chain of circumstances without which the cancero-phobia would not have developed." And so was decided the first case that awarded damages not only for the scars that had already occurred, but also for fear of the unknown.

The medical malpractice mess

Medical malpractice cases have become such a serious problem that doctors are coming up with some novel ideas on dealing with those lawsuits. One doctor called me recently and told me that he had made himself judgment-proof; I asked him how he had done that, and he said that he had very simply taken everything he owned and put it in his wife's name. I reminded him that divorce and domestic difficulty are now just about as prevalent as medical malpractice and that the chances of his losing everything were probably greater by putting things in his wife's name than by taking his chances on an action for malpractice.

A novel thrust was reported recently. It's the case of a doctor who sued both the patient who had sued him and the patient's lawyer for bringing the malpractice case to begin with—and the doctor won. One report stated that this was the most significant victory yet in the medical profession's counterattack on malpractice suits.

The facts were reported as follows, and it is important to note that these reports are based on a case that was won at the trial level only and that will probably be appealed to a higher court in Illinois. The patient had originally sued the doctor for two hundred and fifty thousand dollars because of the doctor's failure to diagnose a small fracture suffered in a tennis accident; the fracture was later diagnosed by another X-ray. When the suit was filed, the doctor immediately countersued the plaintiff for bringing the case without reasonable cause. The countersuit had the desired effect because the plaintiff decided to drop the malpractice suit. But the doctor persisted in his action. The jury deliberated only fifteen minutes and found for the doctor in the amount of two thousand dollars compensatory damages and six thousand dollars punitive damages. The president of the American Medical Association was quoted as saying, "The verdict should discourage the filing of frivolous nonmeritorious cases against doctors and put lawyers on notice that they are placing themselves in jeopardy if they do not adequately investigate a case before filing suit."

Before doctors rush out to sue their patients and their patients' lawyers, however, they should be aware of a recent Arizona case in which the same thing was tried, but the countersuit did not succeed. The problem is, as the Arizona Supreme Court noted, that these countersuits are based on a theory of malicious prosecution, or abuse of process, as it is sometimes called. To succeed, one must prove that the original suit was filed maliciously and with the intent to harass, and one of the most difficult things to prove is that a person acted with malice.

Many doctors and lawyers feel that suit and countersuit, like making oneself judgment-proof by giving away all one's assets, do not hold the answer to the medical malpractice crisis. Instead, more fundamental changes in the system by which reparation for medical injury is made are in order.

The captain of the ship

Is the captain of the ship going down with the vessel? That was the question put recently before the Texas Supreme Court. The case was one of medical malpractice that involved the captain of the ship doctrine. That doctrine says the surgeon in charge of an operation is responsible for anything that goes wrong in the operating room, regardless of who makes the mistake. The theory is that unless somebody is in charge, chaos could result.

The case involved a sponge that remained in the plaintiff's abdominal cavity after an operation. What had happened was that the nurse responsible for counting all the sponges after the operation counted wrong. The surgeon could not see the sponge because it was so small and relied on the fact that the nurse would count correctly.

The lower court found that while the hospital would be liable because the nurse worked for the hospital, the doctor was not responsible because the nurse wasn't his employee or his agent. The appeals court reversed the lower court judgment on the basis of the captain of the ship doctrine, which holds that the doctor remains responsible for what the rest of the crew may have done.

But the Texas Supreme Court reversed and reinstated the lower court's decision in favor of the doctor. The court noted that in navy talk, the captain of the ship is in full command and charged with the responsibility and care of his ship and the welfare of his hands, but he does not assume personal responsibility for acts of misconduct or for criminal deeds committed by the individuals aboard his ship. The high court held that the sponge nurse had been hired by the hospital, was the employee of the hospital, and had followed procedures established by the hospital. In fact, she did everything right except that she counted wrong, something the doctor probably could not have prevented no matter how much he might have wanted to.

There was a strong dissent, with that judge saying that a surgeon has to remain responsible for everything that goes on in the operating room; but the majority ruled, and the surgeon who used to be captain of the ship may become just another hand.

Isn't he a cute plaintiff?

Can a baby sue its mother's doctor because of what the doctor didn't say? The answer is yes, according to a New York court opinion that has taken the doctrine of informed consent yet another step.

The doctrine of informed consent is the legal requirement that obliges a physician to get the consent of his or her patients for any procedure, and it must be consent that is obtained after a discussion with the patient of all of the risks and benefits of the particular procedure. If the doctor fails to get the informed consent of the patient and an injury results to the patient, the doctor will be automatically liable without proof that he or she didn't act as skillfully as another doctor might have acted.

The New York case involved a woman who was pregnant and was being seen regularly by her obstetrician. But the obstetrician didn't discuss with the woman the precise manner in which she would give birth—presumably, whether or not the delivery would be a natural one or would be by Caesarean section. When the birth occurred, the infant was severely injured. Suit was brought by a representative of the baby against the physician, with the claim being made that the baby as well as the mother had the right to insist that informed consent be obtained.

The court pointed out that it used to be the law that suits by infants based on prenatal care or before-birth injuries were not allowed, on the ground that an unborn child is part of its mother and therefore has no distinct judicial existence. However, the court went on to point out that there has been a definite shift away from this principle, with most jurisdictions allowing suits by children or their representatives for injuries incurred before birth.

Recent changes in New York state law have also redefined what is meant by informed consent; all risks don't have to be explained by the doctor, only those that a reasonable doctor would explain under the same circumstances. But, in the court's opinion, the risks in this case should have been disclosed, and although this obligation runs from the doctor to the mother, the court held that the fetus comes within the area of persons to be protected.

So doctors who spend much of their time worrying about whether their patients understand the risks and benefits of a procedure now will have to think as well about those patients who haven't even yet been born.

Informed consent and full understanding

We just took a look at the dilemma of the doctor who must
secure informed consent from patients before proceeding. Unfortunately, the doctor is often unsure as to exactly what informed consent is, how to get it, how to prove he or she got it
two years later when a lawsuit occurs, and, most important, what
the impact of actually getting the informed consent will be on the
patient.

Informed consent is usually defined as consent given for a
medical or surgical procedure after a full understanding has been
reached of the risks and benefits involved. What must be the
ultimate informed-consent case of all time was reported to me a
few weeks ago. A man who lived in a Connecticut town was
referred by his family doctor to a specialist for a coronary by-pass
operation—an operation that can dramatically relieve the pain
and suffering associated with certain kinds of heart disease. The
specialist and patient, however, apparently didn't hit it off very
well, because early in their conversation the doctor decided that
this was the type of patient who would sue him either in person
or via his estate if the operation did not go as planned. So the
doctor decided to be super-cautious and proceeded to lay out in
great and lurid detail every conceivable risk of the coronary
by-pass procedure. As he did so, the patient became paler and
paler, until he decided abruptly that he didn't want this operation
after all. He left the doctor's office, went home, and died. You
guessed it—suit is now being brought against the doctor for
causing the patient's death by negligently securing his informed
consent.

To secure informed consent, many physicians have turned to
rather complicated forms. Many have told me that the major
problem they face, after the patient struggles through reading
the form, is that the patient almost invariably asks, "What do you
think I should do, Doctor?"

Some courts have suggested that only those risks that the average prudent physician would disclose need be disclosed to the
patient. A few lawyers who have studied the problem intensively
are beginning to ask whether another person should be added to
the process, who perhaps could be called a patient surrogate.
This person's duty would be, in a nonconfrontive, nonadversary
sense, to assist the doctor, whose time for detailed explanation
is necessarily short, and to assist the patient who, though he may
not be mentally impaired, may simply be scared to death.

"Another perfect job" (almost)

We've looked at malpractice problems faced by physicians and dentists who do not act in accordance with what other physicians and dentists would have done in comparable situations. However, the conscientious doctor may still be accused of having proceeded without the informed consent of the patient, in which case it doesn't matter how proficiently the procedure was performed. That's why informed consent has become such a serious problem for physicians.

The issue of informed consent can be very simple, as it was in a case that I learned about during a visit to Louisville, Kentucky. An elderly woman had broken her hip and was brought into the operating room to be operated on by a well-known surgeon. After the operation, which consists of inserting a pin into the hip, the surgeon gathered his residents—who had been observing the operation—around him, held up the X-ray plate, and said, "Look at that—another perfect job; not even a trace of a fracture line." Unfortunately, the reason that there wasn't a trace of a fracture line was that the surgeon had pinned the wrong hip. And, of course, since consent had been given to pin the right hip, and the left hip was actually pinned, liability automatically followed, regardless of how well the procedure had been performed.

By the way, this case was subsequently settled for thirty-two hundred dollars, a rather small amount, but the family thought very highly of the surgeon and the hospital. This proved how important patient rapport is in preventing malpractice actions or in lessening the amount of the settlement if an unfortunate accident does occur.

This case is representative of the classic consent case. The problems escalate, however, when one realizes that not only does consent have to be obtained, but that consent has to be *informed* consent. This means that consent for the procedure must be given after a full understanding of the risks and benefits has been reached by the patient. It is here that legal theory begins to diverge from the realities of the practice of medicine.

The problem is that for the physician to explain fully all the risks of even the most simple of surgical procedures may mean that the patient will be seriously frightened about what is to come. I know from personal experience that being told about the risk of death from a general anesthesia the night before a hernia operation does not make for a pleasant night's sleep. Some courts have resolved the dilemma by holding that the doctor need only disclose those risks that would be disclosed by another prudent physician under the same circumstances, but many courts have said that if the doctor leaves out a risk and that risk occurs, the doctor will be held liable.

The hip hype

The hip, the whole hip, and nothing but the hip. That was the issue in a recent Arizona case that dealt with the issue of just what the doctor means when he or she tells the patient about the operation that's going to be performed. The case reminds us that what the doctor says and what the patient hears may be very different indeed.

The case got started when a man complained to his regular doctor about a pain in his right hip. The doctor referred him to a surgeon. The patient told the surgeon that he had heard that Arthur Godfrey had had excellent success following a total hip replacement operation. The doctor replied that he was not an expert in the total hip procedure, and then described it in great detail to the patient, finishing with the words, "It's a terrific operation." The patient signed himself into the hospital and also signed a consent form that said he was going to have a "hip prosthesis inserted into his right side." The patient later said he had no idea what the words "hip prosthesis on the right side" meant, but thought the doctor was going to perform a total hip replacement operation on him. It turned out that what the doctor did was simply to insert a steel pin into the patient's femur. When complications developed after the operation, the patient sued the physician for not performing the right operation.

The court that first heard the case found for the doctor because of the fact that the consent form had the words "hip prosthesis on the right side," which was exactly the procedure the doctor had performed. The lower court also said that even if the patient thought he was consenting to a total hip replacement, a hip prosthesis insertion was a less serious operation and therefore was included in the scope of the consent.

But the Arizona Court of Appeals reversed the case and sent it back for a new trial. The high court said that the essence of informed consent in medical procedure is what the patient actually agreed with the doctor to have done, regardless of what was written on the informed-consent form.

So doctors who have had their problems without signed informed-consent forms are now having them with the form, depending on what they might have said before the form was signed.

An aborted abortion

What would you do if you became pregnant, decided after a lot of agony to have an abortion, went to the hospital for the abortion—and eight months later gave birth to a baby? Such was the plight of a San Francisco woman, and what she did was to file a lawsuit on her account and that of the child, asking a California court to become the first in the nation to grant damages for a wrongful life. (Another wrongful life case, with a different result, was discussed on page 202.)

The woman who brought the suit was unmarried, unemployed, and a part-time art student with a history of emotional problems. When she suspected she was pregnant, she became frightened at the prospect of having a child and went to an obstetrician/gynecologist seeking an abortion. After discussing her case with her, the doctor decided to grant her request to have an abortion, and she entered a hospital for the procedure.

After the operation, the woman moved to Los Angeles. When going for a checkup and birth-control pills, she was told by a Los Angeles doctor that she was still pregnant. She then called her family doctor, who called the doctor who had originally performed the abortion. These two doctors decided that the abortion had to have been successful and that the positive pregnancy test was probably due to her "bodily chemistry" not having returned to normal. A twenty-day supply of birth control pills was prescribed. By this time the woman had decided to move back to San Francisco, where she sought yet another doctor, who confirmed that she was in fact still pregnant and that it was now too late both medically and legally to have an abortion.

The appellate court held that a jury could find that the first doctor had been negligent in performing an abortion which left the fetus untouched, and that the second doctor also failed to treat her properly. As for the baby's action for a wrongful life, the plaintiff alleged that the baby would not have been born but for the negligent failure of the doctor to abort him and that, although a healthy baby boy, he would suffer all his life for being born out of wedlock. The court refused to recognize the concept of wrongful life, stating that it was unable to weigh the value of life against the nonexistence of life itself.

Born instead of aborted

The question of a fetus that was born instead of aborted was also raised before an Illinois appellate court. This case involved a woman who decided to have an abortion in the first trimester of her pregnancy. She went to a physician who agreed to perform the abortion. Illinois had recently passed a strong right-to-life law, but the abortion would have been legal under the Supreme Court case of *Roe* v. *Wade,* which held that during the first trimester a woman's right to privacy entitles her to an abortion if she and her physician deem it to be medically necessary.

The problem came when the doctor performed the abortion negligently; the result, instead of an abortion, was a healthy infant. The woman brought suit against the physician for negligence. She sought as damages medical and hospital expenses and also asked that the court award her the costs of rearing and educating the child. The doctor raised as his defense the fact that recent amendments to Illinois law made it clear that Illinois favors the right to life over abortion, and therefore his negligence should be forgiven, since it did result in life.

The court looked at other cases, paying particular attention to those in which a man or a woman was supposed to have been sterilized, but in fact wasn't, with the birth of a child resulting. In most of those cases, expenses for raising and educating the child have been denied, either because it's been held that the damages sought were out of proportion to the harm suffered or because public policy is held to preclude the birth of a child from being deemed a compensable injury.

Basing its decision on the right-to-life law passed in Illinois, the court said a public policy that "deems precious" potential life while yet in the womb cannot countenance as compensable damage costs and expenses necessary to nurture that life. The court added that the existence of a normal healthy life is an established right under state law rather than a compensable wrong. But the court did award damages to the woman in the amount of her hospital and medical costs, a Solomon-like decision if there ever was one.

A bad news mistake

What if you get a telegram from a hospital telling you your mother died, and it's really all a mistake? That's what happened to a woman in New York State whose mother was a patient in a state hospital. The daughter received a telegram which read, "Regret to inform you of death of Emma Johnson. Please notify relatives and make burial arrangements."

The grieving daughter notified the rest of the family and engaged an undertaker, who prepared the body for viewing just prior to the funeral. After hearing from relatives that the corpse in the funeral home didn't look like her mother, the daughter, in what the court called a state of extreme distress, took a close look herself and found that it was not her mother after all. It turned out that the woman who died was another Emma Johnson and that the hospital personnel had pulled the wrong record from the record room. Her mother was actually alive and well in another wing of the institution, unaware that her whole family, for a while at least, was mourning her untimely passing.

For weeks after the incident, the daughter was unable to return to work and kept having terrifying dreams of death and open coffins. Two psychiatrists testified that she suffered extreme anxiety because of the incident.

The daughter brought suit against the State of New York, seeking damages for the funeral expenses that she had laid out for the wrong Emma Johnson, and damages for emotional harm. The court of claims that first heard the action awarded her seventy-five hundred dollars for the funeral expenses and the emotional harm, but an appellate court reduced the award to sixteen hundred dollars, the amount of the funeral expenses. The rule is that psychological harm alone, unaccompanied by physical harm, is not compensable in a lawsuit. The reason that such harm is not usually the subject of damage awards was explained by Dean Prosser, who said, "The temporary emotion of fright that does not cause serious physical harm is so evanescent, so easily counterfeited, and usually so trivial, that the courts have been quite unwilling to grant damages."

But New York's highest court reinstated the claim for emotional harm, noting that exceptions to the general rule have involved cases where telegraph companies have sent the wrong message and in which corpses have been mishandled. So the court added another exception, reminding hospitals that when they notify the family, they had better make sure it's the right one.

Saved from syphilis by mistake

What happens when a hospital tells a wife she's got syphilis, and it turns out the hospital made a mistake? That was the question recently raised before the California Court of Appeals for the First District. What happened was that a woman had a blood test that allegedly showed she had syphilis. She was told she should tell her husband immediately. While she was telling him the news, she also accused him of having had extramarital relations, picking up syphilis, and transferring it to her. And that was the beginning of the end of the marriage.

Well, it turns out that the hospital made a mistake and the wife did not have syphilis after all. The husband, being extremely upset over the entire incident, went to court claiming that his marriage was ended because of the hospital's mistaken diagnosis. He claimed loss of consortium, which means loss of marital services; loss of consortium is a doctrine that's applied in accident cases where the spouse of the injured person sues for damages from the one who caused the accident.

The court began by noting this was the first case to its knowledge where loss of consortium was claimed without physical injury having been involved. The court reviewed the cases in the loss-of-consortium area, the most recent involving the suit by a wife whose husband was struck on the head by a falling pipe weighing six hundred pounds.

In the syphilis case, the husband claimed that not only did he lose his wife's marital services because of the hospital's action, but that the hospital's negligence caused him direct emotional suffering. However, the court said that what had happened in this was not foreseeable.

One judge dissented, saying the harm complained of certainly was foreseeable, and the average jury could have found what that could do to a marriage. But the majority ruled, and if your marriage ends because your wife was wrongly told she had syphilis, it looks as though you have no case as well as no marriage.

Cutting off your leg to save your life

If you've got gangrene, and you don't want your leg amputated, can the court make you have the operation anyway? The answer appears to be yes—or no, depending on the state you're in. The question has come up, involving elderly persons, in the states of New Jersey, Tennessee, and Massachusetts. So far, it's two to one for the patient's right to make the decision.

The Tennessee case involved a seventy-two-year-old woman who was a patient in the intensive-care unit with severe gangrene of both feet. According to the court, she was in possession of good memory, responded accurately to questions asked of her, was coherent and intelligent in her conversation, and was of sound mind. She felt strongly that her present physical condition would improve and that she would recover without surgery. The problem the court was faced with was that this was a woman who did not express a desire to die, but who, on the contrary, wanted to live while also keeping her gangrenous feet. The court found that while the woman may have been alert and may have had a good memory, she was mentally incapable of comprehending how much danger she was in; to that extent she was incompetent, justifying the action of the State of Tennessee to allow the amputation.

But a similar case was recently handed down by the Probate Division of the Morris County Court in New Jersey. That case involved a seventy-two-year-old man who was taken by a local rescue squad to the hospital emergency room at the request of neighbors. Despite severe gas gangrene of both legs from the knees down, he refused all treatment. The judge accepted the testimony of the psychiatrist to the effect that the man was not mentally ill, and in fact, the judge paid the man a visit. The man told the judge he was hoping for a miracle, even though he really didn't expect one. The judge refused to order the surgery against the man's will.

A court in Massachusetts recently handed down a similar ruling, right after which the woman in the case decided to allow the amputation after all. So what the court orders may depend on what state you're in, mentally, physically, and geographically.

Treatment refused in the middle of the night

What happens in the middle of the night when a person is brought to a hospital emergency ward and does not want to be treated? Most of these cases have involved Jehovah's Witnesses. Members of this faith believe it is wrong for them to receive blood transfusions. In cases where a pregnant woman has been involved, the courts have seen fit to take immediate action to provide the necessary treatment on the theory that the mother cannot be allowed to endanger her unborn child's life. The difficulty comes when a person who isn't pregnant refuses to accept blood or necessary treatment.

The problem is that a person is considered competent to make legal decisions such as whether or not to receive treatment unless he or she is deemed incompetent by a judge who has the power to make such a decision. This is why many hospitals have a judge on call. What usually happens is that the judge finds the patient incompetent and appoints the doctor temporary guardian for the limited purpose of providing the necessary medical treatment. In the event of a later lawsuit claiming deprivation of constitutional rights, the courts have usually found that since the person has recovered, the matter is closed.

In one case, a judge refused to find a person temporarily incompetent, but said that to refuse treatment would force the doctor to violate his Hippocratic oath. Since the judge had to choose between two moral stands, he chose the side of the physician, since the person was voluntarily in the hospital and could not demand that the doctors stop short of saving a life.

What really happens if the life-saving blood or treatment is or is not given? Well, if it *is,* the worst would be a lawsuit for assault with intent to save, or violation of a living person's constitutional rights to privacy. That lawsuit would be far easier to defend than a suit for wrongful death by the family of a seriously injured person who didn't want to accept blood, but still might have wanted very much to live.

"Do Not Resuscitate"

What would you think if you were thumbing through the hospital record of a close friend or relative who had died, and you came across the capital letters DNR—and when you asked what they stood for, you were told they meant Do Not Resuscitate? A recent article in the *New England Journal of Medicine,* widely reported in the lay press, dealt with the difficulties faced by families, nurses, doctors, and hospital administrators in dealing with the problem of the patient who should *not* be resuscitated.

Once again, medical and scientific progress has caused the dilemma. Properly performed, cardiopulmonary resuscitation can restore circulation and respiration in a person who is clinically dead. Ordinarily it is a procedure that should be and is used routinely by properly trained personnel in and out of hospitals when sudden death occurs. The problem comes with the agony of terminal illness and the fact that there are people who should be allowed to die in peace and not have heroic measures taken when the heart finally stops. How not to handle this situation was typified by the actions of an English hospital a few years ago that issued a regulation stating that before patients over sixty-five were resuscitated, the hospital administration had to be called. The British press took off on the regulation, and there were cartoons like the one showing elderly patients trying to escape from hospitals by tying bedsheets together, and another showing a patient with a hand-lettered sign on his chest that read, "Patient asleep—not dead."

The Beth Israel Hospital's suggestion is that if the patient doesn't make the decision, an ad hoc committee should be set up consisting of the patient's physicians and nurses, others involved in the care of the patient, and at least one other staff doctor not directly involved in the patient's care. In the case of an incompetent patient, approval of an order not to resuscitate has to be given by at least the same family members who would have the right to consent to an autopsy.

The Standards of the American Heart Association state that in cases of terminal irreversible illness where death is not unexpected, resuscitation may represent a positive violation of an individual's right to die with dignity. The power to control the moment of death carries with it awesome responsibilities.

When is a dead man really dead?

When is a dead man really dead? That was the question recently raised before the Supreme Judicial Court of Massachusetts in one of the first cases in the country in which a court changed the definition of death. The case involved a man who was convicted of murder in the first degree and who appealed his conviction on the grounds that he didn't kill the victim when he hit him over the head with a baseball bat, but that the doctors killed him when they turned off his respirator.

The victim was a thirty-four-year-old man who came out of a store in Boston's Dorchester section and was struck over the head with a bat by an eighteen-year-old youth. (When asked later why he struck the man, the youth answered, "For kicks.") The victim was taken to a hospital, and a part of his skull was removed to relieve pressure on his brain. He was placed on an artificial respirator. After four days, he was declared dead and the respirator was turned off. The problem was that the traditional legal definition of death is the cessation of heartbeat, or circulation, something that can now be kept going practically indefinitely.

At the trial the defendant claimed that the jury should be instructed in accordance with the traditional definition of death and not with a new definition based on brain death. The judge gave the new instruction, however. The defendant appealed on the basis that the judge had wrongly instructed the jury and that only the legislature—not a court—should be able to change the definition of death. He also urged that even if a judge could change the definition, the change was retroactive, and therefore he couldn't be convicted.

The Supreme Judicial Court found that prior cases said only that the basic legal requirement is that to constitute murder, the victim must die within a year and a day from the time he or she is wounded. The precise question of just when the victim is actually dead had never been before the courts. The court held that the trial judge instructed the jury properly, ruling that he had made an evolutionary restatement of an old rule rather than a substantively new one. The conviction was upheld, and death came by way of being hit with a baseball bat—not by pulling the plug.

Selling bad blood

The sudden death of a hospital trustee in his own hospital in California sends chills down the spine of anyone who spends a lot of time in hospitals—the trustee died because he was given the wrong blood. That death and many others like it raise the question of just what the liability of hospitals and the rights of patients are if the wrong blood or diseased blood is given to a patient.

The most common error is represented by the mistake that is reported to have occurred in a large teaching hospital, where a patient was sent to surgery with somebody else's nameplate. During the operation, the anesthesiologist had occasion to request blood for the patient, and he stamped the blood-request form with the patient nameplate, which he had not checked. Unfortunately, the patient whose nameplate was used had also been cross-matched and blood-typed and had blood waiting in the blood bank. The blood arrived and was given to the patient, who died a short time later of a hemolytic transfusion reaction.

And in another recent case, a nurse and an intern arrived in the
patient's room and told the patient that the blood donated by her
daughter was ready for her. In spite of protests that she had no
daughter, the woman was given the blood and died a short time
later.

There is little question but that the actions which have produced these tragic deaths were negligent, and in most cases proof
could be obtained that the parties involved acted below the
proper standard of care. But in many cases, such as blood carrying hepatitis, proving that someone was negligent is not easy.

Recently, lawyers for the families of the victims have sought to
bring a new legal theory to bear—it's called a warranty of fitness
or merchantability. If that sounds to you like a theory that is more
at home in a department store than in a hospital, you're right,
because the theory is taken directly from the sale of goods rather
than the providing of a service. What it would mean if applied to
blood is that the hospital and the personnel involved would be
liable without proving anybody did anything wrong; all that
would be necessary would be to show that the blood was not fit
for the person who received it. Up to now most courts have
rejected the application of this theory to blood and have held that
providing blood is still a service to the critically ill rather than the
sale of a product.

Publicity by accident

If you were in an accident, would you want everyone to know
about it? Hospital lawyers and public relations people are beginning to take another look at the Code of Cooperation of the
American Hospital Association. That code allows certain facts to
be given out about the patient without his or her consent or the
consent of a family member. For example, the code says that it
is all right in "police cases" for a hospital official to give out
certain items of "public information," a phrase that the code uses
to define private information that is about to become public via
radio, television, or newspaper.

If you are in an accident and taken to the hospital by the police,
the code says the press is entitled to know your name, your
marital status, your age, your address, and your employer. It is
also permissible for the hospital to explain how you got into the
accident, how many fractures you have, and whether or not you
have head injuries, although the code does say that the hospital

should not specify exactly what kind of head injuries they are. Under the code, the hospital official is advised not to say you've been shot or stabbed, but the official can say that the wound was a penetrating one and give the exact location of the penetration. If you've been burned, the hospital can say where you're burned, but is advised only to make a statement about how the burns occurred when the "absolute facts" are known. The code implies that information about other, nonburn injuries can be released even when the hospital isn't certain about the facts.

Those are the rules about patients, but as far as your doctor is concerned, the hospital can only release *his* name to the public with the doctor's consent. The theory behind all this is that when a person in an accident is taken to the hospital by the police, the public gains the right to know a great deal about it.

In the face of federal and state law granting a right to privacy, the whole issue of patient information is being rethought. Many are beginning to think about the legal and ethical problems involved when releasing this information. It's quite possible that hospital officials will soon make it the rule rather than the exception to get the permission of the patient or next of kin before describing his or her injuries to the press.

It's crazy to fly

A few years back I had a client who was a psychiatrist. He had in therapy a commercial airline pilot who had suicidal thoughts from time to time. He continued to treat the pilot without turning him in to the Federal Aviation Administration. This case, while perhaps especially disturbing to those who spend a lot of time flying, raises the question of the confidential nature of the relationship between physician and patient and when it should be breached.

The psychiatrist defended his actions by stating that if he were to turn the pilot in, it would probably mean the end of the pilot's flying career, and you could be sure that the next pilot who felt himself sliding toward mental illness would not seek help because of the consequences. Of course, the psychiatrist did try to reassure me that if he felt that the pilot really *was* going to kill himself, he would take action. (He added that it's crazy to fly anyway.)

The principle is that confidentiality between physicians and their patients should be maintained to encourage people to seek help, knowing that what they reveal about themselves will remain confidential. The only time information should be given out is when the physician believes that imminent danger to society or to the patient himself will occur if disclosure does not take place.

The problem is that psychiatrists are often notoriously poor predictors of human behavior, as witnessed by the student who told his psychiatrist that he was thinking about shooting people. Since the hour was up, the psychiatrist scheduled analysis of this interesting statement for the next visit. A few days later more than forty people were shot from the University of Texas tower in Austin.

Despite the occasional tragedy, the general welfare is clearly better served by confidentiality being maintained than by its breach. One last point. What we've been talking about is the voluntary disclosure of information by the psychiatrist. Unless your state has a statute allowing a psychiatrist to remain silent, he or she would have to give evidence about you if summoned into court. One California psychiatrist recently went to jail for contempt for refusing to cooperate and give information about his patient. But unless you know your psychiatrist quite well, I would not bet on this being the usual result.

Quick to commit and slow to let go

I have been worried about medical malpractice suits for several years now, but things have lately become much more serious. Even the psychiatrists are getting sued, which is unusual because psychiatrists are usually thought to be expert in handling the hostility of their patients.

I read recently of the psychiatrist who was treating a man who was quite ill and had been in a mental hospital for several months. The doctor decided that the time had come to ease the patient back into the community, so he let the patient leave the hospital for a visit to his wife's lawyer's office to discuss their domestic relations problems. During the discussion, things got a little bit heated and, without any warning, the patient jumped across the wife's lawyer's desk and bit the wife's lawyer's nose off. This resulted in a serious medicolegal problem. Suit was brought by the lawyer—not against the patient, who was obviously mentally ill, but against the psychiatrist for negligently allowing a known nose-biter to roam the community. The result was a two-hundred-thousand-dollar settlement paid to the lawyer by the doctor's insurance company.

One might draw from this case the moral that the psychiatrist should be quick to commit and slow to let go. But the other side of the coin is equally treacherous, as illustrated by the case of the lawyer who was committed against his will. Upon being released, he sued the police officer who responded, the family physician, the receiving hospital, the doctor who admitted him, the superintendent of that institution, the mayor of the city, the commissioner of mental health, and the newspaper that reported the whole story.

The doctor faces a serious dilemma. If the patient is committed and it is later held to be improper, the doctor can be sued for false imprisonment; if the doctor doesn't commit and someone, including the patient himself, is either killed or injured, the doctor can be sued for carelessly allowing a dangerous person to remain in the community. Cases indicate the only way out of this dilemma is for the doctor to use common sense and the best clinical judgment and take action to commit if he or she genuinely believes there is imminent and serious danger to the person or to others if commitment does not take place.

Knowing where the bodies are

What happens when a client tells his lawyer that he killed two people, and then tells the lawyer where to find the bodies? That was the subject matter of a recent opinion of the New York State Bar Association Committee on Professional Ethics. The case was a bizarre test of the canons of ethics that guide the professional conduct of lawyers. One of those canons requires that lawyers keep confidential information they get from their clients.

The New York case involved a lawyer who was representing a man charged with murder. As the lawyer was preparing his case, his client told him that he had killed two other persons, in homicides completely unrelated to the one the lawyer was working on. At first the lawyer didn't believe it; then his client told him where the bodies were. The lawyer went to the location, and sure enough, there were the bodies of two young people whose families and friends had been combing virtually all of upper New York State looking for them.

The lawyer photographed the bodies, diagrammed their positions, and made a record of his conversation with his client. And while he didn't do anything to conceal the bodies, he also didn't tell the authorities about them. In fact, not only didn't he tell the

authorities, but also he didn't tell anybody, and a short time later
he destroyed the photographs, the diagram, and the note of his
conversations. Later, however, during plea bargaining in the
original case, the lawyer suggested that he was in a position to
provide information about two unsolved murders still under investigation in return for more lenient treatment of his client in
the original case.

The bar association committee had to decide whether what the
lawyer did was ethically proper. The committee decided it was
not improper for the lawyer not to tell the police about the
bodies. In fact, said the committee, if he had informed the authorities, he would have violated the canons of ethics. The association said that the confidentiality must be complete, with the only
exception being a case in which the lawyer finds out his client is
going to commit a future crime or fraud. Since it was proper not
to tell the authorities, it was also proper to destroy the photographs and other material related to the disclosure.

On the plea-bargaining point, the committee said that it was
proper to use the knowledge of the murders in that situation,
since the client had given permission for disclosure. So, according to the New York State Bar Association at least, a lawyer must
keep his client's past secrets, no matter what they are.

When the lawyer knows too much

We just looked at the case of the lawyer who found the bodies
of two people killed by his client, but did not tell the police.
Another case, recently decided by the Alaska Supreme Court,
involved a similar question: When the lawyer comes across evidence that proves his client is guilty, what does he do next? The
case involved a man accused of kidnapping an eighteen-year-old
university coed for a period of eight days. One of the key pieces
of evidence that convicted him was a document he had written
that laid out the entire plan for the kidnapping. Whether that
document should have ever gotten into evidence was the question before the Alaskan high court.

At the time the defendant was arrested, he told a man to clean
out his car. During the cleaning, the man found the document
that was to lead to the conviction. When he found it, he realized
its significance and immediately brought it to the lawyer who was
defending the accused.

The lawyer realized he had a serious problem on his hands. If he said nothing about it out of allegiance to his client and his duty to maintain a confidence, he would run the risk of involving himself in keeping a highly relevant piece of evidence from the court. If he turned the document over to the police or the prosecution, he would run the risk of a suit by his client for breaching the lawyer-client privilege. Either way, he would run the risk of his conduct being deemed unethical by the Alaskan Bar Association or the Alaska Supreme Court, which regulated the conduct of attorneys.

So the lawyer decided to play it safe and in advance of doing anything asked the Alaska Bar Association for an advisory opinion on the question. The ethics committee of the association advised him to return the document to the man who had found it and at the same time explain to him the laws about concealment of evidence. The lawyer did as he was told. The man then gave the document to the police, and the lawyer withdrew from the case because it became clear that he would have to testify as to his part in the handling of the document.

The court said that there was no question but that a lawyer who comes across evidence has the duty to turn it over to the authorities. Otherwise, he is actively concealing evidence, which could result in his being charged and convicted of a crime. Also, said the court, every lawyer is an officer of the court, meaning that he or she has an ethical obligation to be certain that a court is not misled about a case. As for the lawyer testifying about the incident, the court said this would be a very difficult question if the evidence had been given to a lawyer by his client, but since a third person was involved, no lawyer-client privilege covered the information.

So it looks as though the only way your lawyer can remain silent about evidence he discovers is not to discover it in the first place.

Picketing your lawyer

Can the law stop you from picketing your lawyer? That was the question recently decided by the Pennsylvania Supreme Court. What happened was that an indigent woman went to a Pennsylvania lawyer for help in dealing with a workmen's compensation claim. The lawyer settled the claim for her, and when it came time to distribute the proceeds, he deducted one hundred fifty dollars from the total amount and paid it to the psychiatrist who had testified in the woman's behalf at the hearing. Although the law-

yer had a bill from the psychiatrist and a cancelled check, the
woman became convinced the lawyer had never paid the money
to the psychiatrist but had kept it.

So she took to the streets in front of the lawyer's office wearing
a sandwich-board sign. The sign bore the name of the law firm
and a statement that "they stole money from me and sold me out
to the insurance company." Several hours every day, rain or
shine, the woman would walk back and forth bearing her sign and
pushing a shopping cart on which she had placed the American
flag. In addition, as she walked, she continuously rang a cowbell
and blew a whistle to further attract attention. As you can imagine, such a testimonial from a former client was not overly helpful
to business, and the law firm went to court to get an injunction
to stop the woman from picketing.

A lower court granted the injunction, concluding that the
woman's belief that she had been defrauded was a "fixed idea
which, either by reason of eccentricity or an even more serious
mental disability, refuses to be dislodged, even by the most convincing proof to the contrary." Undaunted, the woman appealed
her case to the Pennsylvania Supreme Court, which reversed the
lower court, stating that the order enjoining the former client's
demonstration was prohibited by the Pennsylvania and the U.S.
constitutions.

The court said that such an injunction would be a prior restraint on the exercise of an individual's right freely to communicate thoughts and opinions. The court added that the lawyer did
have a right to sue the woman for libel or defamation, even
though the court specifically recognized that such a lawsuit would
be futile because the woman was penniless. The exercise of the
constitutional right freely to express one's opinion, said the

court, cannot be conditioned upon the economic status of the individual asserting that right.

And so the woman will be able to go back on the streets with her sandwich board, her pushcart, her bell, and her whistle.

Is a law student good enough?

If you're in trouble and the best you can get to defend you is a law student, is that good enough? That was the question recently raised before the California Court of Appeals for the Fourth District. Throughout the country, law schools have instituted clinical programs designed to better train law students for the courtroom and at the same time relieve the shortage of attorneys available to people who cannot afford a lawyer of their choice.

The California case involved a man who was arrested and convicted of second-degree burglary. You might say he was caught holding the bag, since the evidence against him was that he was in possession of two large bags containing brand-new merchandise "with the price tags yet affixed thereon." Patrolling officers in the vicinity of Derazo's Men's Store in Colexico, California, heard breaking glass and saw the defendant carrying the bags away from the shattered front glass door. The defendant claimed he'd found the bags on the sidewalk outside the store; he did have some problems, however, explaining how he had cut himself and why he had glass all over his hands and arms.

His defense was handled by a law student who was introduced to the court by a lawyer who was supposedly supervising him while he tried the case. The lawyer was in court the whole time, but didn't say a word as the law student went about defending the man to the best of his ability. The defendant was convicted, and he appealed his case to the California Court of Appeals on the grounds that his constitutional right to counsel was violated by the fact that his lawyer was only a student.

The California court looked to the Sixth Amendment to the Constitution, which provides that an accused person must have the assistance of counsel. The court said there simply was not enough evidence that the defendant intelligently consented or even knew he was going to be represented by a law student, and therefore he did not waive his Sixth Amendment rights. The court found the mere presence of the supervising lawyer just wasn't good enough.

So the defendant's conviction was reversed, and he'll be getting a new trial. As for law students, they may just have to wait to become lawyers to learn how to try a case on their own.

When your client swears to tell

If a client answers a question with a commonly used four-letter word, can his lawyer be held responsible? That was the question before the Eighth Circuit Court of Appeals in the case of *Schleper* v. *Ford Motor Company.* The case grew out of an arbitration proceeding in which a Ford employee contended he had gotten a raw deal from both his employer and the union. One of his claims was that he was continually harassed by obscene and abusive language, which was shouted at him by representatives of his employer and the union. He went to court claiming he didn't get a fair arbitration hearing because the people shouting the obscenities weren't called to the witness stand.

As the case was being prepared for trial, a set of interrogatories was sent to the employee for him to answer. Interrogatories are written questions submitted before trial by one party to the other so people can find out what the case is all about. One of the questions asked of the employee was to name witnesses who should have been called at the hearing and to say what they would have testified if they had been called. The employee's answer was "____ you." And the lawyer filed the papers carrying that simple, straightforward answer in court.

After the answer was filed, everybody got a little upset, since the system of justice is not used to such cryptic replies, at least in interrogatories. The attorney representing Ford took the answer as a personal insult and asked that the court dismiss the case because of it. The lawyer who filed the answer then filed an amended answer that read, "Persons would have testified that the foreman said, '____ you'." But that didn't seem to help much, and while the judge refused to throw the case out of court, he did hold the lawyer in contempt and fined him for filing the answer.

The lawyer appealed the contempt citation to the Eighth Circuit Court of Appeals. In the calm light of reflection that an appellate court sometimes brings to issues that get a little heated below, that court said, "When scandalous, abusive, or improper language is included in court pleadings, the common practice is simply to strike the objectionable language with leave to amend." The court said the unexplained and unqualified use of obscene language in the interrogatory could not be condoned, but contempt was too drastic a remedy.

So the interrogatory will go in as amended, the contempt will be removed, and next time at least one lawyer will see to it that his answers are in complete sentences.

It's the story of my life

Can you pay your lawyer with your life story? That was the question recently decided by the California Court of Appeals for the Second District. The case involved a man charged with ten separate counts of murder. He had no money and needed a lawyer to defend him, so he and his lawyer worked out an interesting agreement. In return for his full legal defense, the man transferred to his lawyer the full and unconditional literary rights in the story of his life and in the pending criminal prosecution and trial. The defendant would retain an interest of 15 percent of the profits; the lawyer would get everything else.

The deal was in writing, and the man was in fact informed that he had the option to have a court-appointed attorney represent him free of charge. The agreement also explained in detail that the arrangement gave the lawyer a possible conflict of interest, since he now had a monetary interest in the case; but the agreement went on to say the lawyer would not be influenced by that interest and would raise every available defense to the charges.

The man signed the agreement and the case proceeded. Because he was indigent, his lawyer went to court and asked for a court-appointed investigator to gather the facts. In the course of that hearing, the subject of how the lawyer was being paid came up, and when the court heard of the agreement, it ordered a special hearing to see if that arrangement should be permitted. The man testified that he understood the entire arrangement and that he realized there could be a conflict of interest. Nevertheless, he claimed he wanted to be represented by this lawyer and wanted to pay him by giving him the rights to his life story. In fact, he claimed he had a constitutional right to have a lawyer of his choice and claimed that he could pay him any way he wanted.

But the California Court of Appeals did not agree and ordered the lawyer removed from the case. The court said the incentive to maximize royalties could lead to mishandling of the case and that it simply could not be allowed. The court said that representation in a court of law is not something that just goes on between the parties; the integrity of the court itself is involved, and this arrangement was an affront to that integrity.

One judge dissented, saying a person ought to be able to have the lawyer of his choice when he goes on trial for murder. But the majority ruled, and you can have the lawyer of your choice represent you, but you'll have to sell your life story to someone else.

Punishing a prisoner because of his lawyer

Can you punish a prisoner because you don't like his lawyer? That was the question recently decided by the Fifth Circuit Court of Appeals. The case involved a lawsuit by twelve Texas prisoners and their attorney, a woman by the name of Frances Cruz. Mrs. Cruz had brought all kinds of lawsuits on behalf of Texas prisoners, seeking to overturn convictions, charging violations of civil rights, and challenging the constitutionality of various prison practices and conditions.

As you can imagine, Mrs. Cruz wasn't very popular with the prison officials, and there wasn't much they could do about it— to Mrs. Cruz. But as far as her clients were concerned, that was a different story. The word went out that prisoners were forbidden to use Mrs. Cruz as their lawyer, and men who wanted to remain clients of Mrs. Cruz were ordered moved to a separate unit of the prison. While segregated, they were treated very differently from the other prisoners, facing poorer living conditions and being prevented from participating in various prison programs. Release from the special punishment unit was conditioned on a prisoner's firing Mrs. Cruz as his attorney.

The court concluded there was no question but that the civil rights of the prisoners and the attorney had been violated. The court refused to accept the defense's argument that all these actions were justified because the attorney's activities were "inflaming unsettled prison conditions." The court specifically found that neither Mrs. Cruz nor her clients did anything to provoke the actions taken against them.

The Court of Appeals next had to decide whether or not the prison official responsible could be held personally liable in damages. The court said there can be personal liability if the public official involved has abused his authority and acted in bad faith. The court upheld the findings that the actions of the official were prompted by his long-standing antagonism toward Mrs. Cruz and that he did act unjustifiably and in bad faith.

So the case was sent back for damages, and if you don't like a prisoner's lawyer, you can't take it out on the prisoner.

A public defender on the defensive

How public is a public defender? That was the question recently decided by the Pennsylvania Supreme Court. The case raised the question of whether the client of a public defender can sue the public defender for malpractice or whether the public defender should be considered a public official and get the immunity given to other public officials.

The case involved a client who was involuntarily confined for seven days in a state psychiatric hospital. After the man was released, he sued the county public defender, claiming the attorney had been negligent, and that's why the man ended up a committed mental patient. The court that first heard the case dismissed it on the grounds that a public defender is entitled to immunity.

But the Pennsylvania Supreme Court reversed the lower court and held that public defenders can be sued and should not be able to defend the suit on the basis of being public officials. The court said it's true that public defenders occupy positions that are publicly funded and authorized by statute, but they are much more like private attorneys than public officials. In fact, said the court, they often oppose the state or the county on behalf of their clients.

The court said that once the appointment of a public defender is made, his or her public function ceases. Public defenders, said the court, are like physicians rendering professional services that are paid for out of public funds; like those physicians, they ought to be subject to liability for wrongful conduct.

One judge dissented, saying that defenders ought to be given immunity for the simple reason that they had to take all comers and were not free to decide whom they would or would not represent. But the majority ruled, and when it comes to being sued, a public defender isn't so public after all.

When your lawyer isn't a lawyer

What happens when you find out your lawyer wasn't really a lawyer after all? That was the question recently decided by the New York Court of Appeals. The cases were brought by a group of convicted criminals who had been represented by one Albert Silver, who, although everybody thought he was a lawyer, never had been admitted to the bar in New York or any other state. The court agreed that everybody thought Silver was a lawyer, and in fact, he had maintained a law office in Nassau County for more than twelve years. At one time he had even been appointed city attorney. But in 1976 that chapter of Albert Silver's life came to a close, and he pleaded guilty to attempted unlicensed practice of law.

Then came the question of what was to happen to all of the people Albert Silver had represented, particularly those who had been found guilty of crimes during that representation. This case involved four convicted criminals, two of whom had pleaded guilty on Silver's advice, and two of whom went to trial and were convicted after trial. In two of the cases Silver had been assigned as counsel by the court, and he so impressed the two other criminals that they retained him while he was acting as counsel for the first two. All four were now appealing their convictions, claiming their right to counsel guaranteed by the Sixth Amendment had been violated, since their counsel wasn't a lawyer.

The lower courts rejected their claim, holding it was harmless error, because even though Silver wasn't a lawyer, the men had had excellent representation. The lower court found that Silver had represented each defendant diligently, competently, and conscientiously and that there was no reasonable possibility that his not being a lawyer in any way contributed to their convictions.

But the Court of Appeals reversed, finding the error was not harmless after all. The court said that the word *counsel* as used in the Sixth Amendment can mean nothing less than a licensed attorney at law and that a lay person, regardless of educational qualifications or experience, is not a constitutionally acceptable substitute for a member of the bar. The assistance of counsel, said the court, is among those constitutional rights so basic to a fair trial that the infraction can never be treated as harmless error.

So at least four convicted criminals will get a new trial, this time with a real lawyer rather than a great imposter.

Can you sue your astrologer?

Can you sue your astrologer if what he says is going to happen doesn't? That was the question recently decided by the Hawaii

Supreme Court. The case involved a woman who liked to visit astrologers and others who made their living by predicting the future. She saw this particular astrologer for about a year, during which time he offered some startling revelations about her future. She was told that in order to prevent her daughters from becoming pregnant out of wedlock it would be necessary for her to purchase pendants for them at a cost of eighteen hundred dollars. She was also told she wouldn't have to worry about money any more because she would be receiving a fifty-thousand dollar check in the mail and her income would be tripling in just a few weeks. Last, she was told that she would become the owner of three apartment buildings and a four-bedroom condominium.

Well, none of the predictions panned out. The woman went to court claiming that she'd been defrauded and asking that she be repaid the ten thousand dollars she'd paid to the future forecaster. The Hawaii Supreme Court had to decide whether predictors of the future can be sued for fraud when their predictions do not come true. The court began its opinion by defining fraud, which it said is based on misrepresentations of facts, which misrepresentations were actually known to be false.

The court said that these misrepresentations related to the happening of future events and therefore could not be known to be false. The court also said that fraud cannot be predicated on statements that are mere promises or erroneous conjectures as to future events, even though somebody relied on them. The court said, "We hold that representations made by the astrologer constituted mere prognostication or prophecy as to the happening of future events." And it was utterly unreasonable for the woman to have relied on such representations.

So the case was dismissed, and when you look to the stars for the future, you can't turn to the courts when that future doesn't come true.

Rent-a-car; get-a-ticket

When Hertz puts you in the driver's seat, who pays for the parking ticket after you're gone? That was the question recently decided by the Illinois Supreme Court in a case that made car rental companies very unhappy. The case involved the interpretation of an ordinance of the city of Chicago which said that when a vehicle is parked in violation of any law prohibiting or restricting parking, the person in whose name such vehicle is registered shall be prima facie responsible for the violation. The city decided to move against the car rental companies, which had run up nearly $2 million worth of tickets. For starters, it brought suit against Hertz, Avis, and Chrysler Leasing.

The court began its opinion by saying that "The law has to be read the same for those who lease vehicles as for those who lend their vehicles to family members or friends." The car rental companies claimed that if they proved someone else was driving the car at the time of the violation, that person should be responsible for the fine rather than the registered owner. But the Illinois Supreme Court disagreed. The court said after reviewing similar ordinances in Missouri, Ohio, and Iowa that the words "prima facie" meant that there were only two ways to escape the consequences of the law. Either you proved that you were in fact not the registered owner of the car or you proved that the violation did not in fact occur. Since the companies couldn't prove either of these claims, they lost.

The companies also claimed that to make them pay the fines when they didn't actually commit the crimes was to impose vicarious liability, and that was unconstitutional. But the court responded that vicarious liability has been around for a long time, particularly in criminal cases involving automobiles. The court cited a Kansas case in which an innocent party loaned his car to somebody who used it to bootleg illegal liquor; the car was forfeited to the authorities even though the owner didn't know what the car was going to be used for.

New York courts have recently upheld similar city ordinances, but New York authorities will at least send a bill to the driver if the name and address is supplied by the owner. However, if the driver doesn't pay the fine, the owner has to pay. So whether you're number one or just trying harder, or any of the thousands of other car rental companies, those tickets will just have to be paid.

7-Up is down

If your name is on it, you may be left holding the bag. That's the result of a recent case handed down by the Sixth Circuit Court of Appeals in a case that should make us all a little more careful when we go to the supermarket. The case involved a woman who reached up on the shelf for a carton of 7-Up. As she took it off the shelf and was about to put it under her arm, one of the bottles slipped out of the carton and fell to the floor. It immediately exploded, and she was blinded permanently in one eye.

The carton was described by the court as a so-called over-the-crown or neckthru carton which is designed to be held from the top and which is made without any strips on the sides to prevent a bottle from slipping out. The woman brought suit against 7-Up, which in this case was the franchisor—the entity responsible for distribution of the product. The franchisor claimed it didn't have anything to do with the design or manufacture of the carton, but just licensed those who were distributing it, and that it should not be held responsible for this tragedy.

The court said the question was whether the principle of strict liability extends to a franchisor who retains the right of control over a product but does not actually manufacture or sell it. The court concluded that the franchisor did have responsibility, because without the franchisor there would be no franchisees, and without franchisees, that carton of 7-Up would never have made it to the supermarket.

The court said that the franchisor not only "floated its franchise and the bottles of its carbonated soft drink into the stream of commerce," but also assumed and exercised a degree of control over the type, size, and design of the carton in which the product was marketed. In fact, said the court, the franchisor was shown the carton and should have known about the design and its defects; and the court added that when a franchisor consents to the distribution of a defective product bearing its name, it may be obliged to compensate an injured consumer. So whether you handle cola or un-cola, it has to be heads up all the way.

Strict liability is strict indeed

Strict liability can be strict indeed. That's the message of a recent case decided by the Texas Supreme Court. The case involved a lawsuit against General Motors and a GM dealer and involved the doctrine of strict liability. That doctrine means that a company can be held strictly liable for an inherently dangerous product, or instrumentality. Being strictly liable means that the plaintiff doesn't have to prove that anything was done carelessly in the manufacture of the product. All the plaintiff has to show is that the product was inherently dangerous and that he or she was injured while using it.

This particular case involved a man who had to swerve to avoid a collision with a truck. As a result of the sudden maneuver, his car rolled over. The roof caved in at the driver's corner when the car struck the ground. The driver had his seat belt on and didn't suffer the usual fate of being thrown out of the vehicle. Instead, he was struck on the head by the roof of the vehicle, which crushed his vertebra, paralyzing him. He brought suit against GM and the dealer on the basis of strict liability and invoked another doctrine: that of crash-worthiness.

The doctrine of crash-worthiness holds that a manufacturer and a retailer may be held liable for a defectively designed automobile that causes an injury, even though that design defect did not cause the accident. GM said that in cases where the defect causes the accident, there is little question but that the manufacturer can be held responsible. But where the defect did not cause the accident, GM claimed, the law shouldn't be as hard on the manufacturer; in such cases there should have to be proof that the manufacturer knew or should have known that when the car landed on its roof it would collapse.

The Texas Supreme Court did not agree with GM and upheld the verdict for the injured driver. The court said that collisions and what happens to cars after collisions are clearly interrelated and that a roof collapsing after a collision is an event which is a foreseeable risk that the manufacturer should assume. Cars that crash will have to be worthy regardless of what caused the crash to begin with.

Skating on thin ice

If you sell a defective hockey helmet, you're skating on thin ice. That's the message of a case recently decided by the Supreme Judicial Court of Massachusetts. The case involved a seventeen-year-old boy who was struck in the head by a puck while wearing what was known as a pender helmet. The helmet was a three-piece model consisting of high-impact plastic, shock foam, and leather straps. The problem was that because of the way the helmet was designed, there were gaps between the leather straps where nothing covered the head.

The injury occurred when the boy threw himself into a horizontal position on the ice to block a shot about ten to fifteen feet in front of a shooting player. When the puck was fired, it struck the boy above the right ear, causing a fractured skull requiring a permanent steel plate, and resulting in headaches that were expected to continue for the rest of the boy's life.

The boy and his family brought suit against the manufacturer of the helmet, the sporting goods store where it was bought, and the school on whose hockey team the boy was playing. The suit was grounded in two theories: first, that the helmet was negligently manufactured and everybody through whose hands it traveled should be held responsible; second, that the manufacturer should be held responsible under the doctrine of strict liability, meaning that a hockey helmet is a dangerous instrumentality and if someone is injured because of it, the manufacturer has to pay regardless of whether or not the helmet was negligently manufactured. The defense was that when you play hockey you assume the risk of a fractured skull.

The court held there was sufficient evidence for the jury's award of eighty-five thousand dollars, on the basis that the helmet manufacturer should have known that a three-piece helmet with gaps in it wasn't safe, and the sporting goods store and the school should have realized that too. As far as the boy assuming the risk of his own injury, the court said he clearly didn't realize that the helmet was dangerous; on the contrary, since it was supplied to him by his trusted coach, he assumed it would protect him.

The court said that the manufacturer could be held liable on the basis of strict liability as well, since it was clear that the helmet was made according to a dangerous design and didn't meet the wearer's reasonable expectations as to its safety. So on all counts the manufacturer, the store, and the school were held responsible for a helmet that missed its goal by a long shot.

Cooking with elephant's-ear

What happens when you buy a new cookbook, try out an exotic-sounding recipe, and get poisoned? That was the question recently looked at by a Florida appeals court. What happened was that a housewife went into a bookstore and bought a book called *Trade Winds Cookery.* The woman eagerly plunged into the book and carefully followed a recipe for the cooking of the dasheen plant, which is sometimes known as elephant's-ear. While preparing the roots for cooking, she did what many of us amateur cooks do; she snitched a small piece of one of the roots before she cooked it and, according to the court, immediately experienced a "burning of the lips, mouth, throat, tongue, and intense stomach cramps." Unfortunately, what she didn't know was that uncooked dasheen roots are poisonous.

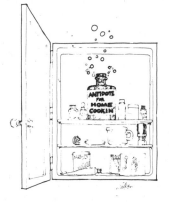

The woman sued the bookstore and the author of the book. The suit against the author of the book was later dropped due to a technicality, but the case went forward against the bookstore. The woman claimed that she should have been warned that uncooked dasheen roots were poisonous, and that the recipe for dasheen dishes was inadequately tested to assure safety for human consumption. She also claimed that books carry with them an implied warranty that everything in the book is safe and that her injury was caused by a breach of that implied warranty.

The question of implied warranties is covered in Florida, as in most states, by the Uniform Commercial Code. One provision of the code says that there is implied in a contract of sale a promise that goods are salable and that they are not inherently dangerous.

The store claimed in its defense that although the code didn't say so, implied warranties had to be limited to the physical characteristics of goods sold. For instance, if a book blew up when it was opened, or fell apart because it was improperly printed or bound, that would be one thing. But as for what was contained within the pages of the book, the store claimed it could not possibly be held to have guaranteed the contents.

The Florida court agreed saying, "We must distinguish between the tangible properties of goods, and thoughts and ideas conveyed by them." So if your recipe lands you in the soup, you may have only yourself to blame.

In the soup

Those of you who travel to or through New England this year would do well to sample some of our delicious seafood, but you would also do well to keep in mind a recent case. It was brought by someone who sampled some seafood and ended up with a bone in her throat that could only be removed after two eso-phagoscopies, causing the plaintiff a lot of trouble.

The problem began when the plaintiff went to a restaurant that was located on the third floor of an old building on Historic Wharf and that she characterized as "quaint." The woman, who the court pointed out was born in New England (a fact that the court characterized as important), ordered a cup of fish chow-der. She stirred her spoon through it, and there was some dispute over whether she was looking for something or whether, as she claimed, she wanted an even distribution of fish and potatoes.

In any event, after the fourth spoonful, she ended up with a bone lodged securely in her throat. The court stated, "We must decide whether a fishbone lurking in a fish chowder constitutes a breach of implied warranty under the applicable provisions of the Uniform Commercial Code." Put more simply, the question for the court was, did the restaurant fail to deliver what any restaurant worth its salt promises to serve its customers?

The judge at the trial level summed up the problem by noting appropriately, "The bone of contention here is whether the fishbone was a foreign substance that made the chowder un-wholesome or not fit to be eaten." The plaintiff cited many cases in which restaurants had been held liable for violating this im-plied warranty of fitness; unfortunately for the plaintiff, they in-volved things like several large stones found in a plate of baked beans or trichinae present in pork.

The court delved into the case with gusto and said that the court took judicial notice (which means that the something is so obvious that it doesn't have to be proved) of the fact that "we are not talking of some insipid broth as it is customarily served to convalescents." In fact, the court quoted from the brief, or written argument, filed by the defense attorneys defending the restaurant. The court then traced the history of fish chowder, including a reference to the fact that Daniel Webster had a recipe for fish chowder that has survived into modern cook-books, and in which the removal of fishbones is not mentioned at all.

In closing, the court said we should be prepared to cope with the hazards of fishbones, the occasional presence of which in fish chowder is, it seems to us, to be anticipated and which, in the light of a hallowed tradition, does not impair its fitness or merchantibility. So next time, be sure to chew your chowder with care.

How safe is summer camp?

How safe is summer camp? Senator Ribicoff of Connecticut doesn't think summer camps are safe enough. In a statement in the *Congressional Record,* the Senator pointed out that approximately 8 million youngsters go to ten thousand summer camps each summer. And each year as many as one hundred of these youngsters will be killed in camp accidents, with more than a quarter of a million serious incidents occurring at camps around the country. A study of the subject by the Department of Health, Education, and Welfare showed that many states have no regulations concerning medical aid, out-of-camp trips or day camps, and ten states had no rules relating to supervision of waterfront activities.

The senator has been assisted by many people around the country, one of the most visible of whom is a Mr. Kurman of Westport, Connecticut, whose fifteen-year-old son was killed twelve years ago on a canoeing trip in Maine while the boy was attending summer camp. Mr. Kurman claims that the boy's death was needless because it occurred on a trip down a raging boulder-strewn river, and no life preservers were in any of the canoes.

Senate Bill 258 filed by the senator from Connecticut would require each camp operator to provide each camper "safe and healthful conditions giving due consideration to conditions existing in nature, facilities and equipment which are free from recognized hazards which cause or are likely to cause death, serious illness, or serious physical harm, and adequate supervision to prevent injury or accident."

This legislation seems destined to suffer the same fate as the bills he has filed over the last ten years. The reason for the continued defeat is a combination of things. There is a fear that the whole question of camp safety could become another bureaucratic nightmare that might drive many good camps out of business while failing to catch up with those that really need the policing. Many also feel that camp safety should remain an issue of state control rather than being taken over by the federal government, and that most camps are doing a good job.

But until the laws are changed, responsibility for camp safety will rest with the camp—and with parents, who should not be afraid to find out just how safe their child's camp really is.

If your new car's a lemon

Are you having problems with your new car? Well, if you are, you may be able to get rid of the whole thing. That's the message of a series of recent cases, one of which was handed down by the New York Supreme Court. Many new car purchasers just live with their lemons, taking them back week after week for repairs that just don't succeed. Most new car warranties provide that if there's anything wrong with the car within the first year, it will be fixed —but there's no escape hatch allowing you to get your money back if it really can't be fixed.

Well, things are changing. In the New York case a man took delivery of a brand-new Cadillac Eldorado. He drove it out of the showroom, and after going seventeen miles, the car burst into flames due to a faulty electrical system. The dealer repaired the car, but the owner just didn't want it any more, claiming he had lost confidence. He wanted his money back, but the dealer refused. The owner went to court, suing both the dealer and General Motors.

The manufacturer and the dealer claimed that the warranty was a contract and the buyer had agreed they were obliged only to repair the car, not to give him his money back. The court disagreed, citing two recent cases that allowed the buyer to cancel the deal. In one of those cases, a New Hampshire man drove his new car out of the showroom; at the first traffic light it stalled, and when he started it again, it would only go in low gear. And in a New Jersey case, a man drove his new car over one thousand miles in three days, when it refused to move any more. Both buyers got their money back.

The New York court said that for a majority of people the purchase of a new car is a major investment, rationalized by the peace of mind that flows from its dependability and safety. Once that faith is shaken, the vehicle has lost its value. As for the warranty, the court held it was a contract of adhesion, which means that one of the parties couldn't really negotiate the terms of the contract before he got stuck.

Would you buy a used car from this man?

Have you bought a used car lately? Well, if you have, I hope
you've had better luck with it than some of the people who testified before a recent hearing held by the Federal Trade Commission on proposals to regulate used-car sales.

One New Hampshire woman testified that when she got home
with the car she had just bought, she rolled down the window and
the whole side of the car began to rattle. Within a week she had
to have a new battery, two new tires, new plugs, and new points.
She then found the gas tank had been smashed, a tie rod was
completely bent out of shape, the shocks were leaking fluid, and
just about the whole car was covered with bonding material used
to repair accidents when the metal is torn, dented, or nonexistent. To top it off, during the first rainstorm, the trunk and
driver's compartment leaked.

When she complained to the dealer, he said, "Lady, where did
you do all that?" She ended her testimony saying, "There ought
to be something done so people won't get rooked any more."

Well, if the Federal Trade Commission has its way, a lot will
be done. Leading the list of changes will be a very large sticker
on the right rear window of the car. The sticker has sixty-five
items on it that have to be checked by the dealer. They include
such comforting things as "cracked block," "visible leakage,"
and "vehicle does not stop in a straight line." The regulations
would also require that if the car is sold as is, without a warranty,
the document must say in large capital letters: "The purchaser
will have to bear the entire expense of repairing or correcting any
defects that exist or may occur in the vehicle."

At the hearing, consumer representatives said that the changes did not go far enough, and selling the car "as is" should be prohibited altogether. The used-car salesmen and dealers turned out in force and testified that consumers would tend to reject vehicles with lengthy repair lists and might assume that such lists indicated vehicles of poor quality. They also said that to have to disclose all repairs done might cause dealers to perform fewer repairs so they wouldn't have to disclose them. Another said that the sticker on the right rear window would cause a safety hazard for people who wanted to test drive the car; another said the system wouldn't work because some cars don't have right rear windows.

The government is reviewing the testimony, but it looks as though it will be a while until the sticker protects you from getting stuck. In the meantime, if you would buy a used car from that man, ask him a lot of questions, and get the answers and the promises in writing.

When your siding starts sliding

How's your aluminum siding holding up? If the answer is that it isn't holding up very well and you feel you've been held up instead, you might be interested in a case recently decided by the Sixth Circuit Court of Appeals. The case involved a homeowner, an aluminum-siding contractor, and a bank. The way it worked was that the contractor sold the homeowner on the fact that aluminum siding for his home was an absolute necessity. The homeowner of course did not have the money, but the contractor said, that's no problem, we'll help get you the money from a bank —all you have to do is sign a note. The papers were signed, the bank paid the contractor, the siding went up on the house, and the homeowner began paying the bank.

And then the siding began sliding off the house, and the homeowner decided he didn't want to pay the bank any more. The reason he claimed he didn't have to pay the bank was that the bank violated the truth-in-lending law by not telling the homeowner the whole story about the loan. The bank said it did tell the homeowner everything, such as what the interest on the loan was and the fact that the homeowner could have cancelled within three days.

That's true, said the court, the bank did make all the disclosures required—except for one. It forgot to tell the homeowner that if the bank for some reason didn't pay the contractor, the

contractor would have a mechanics' lien on the home, which
meant the homeowner could actually lose his home or at least be
prevented from selling it. The court said the truth-in-lending law
requires that any conceivable security interest that could arise on
that property had to be disclosed by the bank, even if the bank
didn't fully control that security interest.

The court held that because the bank hadn't disclosed everything it should have, the chance to get out of the contract didn't
end after three days, and the homeowner could stop it any time
he wanted. So the contractor is probably working on somebody
else's house, the bank has seen its last payment, and the homeowner is home free.

When your dream house becomes a nightmare

What happens when you build the house of your dreams, and
it turns into a nightmare? That was the question in a case recently
decided by the Alabama Supreme Court. The case asked: If your
new house drives you up a wall, can you collect not only for the
actual damage to the house, but also for your emotional upset?

The case got started when an Alabama couple bought a piece
of land and entered into a written agreement for their dream
house to be built on the lot. As the house was being constructed,
the wife noticed a hairline crack in the slab that was the main
foundation of the house. She complained to the builder, telling
him the crack was getting longer daily and already stretched from
the front porch to the den. The builder told her not to worry, that
such cracks were common. After the house was completed, the
couple moved in, and a short time later the crack stopped grow-

ing longer and began growing wider. Eventually it caused severe damage to the house and, according to one expert, rendered the house worthless.

The couple brought suit asking not only for damages related to the decreased value of the house, but also for damages for mental anguish. The general law in Alabama, as in most states, is that mental anguish is not a recoverable element of damages arising out of a breach of contract. The reason is, it's too remote, and if every broken contract ended up with damages for mental suffering, there would be no end to such litigation.

But, said the court, there are exceptions, and one of those exceptions is when the contract is so coupled with matters of mental concern that the party breaching the contract knows in advance that breach of the contract will certainly result in mental anguish. The court said a house is the largest single investment most individuals make in a lifetime, one that places the purchaser in debt for from twenty to thirty years. A builder could easily foresee that an individual would undergo extreme mental anguish if his or her newly constructed home fell apart.

The builder claimed that at least such cases should be limited to mental anguish corroborated by physical symptoms, but the court did not agree. It ordered payment of fifty thousand dollars, proving that sometimes dreams that turn into nightmares do have a happy ending.

A working criminal

Isn't it a crime the way some workmen work around your house? Well, even though you may think it's a crime, it isn't. That's the result of a case recently decided by the New York Court of Appeals. The case involved a section of the New York City Administrative Code that made it a crime for a worker to start work on a project and not finish it. Specifically, the law made it a misdemeanor for a person to abandon or willfully not perform a home-improvement contract.

What happened in this case was that after being paid to do a job, a workman came to a building and did a super job ripping out the walls, the ceilings, the heat, and the toilets. And that was basically it. From then on, he never showed up to put back what he had taken out. The homeowner, being upset with what had happened to his house, complained to the city, and the building contractor was convicted of having violated the law.

He appealed his conviction, claiming that the law was unconstitutional and violated the Thirteenth Amendment, which prohibits slavery. He argued that he certainly could be sued for money damages in connection with the work, that he might even be able to be jailed for fraud if it could be proved that he took the money without ever intending to perform his contract, but that he could not be convicted of a crime because he had merely refused to complete the work.

The New York high court agreed with the contractor. The court cited a U.S. Supreme Court case *(Pollock* v. *Williams),* which held that if a person ends up owing money to another person, he cannot be forced to work for that person, and it certainly cannot constitutionally be made a crime for him to refuse to do so. To do otherwise, said the court, would be in fact imposing involuntary servitude on a person, and that would violate the Thirteenth Amendment to the Constitution, which outlawed slavery.

So while you may think it's criminal for someone to take your money, tear up your house, and leave, in the opinion of a New York court at least, it's a crime for which no one can be convicted.

If you lose your *Life,* it's about *Time*

If you lose your *Life,* what can you do about it? That was the question decided by an Illinois appellate court in a case brought by a subscriber to *Life* magazine who didn't like what happened after his *Life* ran out. The case got started when Stephen D. Pearlman renewed his subscription to *Life* magazine. He contracted for delivery of seventy-eight issues of *Life,* paying in advance a total of $11.95. Three months later, Time, Inc., which was the publisher of *Life,* decided that *Life*'s time had come and ceased publication, leaving Stephen D. Pearlman sixty issues short.

Immediately following the suspension, Time, Inc. wrote a very nice letter to Stephen D. Pearlman and all the other *Life* subscribers, offering a choice of a cash refund for the undelivered issues or a substitute subscription to any one of thirty-three different magazines. The letter went on to say that "we have a commitment to you and we would like to keep you in our family of readers." Well, Mr. Pearlman decided to stay in the family and selected *Time* magazine instead of the $9.19 he would have been entitled to if he had taken the cash refund. So *Life* gave way to *Time* without incident.

The trouble came when *Time* stopped after only forty-three issues. Mr. Pearlman wrote to *Time* asking for the seventeen issues he claimed were due to him, and *Time* responded that forty-three issues of *Time* equaled sixty issues of *Life*, because *Time* was more expensive than *Life*. Mr. Pearlman said that what really mattered was the number of magazines, not the cost of each individual magazine, and he brought suit charging Time, Inc. with common-law fraud, unjust enrichment, and breach of contract.

An Illinois circuit court dismissed Stephen's case, holding that he had received the monetary value of his bargain. The appellate court reversed, saying that while it may be true that the basic subscription rate of 50¢ may have equaled the *Life* contract price, everybody knows that the basic subscription rate is often much higher than actual subscription prices—an average of 16¢ per issue in the case of *Time*. The court held further that Time, Inc. may have known or was culpably ignorant of the fact that its statements were false, so the case went back for full trial.

A lot of litigation for $9.19, but who knows—Stephen D. Pearlman may be having the time of his life.

Life insurance and heroin death

If a person kills himself with an overdose of heroin, will his double-indemnity life-insurance policy pay off just the same? That was the question recently decided by the Nevada Supreme Court in a case that involved a heroin addict who one night injected an overdose into his vein and died as a result.

This man had taken out a life-insurance policy, and it was a double-indemnity policy, which means that the policy pays double if death is caused by an accident. The company refused to pay the double indemnity, claiming that the man intended to inject heroin into his veins, and his death was therefore not accidental.

But the court refused to accept the company's reasoning and held that the double-indemnity benefits had to be paid just the same. The court said no matter how daring, reckless, or foolhardy a person's conduct may be, if death itself is not intended, then the death is an accident.

The court said that insurance policies have to be understood in plain and ordinary language and that any ambiguity in an insurance policy will be strictly construed against the insurance company. Injecting oneself with heroin, said the court, is not a

self-inflicted injury and it's not a disease, and therefore the death
was accidental.

One judge dissented, saying the injection of heroin by the
insured was a bodily injury inflicted upon the individual by himself. The judge said piercing of one's body with a needle is intentional, and death from heroin injection is such an ever-present
reality that it should have been expected and foreseen. Another
dissenting judge pointed out that the man had been using various
illegal drugs including heroin for about three years before his
death. In this case, said the judge, the dead man's self-infliction
of drugs was tantamount to suicide.

But the majority ruled, and injecting oneself and dying from
an overdose of heroin may be a lot of things, but it's no accident.

What's good for NOW

What's good for NOW may not be so good for Shere Hite.
That's the result of a recent case decided by the New York Supreme Court. The case involved a lawsuit brought by the National Organization of Women against Shere Hite, who is the
author of *The Hite Report,* a controversial and very successful book
dealing with the attitudes of contemporary women about sex.
NOW claimed that Shere Hite used NOW's name to get responses to her sex survey, that she used NOW as a mail drop to
collect the survey, and that she used NOW's name to promote
and sell the book. But, said NOW, Hite had given none of the
profits to NOW even though, according to the lawsuit, she promised to take care of NOW in the future.

NOW tried six different legal theories to collect from Hite,
and all but one were thrown out of court. NOW alleged that
Hite had promised verbally that if her book were successful, she
would make "a substantial contribution to the organization";
since NOW had gone ahead and let its name be used based on
this promise, it was a valid contract. Not so, said the court,
holding that the promise to a make substantial contribution was
simply too vague to constitute a contract. The court cited a previous case in which an employer had promised to pay the employee a fair share of the company's profits, but the promise, as
in this case, was too vague, indefinite, and uncertain to be enforced.

NOW also claimed fraud and misrepresentation, saying that
when Hite said she'd make a substantial contribution she knew
at the time that she wasn't going to. The court came out on Hite's

side on this point too, saying it's well-settled law that an intention to perform a future act cannot give rise to an action based on fraud.

So it looked bad for NOW and good for Hite, but then the court turned to NOW's claim of unjust enrichment. The claim of unjust enrichment is not based on contract and it isn't based on fraud. It's a principle of law that says regardless of the intent of the parties, one party has ended up richer at the expense of another, and despite the absence of a contract, the party who was unjustly enriched has to pay. It's as if someone comes on your property and builds a house by mistake, thinking he's on his own land; you can't just stand there and reap the benefits.

The court said that Hite had used NOW's name and that even though there wasn't any specific contract or provable fraud, Hite was enriched by using NOW's name; if she didn't pay anything in return for that enrichment, it would be unjust. So this case is over, for now.

The case of the purloined parrot

The exploits of Chester recently resulted in an opinion rendered by New York's Civil Court for Queens County. The case will probably not be appealed, and while some may consider its subject matter flighty, it is certainly worthy of a close look. Chester was a parrot; his description played an important part in the case. He was fourteen inches tall, with a green coat, a yellow head, and red splashes over his left shoulder. Chester was employed by the American Society for the Prevention of Cruelty to Animals as a show parrot who took part in educational exhibitions for groups of children.

According to the court's opinion, on June 28, 1973, during an exhibition in King's Point, New York, Chester flew the coop and took refuge in the tallest tree he could find. All fire department ladders proved to be too short, and offers of food were steadfastly ignored. During the night Chester took off. Six days later, the plaintiff in the case, who lived in Belle Harbor, Queens County, happened to see a fourteen-inch parrot with a green coat, yellow head, and red splashes seated in his back yard. He brought the parrot some food, which Chester eagerly accepted, and every day for two weeks the parrot returned to the plaintiff's back yard. Finally Chester began really to trust the plaintiff and entered his home, whereupon he was immediately placed in a cage.

The plaintiff then made a fatal error; he called the ASPCA and requested its advice as to the care of a parrot he had found. The ASPCA immediately sent two representatives to the plaintiff's home. The plaintiff was probably surprised at the alacrity with which the ASPCA responded to his request for help, but when the representatives got there, they inspected the parrot, claimed it was the ASPCA parrot, and removed it from the plaintiff's home. The plaintiff sued for the parrot's return.

The court stated, "The issues presented to the court are twofold: One, is the parrot in question truly Chester, the missing bird? Two, if it is in fact Chester, who is entitled to its ownership?" The plaintiff presented ordinary witnesses who said that such a parrot was seen in the neighborhood prior to the time Chester had escaped and an expert witness who said that a parrot could not possibly fly the distance between King's Point and Belle Harbor in so short a time; therefore, said the plaintiff, the bird in question was not in fact Chester.

With regard to the first issue, the ASPCA claimed it *was* Chester and that he could say "hello" and dangle by his legs, which he, of course, refused to do in court. The court also called upon the parrot to indicate by name or other mannerism an affinity to either of the claimed owners; as the court stated, "Alas, the parrot stood mute." But the court found that it was indeed Chester and that it had to be returned to the ASPCA. It also found that it was not a wild animal, which from the point of view of the ASPCA was fortunate, since the law is that the moment a wild animal escapes, all ownership in it is extinguished.

In closing, the court stated that it wished to commend the plaintiff for his acts of kindness and compassion to the parrot during the period that it was lost and was gratified to receive the defendant's assurance that the first parrot available for adoption would be offered to the plaintiff.

A contract with a kidnapper

Do you have to keep a contract with a kidnapper? To answer that question, let's look at a contract made recently under rather unusual circumstances. A man was unhappy that a mortgage company was foreclosing on his mortgage and kidnapped an executive of the company, holding him hostage for sixty-three hours with a sawed-off shotgun wired to his neck. The reason the kidnapper finally let his hostage go was that he made a bargain with the police: If he would release his hostage, he would receive immunity from prosecution and would himself be free.

You might wonder whether such a contract is valid. The kidnapper was arrested and charged just the same. Some argued the reason the contract was broken was because the kidnapper didn't keep his side of the bargain to let the hostage go immediately as he had promised; instead, he held on to the hostage for a while after the contract was made. Others claimed there never really was a contract to begin with, because the law-enforcement authorities never intended to let the kidnapper go anyway; in fact, one of the deputy sheriffs was quoted as saying, "I would have promised him title to Hawaii if I could have gotten that guy out of there."

The real reason the kidnapper didn't have a lawsuit for breach of contract was because a contract entered into under duress is not valid in the eyes of the law. Duress is defined as subjecting a person to a pressure that overcomes his will and makes him do things he would never do if he was acting under his own free will.

This incident involved a promise made by and broken by state authorities. U.S. Attorney General Bell was asked to do the same thing and grant immunity for federal crimes, with the knowledge that the contract wouldn't mean anything because it was made under duress. The Attorney General refused, saying that we ought not to bargain with someone who is holding a hostage. A few days later, he was asked on the television program *Face the Nation* if he would stick with immunity if he ever did promise it. His answer was yes, and he added, "I don't think the government ought to lie."

Is the Rozelle rule reasonable?

Does the Rozelle rule run afoul of the rule of reason? The courts have answered yes and sent the Rozelle rule packing. For those of you who may be uncertain as to just what the Rozelle rule is, it's a rule of the National Football League that gives the commissioner the right to settle a dispute between two clubs just about any way he pleases. Any player whose contract with a club has expired becomes a free agent. According to the rule, if he signs with a different club than the one he just left, the commissioner can award additional compensation to the club he feels is getting the poorer deal. This compensation can take the form of additional players from the active reserve list or prime draft choices.

The plaintiffs in the group were eight National Football League players, and the case went on for fifty-five days, generating four hundred exhibits and more than eleven thousand pages of testimony. The plaintiffs claimed that the Rozelle rule violated the Sherman Anti-Trust Act by restraining free movement around the league by players. Clubs were naturally reluctant to pick up free agents because they didn't know in advance whether or not the deal would be acceptable to the commissioner, who might make an award of unknown compensation under the rule.

An example was the 1971 deal involving Phil Olsen. In that transaction the Rams picked up Olsen, who was with the Patriots and had become a free agent. Rozelle, apparently unhappy with the deal, awarded to the Patriots the Rams' first-round draft choice in 1972, and also gave away the Rams' third-round draft choice, which had been acquired from the Washington Redskins. Rozelle then ordered the Rams to pay the Patriots thirty-five thousand dollars.

The court held that the rule constituted a perpetual restriction on a player, following him throughout his career, and was therefore unreasonable. So the Rozelle rule was an unreasonable restraint of trade and it did in fact run afoul of the rule of reason.

Yazoo Smith won at last

Well, Yazoo Smith won, the Washington Redskins lost, and the impact of the case of *Smith* v. *Pro-Football, Incorporated,* will be felt for a long time to come. Pro-Football, Incorporated, is the legal name of the Washington Redskins, and they, along with the National Football League, were defendants in the case Yazoo brought under the Sherman Anti-Trust Act.

Yazoo Smith was an All-American college football player at the University of Oregon and was drafted in the National Football League's annual player-selection draft as the Redskins' first-round choice. He signed the standard player contract required by the NFL, which gave him a twenty-three-thousand-dollar bonus for signing, an additional five thousand dollars if he made the team, and a starting salary of twenty-two thousand dollars. What he did not get was a clause that would guarantee him against loss of earnings in the event of injury, because clauses like that simply weren't in the standard player contract, and when you're drafted, you don't have much say about how your contract reads.

Yazoo suffered a very serious neck injury that suddenly ended his career just after it had begun. He sued, claiming that because of the draft, he was unable to negotiate a contract that reflected the free-market or true value of his services and one that contained adequate guarantees against loss of earnings in the event of injury. Yazoo claimed that the draft was really a group boycott and therefore illegal under the antitrust laws.

In a lengthy and complicated opinion, the court concluded that the owners of the teams have agreed among themselves that the right to negotiate with each top-quality graduating college athlete will be allocated to one team, and no other team will deal with that person and that this "outright, undisguised refusal to deal constitutes a group boycott in its classic and most pernicious form, a device which has long been condemned as a per se violation of the antitrust laws," and constitutes "naked restraint of trade with no purpose except stifling of competition."

The court awarded Yazoo triple damages of two hundred and seventy-six thousand six hundred dollars plus attorneys' fees, and the football draft, pending all the appeals, may soon be a thing of the past.

You can't tell a wine by its label

You can't tell a wine by its label. This was the complaint of a group of sophisticated wine consumers who went to court because, while they liked American wines very much, they didn't like the way they were labelled.

American wines are labelled under the authority of the Federal Alcohol Administration Act. The connoisseurs complained that the act and its regulations didn't give enough information about the wine. They were most upset about the varietal rule, which allows wine labels to carry the name of a single grape variety without disclosing that other possibly inferior grape varieties may compose up to 49 percent of the wine. They also complained about the geographic rule, which permits wines to be labelled as coming from grapes in one geographic region, without disclosing that as much as 25 percent of the wine may come from grapes grown in other less-celebrated regions of the country. The consumers were also upset by the provisions that allowed a winery to say it produced a certain wine when as much as 25 percent of the wine was in fact fermented and clarified by somebody else.

The consumers said that they were not insisting that wines be 100 percent perfect, but rather that the labelling process be reformed so that at least you knew what you were or were not drinking.

The court said that the act prohibits false, misleading, or deceptive statements. "The question," said the court, "is whether the label Chardonnay, for example, which may have nearly half the wine made from grapes other than Chardonnay, is false or misleading." The court noted that although the label merely reads "Chardonnay," not "all Chardonnay" or "100 percent Chardonnay," the ordinary wine drinker would conclude that he or she was drinking wine made from Chardonnay grapes. This, according to the lawsuit, is rarely the case. The court held that regulations must be changed to tell with more particularity just what is in the bottle and where it came from.

So the next time you toast a special event with Chardonnay, you might think about the fact that when it comes to the Chardonnay, your glass may be only half full.

Knowing what you pay for

Did you ever wonder why more consumers don't get involved in public utility rate-setting procedures? A recent article in the *DePaul Law Review* concluded that one reason is that the whole subject is so confusing. The battle is also one-sided, said the author, who found a lot of very good reasons why consumers in Illinois, as in most other states, have had very little to say about their utility rates.

One of the biggest problems is that it's almost impossible for anybody to keep up with the utilities. Up to 1973, for example,

Illinois Bell Telephone never lost a case. The utility has been in the Illinois courts fourteen times, appealed any lower court decision that didn't come out the way it wanted, and even pursued one appeal for seventeen years. According to the article, a few years back Illinois Bell received a rate of return in excess of 9 percent; ten months later, it filed for another increase, and when the rate fell back to 8 percent, it refiled rate increase requests five times in the following five months. Some states prohibit a utility from coming back within two years after a decision, giving everybody a rest between hearings.

Another area of controversy is how the utility fixes its rates. One of the most important factors used by the utility in fixing its rates is the valuation of its assets. If it values them at what it would cost to reproduce them, it will naturally have a far higher rate base than if the assets were valued at their current fair market value. Most states have forced the use of fair market value as opposed to reproduction costs; but the Illinois Supreme Court has recently ruled that reproduction cost can still be used in Illinois.

The court did strike down some expenditures that had figured into the rates, including contributions to the officers' favorite charities, money spent to lobby in the legislature, and payments to the parent Western Electric for equipment that was bought at a profit rate higher than Illinois Bell itself could earn. According to the author, Illinois Bell promptly went to the Illinois legislature and had the court's decisions with regard to charitable contributions and the Western Electric payments nullified.

So the next time you get your gas, electric, or phone bill, rather than getting irate over the rate, you might think about what you're really paying for.

Getting your dog's worth

What happens when someone promises to give your pet poodle a decent burial and buries a stray alley cat instead? That was the question in a case recently decided by New York's Civil Court for Queens County, a case that looked at how much value the law puts on pets.

The case got started when a lady brought her fifteen-year-old poodle to a local dog and cat hospital for treatment. The doctor, after examining the dog, recommended that it be put to sleep. The woman agreed, but on condition the poodle be given an elaborate burial complete with headstone, epitaph, and graveside attendance by the poodle's owner, her two sisters, and a friend. The dog and cat hospital promised to turn the remains over to an organization that specialized in elaborate pet funerals.

The big day arrived, and the grieving woman decided to open the casket for one more look at her deceased poodle. What she saw when she opened the casket was a dead cat; the poodle was nowhere to be found. The woman brought suit against the dog and cat hospital claiming damages for mental suffering as well as for the fair market value of the dog.

The defense was one that usually wins in these cases, that there can be no damages for mental suffering, and no damages other than the fair market value of a fifteen-year-old poodle. But the court disagreed and said, "This court now overrules all precedent in this area and holds that a pet is just not a thing, but rather occupies a special place somewhere in between a person and a piece of personal property." The court said a pet is not just an inanimate thing that receives affection; it also returns affection. This woman, said the court, had an elaborate funeral plan and had intended to visit the dog's grave in the years to come and was denied that right.

The court cautioned that its decision was not intended to be extended to family heirlooms, since those things are inanimate objects and cannot return love and affection. The court said that losing the right to memorialize a pet rock or tree or family picture album is one thing, but a dog, that's quite another.

So the court overturned a lot of old law, broke new ground, and awarded seven hundred dollars to the woman. And when it comes to the law, it's not true that pets don't mean a thing any more.

False and misleading

As you go about your Christmas shopping this year, you may wonder about comparing similar products, and whether you can depend on the company's advertising to tell you which one is really better. You might also wonder whether one company can knock another company's product, and if it can, why it isn't done much more often. A recent article in the *Federal Bar Journal* by Julius Lunsford analyzes the protection we have from false and misleading advertising and traces the history of the law in this area.

An early case dealing with regulating what companies can do about cheap imitations was the *American Washboard* case. It was decided in 1900, when the washboard had not quite been replaced by the washing machine. The plaintiff made and sold genuine aluminum washboards and tried to prevent a competitor from advertising that its washboards were made of aluminum, when they were really made of zinc. While the court held that such behavior was morally wrong, it said it couldn't stop the behavior unless the other company's product was actually being sold under American Washboard's name.

This case was in conflict with Judge Leonard Hand's opinion in the *Mosler Safe* case, from another federal court, which stopped a Mosler competitor from advertising that it too had explosion-proof chambers in its safes, when it really didn't. Justice Holmes of the Supreme Court settled the conflict in these cases by coming up with the Holmes-Hand doctrine, which basically says that competitors cannot take away a person's customers by misrepresentation.

Years later, Congress enacted what is known as the Lanham Act, which provides that any person who misrepresents as to the place of origin of his goods, or their nature and quality, can be sued by any other person who believes he is damaged by that misrepresentation.

But honest use of another company's trademark to advertise your own goods *is* permitted. So when Saxony products claimed that its Fragrance S was like Guerlain's Shalimar, the court sent the case back to determine whether or not Fragrance S really was like Shalimar, with the implication that if it was, it was then okay to say so.

Mr. Lunsford's *Bar Journal* article concludes that a major problem with the law is that it seems to give the right to police each other only to the companies, while those of us who do all the buying are kept on the sidelines.

Fleeing Georgian fleas

In the course of a year, you probably find yourself traveling at one time or another, and travel usually involves staying in hotels or motels. A recent case heard by the U.S. District Court for North Carolina reminds us that politicians are not the only ones who may encounter strange bedfellows—but that all of us may find unexpected bedmates as we roam around the country. In this case the unexpected visitors were a rather large contingent of fleas who attacked a mother and son while they were asleep in a Georgia motel.

According to the court's opinion, the plaintiffs, while guests of the establishment, were each bitten by numerous flealike insects that caused them grave personal injuries. Suit was brought for breach of contract, the contract being that one makes payment for a room and has a right to expect as part of the bargain a bed that will not be roaming with small vicious insects. Suit was also brought for negligence, claiming that the motel breached its duty of care to the plaintiffs by not taking proper precautions to prevent the invasion.

Unfortunately for the plaintiffs, however—while perhaps sound in concept and doubtlessly having the support of the millions who have stayed in hotels and motels and wished they, too, could have brought a lawsuit the next morning—the case did not get very far before it was dismissed. One of the things a lawyer worries about when he or she files any case is whether the case is filed in the right court. We call this the question of proper jurisdiction, and many a case has gone down to defeat because it was not brought in the proper forum.

This case was brought in federal court, which has more stringent jurisdictional requirements than state courts. While much litigation in the federal courts involves questions relating to federal laws and regulations, actions can also be brought in cases where there is a diversity of citizenship, that is, where the plaintiff and defendant are citizens of different states. These plaintiffs claimed that since they were residents of North Carolina and the motel, and presumably the fleas, were residents of Georgia, diversity of citizenship was present.

The federal court rejected these contentions and dismissed the case—but without prejudice to begin the action in another court, presumably in the state of Georgia. So the plaintiffs will perhaps have a second bite at the issue, and let's hope they find a nice quiet campground to stay at while they're waiting for the trial.

Paying your rent in gold

How would you like to have to pay your rent in solid gold coin? That was the dilemma faced by a tenant who went to court last year to see if he could pay his rent in dollar bills like the rest of us or whether the gold clause in his lease could be enforced by the landlord.

It seems that the tenant signed a lease back in 1927 in which he agreed to pay rent at a monthly rate of fifteen hundred dollars, but the catch was that the lease had a gold clause, which meant that the rent had to be paid not in paper money, but in solid gold coin, valued as of May 1, 1927. Now it just so happens that that fifteen hundred dollars worth of gold coin back then equaled seventy-two ounces of fine gold. Today, seventy-two ounces of fine gold is worth more than thirteen thousand dollars, and that is the rent the landlord claimed was due.

Six years after the lease was signed, in 1933, Congress made it illegal for American citizens to own gold, and also provided that any debt payable in gold coin had to be satisfied in good old U.S. currency. So what looked like a stroke of genius on the part of the landlord lost its luster, and since 1933 the rent had been paid in fifteen hundred dollars worth of paper money.

Then came 1974, when Congress passed a law repealing the resolution prohibiting private ownership of gold. When this happened, the landlord demanded the rent based on the value of the gold and the case went to court. The question for the court was whether the 1933 law was repealed completely or whether just that part of it prohibiting private ownership of gold was repealed. The tenant argued that private debts still couldn't be paid in gold.

After reflecting on both sides, the court held that the purpose of the 1933 law was not only to prohibit gold ownership, but also to be sure that debts were made payable only in a uniform currency and that to allow debts to be payable based on a variable substance like gold would upset the whole uniformity of the monetary system. So the court ordered that forever more the rent will be fifteen hundred dollars in paper, and the glint went out of the gold clause.

If your landlord doesn't take care of you

If your landlord doesn't take care of you, you don't have to take care of your landlord. That's the message of a case recently decided by the Supreme Judicial Court of Massachusetts. The case involved a woman who had leased an apartment for two hundred forty-five dollars a month. A few months after the lease was signed, there was a break in some underground piping, and she lost her heat and hot water for about twelve days. She withheld thirty-five dollars from the next month's rent; the landlord refused to accept her check and sued to collect the full rent and evict her.

The tenant said she had a perfect right to stay in the apartment and withold the rent. She claimed that loss of adequate heat and hot water was a breach of the warranty of habitability, which means that an apartment isn't fit to live in. A lower court agreed with the tenant and found she could remain in possession, could withhold the rent, and could even get damages for the breach although there was no evidence that the landlord had delayed fixing the pipe or acted in bad faith.

The Supreme Judicial Court said there were two questions it had to decide: Can a tenant withhold rent if a landlord fails to maintain an apartment in a habitable condition; and can the tenant withhold rent even if the landlord is trying to fix the problem? The court answered yes to both questions.

The court said a tenant's right to withhold rent occurs as soon as the landlord has been notified that a place isn't fit to live in, and the fact that the landlord is or is not trying to remedy the situation does not matter. The court said its decision was based on a theory that landlord and tenant have entered into a contract, and the moment there's a breach on the part of the landlord, the tenant can withhold the rent.

The landlord said this was an impossible burden, and argued it didn't reflect the true contract because even tenants expect that things will break down; as long as landlords aren't just ignoring the problem, the rent should not be withheld. But the court rejected this argument. The court did not say exactly when an apartment is or is not fit to live in or how much rent can be withheld; but for tenants and landlords, it's the beginning of a long, cold winter.

No children allowed

Can children be kept out of·condominiums? That was the question faced by a Florida court in the latest of a series of cases that have sought to set aside restrictions on the rights of condominium owners to live their lives as they please after they buy their condominiums. Owners of condominiums frequently have to agree to certain conditions of ownership when they accept title to their property. A number of cases have been brought involving restrictions preventing condominium owners from acquiring pets if they've agreed not to, and these restrictions have generally been upheld.

The case that faced the Florida court involved a condominium owner who had broken the condominium rule that prohibited children under twelve from living in the property. The lower court ruled against the property owner, forcing him to give up his property because he broke the rule relating to twelve-year-olds. The owner argued on appeal that the restriction against children was unconstitutional, violating basic and fundamental rights, including the right to marry and procreate, the right to associate freely, and the right to equal protection under the law.

The Florida appeals court agreed that the case involved a number of rights that the United States Supreme Court has declared to be fundamental. Among these is the right to marry and to have children, and the fundamental right of marital privacy. The court also noted that no compelling reason had been shown for refusing to allow children under twelve to live in the condominium, saying, "It is difficult to comprehend that change that occurs on a child's twelfth birthday that renders him fit to live in a condominium."

The court added that there were some families with children under twelve who had moved in before the rule had been adopted and that therefore there was a violation of equal protection. So while prospective pet owners may have a tough time breaking the rules, condominium owners will still be able to marry and have children, thanks to a rather liberal interpretation of the law.

No lawyers allowed

No lawyers allowed. Believe it or not, that was the policy of an apartment house in New York City that became the subject of a recent case handed down by New York's Supreme Court. You've all seen apartment houses that say "no pets," and even a few that say "no children," but have you ever seen one that says "no lawyers"?

The case got started when a black woman lawyer who was also divorced wanted to rent the apartment. The landlord refused to rent it to her, and she brought suit against him, claiming that she was being discriminated against on the basis of her color, sex, and marital status.

The landlord's defense was that he was sure that she would be an undesirable tenant. But the reason he thought she would be undesirable was not because she was black, not because she was a woman, and not even because she was divorced. It was because she was a lawyer. The landlord candidly admitted that he didn't like lawyers and didn't want any as tenants. He said that he was sure that as a lawyer, she would be a source of trouble to him as a tenant, and he prefered to rent to people who were less informed and more passive.

The woman happened to be General Counsel to the New York City Commission on Human Rights, and it was no surprise that the landlord found himself as a defendant in a lawsuit. The New York City Human Rights Law, like most laws dealing with discrimination, prohibits a landlord from refusing to rent an apartment to somebody because of their race, creed, color, national origin, sex, or marital status.

The court concluded that a person is free to do what he wishes with his property unless there's a law specifically telling him what he can't do. The court said, "Regrettable though it may be, a landlord can employ other criteria for refusing to rent; he may decide not to rent to singers because they are too noisy; or to bald-headed men because he has been told that they give wild parties."

So either this landlord has found a new way not to rent to black divorced women, or lawyers have become the latest to join the ranks of the disadvantaged.

Banking on EFT

Have you heard about EFT? Well, if you haven't, you soon will. EFT means Electronic Funds Transfer, and it may mean the end of the problems you've had trying to balance your checkbook or remembering to enter checks you've ripped out in a hurry. It may also signal the end of carrying cash. According to a recent article in the *Commercial Law Journal,* Electronic Funds Transfer has arrived, and with it have come many difficult commercial- and consumer-law problems.

One way in which EFT may work is that when you buy an item, you'll present a plastic card just about the same way that you now use a credit card; only instead of getting credit and having to pay the bill at the end of the month, the card will electronically transfer funds out of your bank account into that of the seller, right on the spot. Congress has set up the National Commission on EFTs, which is supposed to investigate "the need to protect the legal rights of users and customers."

One problem that will have to be solved is who bears the responsibility for fraud. Nowadays the costs of fraud are borne by the bank that paid the check or by the merchant, and only rarely by the consumer. Merchants and consumers are likely to try to shift all of the risk onto the banks, which will be at the bottom of the EFT system. Those familiar with the field predict that merchants and consumers will be able to do this if they play their cards right, thus putting maximum pressure on the banks to come up with virtually foolproof code systems, more commonly known as personal identification codes.

Another issue is what happens if the consumer is unhappy with the goods when he or she gets them home. Present laws give you, the buyer, a right in many situations to change your mind within a stated period of time, usually three days. It gets a little trickier to get your money back if it in fact has already disappeared from your savings account as a result of the split-second Electronic Funds Transfer.

Also, consumers are wondering what will take the place of one of the most powerful weapons that a consumer has—the right to stop payment on a check that has not yet cleared. Consumer representatives want to be sure that these hard-won rights are not lost when EFT enters our lives.

If they won't give you credit

If they won't give you credit, they've got to tell you why—or else. That's the message of a recent case decided by the U.S. District Court for Eastern Louisiana. The case involved the Equal Credit Opportunity Act, which requires that if you are denied credit and you ask why, a written explanation of the refusal must be provided to you within thirty days or you can sue the company for damages.

What happened in this case was that a woman applied to J.C. Penney for credit. She was denied the credit and asked why, but did not receive the answer as required by law. She went to court. J.C. Penney claimed that it should not be held liable because it had simply made a mistake in not getting the required answer out in the time provided by law. It argued that the regulations under the law provide that a company won't be liable if it can prove "inadvertent error." But, said the court, inadvertent error is defined in the regulation as mechanical, electronic, or clerical error, and what happened in this case was none of the above.

The evidence is clear, said the court, that what happened in this case is that J.C. Penney simply didn't have enough employees handling credit applications, so there was no way they could have complied with the law. According to the evidence, there were only two employees handling the entire volume of requests for credit, and a backlog was building every day. The court said it was inevitable that there would come a time when requests for reasons for credit denial could not be provided in a timely fashion. The error, said the court, was one of human judgment in not providing enough employees to do the job; it was not the mistake of the people who were doing the job.

So the case will proceed for damages, and who knows, with the money this woman collects perhaps she will be able to get the credit she was looking for in the first place.

CHAPTER

5

STRIKING OUT:

Injury by accident and on purpose (torts without the icing)

Who's liable, and how much is it worth? Those are probably the most common questions of tort lawyers, lawyers who make a living from cases arising from personal injury or damage to property due to another person's carelessness or intentional wrongdoing. Tort law has become a controversial aspect of the law, and the age-old doctrines that govern it are changing. In general, liability for wrong seems to be expanding. The old rule was that in order to be liable, a person had to prove a reasonably foreseeable injury caused by a breach of a duty of care. Physical injury used to be required, but now, in an increasing number of states, liability and damages have been found for emotional disturbance. Children used to be unable to sue their parents—now they can, with the court adopting the premise that friendly suits are justified because there's usually an insurance company to pick up' the tab. Companies are being held strictly liable for injuries arising out of dangerous instrumentalities, regardless of whether they knew or should have known of any defect. Punitive damages—damages beyond those actually suffered—are being levied more frequently, supposedly to deter future similar conduct, and third persons are being held responsible for the conduct of others, i.e., bartenders are held responsible when people they have served drinks to go out and cause a fatal accident. With insurance more widely available, the amount of litigation and the number of successful suits has skyrocketed—as have insurance premiums and court congestion. This is not to criticize the area of tort litigation, for the private law suit can indeed result not only in substantial damages for the injured party but can also help deter future carelessness or misconduct by others. But one cannot help wonder whether we are reaching the limits of liability and related costs and whether all too often there is a great disparity for the injured, with a few getting huge windfalls and many receiving nothing. Much hue and cry has been raised about the method of payment in the tort area, with most cases being handled on a contingent-fee basis whereby the attorney receives a portion (up to a third and in some cases up to one half) of the verdict or settlement. The attorneys who defend the contingent-fee system argue that it is the poor man's key to the court house and that it prevents frivolous suits, for no lawyer will take a case on a contingent basis if he knows that after a lot of hard work he will receive virtually nothing. Those who attack the contingency claim that it fuels greed for lawyer and client alike and that the merits of a case may become submerged in the pursuit of dollars. Tort law today is a high-risk business for all involved, and one can understand the pleas of those who want to change the manner in which tort law is administered.

Lastly, old protections such as governmental immunity are falling away as the focus turns to the victim and away from the safeguards that used to offer protection to those who caused the injury in the line of duty.

Good news for Good Samaritans

What would you do if you were first on the scene at a serious automobile accident? Since it *could* happen, you might want to think about how you would react if you had a chance to be a good Samaritan. And you might be wondering what the law has to say about what you do or do not do.

The basic rules still have not changed. If you aren't involved in the accident, you don't have to do anything, regardless of how badly somebody needs help. The law of this country, with one exception, is still the law of the frontier: You don't have to help a stranger if you don't want to. The one exception is in the state of Vermont, where a person is required to stop and give aid to another if he or she could do so without personal danger or without interference with important duties owed to others. Anyone who fails to help, except under those conditions, can be fined one hundred dollars.

But before you decide not to help, you might be interested in knowing a few facts about good Samaritans. First, there are no cases to speak of in which a person who has been a good Samaritan has been sued. My offer of a twenty-five dollar reward for a substantiated case still stands. I first offered this reward on the Dick Cavett show in the summer of 1973, and I still haven't had to pay out any money. You may have heard of cases where a person stops to be a good Samaritan and saves a life, and the thanks he or she gets is a lawsuit; but chances are you saw it on television, or read it in a magazine, where making up such cases has been popular for years.

Once you do stop, you should remain with the victim until somebody else arrives. The reason is that someone else who would have remained with the victim may not have stopped because they saw you there. Again, although I know of no cases on the question, the law generally requires that you not place a victim in a worse position than when you found him or her, and stopping, looking, and leaving could be said to have done just that.

As for what you do for the victim, most states have good Samaritan laws providing that even if you were sued, you would be protected unless what you did was grossly careless or reckless. So while the law won't force you to be a good Samaritan, it is on your side if you are.

Good Samaritans abroad

My offer of a twenty-five-dollar reward for a documented case of a good Samaritan, physician or otherwise, being sued still stands. I've never had to pay out any money, but I thought at one point that I was going to be in a lot of trouble. I began receiving reports from all over the country about an incident involving an American physician who had been sued for trying to save a man's life in the Virgin Islands and who had to pay two hundred thousand dollars in damages. What bothered me was the great similarity in the various stories that were reported to me from around the country.

Finally, after a lot of effort, I located the doctor and with some trepidation asked him what had happened to him in the Virgin Islands, and he told me the following story. He was vacationing in the Virgin Islands, enjoying himself immensely, when he noticed a commotion down on the dock. He ran down and saw that a man was lying on the dock and that he'd been electrocuted in working with an electric drill whose cord dropped into the water. The doctor tried to resuscitate him, but was unsuccessful. As a last-ditch measure, he opened the chest there on the dock and massaged the man's heart. The doctor's efforts were to no avail, and the man was dead. But here is where fact diverges from fiction. The doctor was never sued. In fact, he was thanked for his efforts by the family of the victim.

I wish that I didn't have to tell you what did happen to him, because I want everyone to stop and help. But remember, he was never sued. Instead, he was arrested, on a charge of practicing medicine without a license, preliminary to a charge of murder, which was to be brought against him as soon as the results of an autopsy were known, which would be in about six months. (They do an extremely thorough job of autopsying people in the Virgin Islands!) He was actually placed under house arrest and told to remain in his hotel, which up to that moment he had really been enjoying.

At this point it's relevant to mention that the governor of the Virgin Islands was then a direct appointee of the President of the United States; the president at this time was John Kennedy, and this was a Cape Cod physician. I'm not sure how he got word back to the mainland—some say a bottle with a note in it finally reached Washington—but he was abruptly told he could leave, as long as he promised to return if they wanted to prosecute him for murder. He said, "You just call me, and I'll be down on the first plane I can get."

Most states have an exception in their medical practice act which exempts emergency situations; unfortunately, the Virgin Islands medical practice act did not contain this exception. And so, the doctor ended up with a ruined vacation and lawyers' bills of three thousand dollars—but he wasn't sued.

A captain must care

When the boating season arrives, those of us who partake of the thrills of blue-water sailing or power boating would do well to think about our responsibilities toward those who frequently put their lives into our hands without realizing it. A recent case tried in the U.S. District Court for Delaware reminds us that the captain of any ship has a duty of care to his passengers, which if breached may cost them their lives and may result in serious liability for the captain—or for his estate if he too dies as a result of his carelessness.

The yacht was the *Ixtapa,* a thirty-one-year-old fifty-two-foot twin-engine pleasure craft which in December 1971 left Marathon in the Florida Keys bound for Cozumel, Mexico, off the coast of the Yucatan, 470 miles away. The vessel was well equipped, having a Loran, flares, and all equipment required by the Coast Guard. There were three people on board in addition to the owner, and the trip was for pleasure. The trip to Mexico was uneventful, and the weather was excellent; the only problem was that they never made Cozumel because of a substantial error in navigation—they ended up forty miles south at Isla Mujeres instead.

After a delightful week, they decided to return to Florida and left on a Saturday evening with one additional passenger. At the time they left, one of the three guests asked the captain if he had checked on the weather. He replied, "Can't make heads or tails of what these Mexicans say." So they left without checking the weather forecasts broadcast from Miami and Key West, which could easily have been picked up by the equipment on board.

During the night, the weather markedly deteriorated, with a heavy northeast wind blowing against a two-and-one-half-knot current from the southwest, setting up vicious steep and short waves causing a terrific pounding. Shortly after midnight the forward deck hatch was torn loose, but the owner decided not to turn back, even though there was a slight lull in the bad weather at dawn. In fact, the captain at one point made contact with a Coast Guard cutter and asked it to radio that they would be a little delayed, but still did not inquire as to the weather.

Then the weather really hit, and even though there were hours of pounding, no Mayday was ever sent. A few hours later, after the captain had gone below and found the batteries lying on their sides in several feet of water, the Mayday *was* sent; but it was too late because all the batteries were dead. At 9:30 that night, everyone aboard climbed into the life raft, and shortly thereafter the *Ixtapa* drifted away just barely above water.

As the court stated, the eight and one-half following days were a nightmare of high winds and seas, thirst, seasickness, and bitter disappointments. On the fourth night, one person became irrational and disappeared; on the fifth night, the captain, who had tried to keep it all together, jumped overboard and drowned. The three survivors sued the captain's estate.

The court concluded that the owner should have checked the weather carefully and should have turned back after he lost the forward hatch; he should also have asked the Coast Guard for a

weather report and should have sent out a Mayday long before
he tried to. Because he did none of these things, said the court,
even though he died as a result of his own carelessness, his estate
and widow were liable for the deaths of those who died.

Finding the pot of gold

There aren't many cases in which a practical joke leads to a
lawsuit, but those of you who are prone to having fun at the
expense of others would do well to remember a Louisiana case.
The case involved the legendary pot of gold that was rumored to
have been buried many years ago by the plaintiff's ancestors. The
woman, like many others in her family, had known of these ru-
mors, but gave them little thought until she met a fortune teller
in Shreveport, Louisiana. The fortune teller told her that her
relative had indeed buried gold on the property and handed her
a map that purported to show its exact location.

The poor woman gave up her job as a perfume saleswoman
and spent several months digging regularly around a house
owned by a Mr. Smith, who was good-natured about all the digging and quite understanding, knowing the woman had spent
some time in an institution for the mentally ill. As the court
noted, "We assume that [his tolerance of the digging] was due
perhaps to the fact that he had a slight hope that she might
[actually] find something and he would receive a part of it."

When nothing turned up, Mr. Smith and his daughter conceived the idea that they would provide the pot of gold for the
explorer to find. They got an old copper bucket, filled it with
rocks and dirt, and buried it where the next day's digging was to
go on. They also put an authentic-looking note on the tightly
sealed lid of the pot, saying that whoever found it should not
open it for three days and that all the heirs of those who'd originally buried it should be notified.

As expected, the woman found the pot. She brought it to a
bank and demanded a receipt; but the banker, with caution one
would expect from a prudent banker, refused to give a receipt for
one pot of gold because he had no proof of what the pot contained. He only gave a receipt for one pot. Later the banker,
throwing caution to the winds, snuck a look in the pot. When he
found only dirt and rocks, he replaced the lid and decided to join
the joke.

Meanwhile, the poor lady was rushing around preparing to live out her life in luxury and even convinced a judge to accompany her to the pot opening so that everything would be done in an orderly manner. When the pot was opened, with everybody else getting a bang out of it, she flew into a rage so serious that she had to be physically restrained. She commenced a lawsuit, but she died in bitterness and disappointment a few weeks before it was heard.

The court stated that while the practical jokers had no intention of willfully doing the lady any harm and injury, the mental suffering and humiliation was unbearable. The court awarded her heirs five hundred dollars, an amount that it stated would reasonably serve the ends of justice. So the case of the pot of gold joined the annals of the common law.

The worst air disaster

The fiery deaths of 575 people in that crash at Tenerife was the worst air disaster in history, and it may well have touched off the most complicated legal accident case in history. The complications are mindboggling. In addition to the 575 lives and the value that must be placed upon them, there is the considerable personal property lost in the crash, as well as the value of the aircraft, each of which was worth in excess of $30 million. And in addition to the question of damages, the determination of who was at fault and why is also sure to be long and complicated.

The release of the tape-recorded conversation between the KLM pilot and the tower indicated the KLM plane took off after hearing the word "Okay" and not hearing the rest of the sentence, which was "standby for takeoff." But proving who actually said what and why will be a long and complicated process. The problem is that it may well be a very long time before we get to the questions of fault and damages, because it may take years before it's even clear who can sue, where the lawsuits will be brought, and which law will govern the outcome.

One issue that has been getting a lot of attention is whether or not aircraft disaster cases can be brought as class actions rather than separate lawsuits. But a recent similar case involving a Pan American flight that crashed into the side of a mountain on the island of Bali on April 22, 1974, held that a class action was improper, since a different measure of damages would have to be applied in the case of each victim. The court also quoted Harvard law professor Kaplan, who wrote that to allow such class actions would create an unseemly rush to bring the first case and would lead to legalized ambulance chasing.

So from seconds at Tenerife will come years of litigation, and perhaps 575 cases instead of 1.

Long-distance suffering via ESP

Can you collect for damages suffered through ESP? Well, believe it or not, that was the subject of a recent case decided by the U.S. District Court for the Southern District of New York. The case is the first on record that we know of where a person claimed damages based on extrasensory perception.

The case began at the instant a Pan Am 747 and a KLM 747 collided and burned on the ground at Tenerife on March 27, 1977. Margaret Fox was on one of those planes and was instantly killed. Thousands of miles away her twin sister Martha was asleep. At the precise moment of the crash she awoke with a start and experienced a painful burning sensation inside her chest and abdomen and had the feeling of being split apart, and of emptiness, like a black hole within her body. She claimed she knew these feelings related to her twin sister, who she knew was traveling at the time, and she knew instantly that her twin sister was dead. She brought suit against the Boeing Company claiming emotional injuries allegedly sustained at her home through the extrasensory empathy that took place at the time of her sister's death.

The court could find no cases on point and admitted that people can recover for emotional injury when a close relative is killed; but the criteria for such recovery is that the person must witness the accident or come upon it very shortly after it has occurred, and this woman was never at the scene. The court said the injury to this woman was not sensory but rather *extra* sensory and therefore outside the realm of foreseeability as defined by the law.

The woman claimed there have been documented studies that pain can be shared by identical twins even though they are apart. But, said the court, the injury that occurred in this case was simply too remote and unexpected to be compensable. So while extrasensory perception may some day be the grounds for a successful lawsuit, that day still appears to be way off in the distance, perhaps just beyond the horizon.

If you're beaten up on a plane

What are your rights if you're beaten up on an airplane? That was the question recently decided by the Sixth Circuit Court of Appeals. The case involved the question of just what law applied when an assault takes place in a jetliner high above a foreign country.

The case involved a group of passengers who were on a charter flight from Rio de Janeiro to Memphis, Tennessee. The fight broke out twenty-nine thousand feet above the Brazilian jungle. The person who committed the assault was a former Tennessee county sheriff; the victim was a lawyer who'd represented a former deputy sheriff who'd been fired. The assault was a vicious one resulting in many broken teeth as well as serious permanent injuries.

The victim sued, and the question for the court was, what are the rights of a person assaulted in a jetliner far away from American soil? The usual rule of law is that the law of the place where the assault occurred governs who wins and who loses in court. But the victim claimed that when an assault takes place in a jetliner, it doesn't matter where the jetliner is at the time, but rather where it took off from and where it's next going to land. The lawyer claimed there were federal criminal laws punishing crimes committed aboard an aircraft within special aircraft jurisdiction of the United States. Special aircraft jurisdiction is defined as any aircraft outside the United States that has as its next scheduled destination or last point of departure the United States.

The problem for the court was whether a private lawsuit could be brought by one passenger against another based on such laws. The court decided that it could, since a suit for damages would be consistent with the overall congressional purpose.

So while the law of the jungle governed for a while in that airplane, it's the law of the United States that governs when things come down to earth.

Unfriendly skies

Sometimes the friendly skies aren't quite so friendly after all. That's the message of a recent case decided by the Appellate Division of the New York Supreme Court. The case involved a woman who sued American Airlines for serving drinks to an intoxicated passenger who later assaulted her during the flight.

The case got started when the plane got started and took off from a New York airport. The woman passenger was seated across the aisle from a man who was continually served drinks by the flight attendant even though he became increasingly intoxicated. Suddenly the man came across the aisle and began making sexual advances to the woman. When she did not respond, he punched her in the eye. The woman brought suit against the airline, claiming that her physical and emotional suffering was caused by the airline's violation of New York State's Dram Shop Act. That's the law that imposes liability for serving liquor to an intoxicated person who later causes injury. She also sued under the Federal Aviation Administration Regulations, which forbid serving alcoholic beverages to intoxicated passengers.

The court first looked at the New York State Dram Shop Law and said that law could not serve in this case as the basis of a successful lawsuit. The reason was that the liquor was not sold and consumed in New York because the aircraft had left the confines of New York State by the time the liquor service had begun. The court said the Twenty-first Amendment, which repealed prohibition, does not grant to any state the power to regulate the sale of alcohol in or over another state. And, the court added, federal law exclusively governs air carriers, and if individual state dram shop laws were to apply, the uniformity of federal regulation would be disturbed.

But while the woman lost under the New York State Dram Shop Law, she won under Section 1421(a) of Title 49 of the U.S. Code. That's the law that allows the FAA to forbid the service of alcoholic beverages to intoxicated airline passengers. The court said the law was intended to protect other passengers, and while it didn't specifically give a private person the right to sue, it didn't prohibit it either. And, said the court, private lawsuits are a good way to encourage compliance with air safety regulations.

So serving liquor to someone who's drunk too much can be hazardous in the air and also, for the airline at least, back on the ground.

When someone else pays for your drinks

This holiday season, if you drive while you're drunk, you could be in more trouble than ever before. That's the result of a case recently decided by the California Supreme Court. The case involved the question of whether a person who gets drunk and then gets into his car to drive can be held liable for punitive damages when he causes an accident.

Punitive damages are those that are assessed above and beyond the damages actually caused, such as pain and suffering, medical expenses, and lost wages. Punitive damages mean just what they say—damages to punish—and they are usually reserved for cases where spite or malice is involved. Many insurance policies don't cover punitive damages.

In this case the drunk driver had been aware for a long time that he was an alcoholic; he had already caused one serious accident driving under the influence and had been arrested and convicted of drunk driving on several other occasions. This time the jury assessed punitive damages as well as ordinary damages. The California Supreme Court had to decide whether it was legally proper for punitive damages to be assessed in a drunk driving case, where there was no claim that the driver actually intended to cause the accident.

The court said for a victim to be awarded punitive damages, the victim must establish that the drunk driver was aware of the probably dangerous consequences of his conduct and that he deliberately failed to avoid those consequences. The court said, "We have no difficulty concluding that someone who willfully consumes alcoholic beverages to the point of intoxication and then gets behind the wheel may be held to exhibit a conscious disregard for the safety of others."

One judge dissented, saying the majority opinion would allow punitive damages for merely proving that someone had drunk too much wine at dinner knowing he'd have to drive home afterward. But the majority ruled, and in California at least, if someone is hurt or killed because you're driving while drunk, punitive damages may be just around the corner.

Riding into trouble

What happens when you go for a bike ride on a spring afternoon and end up in the hospital? That was the question in a case recently decided by the New Mexico Supreme Court. While riding down the curb lane of an Albuquerque street, a young woman was thrown from her bicycle and seriously injured. The reason she left the bicycle was that it came to an abrupt stop when the front wheel slipped through a drain grate in the road. She sued the city for having placed the drain grate in a place where bike riders were known to tread. The case ended up before the New Mexico high court.

The City of Albuquerque claimed it should not be held legally responsible for two reasons: First, as a city it should be immune from suits of this kind; and, second, the bike rider contributed to her injury by her own negligence.

The court disposed of the question of immunity very quickly. New Mexico law specifically provides that cities are not immune for negligence of public employees involved in solid or liquid waste collection or disposal. And the court said that's what a sewer is for.

As for the woman's conduct, the court said it was true that the weather was clear and dry and the sun was out and it was a perfect bike-riding day in Albuquerque. And it is also true, said the court, that a person has the duty to keep a careful lookout for his or her own safety. But, said the court, in this case the woman had no prior knowledge or warning that this part of the roadway was dangerous for bike riders. In fact, the city had designated the lane as a bicycle path. The court said an ordinarily careful person is not denied access to justice in New Mexico merely because he or she did not actually see everything that could have been seen.

The court held that the lower court had made an error in granting summary judgment to the City of Albuquerque and sent the case back for a new trial. So riding into a sewer may not be good for you or your bicycle, but it doesn't mean your case will go down the drain as well.

"The duty to duck and the flying puck"

"The duty to duck and the flying puck." That's the subtitle of a recent article by Boston attorneys Francis Gregory and Arthur Goldsmith that appeared in *Trial* magazine. The full title of the article was "The Sports Spectator as a Plaintiff," and it was prompted by some recent black days in the annals of sports history.

Leading the list is the death of eleven would-be spectators, pushing to get unreserved seats for the Who concert in Cincinnati in December 1979. Although that wasn't a sports event, it graphically illustrated the hazards of being a spectator. That incident was followed a few weeks later by a battle between New York Ranger fans and the Boston Bruins on the ice and in the stands at Madison Square Garden.

It's become clear that going to a sporting event may be becoming more hazardous for the fans than for the players. The *Trial* article looked at ways the fans can fight back in the courts. The authors stressed that their purpose in writing the article was to prevent injury to spectators to begin with, a subject that the authors feel doesn't get top billing by owners and promoters.

As for promotion, the authors said that a promoter should take care with advertisements and pricing policies and should make sure that bleachers and seats and other products are not defective. The list of cases cited in the article reads like a war-casualty list. One patron collected when his arm was broken during roughhousing by some boys hired to pull up seat cushions after the game. A sixty-nine-year-old spectator collected after he was trampled during the rush for a foul ball, and another collected when he was knocked down through an open trap door by a surging crowd at a prize fight.

As for injury that occurs during play, courts used to throw out most cases involving battered balls and flying pucks. But now the courts are looking much more carefully at the owner's duty to provide proper protective screening, especially behind home plate and the hockey goal.

The authors concluded with a question: How do you protect the spectators without spoiling the sport?

Who pays when the guest falls?

Who pays when the guest falls? During the holiday season, people find themsleves visiting friends, throwing parties, and going places other than where they usually live. Unfortunately, some will slip on icy steps, will fall after having too much to drink, or will hurt themselves in the hundreds of ways people hurt themselves every day. The question is, who is liable when somebody does get hurt at somebody else's house? Believe it or not, the answer depends on what the person was doing there to begin with.

For example, there's a big difference if you get hurt when you're visiting a friend's house as opposed to when you're shopping in a store. Even though your injuries may be exactly the same, you probably won't get anything for them if you fell at a friend's, while you might well get paid if you fell while you were spending money.

The reason for all this is that a person who is shopping is known in the law as a "business invitee," while a visiting friend is nothing more than a social guest. Business invitees are owed a much higher duty of care than are guests. The rule is that a guest, despite the fact that he or she might have been encouraged to come over with promises of food and drink, or even a written invitation, is entitled only to be warned of dangers that the owner of the property knows about. So if there's a defective step or if a railing gives way, the owner won't be responsible unless he or she knew about it in advance.

An example is a recent Missouri case in which a woman fell and was seriously injured while a guest at her sister's. It seems that the cat was fed some meat on the back porch the night before, and nobody cleaned up the grease. The injured woman argued that the traditional rules were wrong and what really mattered was whether she had been careful while her host had been careless. But the Missouri Supreme Court, like virtually every other court that has looked at the law on this subject, refused to change the law and repeated that whether you win or not depends on why you were there.

If you're a trespasser, the only way you can be compensated is if you're willfully trapped or shot. If you're a social guest, you can recover only for failure to warn of known defects. Only if you are there on business do the usual rules of carelessness and carefulness apply.

So when you're visiting friends and relatives during the holiday season, be extra careful.

When does a boy become a man?

When a boy runs into trouble on a snowmobile, does he suddenly become a man? That was the question in a case recently decided by the Washington Supreme Court. The boy was driving one of the more than 2 million snowmobiles now in use in the United States. The snowmobile was a big one, with a thirty-horsepower engine capable of speeds up to sixty-five miles an hour.

The boy was thirteen years old and was operating the snowmobile in a mountain area in Spokane. He decided to pull some other kids on an old inner tube using a twenty-foot tow rope. As he started up, a ten-year-old girl had her thumb in a loop of the rope, and the sudden start-up tension caused the loop to tighten suddenly, tearing her thumb from her hand.

A lawsuit was brought against the boy, and the question that went to the heart of the case was the standard of care to which a thirteen-year-old snowmobile operator should be held. The trial judge in his charge to the jury said that a thirteen-year-old should only be held to the standard of care of another reasonably careful thirteen-year-old. That is, how would another child of the same age, intelligence, and maturity have acted in the same or similar situation? The girl's lawyer claimed that was the wrong standard and that when a child runs something as dangerous as a snowmobile, the child should be held to the same standard of care as an adult. The case ended up before the Washington high court.

That court reviewed the cases in the area and found there were other situations around the country that did hold that children should be treated as adults when they operate dangerous machinery. There was a Minnesota case involving a motorboat, a Kansas case involving a motorcycle, and one in Illinois involving a mini-bike. The court said that when a child engages in activity that is inherently dangerous, the child should be held to an adult standard of care. Such a rule, said the court, protects the need of children to be children but at the same time discourages immature individuals from engaging in inherently dangerous activities.

As for this case, it headed back for a new trial, and this time the jury will be told all about snowmobiles and how a boy becomes a man.

Maleficent tintinnabulation

What happens when the ringing of a church bell causes convulsions to a neighbor who suffers from congestion of the brain brought about by sunstroke? Such was the situation in a case that, as you might guess by the medical diagnosis, is about one hundred years old. The case offers us an interesting look at the law of *nuisance,* which hasn't changed very much since 1883, when Justice Knowlton of the Supreme Judicial Court of Massachusetts dealt with an appeal about the peal . . . of bells.

The plaintiff was being treated by a doctor for his sunstroke, which allegedly caused his convulsions. After making the diagnosis of "congestion of the brain," the doctor left his patient for the night, only to find him worse the next morning because of the ringing of the church bell. The good doctor went to the church sexton and explained that the plaintiff's recovery from brain congestion was being retarded by the bell ringing. The sexton took an unequivocal position, which he happily recounted during cross-examination at the trial. He said, "If a man was sick and that would kill him, I should probably not stop the bell. People are dying every day," he went on, "and I would not stop ringing the bell for my sister or my brother."

The judge noted that the defendant was the custodian of a church used for religious worship. He pointed out that the fundamental question was by what standard is someone's right to use his real estate to be measured as against the interests of his neighbor—a particular problem, the judge noted, in the densely populated cities of the late 1800s.

The judge then stated the general rule that represents the law even today. He said that it is necessary to determine the natural and probable effect of the sound upon *ordinary* persons, not "how it will affect a particular person who happens to be there today, or who may chance to come tomorrow." To buttress his decision, the judge cited the case of the man whose windows looked out on the yard of an undertaker, where all sorts of discomforting sights could be viewed. Then the court stated, "If one's right to use his property was to depend upon the effect of the use upon a person of particular temperament or disposition . . . the standard for measuring it would be so uncertain and fluctuating as to paralyze industrial enterprises."

And so the appeal failed, and the pealing continued, sunstroke and congestion of the brain notwithstanding.

Bitten by your best friend

What happens when man's best friend bites him? That was the question recently decided by the District of Columbia Superior Court. The case is best described by Judge Schwelb's opening paragraph: "The dog is known as man's best friend; nevertheless, he sometimes bites his human companion." When a woman's dog bit a man, probably neither he nor she foresaw the intriguing procedural and substantive problems the incident would present to this court.

The judge noted in a footnote attached to the paragraph that his own dog, Alfie Romeo, whom he described as the most distinguished, sociable, and upright canine with whom the court was acquainted, had on occasion nipped at a stranger's trousers.

The man sued the dog's owner for the amount of the doctor bills. But the woman didn't answer the complaint and never showed up in court. The first question for the court was whether it could order damages against a person who didn't show up. On this point, the court said that if a person defaults and does not answer a complaint, the complaint stands as proved.

But then the court had to decide whether the dog owner was legally liable to pay the doctor's bills. Just because a dog has bitten someone, that is a far cry from establishing legal liability. In common law, a dog is entitled to one bite before legal liability can be fastened on its owner.

What finally brought defeat to the woman and her dog was the fact that the District of Columbia had a leash law. Since the dog wasn't secured, whether this bite was the first bite didn't matter, since there would have been no bite if the leash law had been observed. So if you own a dog, be sure you control it and that it stays man's best friend. It's the leash you can do.

If it's one for the road

If it's one for the road, make it coffee. This could well be the moral drawn from some recent cases that have fastened legal liability on bartenders and restaurants serving more liquor to someone who's intoxicated. These cases raise some very difficult questions.

Many states have laws making it a crime to sell liquor to someone who is drunk. Massachusetts law, which is typical, provides that "no alcoholic beverage shall be sold to a person who is known to be a drunkard, to an intoxicated person, or to a person who is known to have been intoxicated within the last six months." Violation of the law carries a fine and can lead to loss of a liquor license.

But the question is, if the restaurant violates the law and the person who is served the liquor goes out and kills or injures someone in an automobile accident, can a successful suit be brought against the restaurant as well as the drunk driver? The answer is a clear yes in most jurisdictions. One case interpreting the Massachusetts law said that the statute was "undoubtedly enacted with the purpose of safeguarding not only the intoxicated person himself, but members of the general public as well."

Unfortunately, the problems don't end at this point. Suits against bartenders and restaurants are on the increase and premium charges for liquor liability insurance have more than doubled, costing the careful as well as the careless bartenders and restaurants thousands of dollars a year to protect themselves from the increasing frequency of these suits. The major problem in such cases is the great difficulty in ascertaining just how drunk a person was when he came to a restaurant or bar, how many bars he went to, and how much liquor he was served at each one. And when a jury is faced with an injured or dead innocent victim versus a bar and an insurance company, it's not too difficult to predict what the jury will do.

So bartenders and restaurateurs are being advised to be extra cautious, especially at holiday season. And someday you may have to take a Breathalyzer test when you order your next drink.

When the rescuer is hurt

Who's responsible when the rescuer is hurt? Sometimes police officers, fire fighters, and other rescuers are injured or
killed as they go about their work helping people who get themselves into trouble. Recently several courts have looked into the
question of whether the person who caused the trouble to
begin with can be held responsible for what happens to the rescuer later on.

One case involved an automobile accident in the state of Washington. A state trooper arrived at the scene and saw that one of
the drivers was in urgent need of medical attention. He put in a
call for a military helicopter and, on the way to the accident, the
helicopter crashed, killing all on board. The families of the three
men who were killed sued the driver of the car for negligently
creating the situation that led to the men's deaths.

The Washington Supreme Court said there is such a thing as
the "rescuer" doctrine, which under certain situations does
allow a person who is injured rescuing another successfully to
sue the person who caused the trouble to begin with. It must be
proved that the person who caused the peril was careless, that
a real emergency existed, and that the rescuer acted reasonably.
The families of the helicopter crew might well have collected,
except for one more element added by the court that brought
down their case. That was that the men were "professional"
rescuers, and while professional rescuers can collect under
some circumstances, their injury has to be caused by something
unusual. Since helicopter crashes are one of the well-known
risks for rescuers who pilot helicopters, the case had to be dismissed.

But in a Florida case, when a police officer arrived at an accident, he confronted an hysterical woman who told him her husband had suffered a heart attack after the accident. He tried to
get to the man, who was slumped over the wheel, but because
of other wrecked vehicles, he couldn't do it. So, with other
officers, he picked up the car that was in the way and moved it,
seriously injuring his back as he did so. The officer sued the
truck driver who had caused the accident, and won, with the
Florida District Court of Appeals holding that picking up and
moving a car was not within a police officer's normal, expected
line of duty.

So in some situations, the courts will come to the rescue of a
rescuer.

Heads up

A jury awarded thirty-nine thousand dollars to a policeman in Lahaina, Hawaii, who was hit on the head by a falling coconut. Sergeant James Walker brought the suit against Lahaina Properties Limited, alleging that the company was negligent in failing to properly maintain the coconut tree. It seems that the policeman was on patrol duty and was removing coconut fronds from a sidewalk when a coconut hit him on the head, causing him "severe and permanent physical injury and distress."

The circuit court jury found the Lahiana Properties responsible for 83 percent of the damages, presumably for not properly shaking out the misfits from its operation, but the jury reduced the damages due Sargent Walker by 17 percent because he was partly to blame for not wearing a safety helmet issued by the Maui Police Department.

Sex in the subway

When you get on the subway train, you'd better keep your hands in your pockets. That's the message from a recent New York case that got its start on a New York subway train during rush hour. Some time during the ride on the crowded train, the defendant allegedly touched a woman passenger on the buttocks. He was arrested and charged with a violation of a New York State law that prohibits sexual contact with a person's intimate parts. The law defines sexual contact as any touching of the intimate parts of a person to whom you're not married for the purpose of gratifying sexual desire.

The man's defense was that buttocks are not intimate parts as defined by law. His lawyer cited several cases that excluded the buttocks and one case that specifically held that touching someone's buttocks in a crowded subway train simply was not a crime.

But this court took a different view and said that the wording in the new law was intended to broaden, not narrow, the prohibited bodily areas. The defendant claimed that at worst he was guilty of harassment, or maybe even assault, but not sexual abuse of the woman involved. But the judge would not relent; he noted that if the charge were assault, it wouldn't stand because actual physical injury would have to be proved. As for harassment, the court said that wouldn't work because the maximum punishment for harassment was only fifteen days in jail—not enough, said the judge, if the harassment was of a sexual nature.

The judge did take into account different cultural mores. He said that if it had taken place "in an area where social mores condone the unconsented touching or pinching of the buttocks, as in Italy for example, perhaps the defendant's position could be sustained." But in this country, said the judge, the touching of a woman's buttocks without her consent is not treated as cavalierly as elsewhere.

It isn't clear what this case will do to alter behavior in the subways of New York, but don't be surprised if you soon see a sign that reads: "Buttock Bumping Will Be Prosecuted to the Full Extent of the Law."

If the paroled rapist rapes again

If the paroled rapist rapes again, who pays the victim? That was the question before the District of Columbia Court of Appeals, which handed down a decision holding serious implications for those who have the responsibility of paroling people from prison.

The parolee had a long history of assaults on women. When he was thirteen years old, he killed an elderly woman who he said had excited him sexually, and he was committed to St. Elizabeth's Hospital. Six years later, while he was on a conditional release program from St. Elizabeth's, he assaulted a female cab driver and was convicted of robbery and assault with intent to commit rape and sentenced to serve six to eighteen years. Nine years later, he was paroled and shortly afterward became a suspect in the rape-murder of a woman and the murder of her small child in Brentwood Village, a Washington apartment complex. A short time later, he quit his job, after telling his parole officer he was under suspicion in the murders.

His parole officer then helped him get a job at another complex. Not only helped—the officer also did not tell the employment counselling firm that placed the man that he was a convicted murderer and rapist; only his robbery conviction was mentioned. The man went to work as a maintenance man in an apartment complex that included dormitories reserved for women. A short time later, he entered the room of a woman resident and raped and strangled her.

Suit was brought against the parole officer and the District of Columbia, which employed him. The theory of the case was that the parole officer failed to inform those who would be hiring the parolee of his real record. It was also charged that the parole officer failed to supervise his parolee adequately.

The court recognized that there has been reluctance to hold public officials responsible for their actions, but that this was changing because of the large number of persons who could be injured as a result of the defective provision of public services. In this case, the court held the actions of the parole officer were ministerial—that is, they didn't involve policy setting, where some immunity may still remain. Therefore, said the court, he owed a duty to the dead woman to have disclosed this man's record, and, failing his duty, he caused her death.

So parole officers have got to be careful for the sake of the community, and for their own sake as well.

CHAPTER

6

LEARNING TO BELIEVE:

Schools of Thought, Thoughts on Schools, and Do we have a prayer?

At no time are the passions of a people fanned to flames more than when one ventures near its schools or its religions. The zeal with which these institutions are guarded has remained constant through the years, and whether it's burning witches in the seventeenth century or books in the twentieth, the fervor has remained. One would think that learning and praying would be quiet activities, but more havoc has been wreaked in the name of academia and religion than most other forces combined.

Schools, particularly public schools, are for the most part in more trouble than ever before in the history of the nation. Forced busing has strained the patience of many people and absorbed the time of many federal judges and the courts. Many now believe that busing is not the answer and has, in fact, led to the inverse result of what was intended and is weakening the fabric of the entire public school system as thousands have engaged in white flight and headed for the private sector. But busing is not the only problem facing the public school system: rising costs, lowered morale, and difficulties from every quarter assail it. The next few years will increasingly tax our ability to deal with the question of public and private education and the relationship between the two. It is becoming virtually impossible for people to pay large property taxes as well as large private school and day care tuitions. It is clear that in the next several years there will be mounting pressure to bridge the gulf between public and private education, particularly by those who are forced to support the one but prefer to utilize the other.

Of all our institutions, religion has remained relatively unscathed, its freedom zealously guarded by the Constitution and those charged with interpreting that document. This remains true despite the fact that some rather unfamiliar religions have sprung up of late. There is little question but that the freedom of religion must remain paramount and undisturbed, but one cannot help but wonder about some of the newer cults which claim and are accorded religious status, and whether their freedoms are not something quite different from that intended by the founding fathers. But the courts have thus far been reluctant to begin drawing lines, for fear that any line might well encompass far more than intended. One line that may perhaps become clearer and brighter in the years to come is that between commercial and non-commercial activities, and resultant tax ramifications.

Some of the cases that follow deal with the relationship between schools and religion and the continued barrier between the two. Although this barrier is necessary, one wonders if our system can indefinitely sustain a denial of state aid to private schools on the basis that many are part of religious institutions. Also, total absence of religion from schools may contribute to total absence of religion and religious values from our children.

Lastly, a word of warning—the bureaucratization and increasingly top-heavy administrative structure of many of our educational and religious institutions is cause for deep concern, and it is hoped that those in the business of belief and learning will improve their lot, on their own.

Can school drive you crazy?

Can school drive you crazy? That was one of the questions in a case recently decided by the Wisconsin Supreme Court. The case involved a former law student who claimed that law school had driven him crazy and should have to pay him $3 million in damages. The former student claimed that he had been admitted to law school and that since he was a black minority student, the school encouraged him to take some special courses taught outside the law school. One of the special courses was a mind-control course. The law school had entered into a contract with the mind-control school so law students could take a mind-control course for a low tuition fee.

The student claimed that not only did the school encourage students to take the course, but it also said the course would help students' grades in their regular courses if they went and hurt them if they didn't. The student said that under duress he began to attend the mind-control course. A few weeks later he was admitted to a mental hospital, where he remained for six months. He never could go back to law school. His claim was that the law school should have known that the mind-control course was dangerous, and that the school improperly delegated its responsibility to teach to someone else.

The court held that the former student had no case because he hadn't set forth sufficient facts. The student claimed merely that he was taught mind control, but was not taught how to control the mind control. That just wasn't enough to prove his case.

The court stated that society demands that schools perform an ever-growing number of functions and services in order to prepare the future adult for the many complexities of human life. Unless an unreasonable risk of harm was known, said the court, schools simply cannot be held liable in cases such as this.

So school may drive you crazy, but there isn't anybody you can sue if it does.

Flunking kindergarten

What can you do if your kid flunks kindergarten? Well, according to a recent case in the U.S. District Court for Eastern Pennsylvania, you can sue. The case was brought by the parents of a five-year-old kindergarten student named Vincent who, in the opinion of his kindergarten teacher, just didn't make it.

According to the papers filed in the case by Vincent's lawyers and those representing the Northern Pennsylvania School District, Vincent was absent a lot—about seventy-two out of one hundred and eighty days—and, according to the defense, Vincent sometimes had trouble concentrating, had trouble recognizing alphabet letters, and "lacked interest in the printed word." Because of all this, the school officials said that, in essence, Vincent had flunked kindergarten and had to take it over again.

Vincent's mother was quoted as saying, "I just couldn't believe that they could do something like that." She refused to send Vincent back to kindergarten and, in fact, kept him out of school altogether. Vincent's mother was then prosecuted for violating the school attendance laws. The county judge involved in that case threw it out of court, however, on the basis that "it is well settled that kindergarten is not a mandatory part of a child's education, and since a child can not be made to attend kindergarten once, he clearly can not be made to attend twice."

Vincent's mother then went on the offensive and sued the teacher, the principal, and the school board for violation of Vincent's civil rights. The defense lawyers tried to have the case dismissed on the theory that Vincent had no constitutional right to an education to begin with and that therefore to deprive Vincent of his right to go into the first grade didn't give rise to constitutional protection. But the court disagreed, citing the Supreme Court case of *Coss* v. *Lopez,* which held that a student does have a right to due process if he or she is suspended, and saying this case wasn't all that different.

So Vincent's case went to the jury and it brought back a verdict of six thousand dollars—enough to send Vincent to private school.

Understanding the *Bakke* case

What the *Bakke* case stands for and against is becoming clearer. Allan Bakke successfully sued the University of California on the basis that he'd been discriminated against because he was white. One of the most recent cases citing *Bakke* was decided by the Fourth Circuit Court of Appeals.

The case involved two University of North Carolina regulations, one of which required the class president to appoint two minority students to the campus legislative body if two were not elected in the usual course. The other regulation required that a student accused of a disciplinary infraction be entitled to have a majority of the judges be of his or her race or sex.

A group of white students brought suit claiming that the regulations were illegal because they set up a racial quota system in their student government. They claimed that white students were disqualified if the right number of minority students weren't elected. They also claimed that forcing a majority of student judges to be of the same race as the accused placed a cloud over the entire student disciplinary system.

The Court of Appeals said the *Bakke* case held that in state educational institutions race may be a consideration in fixing the rights of students, but that race cannot be the sole determination. The court said that the regulations in question had the effect of keeping white students out of the legislature and from sitting as judges solely because they were white.

The court held that the regulations imposed an artificial racial structure barring nonminority students and that "this resort to race affronts *Bakke.*" Although the purpose of the regulation was to provide protective representation, the court said its effect was to establish a racial qualification, since it relied exclusively on race to preclude nonminority students from enjoying opportunities and benefits available to others.

One judge dissented, saying that he read *Bakke* differently and that it allowed the use of racial criteria to redress wrongs in clear instances of racial discrimination. But the majority ruled, and the repercussions of the *Bakke* case are just beginning.

Bakke is back

The *Bakke* case is back again, and this time it's a law school that has failed the test. That's the result of a recent case decided by the California Court of Appeals for the Third District. The case involved the University of California Law School, which selected students on the basis of a formula. That formula included a combination of academic grades, law-school admission tests, and ethnic-minority status, which could raise low scores. It wasn't quite a quota, but ethnic background made a lot of difference.

The appeals court began its opinion commenting on the *Bakke* case. It said, "The long-awaited opinion of the United States Supreme Court in the *Bakke* case proved weak and inconclusive; instead of collectively and forthrightly addressing the Fourteenth Amendment issue, the Supreme Court Justices intellectualized themselves into decisional obscurity." The California court said the *Bakke* case outlawed the use of quotas, but sanctioned their equivalent by allowing ethnicity to be used as a factor in admissions criteria.

The California court, however, said the *Bakke* case was not the last word; while the law school's criteria for admission would probably withstand the *Bakke* test, they could not withstand a more stringent test under the California constitution. The California court said it's undeniable that the preference accorded minority applicants denies admission to nonminorities solely because of race, and gives to Indians, blacks, Philippinos, Asians, and Chicanos a special privilege it denies to all other Americans. This, said the court, violates the California constitution.

One judge dissented, saying the majority opinion offers the ideal of legal equality but the degradation of actual inequality. But the majority ruled, and in California everyone will soon be treated the same—or will they?

When the teacher won't go to school

What happens when the teacher refuses to go to school? That was the question recently decided by the U.S. Supreme Court. The case involved a teacher who had tenure but was fired because she refused to comply with the continuing-education requirement laid down by the school district. Teachers, like doctors, lawyers, and other professionals, are increasingly being required to go back to school to keep up with changes in their profession as a condition to keeping their shingle, license, or certification.

The particular teacher involved was hired in 1969 by the Harrah Independent School District in Oklahoma. She refused to comply with the continuing-education requirement and even forfeited salary raises that were withheld because of her refusal. Then the Oklahoma legislature passed a law requiring salary raises to be given whether or not teachers had complied with the continuing-education policy. Since the school system couldn't withhold salary raises any more, they fired her.

She brought suit in the U.S. District Court for the Western District of Oklahoma, claiming that the action of the school district violated due process of law and equal protection. The federal Court of Appeals agreed with her, holding that she had a constitutional right to retain her employment as a teacher and that to fire someone for not complying with continuing-education requirements was arbitrary and capricious. The school district appealed to the Supreme Court.

The High Court stated that, "While our decisions construing the equal protection and due process clause of the Fourteenth Amendment do not form a checkerboard of bright lines between the black and red squares, neither do they leave courts quite as much at sea as the Court of Appeals apparently thought was the case."

The court said this teacher was accorded both substantive and procedural rights. She had a hearing at which the board found her guilty of willful neglect of duty because she failed to go by the book when it came to her continuing-education requirement. And as far as those requirements were concerned, the court said it was a perfectly rational way to assure that students had competent and well-trained teachers.

So at least one teacher who refused to go back to school has been taught a lesson.

It's a matter of degree

Can a college refuse to grant a degree just because the man receiving it is homosexual? That was the question recently decided by the Kentucky Court of Appeals, and the answer is yes. The case involved the Lexington Theological Seminary and a man named Vance who, according to the courts, was "an avowed homosexual."

Nine months before graduation, Vance informed the dean that he was homosexual and "had been married to another man for six years." The president of the seminary told Vance there was a chance he would not be granted a degree. In May, just before graduation, the faculty recommended Vance be granted the degree. But the executive committee of the board of trustees voted not to grant the degree, and the full board of trustees ratified that decision.

Vance went to court, and the trial court ordered the degree be granted on the ground that the catalog of the school was in effect a contract, and since Vance had fulfilled all the academic and financial requirements, he should get the degree. As for the character standards mentioned in the catalog, the court said they were not expressed with sufficient clarity to become part of the contract. The seminary then appealed to the Kentucky Court of Appeals.

That court reversed the trial court's findings, saying that the portion of the catalog referring to character was not vague at all. The catalog used phrases such as Christian ministry and gospel transmitted through the Bible, and said that persons graduating must display traits of character and personality that indicate probable effectiveness in the Christian ministry. The court said, "Besides having meaning to anyone with enough intelligence to be admitted to college, we believe these words should have even greater meaning to a student who is actively seeking a degree in a religious field of study." The court also said the seminary had

a compelling interest in seeing that its graduates who went forth
with the divinity degree be persons possessing character of the
highest Christian ideal.

One judge dissented, saying that once aware of Vance's life-
style, the seminary could have expelled him, but kept on accepting his tuition instead. But the majority ruled, and while Mr.
Vance may preach about virtue, it won't be with a masters degree
from the Lexington Theological Seminary.

It's all over for all-girls volleyball

The all-girls volleyball team won't be all girls anymore. That's
the result of a recent decision of the U.S. District Court for Rhode
Island. The case involved one Donald Gomes who was a senior
in a Rhode Island public high school. Donald went to court
against the Rhode Island interscholastic volleyball league claiming he was prohibited from participating in volleyball competition solely because of his sex. All the teams in the conference
consisted only of women, and, in fact, any team that had a man
on it would be disqualified just for that reason.

Donald claimed a violation of Title 9 of the Education Amendments to the Civil Rights Act and the Fourteenth Amendment to
the Constitution. But the court found it wouldn't be necessary to
get to the Constitution, since Title 9 gave Donald all the points
he needed. Title 9 provides that no person shall be excluded on
the basis of sex from any educational program or activity receiving federal financial assistance.

The judge began his opinion noting that high school males
differed physically from high school females, particularly in their
relative ability to compete in volleyball. And he said that open
competition among the sexes would probably relegate the majority of females to second-class positions as benchwarmers or mere
spectators.

The volleyball league argued that Title 9 did not require it to
provide males an opportunity to compete on all-female teams, or
to provide separate all-male teams, because the purpose of Title
9 was to benefit women, not men. But the court found no such
intent. It said the regulations simply provide that when a school
operates a team in a sport for the members of one sex but no such
team for the members of the other sex, and athletic opportunities
for members of that other sex have previously been limited,
members of the excluded sex must be allowed to try out for the
team unless a contact sport is involved. Since athletic opportuni-

ties in volleyball had previously been limited for males, Donald had to be permitted to play on the female team.

So womens' volleyball, in Rhode Island at least, will continue to consist of all women—and Donald Gomes.

Nazis in the ROTC

What happens when a self-proclaimed Nazi wants to join the U.S. Army? That was the question recently decided by the U.S. District Court for Eastern Wisconsin. What happened was that a college student applied for enrollment in an advanced ROTC program at his college. His application was denied for a number of reasons, one of which was that he proclaimed himself to be a Nazi.

After his application was denied, he brought suit in federal court claiming that his First Amendment constitutional rights had been violated. The court said because the student had raised such an important constitutional question, it would take jurisdiction of the case rather than leaving it, as in most cases, to the military justice system.

The court began by noting that the government has a compelling interest in recruiting qualified military officers as a crucial element in the nation's defense. It also said that recruiting officers who go to the nation's college campuses are responsible for recruiting "the best qualified" students and enrolling them into the advanced ROTC program. Anyone who makes it into that program is well on the way to becoming an officer, and such a person would be leading people of various races and religions.

The court said that officers must demonstrate the ability both to lead and to gain effectively the respect of persons from diverse backgrounds. Therefore, said the court, it was proper for the recruiting officer who denied the application to take into account the student's personal beliefs and decide that the student's view on racial relations made him an unlikely candidate for a successful officer in the U.S. Army. The court did say that the First Amendment does protect a person's right to hold and disseminate political beliefs, but it does not stop the military from considering those beliefs when it chooses future officers.

So the court upheld the denial of the student's right to join ROTC, and students—or anybody else, for that matter—can proclaim themselves Nazis, but not if they want to become officers in the United States Army.

All for one

What happens when you turn your home into a school, and your child is the only pupil? That was the question recently decided by the Nebraska Supreme Court.

The case involved a couple and their thirteen-year-old daughter who were born-again Christians and who were dissatisfied with the quality of public education. They claimed that the curriculum of public schools was not religiously oriented, and so they decided to send their child to school at home. They actually built a classroom for their daughter and founded what they called an academy, with the girl's father as the headmaster, her mother as the teacher, and the child as the only student. They had textbooks, lesson plans, reading lists, problems, and tests that they secured from an out-of-state organization that supported the school-in-a-home idea.

As might be expected, the academy that the parents had founded was not approved by state education officials, and they moved against the parents for violating the child-neglect laws. The state claimed that the parents had violated the child-neglect law because that law required parents to provide proper education for the health, morals, and well-being of a child, and because these parents had failed to provide that education in a state-approved school.

The Nebraska Supreme Court disagreed and said that the state's reading of the child-neglect law simply ignored the history of that law. The court said it was clear that the legislature's intent was to help those children who, for all practical purposes, had been abandoned by their parents. The compulsory school-attendance law and the statute regarding neglect of children are not related, said the court; since a legislature must be presumed to have knowledge of all previous legislation on a given subject, if it had intended to equate nonattendance under the compulsory education laws with child neglect, it would have done so.

So at least one child will continue to go to school at home.

When a Catholic school goes public

What happens when a Catholic school goes public? That was the question in a case recently decided by the U.S. District Court for Western Michigan. The case involved a Catholic school system that, for financial reasons and other problems, decided to close its high school. As a result, six hundred children were going to be forced to enter the public school system, and the public school system had no place to put them. So the public school system decided to lease the part of the building that had been the Catholic high school. The lease was carefully drafted and provided for an annual rental to be paid, for the removal of all religious objects, and for the posting of signs designating the premises as a public school annex. The six hundred students would continue to attend classes in that building.

The case was filed by a group called Americans United for Separation of Church and State, which claimed the arrangement violated the First Amendment. First, the court said that to be upheld, a law or governmental action must have a secular and not a religious purpose; second, its primary effect must be one that neither advances nor inhibits religion; third, it must not foster an excessive government entanglement with religion.

The court said that this arrangement met the secular-purpose test, since the public school system was faced with a serious problem of overcrowding in the public schools. But, said the court, when it comes to the second and third tests, the school arrangement flunked out. The court said this arrangement did have the primary effect of advancing religion; the student body remained intact, and in reality was an entity separate from the public schools, but supported by the public school system.

In short, said the court, the state provided the greatest benefit it could bestow upon a sectarian school—the financial ability to continue its educational functions without bearing all of the costs of doing so. So Catholic students can go public, but their schools can't cross over to the other side.

Courting the devil

In these days of *The Exorcist, The Omen,* and other books and films dealing with the supernatural, it was only a matter of time before someone would try to bring a lawsuit against the devil. Well, it really happened; the case is *Mayo* v. *Satan and His Staff* and was brought in the District Court for Pennsylvania in 1971.

The case was brought in forma pauperis, which means that the plaintiff could not find a lawyer to bring the case so he decided to go it on his own. It was also brought as a class action on behalf of people everywhere who are upset with the devil. The plaintiff chose as his jurisdictional basis Section 1983 of Title 28 of the

U.S. Code, which deals with alleged violations of one's civil rights. The plaintiff alleged that Satan "has on numerous occasions caused plaintiff misery and unwarranted threats, against the will of the plaintiff, and that Satan has placed deliberate obstacles in his path and caused plaintiff's downfall and thus deprived him of his constitutional rights." And he sought a restraining order preventing the devil and his staff from further harassing him and asked for substantial damages.

"The court has serious doubts that the complaint reveals a course of action upon which relief can be granted and we question whether the plaintiff may obtain personal jurisdiction over the defendant in this judicial district." The court went on to point out that while the official reports disclose no case where this defendant has appeared as a defendant, there is an unofficial account of a trial in New Hampshire where the devil filed an action of mortgage foreclosure as a plaintiff. In that case, the defense was represented by Daniel Webster, who raised the issue that the plaintiff was a foreign prince with no standing to sue in an American court.

Last, the court noted with some serious trepidation that the plaintiff failed to include in his complaint the required form of instructions for the U.S. marshal as to how the devil could be served with a summons. And so the devil, even without counsel, emerged victorious once again.

Run over in church

What happens when a worshiper at a church revival service is overcome by religious fervor and tramples another worshiper?

That was the question recently asked of the Louisiana Supreme Court.

The case got started at a revival service held at the Shepherd's Fold Church of God. There was quite a turnout this particular night, and there weren't enough seats for all those who had come to worship. As a result, a lot of people, including a lady by the name of Mrs. Bass, were standing in the aisles when the service began. The preacher began his sermon and worked those assembled up to a fever pitch. One Mr. Fussell began running up the aisle. He ran into and over Mrs. Bass, who was standing in the aisle praying with her head bowed. Mrs. Bass was bowled over and seriously injured when she fell to the ground.

Mrs. Bass sued Mr. Fussell and the Shepherd's Fold Church of God, claiming that Mr. Fussell was guilty of heedless running in the aisle of the church and that the church was guilty of not having enough seats for its parishioners and of getting Mr. Fussell so excited.

Mr. Fussell and the church raised a number of interesting defenses. Mr. Fussell claimed he was "trotting under the spirit of the Lord" and didn't remember running into Mrs. Bass. Mr. Fussell and the church claimed that Mrs. Bass contributed to her own injury by standing in the aisle with her head down when she should have known that people were prone to running around the church during a revival service.

The court addressed all these defenses and knocked them out one by one. As for Mr. Fussell not knowing what he was doing, the court said that that could be compared to voluntary intoxication, which will not excuse a person from responsibility. Apparently, in the opinion of the court at least, trotting under the influence of the spirit of the Lord isn't very different from trotting under the influence of other spirits.

The court added that a worshiper in church has no more right to run over a fellow worshiper in the aisle than a passerby on the sidewalk. The court also said the preacher should have known that the church was just too crowded that night and that people should not have been encouraged to run through the aisle. As for Mrs. Bass, the court said that she was standing and praying quietly and could not have known that she was in imminent danger of being run over by an out-of-control fellow worshiper.

Three judges dissented, but the majority ruled, and now the courts will come to your aid if you're run over in church.

When the Old West comes to the Big Apple

What happens when a piece of the Old West is transplanted to the Big Apple? That was the question in a case recently decided by the U.S. Court for the Southern District of New York. The case was brought by a group of New York City residents who claimed they should be able to use peyote for religious purposes just like the Native American Indian Church out west. Peyote is a hallucinogenic drug, the possession of which is forbidden by federal law for anyone except the Native American Indian Church, which for years has not only used peyote for religious purposes, but has actually worshipped the drug as a god.

Well, what's good for the goose is good for the gander, claimed Alan Birmbaum, who founded the Native American Indian Church of New York. That church consisted of approximately one thousand New York residents, and while it's not related to the other Native American Indian Church, it claims to have exactly the same feelings about peyote. The question for the court was whether the exemption from the law should only apply to the original Native American Indian Church or to the Native American Indian Church of New York as well.

The court reviewed the legislative history of the Comprehensive Drug Abuse Control Act of 1970. There was concern at the time the law was passed that the use of peyote for religious purposes would be outlawed. Michael Sonnenreich, a representative of the Bureau of Narcotics and Dangerous Drugs, assured Congress that the exemption for the church would continue, because the Native American Indian Church is sui generis, the only one of its kind.

The court said that was true at the time, but what made the Native American Indian Church sui generis was the fact it was the only church around that actually worshipped peyote as a god. Now, said the court, we are faced with another group, the Native American Indian Church of New York, which also worships peyote. Therefore, it would be unfair to limit the exemption to the one group and not give it to the other. And so the Native American Indian Church will be able to use its peyote, whether it is on the deserts of Arizona or in the streets of New York City.

Hare Krishna at the airport

Hare Krishna and Sankirtan—but at the airport? If you've been traveling lately, you may have noticed an increase in members of the Krishna and other sects soliciting at airports around the country. Sometimes you may have been annoyed by their behavior as they go about performing their chanting religious ritual called Sankirtan, just as you are about to miss the 9:00 shuttle.

Well, the city of Chicago, which operates O'Hare airport, decided to do something about the Krishna. It passed an ordinance that started out broadly, proclaiming that people can distribute literature or solicit contributions in public areas at the airport. Then, in a series of subparagraphs, it listed the public areas that were excluded. These were all aircraft departure lounges and concourses leading to them, all search and security areas, all ticket counters, baggage pick-up or collection areas, washrooms, and areas leased to concessions, and any place where people stand in line.

The ordinance went on to state that, even assuming there were any public places left to solicit, no one could do so unless they registered between 9:00 and 9:30 each day with the airport manager, who had full discretion to deny the permit if he felt like it. Assuming a Krishna got by all this, he or she had to solicit in silence, since the ordinance allowed no noise; also the airport manager could suspend the solicitation at any time he wanted to because of bad weather or "emergency security measures."

The Krishnas brought suit in the federal district court, alleging that the ordinance restricted their right to free speech. The court agreed, holding that since a person of common intelligence couldn't figure out any public places that weren't prohibited, the ordinance was vague. Also, the court said that the unbridled discretion of the airport manager and the failure to define "emergency security measures" combined to make the regulations unconstitutional.

So while the court said that reasonable regulations would be permitted, regulatory overkill was not, and the Krishna won't be taking off from the airports after all.

Ask and ye shall receive—later

Asking for money is one thing; actually getting it is another. That's the message of a case recently decided by the Fifth Circuit

Court of Appeals. This was another case involving the International Society for Krishna Consciousness and its continuing battle to solicit funds at airports. This case involved the Atlanta airport, which came up with a new twist.

What the city of Atlanta did was to pass an ordinance allowing members of the group to ask for money anywhere in the airport but actually to receive the money at special solicitation booths located around the airport. If you were traveling through the Atlanta airport, a Krishna could ask you for money. If you said you were willing to give some, the Krishna could not accept it on the spot; you would have to go to a special solicitation booth where the money could be received.

The Krishnas went to court claiming the ordinance was illegal and unconstitutional. They claimed they were losing a great deal of money because by the time a prospective giver found the soliciation booth he might well have changed his mind.

The city claimed it wasn't interfering with free speech. In fact, it allowed the Krishnas to talk with people anywhere and even allowed the Krishnas to give things to the people. The only thing not allowed was the giving of money to the Krishnas. The reason the city did not allow money to be given was that noncommunicative aspects of transferring money were causing problems in the pedestrian traffic flow. The city said the fumbling through pocketbooks or wallets and searching for the right amounts of money and making change at a busy airport terminal caused congestion.

The court said the regulation did not interfere with freedom of expression because Krishnas could express their ideas wherever they wanted to. As for the reasonableness of the solicitation-booth requirement, the court said, "While we do not doubt that this is burdensome, it is not obvious that the loss is very great, and further, the benefit to the city of reducing disruption outweighs the burdens the law places on the religious practices."

So, as it is written, ask and ye shall receive, but only at the booth.

When a moose meets its maker

What happens when you kill a moose out of season, but it was because of your religion? That was the question recently decided by the Alaska Supreme Court. The case got started when an Alaskan Indian named Denor Charlie died in the village of Minto. Immediately after his death Denor Charlie's fellow villagers began the preparation of the potlatch, which is an age-old native Alaskan ritual. The funeral potlatch lasts for several days and culminates in a feast eaten after the deceased is buried.

The villagers made ready for the potlatch. The traditional meal is moose meat. Twenty-five men, including the defendant, an Indian named Frank, took off in search of moose for the potlatch. They found a cow moose, shot it, butchered it, and consumed it. Everything was just right for Denor Charlie's funeral except for one thing; moose was out of season, and Frank was charged with unlawful transportation of game illegally taken.

Frank contended he couldn't be convicted of a crime because he was engaged in carrying out a religious ritual, securing moose meat for the potlatch. The court that first heard the case decided that it was true that the potlatch was an integral part of the cultural religious beliefs of the Indians; but the judge concluded that while moose meat may be desirable, some other meat could have been used. Frank was convicted and appealed his conviction to the Alaska Supreme Court.

That court reversed the conviction and held that the free exercise of religion clauses of the First Amendment protected Frank's conduct, and that the State of Alaska did not demonstrate reasons that justified prohibiting the conduct. The court said that the evidence revealed that the funeral potlatch is the most important institution in Indian life and that food is the cornerstone of the ritual, since the deceased is thought to partake of the meat to help the spirit on its long journey. As far as the moose is concerned, the court said that moose does occupy a special place, that Alaskans perceive moose meat as the staff of life, and that there was testimony that the Indians did not want to risk showing disrespect to the dead.

One judge dissented, saying that he didn't believe that freshly killed moose meat was indispensable. But the majority ruled, and wherever Denor Charlie's spirit may travel, it will have freshly killed moose meat to eat along the way.

Can Satan be barred in prison?

Can a prisoner practice the Satanic religion—in prison? This was the question raised before the Tenth Circuit Court of Appeals, and it has to go down as one of the more unusual cases of the year. Three inmates of the Wyoming State Penitentiary filed a civil rights suit against the warden and other prison officials.

The complaint, which is the document that starts off any lawsuit, was filed pro se, which means by oneself without a lawyer. Documents filed pro se are supposed to be liberally interpreted so they don't get thrown out on technical violations of the court rules.

The complaint claimed that the prisoners weren't able to post religious information on the inmate bulletin board and that prison officials had initiated disciplinary action against one of the prisoners because he had misused state paper by writing religious information on it. It also claimed that officials had refused to permit a religious study group and had denied the prisoners the right to keep the necessary ritual items in their cells, which items consisted of candles, robes, a holy water sprinkler, parchment, incense, and a bell.

The lower court dismissed the case, chiefly on the grounds that while freedom of religious belief is absolute, the freedom of exercise is not, and the restrictions put on the Satanists were reasonable. But the lower court judge dismissed the case without hearing any evidence, simply declaring as a matter of law that religious belief wasn't involved but, rather, religious exercise.

The court of appeals did not agree, stating, "We cannot agree that on the basis of this complaint a court may declare as a matter of law that no religious belief is involved." The court added that some overt acts prompted by religious beliefs or principles are subject to some regulation, and the fact that these plaintiffs were in prison was a factor that certainly bore on the reasonableness of any regulation. But the court went on to point out that the lower-court dismissal was made before there was any assertion by the prison authorities that their actions were taken as necessary security or control measures in the prison, and without any proof that this was the case. So the case went back for further proceedings, and the Satanists may get their robes and candles after all.

7

A WORKING RELATIONSHIP:

Getting Hired, Getting Fired, and In the Middle

Perhaps the reason that there are so few strikes in many West German companies is that many of them are owned in equal shares by those who manage and run them and those who work in them. Each group knows that the best thing they can do is keep things humming, with productivity and profits as high as possible. It is unfortunate that such harmony is not always the rule in this country—indeed, it may be becoming the exception. It is difficult to assess fault: Management will say that it is the fault of the unions demanding more money and more benefits for less and less work; the unions will say that loss of productivity is the result of poor management decisions, inability to assess demand, and failure to refurbish plant and equipment. Whatever the reason, there is no question that productivity is down severely; and exacerbating the problem is the loss of harmony between employer, employee, and employee representatives.

Since 30 percent of Americans are at the top of the economic ladder, 20 percent are at the bottom (a figure common to most societies from time immemorial), and 50 percent are in the middle, it makes little sense to try to pull down those at the top in the belief that this will help those at the bottom. This is particularly true in a country that while comprising less than 5 percent of the world's population uses up more than 30 percent of the world's resources (on an annualized basis) and still owns outright more than half of the real wealth of the entire world. We ought to be able to do much better all around.

One direction in which much hope may lie is the enlargement of the pie from which we all partake. To accomplish that, we ought to begin to explore ways in which we can work together instead of sharpening the tools which drive us apart. Also, perhaps we can look to professionalizing many more jobs; if we work it right, there can be a greater measure of pride, dignity, and money (buying power) for all.

The stories that follow raise the question of whether or not the various labor relations tools, such as the NLRB and the EEOC, are serving to better the lot of the labor force of this nation or whether they are spending far more time and effort building their own nonproductice bureaucracy, hassling employers, and causing everyone to lose far more than is ever gained. There is much to be gained when employers and employees work together; perhaps they actually could if there weren't so much in between.

"Have you ever been arrested?"

"Have you ever been arrested?" is a question found on many employment application forms. If you have been arrested, you might not get the position you're looking for, even if you weren't convicted. Well, an increasing number of states are making it illegal for this question to be asked at all and in fact are passing laws that help people get "unarrested."

The process of getting arrested is now pretty well known, thanks to the hundreds of thousands of arrests made yearly in real life and on television. There is the apprehending, the conveyance to the local police station, the booking, the fingerprinting and the photographing, and the appearance in court, which may or may not be preceded by a short stay in a cell. But relatively little attention has been given to what happens if the police have made an obvious mistake in identification, or if the case is dismissed for other reasons, or if the person is simply found not guilty of the offense with which he or she is charged.

What happens to all those fingerprints, photographs, and arrest records? Well, typically, they just stay on file and become a part of a person's criminal record and can be the source of great difficulty in years ahead. And, although most states have statutes allowing only certain authorized persons to get ahold of your criminal record, prospective employers and other nonofficials are often able to get access to these records anyway.

A recently enacted New York law requires that if a person is not found guilty, every photograph and photographic plate or proof, and all palmprints and fingerprints taken, and any duplicates, must be returned to the person or the person's attorney. In addition, all arrest records are to be sealed and not made available to any person or agency, private or public. The record is available if a court orders it to be produced in a specific proceeding. The law also provides that no one can be required to give out information about an arrest and makes it unlawful discriminatory practice for any person or company to ask whether or not a person has been arrested. The only exception to this is on an application to carry firearms.

As for what happens if you run across the question anyway, the New York Civil Liberties Union has offered to provide legal aid to anyone who answers no to the question, even if the answer is a lie.

Hang-ups and the telephone company

Sex—a three-letter word that means different things to different people. Just exactly what it means was the subject of a recent decision of the Ninth Circuit Court of Appeals. The case got started when the Pacific Telephone and Telegraph Company made it clear it wasn't going to hire any homosexuals. A group of homosexuals who wanted to work for Pacific Telephone went to court, claiming that Title 7 of the Civil Rights Act prohibited employment discrimination based on sex, and that sex meant sexual preference as well as gender.

The homosexuals, all of whom happened to be male, argued that discrimination against homosexuals disproportionately affects men because there are more male homosexuals than female homosexuals. But the court refused to accept that claim, saying it was nothing more than a bootstrap argument which, if adopted, would frustrate the goals of Congress when it enacted Title 7.

The homosexuals next argued it was discriminatory to treat a male employee who preferred a male as a sexual partner differently than a female employee who preferred a male partner. Since both preferred male partners, they ought to be treated equally under the law. But the court also refused to accept that argument, stating, "Whether dealing with men or women, the employer used the same criteria; it refused to hire or promote a person who prefers sexual partners of the same sex."

But still the plaintiffs didn't give up. They said they had a viable claim under Section 1985 of Title 42 of the U.S. Code. That law, known as the Klu Klux Klan Act of 1871, was enacted to provide federal assistance to blacks in the Reconstruction South. The homosexuals argued that just like the blacks who were discriminated against back in 1871, homosexuals are being discriminated against in 1979, and the law should apply. But once again, the court said no, stating that the law only applied when there was some racial or otherwise class-based invidious discrimination, and homosexuals just didn't qualify.

One judge dissented, but the majority ruled. And the next time you run into an employee of Pacific Telephone, you can bet he won't be a homosexual. But just in case, don't keep your telephone in the closet.

When gossip costs you your job

What happens when giving gossip to the government costs you your job? That was the question in a case recently decided by the U.S. District Court for the Southern District of New York. The case got started when a young woman applied for a job as a White House Fellow. That's a very prestigious position and because it involves a close relationship with the President and the White House, extensive investigation is carried on by the Civil Service Commission and other authorities.

In this case the commission conducted a field investigation, speaking with more than thirty-five people, most of whom said very nice things about the woman; but two people told the investigators that she had engaged in petty theft while she was a college student. The commission filed its report with the Commission on White House Fellowships, and the woman was turned down. When she found out she wasn't going to be chosen, she filed a request under the privacy act seeking access to the investigative files. When she saw the statements about stealing, she asked the Civil Service Commission to delete them, because they weren't true.

The commission refused, and the woman went to court, seeking to have the court force the deletion of the information and also seeking monetary damages from the officials involved. She claimed the commission violated the privacy act by putting into her file unverified information. She claimed the commission should not have depended on just what someone told it, but should have conducted an independent examination of the facts and also given her the opportunity to refute the charges.

The court agreed with the applicant that her rights had been violated. The court said that the Fifth Amendment prohibits the government from depriving an individual of liberty without due process of law and that a person's reputation is a part of that liberty and cannot be stripped away without due process.

The government claimed that if it had to have a hearing every time someone gave information, nobody would give information any more, and that informers' privilege should protect the information. But the court did not agree, and sent the case back for further agency review and possible damages. It looks as though government files on people are going to get much thinner.

Can you be fired for quoting the law?

Can you be fired for quoting the law? That was the question in a case recently decided by the Seventh Circuit Court of Appeals. The case involved a woman who was a personnel officer for a manufacturing company. One of her duties was to answer questions about employee benefits, including specifically the employer's disability insurance program. The program covered employees for accidents or illness, but did not cover them for disability due to pregnancy.

This woman took her job very seriously and enrolled in a course at a local college. During that course she learned from a lawyer instructor that the Wisconsin Supreme Court had said an employer could no longer lawfully exclude pregnancy from its disability benefits. The woman then gave an employee a copy of the court's decision and explained that the employer's policy was completely illegal. When a supervisor asked the woman if she had in fact criticized the employer's personnel policy, she answered she had, and she was fired.

The employee sued her employer, claiming that she was fired in retaliation for merely telling fellow employees about their legal rights. Title 7 of the 1964 Civil Rights Act provides that it is unlawful to discriminate against any employee because he or she has opposed any practice which is unlawful. The employer claimed that the question of legality of pregnancy benefits wasn't all that clear, and the woman should not have been handing out court decisions that undercut the position of the employer. The U.S. Supreme Court in fact had ruled in the *General Electric* case that a disability plan did not violate the law just because it failed to cover pregnancy. But then Congress changed the law to make it unlawful to discriminate against employees because of pregnancy, and that's the present law of the land.

The appellate court said regardless of the precise legality of the situation at the time, the woman clearly entertained a reasonable belief that the employer's practices did violate the law. Further, said the court, her interpretation of the law coincided with that of the Equal Employment Opportunity Commission, three dissenting justices of the U.S. Supreme Court, and Congress. Therefore, she should be protected and not be fired for quoting the law.

Talking about tendencies

Talking about it is one thing, doing it another. That's the message of a case recently decided by the U.S. District Court for Eastern Wisconsin. The case involved a U.S. Army reservist who was discharged under a regulation that allowed the discharge of a soldier who "evidences homosexual tendencies, desire, or interest but is without homosexual acts." In other words, you don't have to commit any homosexual acts—you just have to show tendencies, and that's enough to end your army career.

This reservist was a woman who had told fellow reservists she was indeed homosexual and, in fact, admitted it to a reporter for her division newspaper and talked about it in a class she was teaching for drill sergeants. However, other than doing a lot of talking about it, there was no proof that she ever actually committed a homosexual act. In fact, the army admitted she was a capable soldier and an excellent instructor. But they discharged her anyway, and she went to court claiming violation of her constitutional rights.

The court pointed out that ordinarily courts restrict themselves in dealing with military regulations. But this regulation just could not pass muster. The court said the woman engaged in no known homosexual activity and that her homosexuality caused no disturbance except in the minds of those who chose to prosecute her. And the broad sweep of the regulation substantially impinged the First Amendment rights of every soldier to free association, free expression, and free speech.

The army argued it had to protect the national defense and maintain discipline and uphold the law of obedience under the peculiar conditions of military life. The court said it respected all of that, but it was outweighed by the chill imposed on the First Amendment liberties of soldiers.

The court said the privacy of one's personality is fundamental to the concept of ordered liberty. And so this woman will be back in drill instructor class, U.S. Army regulations notwithstanding.

Can you be fired because you're afraid?

Can you be fired because you're afraid? That was the question in a case recently decided by the Tenth Circuit Court of Appeals. The case began when three employees were directed by their supervisor to melt down four hundred pounds of lead and pour it around the base of machines to prevent vibration. The employees didn't like the job from the very beginning and liked it even less when they found out the lead they were supposed to melt down had been used by a hospital to store radioactive cobalt and radium. The employees became afraid that the lead was radioactive and refused to carry out their supervisor's orders.

The supervisor told the men that the company had been in touch with an expert on the subject the night before and had been assured that the lead was perfectly safe. The employees responded that if it was so safe, the company president should put it in writing and assume any responsibility for radioactive contamination; but the supervisor would not give such a statement and ordered them to get started with the meltdown. The men continued to refuse, and they were fired.

The employees went to the National Labor Relations Board and claimed that the company had violated the law by firing them. They claimed that they had the right under the law to be afraid and that it was illegal to have fired them because of their fear. They also claimed that their refusal with the lead was concerted protected activity. Section 7 of the National Labor Relations Act provides that employees shall have the right to engage in concerted activities for the purpose of mutual aid or protection. When the case went to court, the court of appeals said the section applied and prevented discharge even though no union activity or collective bargaining was involved.

The only remaining question was whether the men should have continued to be afraid once they had been assured by the company that the lead was not dangerous. The court agreed with the finding of the NLRB administrative law judge that it was not necessary for the employees' fear to be reasonable if, as a matter of fact, the fear was real. The court ordered the employees reinstated with full back pay.

So it may be that there is nothing to fear but fear itself, but when it comes to your job, fear of working won't lose it.

Losing your job with the FBI

Can you lose your job with the FBI just because you're a homo-sexual? That was the question recently raised before the District of Columbia Court of Appeals. The case involved a man who worked in the mail room at the FBI. He had been given a temporary indefinite appointment as a mail clerk and assumed along with all the other temporary indefinite workers that he could keep his job as long as he performed it in a satisfactory manner.

One day the employee was summoned up from the mail room into the office of a special agent and told that an investigation had resulted in his being implicated in homosexual activities. Answering specific questions put to him by the agent, the man admitted he was a homosexual, but told the agent that no other FBI employees knew about it because he had been so discreet. The employee was told he had to leave the bureau immediately and that if he didn't resign he'd be fired on the spot. The man did resign, but later went to court claiming he had submitted his resignation only because he had no possible alternative.

You might think that a government employee who has a job cannot be deprived of his job without a hearing and due process of law. But the FBI claimed that because all FBI employees are exempted from competitive civil service, they do not have the rights guaranteed to other governmental workers. The court agreed that FBI workers were different; but while they might not have full due-process rights, the FBI itself had given the understanding to its employees that they could lose their jobs only if they didn't do their jobs well, not for non-job-related reasons.

The court referred to the *FBI Handbook,* which gave employees no notice that they could be fired at will without warning for non-job-related reasons. When people come to work for the FBI, said the court, they know they're leaving civil service and all that goes with it behind, but they do not know they're expected to give up their right to fundamental fairness when it comes to whether or not they're going to keep their job.

So this employee will be back in the mail room—not quite as discreet as before, but back in the mail room just the same.

Sex in the office

Most people will agree that sex in the office is not a very good idea. The attempted violation of this immutable rule led to a recent case brought under Title 7 of the Civil Rights Act, more popularly known as the equal employment opportunity law. The facts of the case are simple, but what followed from them is the first court enforcement I've seen of the no-sex-in-the-office rule —particularly if one of the parties is not a willing participant.

The employee worked as a public information specialist for the Department of Justice, of all places. As the testimony showed, she had a good working relationship with her supervisor until she refused a sexual advance by him a few months after she'd been working there. Apparently the supervisor was rather unhappy at his rejection. Three months after she had refused the sexual advances, she was fired.

She sued under the equal employment opportunity act, which provides redress for termination of employment based on sex discrimination. Believe it or not, she lost at the administrative level because the hearing officer felt that this was not sex discrimination, but rather simply action based on refusal to grant sexual favors. The officer stated, "The female employee is in no different class from other employees in the Department of Justice, regardless of their gender or sexual orientation, who are made subject to such carnal demands."

The U.S. District Court for the District of Columbia reversed the agency, stating that while this argument was appealing, it obscured the fact that in this particular case the conduct of the supervisor created an artificial barrier to employment that was placed before women and not men. Judge Richey stated that the statute prohibits any discrimination based on sex and that it is not only the usual sex stereotypes that can give rise to an action under the law. He also noted that a finding of discrimination could be made where a female supervisor made similar demands on the men in the office, or where a homosexual sought such liberties with those of his or her own sex. He was singularly unimpressed by the argument that no discrimination could occur in the case of a bisexual supervisor who made equal demands on both sexes.

15 percent to blame

Take heart, fellow Americans. When it comes to the legal system, the grass is not always greener on the other side of the ocean. That's the message I received from reading the *Daily Telegraph,* which was one of the few English-language newspapers

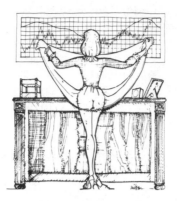

available on a recent trip to Spain. The following article appeared in the *Telegraph* under the headline, "Tribunal Rules Sexy Secretary Critics Too Prudish," and the article read as follows:

"A sexy secretary, sacked after five colleagues complained about her behaviour, was unfairly dismissed, an industrial tribunal ruled yesterday. Mr. William Cariuthers, chairman of the tribunal, said in a written opinion that office staff should not be too prudish. But, said Mr. Cariuthers, Ms. Janet Lawfer, twenty-seven, who was alleged to have flashed her french knickers and to have asked a male colleague for a quick grope, was 15 percent to blame."

I tried in vain in Spain to find out what french knickers were (I have since learned that french knickers are the complete absence of underwear) and also exactly what constituted a quick grope, but since no one spoke English and I didn't know the Spanish translation of the terms, I'll just have to let the facts as stated speak for themselves.

"Mr. Cariuthers continued, are not the persons who objected to her language and actions just being overly prudish? After all, it's not very different than showing one's operation scar, gyrating as a stripper, or showing underwear, and we cannot see a great deal wrong with that." And he ordered Ms. Lawfer rehired despite her being 15 percent to blame.

That was the last I ever expected to read about Ms. Lawfer and the case of the sexy secretary. But the next day, when I plunked down my sixty pesetas for another *Daily Telegraph,* there she was again, this time on the editorial page. The opening line of the editorial was "What Constitutes Sexy Behaviour and What Does Not." It asked, who can deny that the extent of Ms. Lawfer's alleged sexiness is a ludicrous subject for any tribunal? The editorial said the best protection for Ms. Lawfer lies not in tribunals, but within the terms of a proper contract.

Well, as for Ms. Lawfer, she'll be back at her desk. And as for me, it's good to be back in the United States, where our courts only deal with important things.

Can you keep a secret?

Can you keep a secret? If you can't, at least make sure you don't promise in writing that you will. That's the message of a case recently decided by the U.S. Supreme Court. The case raised the freedom of the press and the right to criticize the government on the one hand, and a vow of silence on the other.

The case had its beginning back in 1968, when Frank Snepp went to work for the CIA. One of the first things he had to do was sign an agreement promising he would not publish any information about the CIA, either during or after his term of employment, without the prior approval of the agency. Snepp then left the agency and wrote a book entitled *Decent Interval,* which told about certain CIA activities in South Vietnam.

The government sued Snepp, seeking to enjoin him from any future breach of the contract and claiming that any money he made on *Decent Interval* should be turned over to the government. The lower court agreed that he'd breached the agreement, but refused to order the money turned over on the ground that Snepp had a right under the First Amendment to write about unclassified information.

The Supreme Court agreed with the lower court that Snepp had broken his agreement, but disagreed that only nominal damages should be the result. The court said the agreement Snepp signed was not just an ordinary agreement, but rather it gave "life to the fiduciary relationship" and invested in Snepp the trust of the CIA. And the court said a constructive trust existed. A "constructive trust" means that even though there was no formal instrument creating a trust, a person's behavior and relationship to the injured party was such that a court could create a trust anyway. In this case, the constructive trust meant that every penny Frank Snepp earned from the book would be held for the benefit of the United States and turned over to it. The court said whether the information in the book was or was not classified did not matter.

The present director of the CIA testified that the book had seriously impaired the effectiveness of the American intelligence operation. The court said that the only appropriate punishment was to take the money. The trust remedy, said the court, simply required Frank Snepp to "disgorge" the benefits of his faithlessness. Three justices dissented, but the majority rules, and *Decent Interval* is now reaping profits for the United States.

Black women have rights on their own

Black women do have rights all their own. That's the message of a case recently decided by the Fifth Circuit Court of Appeals. The case involved a black woman who sued her employer on the grounds that she was discriminated against because she was black. She'd worked for the company for seven years, and for the last four years she'd applied unsuccessfully for various promotions. Then came a promotion she really wanted. She applied again, only to find out on the day she applied that a man had already been hired for the position. The woman concluded she was the victim of discrimination and fired off several complaints to the Equal Employment Opportunity Commission. She was then fired, and the case went to court.

The district court dismissed her case because the man who had gotten the promotion was black as well. The court said there was no question but that the woman failed to prove racial discrimination, because where a person seeking to be promoted and the person actually promoted were both black, racial discrimination could not have played a part in the failure to promote.

The woman appealed her case to the Circuit Court of Appeals. That court agreed with the district court that the claim of racial

discrimination had to fail, but disagreed with the district court on
the question of sex discrimination. The woman argued it might
well be true the company did not discriminate against blacks, and
even that it did not discriminate against women; but it was still
possible that it did discriminate against black women. The court
agreed, and said that black females have to be considered as a
class separate and apart from blacks or women in deciding
whether discrimination has occurred.

So the case was sent back for a new trial with a new and different standard for judgment. And when it comes to discrimination,
black women are truly on their own.

East, West, and women

What happens when East meets West on the subject of women?
That was the question recently raised before the U.S. District
Court for the Southern District of New York. The case got started
when a group of women secretarial employees of the Sumitomo
Shoji American Company brought suit claiming that because
they were women they were restricted to clerical jobs and not
promoted to executive positions. They claimed that Sumitomo
kept those choice positions for male employees. They claimed a
violation of Title 7, which forbids discrimination in employment
based on sex.

Now as you might imagine, when it comes to employment,
women in Japan are several steps behind their American counter-
parts, and Sumitomo Shoji is a wholly owned subsidiary of a
Japanese corporation. As its defense, the Japanese company admitted that women might not be doing so well, but there was
nothing an American court could do about it because of a 1953
treaty between the United States and Japan. That treaty provides
that "nationals and companies of either party to the treaty shall
be permitted within the territory of the other party to engage
executive personnel of their choice." Since Sumitomo preferred
men to women for important jobs, it was tough luck for the
women.

Not so fast, said the district court. "We believe an initial inquiry
must be made as to the nationality of Sumitomo Shoji," it said,
and referred to another treaty that hadn't been mentioned by the
Japanese. That treaty said if a company is incorporated in the
other country, then it's deemed a citizen of that other country.
Although all the principals and shareholders in Sumitomo were

Japanese, Sumitomo happened to be incorporated in the state of New York. Therefore, said the court, it's a U.S., not a Japanese, company; what counts for the citizenship of a company is the place of its incorporation.

Since this was an American company, American law applied on the subject of women's rights. Sumitomo pointed to a letter it had received from the State Department promising it would be able to fill executive positions with persons of its own choice. But the court said that argument was not persuasive. So women may be on the way up at last, at least at Sumitomo Shoji American.

Only men need apply

"Dear Mrs. Davis: You are an able, energetic, and very hard worker, but I have concluded it is essential that the understudy to my administrative assistant be a man." So wrote Otto S. Passman, former congressman for the Fourth Congressional District of Louisiana. When the former congressman wrote those words, he probably didn't have in mind Title 28 of the U.S. Code, which provides that federal district courts have jurisdiction in all civil actions involving more than ten thousand dollars and that arise under the Constitution of the United States.

Mrs. Davis brought suit against the congressman, claiming his conduct discriminated against her on the basis of sex in violation of the due process clause of the Fifth Amendment to the U.S. Constitution. She won in a lower court, but lost when a court of appeals held that a private right of action cannot be implied from the due process clause of the Fifth Amendment. Mrs. Davis appealed to the U.S. Supreme Court.

That court reminded us that recent cases have clearly stated there is a private right of action for damages under the Fourth Amendment to the Constitution. The court cited the case of *Bivens* v. *Six Federal Agents of the FBI*. That case held that a citizen who suffers an unconstitutional search and seizure does have a private cause of action. The court pointed out that Mrs. Davis had no other recourse at the time of her discharge, and for Mrs. Davis it was either money damages or nothing. Six months after her discharge, the House of Representatives adopted as part of its code of official conduct a prohibition against sex discrimination —a prohibition that has been branded as unenforceable by the House commission on administrative review.

The congressman also claimed as part of his defense the

speech or debate clause of the Constitution, which provides immunity for congressmen. But the Supreme Court said that was a matter that would have to be considered when the case was sent back to trial, adding, "No man in this country is so high that he is above the law."

The Chief Justice and three other justices dissented for reasons including the fact that if a congressman wants a man as his assistant, he should have that right. But the majority ruled, and it looks as though from now on even Congress will have to play by the rules.

When are you too old to serve?

When are you too old to serve? That was the question recently decided by the U.S. Supreme Court. The case involved the foreign service act, which requires persons who are covered by the foreign service retirement system to retire at age sixty. Originally the act included only career foreign service officers in the State Department, but now it includes foreign service reserve officers, information officers, and career staff in the International Communications Agency and the Agency for International Development.

A group of people covered by the law brought suit, claiming that the law violated the Fifth Amendment's promise of equal protection. The reason they claimed it was unfair was that at the time the suit was brought, other government employees did not have to retire until age seventy. And now, as a result of an amendment to the law in 1978, there's no retirement age at all for other civil servants. The foreign service people won in the lower court, where a three-judge panel agreed that the law was unconstitutional. The government appealed to the U.S. Supreme Court. That court reversed the lower court and held that mandatory retirement at age sixty does not violate the Constitution.

The court reminded us that when dealing with equal protection cases, the most important questions are whether the right being protected is a fundamental one and whether those seeking the protection are part of what is known as a suspect group—that is, a group historically discriminated against and needing special attention from the courts. The court said that the right not to retire was certainly not a fundamental right and that foreign service personnel were not a suspect group.

The court said that in the absence of a fundamental right or a suspect group, courts are reluctant to overturn actions of Congress and that "the Constitution presumes that even improvident decisions will eventually be rectified by the Democratic process." The court agreed with the government's claim that it might be rationally assumed that the law would assure professional competence, as well as mental and physical capability and more opportunities for promotion.

Justice Marshall dissented on the ground that the policy was unfair to older employees and was not rationally related to overseas work. But the majority ruled, and if you're in the foreign service and you hit sixty, you'll just have to pack it in and come home.

If your boss drives you crazy

If your boss overworks you until you have a nervous breakdown, can you recover? That was the question recently decided by the Arizona Supreme Court. The case involved a woman who worked for an insurance agency. She was described by the court as a conscientious employee and a perfectionist, and she began having a lot of trouble keeping up with her work. The agency involved had about four hundred thousand accounts. A normal growth rate would have meant that such an agency would pick up about forty thousand new accounts each year; but this agency picked up eight hundred thousand new accounts in one year, and that caused a lot of extra work for and pressure on the employees who had to service the accounts.

One day the plaintiff just couldn't stand it any more and left the office after breaking into tears, following what the court described as an emotional telephone conversation with a client. She went home, took an overdose of sleeping pills, and was admitted the next day to a mental hospital, where her condition was diagnosed as a nervous breakdown.

The woman claimed she was disabled and asked for benefits under the Arizona Workmen's Compensation Act. Workmen's compensation acts are present in just about every state and make it easier for an employee to collect damages for accidents on the job. The question for the court was whether a nervous breakdown caused by overwork could be considered an industrial accident. The company claimed in order for Workmen's compensation to be paid, there must be an unexpected injury caused or accompanied by physical impact or exertion.

The Arizona Supreme Court held the nervous breakdown was compensable. As far as being unexpected, the court said the woman's mental breakdown resulting from too much work was unexpected and thus accidental. As far as the need for physical impact or exertion, the court said that strain and worry were enough, and physical impact or exertion weren't the only things that counted.

One judge dissented, saying what really brought about the breakdown was stress caused by her husband's drinking, her difficulty in relating to her daughter, and her mother's death— not her job. But the majority ruled, and if your boss overworks you until you have a nervous breakdown, recovery may be just around the corner.

And on the seventh day he rested

Can your boss force you to work on Saturday? The end result of recent action taken by the U.S. Supreme Court is no, as long as the reason you don't want to work is related to your religion. The action taken by the Supreme Court, however, was less than a clear statement on the issue, since it was a four-to-four decision. That means the lower court ruling stands.

The case involved an employee of a rubber seal company who was a member of the Worldwide Church of God, which forbids work on the Sabbath, which in that religion runs from sundown Friday to sundown Saturday. The plaintiff testified that shortly after joining the church, he told the plant foreman that he couldn't work on Saturdays and the foreman said okay, as long as it didn't cause any problems. A short time later the foreman told the employee that a number of complaints had been made by another supervisor about the employee not working on Saturdays. The foreman then fired him.

The district court that first heard the case held that it was just too difficult for the company to accommodate itself to the no-Saturday work requirements of the plaintiff. At issue was a regulation of the Equal Employment Opportunity Commission that said that the duty not to discriminate on religious grounds includes an obligation on the part of the employer to make reasonable accommodations to the religious needs of employees.

The appeals court found that the real reason the person was discharged was the company's fear that it would have potential problems with other employees who resented the fact that one of

their number didn't have to work on Saturdays. The court also
did not accept the company's argument that the regulation fostered religion by allowing a person to go to church on Saturday
instead of going fishing. So you don't have to work on Saturday
as long as it's for the right reason.

A uniform appearance

Women have to wear uniforms, but men can dress any way they
please. That order was the subject of a recent case decided by the
Seventh Circuit Court of Appeals. The case involved a savings
and loan association that required all of its women employees to
wear uniforms. Men could wear anything they wanted as long as
it fell "within the range of ordinary business attire." Not only did
the women have to wear uniforms, but the savings and loan
association treated the cost of the uniform as income to the
women and withheld income tax based on the value of each
uniform.

The women employees went to court claiming they were being
discriminated against on the basis of sex and forced to wear
uniforms while men were not. The Court of Appeals found that
the order requiring women to wear uniforms was a violation of
Section 703 of the 1964 Civil Rights Act. That act makes it unlawful for an employer to discriminate against any individual with
respect to the terms or conditions of employment because of the
individual's race, color, religion, sex, or national origin.

The company produced evidence that some of the women
actually liked wearing the uniform, that it made their day sim-
pler, and that even though it was treated as income, it was a lot
cheaper in the long run than having to buy new clothes all the
time. But the court said that was immaterial, and it didn't help
any that some of the women being discriminated against didn't
object.

The court pointed out that other cases had upheld reasonable
regulations such as male employees having to wear a tie. The
court said the employers could promulgate different personal
appearance regulations for men and women as long as they were
reasonable regulations based on commonly accepted social
norms. However, forcing women to wear uniforms crossed over
the line.

One judge dissented, claiming that the majority opinion ignored the fact that men's customary business attire has never

really advanced beyond the status of being a uniform. But the majority ruled, and the women will be free to wear what they please to work. As for the men, it's customary business attire all the way.

Suffering sexual harassment in silence

If you quit because of sexual harassment on the job, can you collect unemployment? That was the question in a case recently decided by the Pennsylvania Commonwealth Court. The case involved a woman who for three years was annoyed by "sexual insinuations" and momentary physical contacts habitually made by her office manager. The woman finally quit and applied for unemployment compensation. Pennsylvania law, like that of most states, provides that if a person voluntarily terminates employment without a compelling cause, unemployment compensation will not be paid.

The question for the court was whether what happened in this case forced the woman to leave, in which case she would be paid, or whether she left voluntarily, in which case she wouldn't.

The court said without question, the woman's termination was prompted by repeated sexual insinuations and physical contacts. But, said the court, the record also indicated that the woman had not used common sense. In three years she had made only one attempt to report the situation to the owner of the company. It is true, said the court, that on that one occasion the owner had said he was too busy to see her, but the court said she should have tried again.

The court admitted that the problem of job-related sexual harassment is a difficult one, but when it comes to unemployment compensation, an employee has to make a reasonable attempt to stay on the job, and this woman didn't. So if you are sexually harassed on the job, yell out loud and clear. It may save your dignity, your job, or at least your unemployment benefits.

Death in the line of duty

Can you discriminate against a heart attack? That was the question in a case recently decided by the Minnesota Supreme Court. The case involved a Minnesota law providing that fifty thousand dollars would be paid by the state to the spouse and children of a peace officer killed in the line of duty. All peace officers were covered and all causes of death were covered except one, a heart attack.

This case involved a fire fighter who died of a heart attack while fighting a fire. There was no question that he qualified as a peace officer, since fire fighters were specifically defined as peace officers under the law, and there was no question that he died in the line of duty. But his widow and children were to receive nothing because, as in many states, heart attacks are exempted from the law.

The fire fighter's family went to court, claiming that to deny benefits to a peace officer killed in the line of duty by a heart attack was discriminatory and violated the equal protection clause of the Constitution. The court said that to withstand an equal-protection attack, a law has to apply uniformly to all who are similarly situated and that if there are distinctions in the law, there must be genuine and substantial reasons for those distinctions. Also, these distinctions have to be relevant to the purpose of the law.

The court noted that there was medical testimony in the case saying that the same stress that triggered the heart attack could have caused respiratory failure or stroke, and if it had, the state would have paid; but since the stress caused a heart attack, there was no recovery for the wife and children. The court concluded that there was no reason to distinguish between heart-attack victims and victims of the same stress who die in other ways. The court said that such a distinction subverted the purpose of the law, which was to provide additional benefits to dependents of peace officers because of the unusual risks such officers face in their work.

So in Minnesota at least, a heart attack may stop a peace officer, but it won't stop his wife and kids from getting some help after he's gone.

Leaving work for good

What happens when you leave work to go to a labor hearing after your boss told you not to? That was the question recently decided by the District of Columbia Court of Appeals. The case involved the Service Employees International Union, which demanded recognition as the bargaining agent for the employees of a warehouse. The union also filed a petition with the National

Labor Relations Board, and a hearing was scheduled by the NLRB on the question of representation.

The day before the hearing the manager of the warehouse assembled all sixteen of the warehouse employees and read a statement refusing them permission to attend the hearing because attendance by all would completely disrupt business for the day. The statement also said that one of the employees would be permitted to leave to attend the hearing in a representative capacity; but the next day thirteen of the sixteen employees left to go to the hearing, virtually shutting down the warehouse, which lost thirty-nine hours of work. When the employees came back, the manager fired them all. The now-former employees filed an unfair labor practice charge with the NLRB.

The NLRB found the employer guilty of unfair labor practices, holding that an employee has a protected right to attend an NLRB hearing. The company appealed to the District of Columbia Court of Appeals, which reversed the NLRB. The court said first, the NLRB wasn't following its own prior cases in the area, citing a case in which the NLRB upheld the firing of two employees (out of 195) who had attended a hearing without permission. The court also said that to uphold the NLRB decision in this case would result in complete disruption of an employer's production activities and that we must bear in mind that "working time is for work." Unless the employee can demonstrate compelling reasons, the employer's right to maintain normal operation should and does take precedence over the employee's right to leave work during regular working hours.

One judge dissented, saying the court exceeded its limited powers of review of agency action. But the majority ruled, and the next warehouse worker hired will have to work and send a representative to the hearing, instead of attending the hearing and leaving a representative to do the work.

Temporary employment is temporary

It may be very wrong, but there isn't much we can do about it. That's the message of a recent case decided by the Indiana Court of Appeals in a case that teaches us that while perhaps there ought to be a remedy for every wrong, there often isn't. The case involved what is known as an employee at will. That's where you get a job without a contract, and it's pretty clearly understood that you'll have the job only as long as your employer wants you around.

In the case that ended up before the Indiana court, an employee at will was fired, but not because there was no work or because he wasn't doing the job well. He was fired because he turned in a supervisor who was demanding kickbacks from him for his having the job to begin with. Because he blew the whistle, he was fired.

The court began its opinion stating that the general rule is that either party may terminate a contract at will or without cause at any time. The court looked at cases throughout the nation that dealt with whether employees at will can or cannot be fired. One case reinstated employees who were fired as a punishment for claiming workmen's compensation benefits after they were injured. Another case provided that people could not be fired for complying with legal requirements, like jury duty, or for refusing to commit perjury on behalf of an employer. But when it came to relief for non-legal reasons, the only winner was a woman who was fired because she refused to go on a date with her foreman.

The court concluded that to fashion a remedy based solely on public policy and to grant damages solely on the basis of public policy, all without any law serving as a foundation, was just too much. Relief in such situations it said, was a matter for the legislature, not for the courts. And so it looks like all's fair in love, war, and temporary employment.

Wearing your wares

How would you like to be able to deduct from your taxes the cost of clothes you wear to work? That was the question recently raised before the United States Tax Court. The case involved a woman who worked in a boutique that specialized in the sale of very fancy clothing, the kind with initials all over it. The woman liked to wear jeans, but when she came to work she was required to wear the initialed clothing because, according to her employer, if you're going to sell it, you've got to wear it. And the woman had to pay for the fancy clothes herself since, as in most places, it was not furnished as a part of her salary or compensation.

The woman claimed that since she had to wear the clothing to work ·and would not ordinarily have bought the clothing, she should be able to deduct the cost of it as a business expense.

The tax code itself is clearly in conflict on this question. On the one hand, Section 162 of the Internal Revenue Code permits a deduction for business expenses, but Section 262 of the Code disallows the deduction for personal living or family expenses, and clothing is usually considered to be personal.

The Commissioner of Internal Revenue argued that the determination had to be made on the basis of objective standards, rather than on the basis of the taxpayer's individual life-style. But the court agreed with the woman, saying that there was precedent for life-style to be taken into account. The court said that while the dramatic, highly fashioned and avant-garde apparel that the taxpayer wore might be used by some members of society for general purposes, it was not the type worn by most women generally, and its cost greatly exceeded the price the taxpayer would ordinarily have paid for her clothes.

So under certain circumstances, you may be able to deduct the cost of clothes you wear to work. I'm still trying to find a rule on three-piece suits.

Eating on the job

When you have to eat on the job, who decides how much you're going to have to pay for your food? That was the issue recently decided by the U.S. Supreme Court. The case involved a suit against Ford Motor Company brought because Ford refused to enter into collective bargaining with the union as to how much food on the job was going to cost.

The case got started at a Ford automobile stamping parts plant in Chicago Heights, Illinois. The plant employed thirty-six hundred production employees, who were paid by the hour. An independent caterer provided the food, but Ford had the right to review its quality, quantity, and price. The problem came when

Ford notified the union that the price of food was going up.

The union first announced a complete boycott of food services, but the boycott failed when more than 50 percent of the employees decided they would rather eat than fight. The union then filed an unfair labor practice charge with the NLRB alleging refusal to bargain contrary to the National Labor Relations Act. That law provides it shall be an unfair labor practice for an employer to refuse to bargain in good faith with respect to wages, hours, and other terms and conditions of employment. Ford argued that food prices and services should not be considered terms and conditions of employment because they did not vitally affect employment and because they were trivial matters over which neither party should be required to bargain.

The Supreme Court noted that it was extremely difficult for employees to eat away from the plant during their shifts, since the lunch period was only thirty minutes long and the restaurants were all over a mile away. The court also noted that some workers brought food to work, but since there were no refrigerated storage facilities provided, spoilage and vermin had become a real problem, particularly in the summer. The Supreme Court said common sense tells us that even minor increases in the cost of meals can amount to a substantial sum of money over time. And the court accepted the NLRB's view that in-plant food and services were conditions of employment and subject to collective bargaining.

So union and management will soon be sitting down at the bargaining table to figure out how much sitting down at the lunch table is going to cost.

From full-service to fast-food

When you convert from a full-service restaurant to a fast-food cafeteria, you'd better check it out with your employees first. That's the message of a case recently decided by the Seventh Circuit Court of Appeals. The case involved a restaurant and a motel that were part of a large franchise chain. The restaurant was a full-service restaurant, including table service provided by six waitresses.

The problem was that business wasn't very good, and faced with declining food sales, the employer decided to convert the restaurant. He laid off kitchen employees and waitresses without notifying the union that he was going to make the change. A few days later the restaurant reopened as a cafeteria, the kitchen staff was rehired, and the waitresses received formal notice of their termination.

The waitresses complained to the NLRB that the union should have been consulted before the change was made. They also said that going from full-service to self-service should have been the subject of collective bargaining because it fell within "the terms and conditions of employment." The NLRB agreed.

The employer appealed to the Court of Appeals. The court agreed with the traditional position of the NLRB, which is that in all circumstances except when an employer has decided to shut down completely, the decision to terminate a position or any part of a business must be the subject of collective bargaining.

The employer argued that he made the change as a matter of economic survival and therefore should not be held to have violated the law. But the court said to force bargaining in such a situation would promote the basic purpose of peaceful settlement of labor disputes, and to further require the employer to bargain about the conversion would not significantly abridge his freedom to manage his own business.

So if you want to keep up with the times and go from full-service to fast food, you might find the going a lot slower than you'd planned.

The Yellow Bird Express

What happens when a group of nurses turns a patient into the "Yellow Bird Express"? That was the question for the First Circuit Court of Appeals in a case that involved a hospital, a group of nurses who were active in a union, and the National Labor Relations Board.

The case got started when a patient was admitted to the hospital with a diagnosis of infectious hepatitis. As the nurses were preparing him for surgery, they decided a little horseplay was in order, and so they dressed the patient in a yellow gown with the words "Yellow Bird Express" lettered on the front. They decided something else was needed, so they put a brown plastic bag on the patient's feet, a surgical mask on his face, and a plastic shower cap on his head. Then they took off down the hall singing, "Here Comes the Yellow Bird Express."

All went well till they came around a corner and ran into the patient's wife, who didn't think the whole thing was very funny, followed next by the operating-room nursing supervisor, who saw absolutely no humor in the situation at all. And when the hospital administration heard about the "Yellow Bird Express," the nurses were promptly fired. As for how the patient felt about all this, there was some question; the nurses said that he joined in the fun, but the patient's wife said that he was drowsy and that when she saw him he didn't seem to be enjoying himself at all.

The nurses appealed their firing to the National Labor Relations Board, claiming they were really fired for their union activities, not for horsing around. An administrative law judge who heard the case agreed with the nurses and ordered their reinstatement. He said it wasn't necessary that the union activities be the *sole* reason for firing, but that if the firing was even partially caused by the union activities, the nurses had to be reinstated.

The hospital appealed the case to the First Circuit Court of Appeals, and that court reversed and held that the termination of the nurses was proper. The court said that while the union activities probably didn't make the nurses very popular with the hospital administration, they wouldn't have been fired but for the horseplay. As for the horseplay itself, the court said the "Yellow Bird Express" was bound to raise serious doubts with patients and other hospital personnel as to the quality of nursing care at the hospital. So it doesn't pay to fool around—especially if you're active in the union.

What's mine is yours, unless it's your mine

What's mine is yours, but what if the mine is mine and not yours—does it make any difference? That was the question in a case recently decided by the Fourth Circuit Court of Appeals. The case involved the question of federal benefits paid for black lung disease and whether they can be paid to a miner who happened to own the mine.

A few years back Congress made miners who contracted black lung disease eligible for special federal funding. The disease, the formal name of which is pnumoconiosus, is widespread among the nation's coal miners, and Congress wanted to help those miners affected by the disease. The problem came over the definition of a miner. The Department of Health and Human Services (that used to be HEW before education was taken out) issued a regulation that said a person could only be considered a miner if he worked in the mine as an employee of a mining company. If he worked as a miner in a mine that he owned or that was owned by a closely held corporation of which he was one of the principal shareholders, he didn't qualify for the benefits.

One miner who was denied the benefits went to court, claiming that what mattered was whether you got black lung disease from working in a coal mine, not who owned the coal mine. The government argued Congress had simply not included those who were part of the ownership and that such people needed the protection of the law less since they were part of the ownership.

The court disagreed, saying the opposite was the case—that where people worked as employees for a large mining company, they might well be treated better than the small self-employed miner. In any case, the court said it was clear that Congress meant to include the self-employed as well as the employee, even if it was less than artful in the way it drafted the original law. And the court set aside the regulation giving the shaft to the self-employed miner.

One judge dissented, writing that if you are part of the ownership of the mine, you can decide what your role in the production will be and can control your own destiny. But the majority ruled, and you'll be able to get black lung benefits even if the mine is yours.

CHAPTER

8

SMALL, MEDIA, AT LARGE:

New Wrinkles in the Press, on the Screen, and in the Air

It is doubtful that the relationship between the law and the press has ever been at a lower ebb than now. The jailing of reporters for refusing to identify sources, decisions of the U.S. Supreme Court allowing search of newspaper offices (recently restricted by an act of Congress) and allowing interrogation of reporters in order to prove malice, are just a few examples of the recent clashes between the courts and the press.

The freedom of the press must not be impinged upon by the courts. Reporters must be able to protect the sources of their information, lest they not receive sensitive information at all.

However, just as there should not be external constraints placed upon the press, so should there be much improved policing of the press by itself, and, more important, by each individual member of the press. Being a member of the press is often a thankless job; the constant deadlines, the difficulty of obtaining reliable information, and other factors give rise to much frustration that is often met with biased, partial reporting in return. The press must use its power fairly, objectively, and with care. Unearthing dishonesty is very different from destructive reporting for its own sake. Tearing down is one thing, but sometimes people might also like to know when a job is well done. The press itself should be on the look-out for the biased reporter who hides behind the cloak of impartial journalism. Such a reporter knows that if his victim complains of unfairness, he or she is written off as a crank and there is no place to go.

This chapter also deals with other fundamental rights which are often in collision, such as the right of privacy and the right to know, and the question of just when a person sheds the skin and protection of a private person and assumes the nakedness of a public person, for whom there is very little protection from the spotlight.

And more changes are coming. The deregulation that has come to the airline industry is on its way to the communications industry. Clear channel stations are vulnerable, new networks will be born, and the battle over how and by whom America will be wired with cables is sure to keep lawyers and the courts busy for many years to come.

One thing is clear, however, the courts and the press are among the most important safeguards of our personal freedoms and it is essential that we begin to solve the many problems that have caused the law and the press to turn against one another instead of working together to protect our privacy and keep us informed.

Dracula is back

Dracula has come back from the grave, but he's lost again. That's the result of a case recently decided by the California Supreme Court. The case had its beginning back in 1920 when Bela Lugosi and Universal Pictures entered into an agreement for the production of the film *Dracula,* in which Lugosi played the title role.

Lugosi died in 1956, and Universal continued to use his picture in advertising and also licensed the use of the Count Dracula character. In 1972 Bela Lugosi's widow and son went to court claiming they were Lugosi's heirs and were thus entitled to all profits made from Lugosi's name after his death. Moreover, they said, they should be able to control the Count Dracula name.

The trial court that first heard the case found in favor of the widow and son on the basis that the essence of the thing being licensed by Universal was "the uniquely individual likeness and appearance of Bela Lugosi in the role of Dracula." The thing that influenced the trial court the most was that even though other actors such as Lon Chaney were playing the role of Dracula, what was used in all the advertising and merchandising was the likeness of the original Count Dracula, Bela Lugosi himself.

But Universal appealed and the California Supreme Court drove a stake through the heart of the trial court opinion and reversed the case. The high court pointed out that Dracula was around even before Bela Lugosi. The character first appeared in 1897 in the novel *Dracula,* written by Bram Stoker, and since

Stoker didn't copyright the book, Dracula is in the public domain and belongs to us all.

It's true, said the court, the law does say if a person ties his name, face, or likeness with a business, product, or service, that can be protected by law. This is where Lugosi's case began to sink back toward the grave, since a right of value is embraced in the law of privacy and only protectable during a lifetime. It does not survive death.

Judge Mosk, concurring, said, "Not unlike the horror films that brought him fame, Bela Lugosi arises from the grave twenty years after death to haunt his former employer." Chief Justice Byrd was the only dissenter, saying that Lugosi's image was so impressed on the public's memory that Universal ought to have to pay when it continues to use that image after death. But the majority ruled, and Dracula is back in the grave, at least temporarily.

Ralph Nader wins again

It may be that Ralph Nader just can't lose. That's the result of a recent case decided by the District of Columbia Court of Appeals. The case involved an article written about Nader by a columnist named Ralph DeToledano. The article was critical of Nader and his opposition to the development of nuclear power as a source of energy for the United States. To build his case that Nader wasn't to be trusted or believed, DeToledano referred back to Nader's involvement in the Corvair automobile controversy. Nader had charged that General Motors had suppressed evidence about design flaws in the Corvair which, he claimed, caused it to flip over and burst into flames with great regularity. Nader had also charged that GM officials had made false statements before a Senate investigating committee.

Nader's charges were thoroughly investigated by Senator Abraham Ribicoff over a two-and-one-half-year period. A Senate report was issued saying there was no substantiation for Nader's claims, but that the committee believed that Nader's charges were made in good faith based on the information available to him. DeToledano wrote that Nader falsified and distorted evidence to make his case against the automobile, and he left out or ignored what the Senate had said about Nader's good faith. Nader sued DeToledano for libel.

The general rule is that when a journalist writes something bad about a public figure, the public figure has to present clear and convincing proof of actual malice in order to prevail. Ordinarily that's impossible, and the public figure loses even before the case gets to trial.

But not Ralph Nader. The court found that the presence of a sentence in the Senate report that said Nader acted in good faith and the absence of that sentence in the DeToledano column meant that a jury could very well find that DeToledano was acting maliciously. The court said the case should not have been dismissed and sent it back for a full jury trial.

One judge dissented vigorously, saying the majority of the court had injected confusion into an area of the law that had previously appeared clear to virtually every court that had confronted it. And the judge said that anyone who is familiar with Senate reports and how voluminous they are would know you could never impute malice because a sentence appearing in such a report was omitted from a newspaper column. But the majority ruled, and Ralph Nader is still riding high.

A human cannonball's right to privacy

Does a human cannonball have a right to privacy? The Ohio Supreme Court had occasion to answer this question and the result was of importance not only to other human cannonballs, but also to the rights of news media to cover various events.

The facts of the case are interesting. As the court stated, "The plaintiff performs the feat of being shot from a cannon into a net some two hundred feet away. The entire performance lasted about fifteen seconds and was staged in an open grandstand area and could be seen without an extra admission charge by anyone attending the fair."

The problem came when one of the blasts was videotaped by a local TV news station and shown on the nightly news, as a feature on how various people spent their time in this particular community. Following the single news telecast, the performer brought suit against the TV station for invasion of privacy, contending that the TV station had appropriated his professional talents for its own use without his permission.

The case raised the questions of just what kind of privilege the news media has to invade privacy and if that privilege was abused in this particular case. There is little question but that appearing on the nightly news without your consent is a violation of your privacy, and we have all seen film clips of somebody trying to prevent himself from being seen on the 11:00 news.

The United States Supreme Court in the landmark case of *Time, Inc.* v. *Hill* set down the general rule, which is that the constitutional protections for speech and press prevent successful actions against the news-reporting media unless it can be proved that the media published or printed something which it *knew* to be false, or in reckless disregard of the truth. This means that the press has the privilege to report matters of legitimate public interest, even though these reports intrude on what might otherwise be private behavior.

As for the human cannonball, one can only say he lost this round, and his only recourse is to be shot from guns in his own apartment.

Can television drive you crazy?

Can television drive you crazy? That was the question recently decided by the Florida District Court of Appeals in the case of *State* v. *Zamora*. Ronnie Zamora was a fifteen-year-old boy who was convicted of the fatal shooting of an eighty-two-year-old woman, his next-door neighbor. The woman had discovered him and a friend burglarizing her home, and Ronnie shot her with a gun she had in her house and then escaped in her car. A few days later he confessed to the crime. And then the case of *State* v. *Zamora* became something quite different from just another murder trial.

The defense that Ronnie's lawyer put forth was that he was insane at the time of the crime and that his insanity was caused by "involuntary, subliminal television intoxication." In short, he claimed he'd been driven crazy by television. Evidence put forth at the trial included the fact that Ronnie was a confirmed TV addict who watched television at least six hours a day and who even refused to eat unless the television was on. There was testimony that he was such a "Kojak" fan that he asked his father to shave his head so he'd look more like Telly Savalas. The defense also included the fact that the crime itself was similar to recent episodes of "Kojak" and a Dracula movie that Zamora had watched the night before the murder. But after all the evidence was in, the jury refused to accept the defense and returned a verdict of guilty of murder.

It was somewhat ironic that the trial itself was televised and was the first such trial to be shown on television under a trial program of making justice more accessible to the public. Following the trial, Ronnie's lawyer appealed the case, claiming that the trial judge had made a reversible error by prohibiting a defense psychologist from testifying at the trial as to the effect of television violence on adolescent viewers. But the court said since the psychologist was not prepared to testify that television destroys the ability to distinguish between right and wrong, her testimony was properly excluded. The lawyer also claimed the judge had erred by failing to allow him to inquire into TV-viewing habits of prospective jurors, but the appellate court said the trial judge acted within his discretion.

The appeals court also commented on a concluding statement in Ronnie's appellate brief that read: "Television was on trial and the trial was on television." The court said this was simply not the case; television was not on trial—Ronald Zamora was on trial for the senseless slaying of an elderly woman.

Dialing for dollars

Dialing for dollars may add up to a lot of trouble. That's what a Utah television station found out when it got sued by a woman who said what she thought about the station's programming. The case involved a gimmick that radio and TV shows use to encourage more listening and watching. This particular station had a program called "Dialing for Dollars"—throughout the day telephone numbers would be selected at random from the phone book, and if the person called was watching the show at the time, he or she got all the money in the kitty.

On this particular day the program emcee called a lady who lived in Salt Lake City and had the following conversation. He started by saying, "This is 'Dialing for Dollars'—do you have your TV set on?" She answered, "No, I don't." He said, "That's unfortunate, because you could have won fifty dollars," and she replied, "Well, I'll tell you; I would rather have peace in my home than all that garbage on television, even for fifty dollars." And that was the end of the conversation but the beginning of the trouble, because what the lady didn't know was that her name and telephone number had been broadcast to all the viewers before the call was made, and the call itself was broadcast live.

The result was that after the call was completed, a lot of viewers who didn't like the implication that they liked watching garbage began calling the woman; only they didn't offer money—they gave obscenities. In fact, according to the court, the plaintiff received calls all afternoon from all over the state of Utah from people who used "rude, abusive, obscene, and threatening language." All of this caused the plaintiff to be embarrassed and humiliated and to fear for her personal safety and well-being.

The woman and her husband sued the station for invasion of privacy, abuse of their personal identity, and violation of a Utah law that prohibits using a person's name or identity for commercial purposes. In short, the plaintiffs claimed their name and number were used without their knowledge and consent for the purpose of advertising the station, and the Utah Supreme Court agreed. That court reversed a lower court, which had held that the woman waived her right of privacy and invited people to call her residence by having her name and phone number published in the telephone book.

So radio and TV stations, beware—when you dial for dollars you may find that giving away money can be very costly indeed.

Cable TV—who will wield the power?

Cable TV—a setback for the government. That's the result of a recent decision of the U.S. Supreme Court. The case began back in 1972 when the Federal Communications Commission adopted some rules saying that a cable TV system serving more than thirty-five hundred customers must have a capacity of twenty channels, four of which must be devoted to public educational or local government use. The rules also said that the decision of what was to appear on the public channels was to be made by those who had access to the channel, not by those who operated the cable TV system.

This was the second time that the issue of cable TV made it to the Supreme Court. The first case dealt with the question of whether the FCC had any jurisdiction at all over cable TV, and the court held by the narrowest of margins that it did. Those early rules required that the cable system originate a lot of its own programming, in addition to just carrying programs from far away. In that case the Chief Justice, while siding with the majority, said, "The rules strained the outer limits of the commission's jurisdiction."

This time a majority of the court held that the FCC had gone too far. What particularly bothered the court was the fact that not only were four out of twenty channels reserved for public access, but the decision of what was to be broadcast over those channels was taken out of the hands of those who operated the cable system and placed in the hands of the public. What this did, said the court, was to take cable TV and reduce it to the status of a common carrier, which was against the law. The court said that through the years, although limited control has been exercised (such as requiring equal time for political controversy), basic control of programming has remained with the broadcasters.

Justices Marshall, Stevens, and Brennan dissented, writing they would have supported the FCC, since the rules increased the number of outlets for community self-expression and augmented the public's choice of programming. But the majority ruled, and while the public will still have a voice in what comes over the cable, it won't be the FCC that controls the volume.

When there is no more room in hell

When there is no room in hell, the dead will walk the earth
. . . and it looks as though the first stop will be the courtroom.
That's the message of a case just decided by the U.S. District
Court for the Northern District of Illinois. The case involved two
horror films, one an old stand-by and the other in the making.

Night of the Living Dead is a horror film that's been around since
1968. It was based on a screen play by George Romero, with the
copyright owned by Dawn Associates. What caused the lawsuit
was that George Romero had written a script for another movie
that was supposed to be called *The Messiah of Evil,* but after being
transferred to another company, it was renamed *Return of the
Living Dead.*

George Romero and Dawn Associates claimed that the other
company, called The Messiah Company, had represented the
new film as a sequel to *Night of the Living Dead* and had used
identical promotional material to advertise it, including the exact
phrase about who is going to walk where when hell is all filled up.
In addition, they claimed that still pictures from *Night of the Living
Dead* were used to advertise the new film, and the words "Horror
Classic" were also used. Last, they claimed that the words "Living
Dead" were so well known that they had acquired a secondary
meaning in the mind of the public, and should be protected.

The defense claimed that it hadn't violated any of the plaintiffs'
rights. First, as far as advertising the *Return of the Living Dead* as
a horror classic, it pointed out that the promotional material also
included the words "all new"; even though the two phrases were
inconsistent, including the words "all new" showed its good
faith. The court did not agree, saying that the law prohibits
deception even if the deception results only indirectly or through
innuendo.

As for the still pictures, the defense said it wouldn't use them
any more. As for the words, "Living Dead," it said that was a
generic term and was merely descriptive of ghouls and zombies
and has been used so often that it is part of the public domain.
Again the court did not agree and said that even though the
phrase "Living Dead" may be generic, this case was based on
unfair competition, not merely a technical violation of the trademark law. What this was, said the court, was palming off your
product as somebody else's.

The court ordered that all advertising and distribution of any
film entitled *Return of the Living Dead* could not proceed. So it

looks as though the "Messiah" may soon return to take the place of the "Living Dead."

Eighty-three hours till dawn

A good story is more than the sum of its parts. That's the message of a recent case that upheld a verdict of $200,000 against Universal City Studios for copyright infringement or, more simply put, for stealing a story and making it a movie.

The case involved the Barbara Mackel kidnapping, which occurred back in 1971. As you may remember, Barbara Mackel was the daughter of a wealthy Florida land developer. She was abducted from an Atlanta motel room and buried alive for five days in a coffinlike container in the Georgia woods.

Sometime later she consented to write a book with a Pulitzer-Prize reporter named Miller. The book was written and called *83 Hours Till Dawn*. The reporter spent more than twenty-five hundred hours researching the facts and writing the book which, according to the court, was similar in technique to *In Cold Blood.* Later, Universal Studios released a television docu-drama which Miller claimed could only have come from his story. Universal had once approached Miller and offered him $15,000 for the story. But he turned it down, wanting $200,000 dollars instead.

The evidence showed that when Universal couldn't buy the story, it took it anyway. The key to the evidence was the fact that many scenes appeared in the TV show that were only in the book, including some errors that Miller had made, such as the location of a want ad the Mackel family used to communicate with the kidnappers.

But what really did Universal in was a memo introduced at the trial—which the court referred to as the "smoking gun exhibit" —in which a Universal script writer said, "All I have to go on is the book, which is verboten." The writer suggested he be provided with a bodyguard when he traveled into Mackel territory.

The jury came back with $185,000 for Mr. Miller, even more than his lawyer had asked for in closing argument. Universal asked for a new trial on the basis that the case involved facts of a crime that had really happened and therefore were not subject to copyright. The court held in denying that motion that while the facts themselves may not be copyrighted, the research and compilation of those facts certainly could be. So a story may be greater than the sum of its parts.

Privacy in a haunted house

Getting into the spirit of things can sometimes cause a lot of trouble. That's the message of a recent case decided by the U.S. District Court for the Eastern District of New York. The case was brought by George and Kathleen Lutz, who owned the house you may have read about in the *Amityville Horror.* This time the Lutzes weren't upset about what went on in the house, but rather what went on in *Good Housekeeping* magazine and the *New York Sunday News.* The *News* ran a story entitled "Life in a Haunted House," and *Good Housekeeping* featured "Our Dream House Was Haunted." Both stories dealt with the Lutzes' frightening experiences with demons and spirits in their Amityville home. The Lutzes claimed these stories were written without their permission and violated the common-law right to privacy and also misappropriated their names in violation of New York State law.

The court began its opinion by looking at New York law, which provides that anyone who uses a person's name or picture for advertising or commercial purposes without first getting written consent commits a crime and can be sued for damages as well. But, said the court, while the law is clear, it's equally clear that use of a name in connection with a news story is not defined as use for commercial purposes. In order for the plaintiffs to win under this law, said the court, they would have to show that the publication of a newsworthy event was solely for the purpose of enhancing sales rather than letting people know about the news.

The court then looked at the common-law right of privacy, noting that while the right of privacy has been making great strides, "it has not as yet found an abiding place in our jurisprudence." The only cases that have upheld such a right in New York have been instances when there has been an extreme intrusion into a person's private life.

Also, said the court, the person who wants to collect for emotional suffering must prove the defendant went beyond all reasonable bounds of decency with extreme and outrageous conduct. While what went on in the Amityville haunted house may have been indecent, extreme, and outrageous, said the court, writing about it in *Good Housekeeping* and the *New York Sunday News* wasn't.

"The Serengeti Incident"

If you've got it and you let it go, you may lose it forever. That's the message of a recent case involving a New Hampshire doctor, the journal *Natural History,* and NBC.

The case got started when Dr. Brian Burke, a well-known New Hampshire anesthesiologist, decided to take a safari on the Serengeti Plain in East Africa. While there, he filmed what the court called "an unusual affray between a zebra and a lioness." What had happened was that the lioness had attacked and killed the zebra foal. The herd of zebras scattered, but the foal's mother returned and attacked the lioness, all while the doctor was rolling his film, which he later entitled "The Serengeti Incident."

A few months after he returned to the United States, an article appeared in *Natural History* that said zebras do not protect their young against lions. After reading the article, the doctor wrote to the journal stating that not only was the article incorrect, but he also had the film to prove it. After the letter appeared, a professor in Germany wrote to Dr. Burke asking if he could get a copy of the film for his lectures and for use on a German public-television station. Dr. Burke sent the film. The professor in turn was contacted by a British company specializing in nature films, which asked for a copy of Dr. Burke's film for use on a special on animal parenthood. The film was provided. Then the special was sold to NBC, containing thirty-three feet of Dr. Burke's film as part of a one-hour special entitled "Parenthood Game."

Dr. Burke then sued NBC, claiming his common-law copyright had been violated and asking for money damages. He admitted he'd let the film be used in Germany, but he'd never given permission for NBC to use his film in a widely publicized network special. The court explained that common-law copyright does remain with the film creator until he permits what is known as general publication, at which point the work becomes the property of the general public.

The court said when it comes to general publication, the intention of the creator is irrelevant. What counts is what he did and whether or not he voluntarily parted with his property. The court found that since the good doctor had sent the film without any restrictions on its use, he had permitted a general publication to occur. So the case of "The Serengeti Incident" rolled to a halt.

Inside information

What happens when a newspaper financial columnist writes about a stock and he just happens to own some of it himself? That was the question in a case recently decided by the Ninth Circuit Court of Appeals. The case was brought against a financial columnist for the *Los Angeles Herald Examiner* charging the columnist had printed favorable information about a company about to be involved in a merger, right after he bought five thousand shares of stock in that company. After the article appeared, the stock went up, and the merger took place on the basis of the temporarily inflated value of the stock. The columnist sold out at a profit.

The suit was brought by the principals in one of the companies claiming that they were done in by a carefully timed newspaper article that led to the inflated value of the stock giving them far less value for their company. They claimed the violation of Rule 10(b)(5), which makes it illegal for a person to use any means of interstate commerce to make untrue statements or omit material facts about securities.

The district court that first heard the case dismissed it, claiming that everyone has a right to make a nickel. The case was appealed to the federal Court of Appeals. That court reviewed the history of the particular columnist and found he frequently discussed the financial conditions of small companies in Southern California and often bought stock in those companies just before he printed favorable comments. During a two-year period, the columnist bought the stock of twenty-two companies shortly before the columns about the companies were published. In twenty-one of the twenty-two cases, he made a profit. In addition, his favorable columns were reprinted as advertisements for the companies in a financial journal in which he also had an interest.

The court said that the columnist's ownership of stock was material and relevant, and that he did have a duty to disclose. The court added that the rule should not be extended to require every financial columnist to disclose his or her portfolio to all, but it does cover the activity of one who uses a column as part of a scheme to manipulate the market and deceive the public.

One judge dissented; but the majority ruled, and financial columnists who own stock will have to take stock in their portfolios and in their ethics.

The courts, the press, and the *Fresno Bee*

Confrontations between the courts and the press are getting tougher. While relations between these two institutions have never been overly cordial, the battles seem to be becoming more frequent and the stakes getting higher. The latest battle involved four reporters from the *Fresno Bee* who were jailed for contempt because of their refusal to answer questions about where they secured their information. While the reporters were recently released from jail and plan no further appeals, their case deserves a close look from those who try to reconcile the prerogatives of the courts, the rights of criminal defendants against pretrial publicity, and the freedom of the press.

The case that ended up in the jailing of the reporters began in 1974 with the indictments of a Fresno city councilman, a well-known land developer, and the city's former planning commissioner. The court knew there would be reporters trying to get a hold of the grand jury transcript, so it kept a careful record of who was given the copies of it. The court then sealed the transcript and ordered silence on the part of all parties involved and their attorneys, as well as the court officers and, in fact, just about anyone who could provide any information whatsoever.

Despite all the elaborate precautions, there appeared on the front pages of the *Fresno Bee* on three successive days extensive quotations from the sealed grand jury transcript. The court took the unusual step of ordering the county attorney to represent the judge in his attempt to find out how the leak had occurred so that the appropriate persons could be punished. When the reporters were called, they refused forty-eight times to answer questions about how they had gotten access to the material.

The key portion of this decision discussed the impact of California's shield law, which provides that reporters cannot be judged in contempt by a court or legislature for refusing to disclose the source of information they may have procured. The appeals court in California virtually ignored this statute, citing the *Far* case, which involved a reporter who was jailed for violating the protective and seal orders in the Manson trial. The court stated simply, "The power of contempt possessed by the courts is inherent in their constitutional status and the legislature cannot declare that certain acts shall not constitute a contempt."

The four reporters cited the law all the way to their cells. And there are a lot of California reporters wondering just what protection the shield law provides.

It's downhill for snowmobiling

How do you feel about snowmobiling? Well, whether you're for it or against it, you'll be interested in a case recently decided by the First Circuit Court of Appeals. The case has a lot of implications for TV advertising and the environment. It got started when a group of opponents of snowmobiling organized themselves and wrote to a local television station that had been running paid advertisements for snowmobiling. The ads said things like, "Ride the machine which changed the winter," and a lot of other thoughts that made the snowmobile opponents very unhappy. They felt the ads presented the viewpoint that snowmobile ownership represented the good life and ignored the danger of the sport and the fact that it was often practiced without any conscious consideration of wildlife, vegetation, ecological balance, noise, or safety.

The opponents wrote to the station and claimed that the fairness doctrine of the Federal Communications Commission imposed a duty on the station to present both sides of the issue. When the TV station didn't respond promptly, the opponents filed a formal complaint with the FCC. The station did sponsor a single half-hour discussion program having to do with pending legislation that would regulate the seventy-five thousand snowmobiles that were in use in Maine, but the opponents felt that a single half-hour program wasn't really enough to counter all the advertising.

The FCC ruled that product commercials that merely advocate the use of one product over another cannot be said to inform the public on any side of a controversial issue of public importance. The Circuit Court of Appeals agreed, saying that the fact that the FCC had once required statements that cigarettes were bad for health when cigarettes were advertised was not relevant, since the FCC had retreated from that position.

So if the antisnowmobilers want to show the bad side of snowmobiling, it looks as though they're going to have to buy time to do so.

Dog Day Afternoon

Remember the movie *Dog Day Afternoon*? That was the one where the bank robbers got caught in the bank with eight hostages on a hot afternoon in Brooklyn. Well, *Dog Day Afternoon* was based on real events that occurred on August 22, 1972, when John Wotkowits and Sal Naturile tried unsuccessfully to rob the Brooklyn branch of the Chase Manhattan Bank. The events of the day, including the arrival of Wotkowits's homosexual mate, who participated in the negotiations, were broadcast live on television. The story ended when Naturile was shot and killed by an FBI agent at Kennedy airport. Wotkowits was captured and is now serving a lengthy prison sentence.

Some time after these events, Warner Brothers produced and distributed the motion picture *Dog Day Afternoon,* which in its opening scene announced that the story was true. Careful reviewers could have noticed a reference in the screen credits to a story in *Life* magazine that appeared in September 1972 and reported the whole story, including the true names of all who were involved. Wotkowits's real wife and two children brought a lawsuit against Warner Brothers for invasion of their privacy. The wife claimed that even though her name and the children's weren't used, they were easily identifiable through the *Life* magazine story. She also claimed that she was portrayed in a false light in the movie since, as the New York Supreme Court put it in its recent opinion, she was depicted as a rather loquacious and unpleasant person, and it could be implied that she was in part the cause of her husband's problems.

A lower court granted relief and damages for the wife and children on the basis that privacy could be invaded even if a person's name or picture was not used. But the New York Supreme Court disagreed and reversed the case on the grounds that New York law specifically said that the right of privacy was hooked to the use of a person's name or picture.

The court added that the law was not intended to give a person a cause of action based on the portrayal of acts and events in a play or novel merely because the acts or events were similar to what really happened. And the court concluded with something that must be considered by everyone who brings private matters into public courts: "It is the plaintiffs who have identified themselves to the public, not the defendants."

Four-letter words on the radio

Can you use four-letter words on radio and TV? That was the question in a case recently decided by the District Court of Appeals. The case got started four years ago when a New York radio station decided to broadcast a segment from an album entitled *George Carlin: Occupation, Fool.* Just before the broadcast, listeners were warned that the selection included some sensitive language that might be offensive to some and that those who might be offended should change stations and come back in fifteen minutes. The monologue consisted of a comedy routine that was, as the court put it, almost entirely devoted to the use of four-letter words depicting sexual or excretory organs and activities.

Of the millions of potential listeners in the New York area, everybody either listened without comment or switched stations —except for one man who was driving in his car with his young son. He decided that he'd rather fight than switch and lodged a complaint with the station and the Federal Communications Commission.

Federal law provides that whoever utters any obscene, indecent, or profane language on the radio can be fined up to ten thousand dollars or imprisoned for up to two years. And the FCC, based on this single complaint, decided that clarification of the word *indecent* was in order. The rule laid down by the FCC was that *indecent* means language that describes in terms patently offensive as measured by contemporary community standards sexual or excretory activities and organs, at times of day when there is a reasonable risk that children may be in the audience.

There was a split within the FCC itself over the issue. Two commissioners believed that such language was inappropriate for broadcast at any time, with one commissioner commenting that garbage is garbage and should be prohibited from the airwaves.

The radio station involved challenged the regulation. It argued that this was censorship, that it would prevent programs of serious literary value, and that there really isn't much time nowadays when children can't be expected to be in the audience, since in fact, studies showed that up until 1:00 A.M. on any given night, there are at least one million children watching television.

The commission replied that it wasn't censoring, but was merely channeling indecent language to certain times of the day. The court disagreed with the commission, stating that it *was* censorship, regardless of what the commission chose to call it. The court also found that the order was too broad and that it would prohibit the broadcast of certain passages from the Bible, Shakespeare, Lord Byron, Hemingway, Lawrence, Orwell, and the Nixon tapes.

Memories can be very painful

Memories can be very painful. That's the message of a recent case decided by the California Court of Appeals for the Third District. The case is sure to cause second thoughts for those who prepare the memory columns in newspapers around the country. It got started when the *Modoc County Record,* a weekly newspaper in Alturas, California, published a story under the caption "Twenty Years Ago in Modoc County." The story gave the name of a man who had killed his brother-in-law twenty years before. He served a prison sentence, was paroled, rehabilitated himself, and lived respectably in society with many friends and family members who were unaware of the incidents of his earlier life.

The man sued, claiming that many of his friends and acquaintances learned about the crime for the first time when they read about it in the paper. He claimed that after the article appeared, he was subject to mental anguish, embarrassment, and humiliation. A lower court threw the case out of court on the basis that the matter was news; even twenty years later, it was still news.

The plaintiff appealed to the California Court of Appeals, and that court reversed and said the plaintiff should not have lost. The court cited as authority for its decision another California case in which the *Reader's Digest* was sued for mentioning a man's name in an article on truck hijacking. The man had hijacked a truck eleven years earlier, but the court found in his favor, holding that there is a difference between recent news and rehashing of old events. In the case of recent news, said the court, there is a reason for the public to know and an important social interest served by the publication of names and facts. But as for long-past crimes, while the facts of those crimes may retain their news value, the names of people who carried them out serve little independent public purpose.

The court went on to say that once legal proceedings have terminated and a suspect or offender has been released, identification of the individual will usually not aid the administration of justice. And unless the individual has reattracted the public eye to himself in some independent fashion, the only public interest served is that of curiosity. The court said that this man who had reestablished his life and had it shattered again was entitled to a full trial on the question of liability and damages.

So "long-ago" columns may trigger some interesting memories as well as some interesting lawsuits.

A time to be born and a time to die

A time to be born and a time to die, and just whose business is it, anyway? That was the question recently before the U.S. District Court for the Northern District of Alabama. The case got started innocently enough when the *Birmingham News* decided it wanted to expand its coverage of Jefferson County's vital statistics. For about eleven years the *News* had been printing all the deaths that occurred in Jefferson County, and just to keep people's spirits up thought perhaps it ought to print all the births as well.

A reporter was assigned the job of compiling the names of the newborn, and she figured that since the Department of Health was providing the names of all those who died, she'd just ask them to provide the names of all those who were born as well. But when she contacted the director of the Bureau of Statistics and Vital Records, he refused to turn over the names.

The county officials said they were afraid printing names of newborns would subject them to commercial exploitation and cited a regulation that prohibited indiscriminate disclosure of records. The paper pointed out that the same regulation applied to births and deaths, and since it had been receiving the deaths, it ought to get the births too. The end result of that comment was that the records of deaths were no longer provided. The newspaper went to court claiming that freedom of the press was being dealt a severe blow in Jefferson County.

The court said the question in the case was whether the *News* had a constitutional right of access to public records and if so, whether that right had been abridged. The court cited language from Supreme Court cases holding that the First and Fourteenth Amendments do not guarantee the press any basic right of access superior to that of the public generally. The court said, "The Constitution does no more than to assure the public and the press equal access once the government has opened its doors."

The court did say it was clear that the function of newsgathering did merit some degree of First Amendment protection, but that the right to speak and publish does not carry with it the unrestrained right to gather information. So while a journalist has the right to seek out something that may not be available to all the public, the government has no affirmative duty to make available to journalists sources of information that it would not make available to the public generally.

The *News* considered an appeal, but in the meantime, if you want to find out who has died and who was born in Jefferson County, you'll just have to wait for an announcement.

Can you slander a city?

Can you commit libel or slander against a city? That was the question recently decided by the U.S. District Court for Eastern Pennsylvania. The case grew out of the lawsuit brought by the U.S. Department of Justice against the City of Philadelphia alleging extreme police brutality. We looked at that case on page 180. It was dismissed by the court because Congress had never given the power to the federal government to protect individual civil rights.

This lawsuit involved the City of Philadelphia against the *Washington Post*. The *Post* had run a story the day after the Justice Department filed its suit. The city claimed that the members of the Philadelphia police department and all of the citizens of the city were libeled by the *Post* story. The city charged that the statements made in the story were published for the sole purpose of falsely and maliciously portraying an official policy of police oppression that reached every encounter with a Philadelphia police officer. They claimed that the article brought disgrace and humiliation to Philadelphia citizens, and that the public generally had been misled into believing that Philadelphia was an unsuitable place in which to live.

The court said a city cannot maintain an action for libel on its own behalf and that a governmental agency is simply incapable of being libeled. If the claim was that certain individuals who worked or lived in Philadelphia had been libeled, then the city was the wrong plaintiff, said the court; those individuals who claimed they'd been libeled would have to bring the lawsuit, and even they would probably lose because of the First Amendment.

The city also sought to justify the suit on the ground of the doctrine of parens patriae, which means that the city has the obligation to play the role of the father of its people; if its people had been libeled, the city must seek redress on their behalf. But the court characterized that argument as being as unpersuasive as the rest. So it looks as though you can say whatever you want about a city, and it will just have to lie there and take it.

Sex discrimination in advertising

Sex discrimination in advertising—what does it mean to the company that writes the ad and the newspaper that runs it? That was the question recently raised before the New York Supreme Court. The ad involved read as follows: "Salesmen, if you are an 18- to 25,000-dollar man, we'd like to meet you personally." That ad was presented to the Binghamton Press by an advertising agency on behalf of an employment company.

Well, as you can imagine, all the women who felt that they were in the $18 to $25,000 class were upset. The president of the Women's Equity Action League filed a complaint with the State Commission on Human Rights charging the newspaper and the company with discriminatory practices. The newspaper and the company were found to have violated the law.

The newspaper appealed, claiming that with all the ads it received, it just couldn't be responsible for checking to see if an ad was discriminatory before running it. The court said there was no question but that the Binghamton Press did aid and abet an illegal act by running the ad. The court rejected the newspaper's argument that simply because it obtained the ad and ran it without changing it, it should not be held to have violated the law.

The court did say that while newspapers could be held responsible for printing an ad that clearly violated the law, they would not be held responsible for making an independent investigation to determine whether every job advertised is or is not exempt from the law.

So newspapers had better start reading their own ads before they publish them—but they don't have to go beyond the words in front of them to decide whether the ad is legal.

Keeping the public out

Yes, the press and the public can be kept out of the courtroom. That's the result of a recent decision handed down by the Appellate Division of the New York Supreme Court. The case involved a thirteen-year-old boy who was the first juvenile to be charged with murder under New York's new juvenile crime law and the youngest person ever to be charged with murder in the state of New York. The crime with which this young man was charged was the subway murder of a man on his way home from work who was pushed from a subway platform into the path of a moving train.

The case involved a pretrial hearing at which the defense lawyers were going to try to have an alleged confession thrown out. The defense attorney moved that the press and the public be barred from the hearing. At first the judge denied the motion, but then went home and turned on his television set and watched a telecast that referred in great detail to the killing and implicated the thirteen-year-old, who had not yet been tried.

The judge returned to court the next morning, told the lawyers what he had seen the night before, and then ordered the press and the public excluded from the hearing. The judge did offer to make available to the press a daily copy of the transcript of the hearing, although any reference to the confession would be edited out. The case was appealed, and the appellate court held that the action of the trial judge was proper. The court said that the boy was not only the first thirteen-year-old to be prosecuted as an adult under New York law, but was also charged with complicity in the vicious murder of a subway passenger, and thus was the subject of intense press coverage.

The court said a trial judge has to insure a proper balance between the defendant's right to a fair trial and the public's right to an open forum. It also said that if closure was not invoked in this case, the details of the confession, at a hearing to see if the confession was to be excluded, could well be disseminated to every prospective juror in Bronx County.

One judge dissented, saying that if the courtroom was closed in this case, it would probably be closed in a lot more; but the majority ruled, and the press and the public won't be within hearing on this one.

9

THE RUMBLINGS OF THE GIANTS:

The Business of Corporations, here, there, and everywhere

Capitalism is a great system. It is unbeatable for the nurturing of incentive and the production of goods and services. It has only a few problems: it does not know when to stop producing, it has major problems assuring an equitable distribution of goods and services, and it can be guilty of huge amounts of waste and inefficiency. Nevertheless, as a study of other countries around the world will show, it is very hard to beat, and we must do all we can to keep our system viable.

The guardians of capitalism are big business, and as one reads down the list of the *Fortune* 500, one realizes that big business is indeed very big. As I have come to know it, big business has one basic problem—on occasion it has difficulty distinguishing between short-term greed and long-term self interest. For some reason, big business has become fixated on the short term and has in some cases forgotten about the long term and the principle that it pays to keep one's customers and consumers happy.

Big business has some rather formidable foes, namely, the press, the government, and consumerists, led by Ralph Nader. The press seems to dislike big business just out of principle; the government seems to be intimidated by the profit motive and resentful of the salaries earned; and consumerists seem to get far more pleasure out of attacking business interests than in working for the consumers who they are supposed to represent.

I suggest that we should not get our kicks from striking out at big business just for the sake of it or because we think that it makes us feel better, for the quality of our lives is to a large extent pegged to how big business is doing. The future of our system may depend in a large part on how the government comports itself—and, even more important—on the responsibility with which big business manages itself. It has been said that there used to be an interesting difference between a worker in Detroit and a French peasant. The Detroit worker stands by the side of the road, and when he sees a Cadillac drive by, he puts his cap back on his head and says to himself, "If I work hard, I can get me one of those." The French peasant, on the other hand, stands by the side of the road, and when he sees a limousine drive by, he can't wait but to make the driver walk. I hope that we will maintain the spirit that made our country the richest and the most powerful in the world and that we will pay close attention to finding ways to make its riches felt far, wide, and deep throughout this nation.

The stories that follow involve the clashes of these giants with each other, with the government, and with the people they serve. More power to them, but only if that power is used reasonably, with care and with understanding for the problems and needs of a troubled nation.

Who owns the rays of the sun?

As the days of solar energy dawn, a question that is beginning to bother some of the solar-energy companies is, who has the right to the rays and what can be done by way of regulating buildings, walls, trees, and all the other things that may block the rays of the sun?

The problem is that sunlight is made available for energy use by being captured in a stationary device known as a cooker. Since most of the sun's rays that reach a particular piece of land strike that land at an angle, very little of the sunlight collected by the cooker comes to it from directly above the land on which it rests. Imagine building a house to be heated by solar energy and then having your neighbor decide to put up a ten-story building on his land next door.

A recent article in the *University of Colorado Law Review* says that Congress could act because of the fact that sunlight travels in interstate commerce just about every day that the sun shines, but that it probably won't act in time. The matter, says the article, will come to the courts, which aren't well prepared to deal with what may very soon become a burning question.

Finding nothing much by way of precedent in this country to help, the article goes back to the Doctrine of Ancient Lights. The author points out that this would have solved the problem, except that the Doctrine of Ancient Lights isn't recognized in the

United States. The Doctrine of Ancient Lights provides that if a
landowner has received light from across his neighbor's land for
a certain time, he has a right to continue enjoying it; and the light
may not be obstructed, for example, by his neighbor's building
a house right up against his window. The problem is that the
length of time to establish this right in England is twenty years,
and the light that you're entitled to is not unlimited light, but
only enough to read a book in a room—an amount that wouldn't
be too useful for a solar-energy cooker.

In concluding, the article recommends that the law of water
rights might be the most help. That law says that a landowner has
the right to the continued flow of a stream, free of unreasonable
interference.

So, the next time you see the sun, you might think about who
owns its rays, and if you get any bright ideas, let us know.

A shady story

If you're going to Florida for your winter vacation this year,
you might be interested in a lawsuit brought a few years back by
the Eden Roc Hotel against the Fontainebleau. The suit was
brought by the Eden Roc to get back its sun, which was about to
be stolen by the Fontainebleau. It seems that the Eden Roc had
a swimming pool that was in the sun most of the day, and the
Fontainebleau decided to put up a fourteen-story addition that
would have the effect of plunging the Eden Roc swimming pool
into virtual darkness about two o'clock in the afternoon.

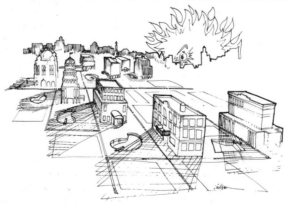

The court's decision made it pretty clear that the two hotels
didn't get along very well, since the Eden Roc claimed that the
Fontainebleau was building its addition maliciously, just to cut off

the flow of sunlight to the Eden Roc's swimming pool. The lower court granted a temporary injunction stopping the building on the basis that a person cannot use his own property in a way that harms another.

The Florida appeals court reversed the lower court, pointing out that it is not quite correct to say that a person cannot use his property in a way that harms another person; rather, a person cannot use his property in a way that injures the lawful rights of another, a very different proposition indeed. Unfortunately for the Eden Roc, there is no American court decision holding that a landowner has a legal right to the free flow of air and light across the adjoining land of his neighbor. Even in England it was pointed out that such a right did not attach until after twenty years of continuous enjoyment of the light in question. And that concept simply hasn't been followed in the United States.

So the moral of the story seems to be, if you're going to have a dispute with your neighbor, first make sure you're on the sunny side of the street.

The Concorde gripe

At long last, the courts let the Concorde land. The refusal of the U.S. Supreme Court to grant any further stay capped the almost two years during which the case traveled at less than supersonic speed through the federal courts.

The first major confrontation was won by the airline when a federal district court judge ruled that the Port Authority could not prevent the Concorde from landing because the decision of the federal government on the matter was supreme. The judge reasoned that since the Department of Transportation had studied the problem and decided that the Concorde could land at Dulles airport, this meant that individual state port authorities couldn't impose a ban.

This decision was overturned a short time later by the Second Circuit Court of Appeals, which stated bluntly that "The conclusion that the Secretary of Transportation's order preempted the power of the Port Authority is simply untenable and erroneous." The court pointed out that the federal government itself said that the order of the Secretary of Transportation was never intended to deprive local port authorities of their jurisdiction to lay down standards at their airports—as long as those standards were reasonable, nondiscriminatory, and nonarbitrary.

While things looked good for the Port Authority for a short

time, the seeds of a nose dive for the authority were in that Court of Appeals opinion. It sent the case back to the district court with orders to conduct an evidentiary hearing on the reasonableness of the ban, which was in its thirteenth month. That hearing was held, and the district court judge found again for the airline. But this time there was a different reason—the fact that the Concorde could comply with existing antinoise regulations and that continued study of the problem was mere harassment.

This time, the judge was upheld by the Court of Appeals, which said that "If there was ever a case in which a major technological advance was in imminent danger of being studied into obsolescence, this was it."

The last gasp of the Port Authority was that since the Concorde emits low-frequency vibrations that are a particular source of annoyance, it wanted a little more time to develop a vibration rattle index. The court said that the authority could develop any index it wanted, but in the meantime, at Kennedy airport, the Concorde will be landing and taking off.

"I can get it for you wholesale"

"I can get it for you wholesale" may soon be a thing of the past. That's the result of a little-publicized decision of the U.S. Supreme Court. The decision, which is now several years old, is just beginning to have an effect on the marketplace—an effect that could make it much harder to find brand-name items in discount stores.

The case involved Sylvania, which had gotten worried about a declining share of the TV market. Like most other TV manufacturers, Sylvania handled its distribution by selling TV sets through independent distributors, who in turn sold to a large and varied group of retailers, including discount stores. When Sylvania's share of the TV market declined to between 1 percent and 2 percent, Sylvania decided to change its method of marketing and began selling directly to a select group of retailers, cutting out the middleman and many of the discount operations.

All went well until Sylvania decided to franchise a company that was about a mile from Continental TV, which had been selling a lot of Sylvania sets at reduced prices. Continental protested but to no avail. Continental finally went to court claiming that Sylvania had violated the Sherman Anti-Trust Act. Continental claimed that Sylvania was engaging in vertical control, that is, controlling its product price after it parted with the product. And Continental won a judgment of $1 million. The leading authority holding that vertical control was illegal was the *Schwinn* case, in which the U.S. Supreme Court held that under the Sherman Act, it is illegal for a manufacturer to restrict its product after it has parted with it.

But that was ten years ago, and today's court is a different court, particularly when it comes to business interests. This court decided to override the *Schwinn* case, holding that it is economically healthy for a company to control its product all the way to the consumer.

Justices Marshall and Brennan dissented, but the majority ruled, and brand-name products will probably be selling at brand-name prices because of it.

Is it a crime to push a Pinto?

Can manufacturing an automobile be a crime? That was the question recently decided by the Indiana Superior Court in the first case of an automobile manufacturer indicted because of the way it made one of its cars. The case involved a Pinto that was struck from behind on an Indiana highway, resulting in an immediate explosion and the fiery deaths of all of the Pinto's occupants. Shortly after the accident, the Ford Motor Company was indicted.

Ford was indicted under an Indiana law that provides that a person who recklessly kills another human being is guilty of reckless homicide. The court, in denying Ford's motion to dismiss the indictment, said that reckless homicide may result from either a positive act that results in death, or a reckless failure to perform an act that one was under a duty to perform. The court said that federal law now places a clear duty on an automobile manufacturer to notify an automobile owner of any safety-related defect and to remedy that defect. The court said that in this case the indictment alleged that Ford knew, or should have known, that the Pinto was likely to burst into flames upon rear-end impact, due to faulty gas-tank design. And yet the Pinto with its faulty design was permitted to "remain on the highways and byways of the country."

Ford claimed that the reckless homicide statutes that used the word "person" only applied to people, not to corporations. But the court said that "person" does include corporation and that a corporation can be indicted and convicted as long as the people carrying out the corporation's business were acting within their corporate authority.

Ford also claimed that it didn't have fair notice of the law, but the court said that while the statute is quite general in its terms, the definition of reckless is specific enough, and people of ordinary intelligence would know what it meant. Last, Ford claimed that when it comes to automobile safety, the federal government has preempted the field, and that for states to use their powers interferes with interstate commerce. But the court did not agree, and upheld the indictment.

Thus the question of whether Ford was a felon continued on track in the Indiana courts. And while Ford was found not guilty in the subsequent trial, the principle of a manufacturer's responsibility under reckless homicide laws remains intact.

How much does your doctor make?

Should how much a doctor earns be made public information? That was the question recently decided by a U.S. District Court for Florida. The suit was brought by the Florida Medical Association. The doctors were upset at a proposal of the Department of Health, Education, and Welfare to publish a list of all the names and addresses of all physicians who were paid by Medicare, and exactly how much they were paid.

The Secretary of HEW claimed he was acting under the Freedom of Information Act and that people wanted to know and had a right to know how much individual doctors were earning under the Medicare program. The doctors claimed that such information was traditionally private and that they would be embarrassed and perhaps even endangered by publication of their names, addresses, and earnings.

The appeals court pointed out that the Freedom of Information Act exempts disclosure of personal and medical files and "similar files" when such disclosure would constitute a clearly unwarranted invasion of personal privacy. The court said that information such as personal earnings hooked to a particular individual would cause special embarrassment and is included within the exemption.

The secretary of HEW claimed that the public has an important and legitimate interest in knowing the amounts of public funds spent in reimbursing Medicare providers, particularly in light of the ongoing debate over national health insurance. But the court did not agree and added that another law, the Privacy Act, also prohibits this kind of information from being made public. The Privacy Act prevents individually identifying information from being released by the government without prior written consent of the individual.

The government debated whether or not to appeal this case, but for the moment, how much your doctor earns will not be part of your bedside reading.

Some doctors are different

All doctors are not the same, at least when it comes to paying them. That's the result of a recent case decided by the U.S. District Court for Eastern Virginia. The case was brought by the Virginia Academy of Clinical Psychologists, which was upset by the way Blue Shield was paying for psychotherapy. It seems that if you got your psychotherapy from a psychiatrist—who is a medical doctor—it would be paid for, but if you got the same therapy from a psychologist, it would not be paid for unless you could prove the psychotherapy was ordered by, supervised by, and billed through a physician.

The clinical psychologists went to court alleging that the Blue Shield policy was the result of a conspiracy between Blue Shield, which was allegedly physician-controlled, and the psychiatric society and as such violated the Sherman Anti-Trust Act. The court said there was no question but that the psychiatrists and Blue Shield did spend a lot of time together during the three-year period in which the Blue Shield payment policy was determined. But the real question, said the court, was whether this cooperation was a conspiracy to restrain trade.

The court decided against the psychologists. Blue Shield's decision, said the court, did not become a conspiracy with the psychiatric society just because both entities took exactly the same position. Also, just because Blue Shield's business decision was helpful to the psychiatrists didn't mean it was a conspiracy. Last, said the court, even if it were a conspiracy, to be illegal it must be one in restraint of trade.

The court said while it may be that psychiatrists and psychologists are equal providers of psychotherapy, psychiatrists—being medical doctors—are capable of providing the full range of psychiatric and medical treatment for nervous and mental disorders.

The court also said if the psychologist has to bill through a medical doctor, that is a good way to show that the treatment given was medically necessary, which is the only type of service Blue Shield is supposed to be paying for, anyway.

The psychologists also claimed their exclusion from payment was an illegal boycott, but the court said Blue Shield wasn't refusing to deal with the psychologists, but merely requiring that they submit their bills through a physician. So the next time you head for your fifty minutes of problem-solving, you and your psychologist just may have one more problem to think about.

WNCN gets a hearing

What happens when a radio station wants to switch to another listener? That was the question in a case recently decided by the Circuit Court for the District of Columbia. The case involved a Connecticut radio station that decided it was going to change from all classical music to a livelier, more popular, and hopefully more profitable format. As you can imagine, a lot of listeners were very upset when they learned of the change, and they formed a group called the WNCN Listeners Guild.

The question for the court was whether stations ought to be able to change their formats in any way they wanted. The most recent case on the matter held that when a significant sector of the listening community protests a format change, the law requires that the Federal Communications Commission hold a hearing as to whether the change is in the public interest. But recently the FCC itself stated that it believed the court was wrong in that case.

Federal law requires radio stations to operate based on the public interest, convenience, and necessity. Diversity of format, said the court, is a very important part of the public interest. If there is no outpouring of protest, a station can go right ahead and change its format any way it wants to. And, said the court, when there is only a committed and vocal minority that engages in significant public grumbling, no formal hearing is necessary. But when the volume of public protest is loud and long, and a unique form is involved, the FCC has to get into the act whether it wants to or not.

The court said it was aware that there were bills pending in Congress that would deregulate the air waves just like the airways, but for the moment those bills were not becoming law. And the court said we must remember that the air waves are priceless property in very limited supply and are owned by all the people, and it's up to the courts and the FCC to make sure the different tastes are gratified.

One judge dissented, saying that all stations are unique and open competition is the way to go. But the majority ruled, and for now there will be hearings on what you will be hearing.

It's alive, it moves

It's alive, it moves, and it can be patented. That's the result of a case recently decided by the U.S. Supreme Court. The case was the first to decide whether a human-made microorganism was patentable under the patent laws of the United States.

The case began when a microbiologist who worked for General Electric filed a patent application relating to a man-made, genetically engineered bacteria which, when spread in straw over an oil spill, would virtually eat up all the oil. But the Patent Office rejected the application on the grounds that the patent law was not intended to cover living things.

The case made its way from the Patent Office to the U.S. Supreme Court, which took the opportunity to review the patent process itself. That process begins in the Constitution, which grants Congress the power to legislate and promote the progress of science and the useful arts. The law, which goes back to 1793, provides that whoever invents or discovers any new or useful process, machine, manufacture, or composition of matter may obtain a patent.

The question was whether a living, man-made microorganism

is a manufacture or composition of matter, and the court found that without question the organism was patentable. The court said that not everything is patentable, but this bacteria was because it was a non-naturally-occurring manufacture of composition of matter, a product of human ingenuity. The court said the distinction is not between living and nonliving things, but between products of nature and human-made inventions. The government claimed that patenting genetic research could be the first step to the destruction of the human race, spreading pollution and disease. But the court disagreed and said the parade of horribles will neither be slowed nor speeded by patentability.

Four justices dissented; but the majority ruled, and man-made living things are patentable. And it's just the beginning.

Grocery coupons—are they legal?

Grocery coupons—are they legal? That was the question recently decided by the U.S. District Court for Western Pennsylvania. The case saw two coffee companies fighting it out to the last drop over discount coupons.

What happened was that Folger Coffee, which dominated the coffee market in the West, decided to challenge General Foods in the East and launched a major marketing campaign. That campaign included a lot of consumer coupons that were distributed by direct mail, newspaper advertisements, and inserts in the Folger coffee packages. The coupons could be redeemed at any retail outlet selling Folger coffee.

Well, the coffee war was waged and as often happens, the victim was neither of the two giants, but rather a third, smaller company. The Indian Coffee Corporation was engaged in the manufacture of coffee primarily in the Cleveland-Pittsburgh area and claimed that as a result of the Folger attack, it went out of business. Indian went to court claiming that Folger engaged in what it called predatory pricing policies in violation of the Sherman Anti-Trust Act. It claimed that Folger violated the law by selling coffee at lower prices in the Cleveland-Pittsburgh area than in other parts of the nation. The lower prices resulted from the use of coupons in the East, while coupons were not available in the West.

But the court threw out the Indian Coffee grounds. The court held that while the law does make it illegal to discriminate among your customers by charging different prices for your product,

Folger customers were the retailers and received absolutely no price concession and merely served as redemption agents for the coupons. The court said that while it's true what Folger did may not have been good for Indian Coffee or even for the forces of coffee competition generally, the law does not simply prohibit an undesirable end result. And so Folger's cup runneth over and the Indian Coffee cupboard is bare, and you can continue to clip your coffee coupons.

Miss Nude USA has a lot of dash

Will the real Miss USA please stand up? That was the question raised in a recent federal district court case in California. The case settled a nasty feud between those responsible for the Miss USA pageant and those who hold themselves out under the Miss Nude USA banner.

Miss USA was one of the trademarks secured by a corporation called Miss Universe, Incorporated, which was responsible for the yearly parade of beauties that many of you have watched on TV for years. The Miss USA Beauty Pageant has been broadcast every year since 1965; in 1976 it was seen by an estimated 60 million people.

The trouble started when a couple named William and Fran Flesher decided to start a beauty pageant of their own on the West Coast. They called it Miss Nude USA. When the lawyer for the Miss USA contest found out about it, he wrote to the Fleshers protesting what he considered the infringement of the Miss USA trademark. He claimed that the Miss Nude USA title was confusing to the public; for example, many parents of Miss USA contestants would object if they thought there was any relation to the Miss Nude USA. The Fleshers refused to stop using the name, and the case of *Miss Universe, Inc.* v. *Flesher* went to court.

The court found that the Miss USA group had spent a great deal of time and money in promoting its trademark, while the economic investment in Miss Nude USA by its founders was only slightly more than was worn by the contestants. The court further found that there was a likelihood of confusion over which pageant was which and that it was probable that Miss USA's trademark would be diluted if Miss Nude USA continued unabated.

But here's the rub: The court had difficulty in fashioning the appropriate remedy, for when you get to the bottom of it, there aren't too many other things you can call a contest of nude misses that takes place in the U.S.A. But the day was saved by simplicity. The court merely required that a hyphen appear between the words "Nude" and "USA" whenever the trademark Miss Nude-USA appeared. One can't help but admire the simplicity of this rather dashing result.

A tough case for Listerine to swallow

I was was a little hoarse for a while because of a cold and the flu. That's why I was very interested to see the case of *Warner Lambert Company* v. *Federal Trade Commission,* involving the question of whether Listerine really did what it said it did, which was to prevent, cure, and alleviate the common cold.

The case had been going since 1972, which really isn't a very long time when one considers that Listerine has been on the market since 1879. In 1972 the government decided to challenge Listerine's claims that it would ameliorate, prevent, and cure colds and sore throats, and ordered a hearing to be held. Four thousand pages and forty-six witnesses later, the FTC concluded that Listerine's claims were false and ordered it to cease and desist in its advertising. What was even more bitter for the makers of Listerine to swallow was that the FTC ordered the company to spend its next $10 million of advertising to correct what the old advertising said. The makers of Listerine went to court to challenge the order of the FTC, and lost.

The District of Columbia Court of Appeals began its opinion reminding us of the rather awesome power that agencies like the FTC really have. A court that reviews agency action does not look at whether what the agency ordered was correct, but only at whether there was substantial evidence for the position. The court said that it was up to the commission to decide whether to believe the two leading pharmacologists called by the commission or the experts called by the makers of Listerine.

Based on the expert testimony, the commission had found that in the process of gargling it was impossible for Listerine to reach the critical areas of the body in medically significant concentrations. As for the four-year study of school children ending with the claim that those who gargled with Listerine had fewer colds, the commission had found that the design of the study was poor and the study was therefore unreliable. The court upheld these findings. The court also agreed that there was sufficient evidence for the commission's finding that the germs Listerine was alleged to be killing by the millions weren't the germs that caused colds.

Now let's look at the part of the court opinion dealing with the question of whether the Federal Trade Commission, in addition to stopping the Listerine advertising, could also order the company to spend its advertising money telling the public that its prior advertising was wrong. The FTC told the company it had to include the following language in its next $10 million worth of advertising: "Contrary to prior advertising, Listerine will not help prevent colds or sore throats or lessen their severity."

The company claimed that such corrective advertising was beyond the scope of the Federal Trade Commission Act, and that since the power to order corrective advertising wasn't specifically listed in the law, the commission couldn't order it. The commission claimed it had the power to order the misleading impressions given to the public corrected. In the case of Listerine, said the commission, a hundred years of false cold claims had built up a large reservoir of erroneous consumer beliefs. The court agreed with the commission.

The company also claimed the order violated its First Amendment right of free speech by telling it what it had to say, and that the order shouldn't stand because nothing like it had ever been ordered before. On the issue of free speech, the court said that deceptive advertising doesn't come under the protection of the First Amendment. As for it never happening before, the court reminded the company that the makers of Geritol were forced to tell you that their product would help you only if you were tired because of iron deficiency anemia, which most people don't have; and companies that make products for baldness and bed-wetting have to tell people those products don't work for most conditions that cause baldness and bed-wetting.

One judge dissented in the Listerine opinion, but it looks as though curative advertising is here to stay.

Sip your Coors slowly

Sip that Coors Beer slowly, 'cause it may get even harder to find. That's the result of a recent decision out of the Tenth Circuit Court of Appeals. The case involved a lawsuit by the Adolph Coors Company against A&S Wholesalers. Coors makes its beer in one brewery in Colorado, and even though it's the largest brewery in the world, there just doesn't seem to be quite enough to satisfy nationwide demand. In addition, the company doesn't pasteurize its beer, which means that, unlike a lot of other beers, continual refrigeration is needed. So Coors limited its marketing area to ten and one-half states in order, said the company, to maintain the integrity of Coors Beer.

What A&S Wholesalers did was to buy Coors from retailers in Colorado and truck it back to North Carolina for resale to other retail outlets at greatly inflated prices. Coors sued to prevent A&S from doing this. The distributor argued that Coors was engaging in unlawful customer and territorial restrictions in violation of the Sherman Anti-Trust Act. The lower court decided that Coors couldn't stop A&S from distributing and in fact let the case go to a jury on the issue of whether Coors had to pay damages to A&S for violating the Sherman Act. Both parties appealed the case to the Tenth Circuit Court of Appeals.

The court looked at the arguments in the case, which were basically that Coors's contention that it was limiting the territory to maintain the integrity of the beer was just a sham and that the real reason was to restrain trade improperly. A&S argued that prior antitrust cases required a ruling that the restrictions were illegal and no matter what the reasons were, they existed. But the court did not agree and sent the case back to the trial court to see if, in fact, the territorial restrictions were really related to the integrity of the product.

So for drinkers of Coors Beer who don't live in the West, there may be some dry days ahead.

Feeding your kitty kitty-food

Can Kitty kill Kal Kan Kitty Stew? This was the question put before the United States Court of Customs and Patent Appeals, which has decided what can only be called a landmark case in the complicated world of pet food trademarks.

The whole mess started when Kal Kan Foods decided to market a product it wanted to call Kal Kan Kitty Stew. This upset the New England Fish Company because, back in 1960, its predecessor company had registered the trademark "Kitty" for cat food. New England claimed that the words "Kal Kan Kitty Stew" were illegal because they encroached on the prior registered trademark of "Kitty." Kal Kan won before the Patent Office Trademark Trial and Appeal Board, and New England appealed to the U.S. Court of Customs and Patent Appeals.

As was pointed out by Kal Kan's attorney—whose name, by the

way, was Grubb—this was not the first battle over cat food to reach the Court of Patent Appeals. In earlier cases the court had held that products called "Here Kitty" and "Pretty Kitty" did violate New England's trademark. But this case, said the court, was very different.

The court pointed out that the dominant visual impact of the label was the use of the words "Kal Kan," which were actually set off from the words "Kitty Stew." The court then discoursed at great length about the plain meaning of the words "kitty stew." The judge stated, that, literally, they could only mean one of two things—either a stew of kitties or a stew for kitties—and he went on to point out that a stew of kitties is improbable in this country.

The court concluded that when "Kitty" is used with other words only as an adjective modifying stew to indicate that the stew is for kitties, it is devoid of trademark character, which means its use cannot be stopped.

So thanks to the U.S. Court of Customs and Patent Appeals, Kal Kan Kitty Stew can be canned for your kitty.

The right to lite (light)

"You light up my life" probably won't be hummed any more by employees of the Miller Brewing Company. That's because the Seventh Circuit Court of Appeals has overturned a lower court ruling preventing other companies from using the word "light" on their beer.

It all started when a now-defunct brewery known as Meister Brau began making and selling a reduced-calorie beer under the name Lite. Meister Brau sold the trademark to the Miller company, which proceeded to spend $12 million a year advertising it. Then a number of other brewers decided to join the trend toward less-filling beers and began marketing their beers with the word "light" somewhere on the label. Miller brought court actions to restrain other brewers from using the word, and initially succeeded.

In reversing the lower court judgment, the court of appeals reminded us that a common or descriptive word simply cannot become a trademark. Miller said it should be able to trademark the word "light" because they spelled it wrong, and that therefore it wasn't the commonly used word after all. Miller also argued that the word "light" as it applied to beer had been meaningless until Miller spent all the money on advertising, causing "light" to take on a secondary meaning.

Miller wasn't helped much by the fact that the *Webster's New International Dictionary* published back in 1940 mentioned beer as an example of the use of the word "light," or by the fact that Pepsi appropriated the word for its nonalcoholic drink with half the calories missing. The court said that other brewers who come up with a beer that is in fact light must have the right to call it light; otherwise a manufacturer could remove a common descriptive word from the public domain, gaining the exclusive right to call his wine "rosé," his whisky "blended," and his bread "white."

But you'll still be able to buy Miller Lite—along with all the others.

Did Bruce Jenner ever really eat Wheaties?

Did Bruce Jenner really eat Wheaties when he was a kid? Although it looks as if that question may not reach the courts, a similar one did get to the Second Circuit Court of Appeals. The question was, just what *was* Wonder Bread doing for your child? The court's opinion had a lot to say about what's being fed to children—on the television set as well as on the table.

The case involved Wonder Bread commercials of a few years back that showed a small child growing to the size of a twelve-year-old in a few seconds, presumably because of the ingestion of Wonder Bread. The commercials also claimed that Wonder Bread was an extraordinary food for producing dramatic growth in children. The Federal Trade Commission filed a complaint against the makers of Wonder Bread, charging them with deceptive advertising practices.

The case was first tried before an administrative law judge, who hears cases before they are considered by the Federal Trade Commission as a whole. For the most part, the makers of Wonder Bread admitted that the bread wouldn't really alter natural growth patterns. Their defense was that most people didn't really believe that Wonder Bread made a child grow more quickly. All that had really happened, they said, was that Wonder Bread has secured a kind of "halo" effect because of effective advertising, and the "halo" effect didn't really relate to an actual nutritional advantage of the product.

The administrative law judge agreed with the company and

decided in its favor, finding that the ads weren't deceptive. But the full Federal Trade Commission overturned the judge's decision, primarily on the fact that there was testimony that the advertising could in fact have a great deal of impact on children. One expert said that children might feel that something was wrong with them if they didn't suddenly grow taller after they had eaten Wonder Bread. Another psychologist testified that young children might be temporarily burdened by the somewhat puzzling portrayal of instant growth.

The Wonder Bread people appealed to the Circuit Court of Appeals. The basis of their claim was that consumers weren't really so unsophisticated as to believe that Wonder Bread could make somebody grow from the size of a one-year-old to the size of a twelve-year-old in thirty seconds, even if Captain Kangaroo and Bozo added their approval of Wonder Bread along the way. And they claimed that the cease-and-desist order at best ought to be limited to children. But the court said that the line between children and adults if often a thin one, and that the ad was deceptive no matter how you sliced it.

Colonel Sanders v. Kentucky Fried

What happens when Colonel Sanders and Kentucky Fried Chicken don't see eye-to-eye any more? That was the question recently put before the Kentucky Supreme Court. The case got started when Colonel Sanders made some statements to a newspaper reporter who was doing a piece on "Is a Chicken Wing White Meat?" In the course of the article, the Colonel was reported to have made some very disparaging statements about the fried chicken empire that he had started, but no longer owned.

The Colonel said things like, "The gravy is horrible—they take tap water and mix it with flour and starch and end up with pure wallpaper paste, and I know wallpaper paste, by God, because I've seen my mother make it." Then the Colonel went on to say, "That new 'Crispy' recipe is nothing in the world but a damned fried dough ball stuck on some chicken."

Well, Kentucky Fried Chicken of Bowling Green, Kentucky, one of five thousand fried chicken franchises, brought a libel suit against the Colonel claiming that the Colonel's statements had held it up to ridicule and abuse and had seriously damaged its business.

The trial court dismissed the suit before a trial, holding that

Kentucky Fried Chicken of Bowling Green had failed to make a case. The decision was appealed to the Kentucky Supreme Court. That court also sided with the Colonel on the ground that the particular fried chicken outlet that brought the suit was not the subject of the Colonel's wrath. Rather, his statements were directed at Kentucky Fried Chicken generally, and therefore no single member of the class of Kentucky Fried Chicken owners was defamed. The court said that there was nothing in the Colonel's remarks that identified the Bowling Green Kentucky Fried Chicken outlet, and therefore it could not collect damages.

So on the basis of this case at least, if you're going to make a statement that gets people upset, keep it general; and if you've got any questions about Kentucky Fried Chicken, just ask the Colonel.

Anacin v. Tylenol

The makers of Anacin may have a headache. The reason they're upset is that they will no longer be able to tell you that Anacin is better than Tylenol. That was the result of a recent decision by the Second Circuit Court of Appeals.

The case came about as the result of two television and magazine ads that began with the statement, "Your body knows the difference between these pain relievers and adult-strength Anacin." The ad proceeded to tell you that Anacin can do things to you that Tylenol cannot and left you with the distinct impression that Anacin is better than Tylenol. The makers of Tylenol protested to the TV networks and magazines, claiming that the Anacin ads were deceptive and misleading—claims that didn't get them very far at all.

The court case was actually started by Anacin, which decided to get a head start by seeking to enjoin Tylenol from further protest and from interfering with the way it wanted to sell its product. Tylenol counterclaimed, saying that Anacin's ads were false and misleading. It said that Anacin is not a superior pain killer compared to Tylenol, that Anacin's anti-inflamation claims were over-inflated, that Anacin really isn't faster-acting than Tylenol, and that Anacin's claim that it won't hurt your stomach was not true.

The district court where the case was first heard held that on the basis of consumer reaction to the Anacin ads, those ads did violate the Lanham Act, which forbids false and misleading advertising. Anacin claimed that it never really said it was better than Tylenol, but the court found, based on an extensive study, that that's what the public believed. The court halted the Anacin advertising.

Anacin appealed on the basis that its ads should not be halted just because the public misinterpreted the actual language. But the appeals court agreed with the district court that what really counts is the message—not the literal words that make up that message. So when it comes to pain relievers, the difference had better really be there.

Collaring the wrong polo shirt

When is a polo shirt not really a polo shirt after all? That was the subject matter of the case of *Polo Fashions* v. *Extra Special Products,* recently decided by a federal district court in New York. The case got started when Extra Special began marketing shirts with the famous polo player swinging his mallet. The polo player looked almost exactly like the polo player used by Polo Fashions which, along with designer Ralph Lauren, had registered the polo player as its trademark. Until Extra Special came along, when you saw a polo player galloping across your shirt you knew what it was all about.

Polo Fashions and Ralph Lauren, being greatly affronted by this latest form of horse stealing, brought suit in district court seeking to enjoin Extra Special from infringing on its trademark. Extra Special claimed it wasn't doing anything wrong. It said that the word *polo* and the figure of the polo player were generic to polo shirts and coats, and therefore could be used by anybody.

Judge Goettel rolled up his sleeves and went to work. He agreed that the term "polo shirt" was a generic term, meaning —for those of you who've always wondered what the legal definition of a polo shirt was—"a close-fitting pull-over shirt for sports wear, with a turn-over collar, or a rounded, banded neck." But the court went on to point out that there are a lot of other factors that go into the decision of whether competition is unfair and a trademark is being infringed. The court held that while the defendant could continue to sell polo shirts, when it put the polo player on the shirt it was infringing the trademark and stepping on Ralph Lauren's toes.

What really did it for the court was the fact that there was great confusion among the public, as was shown by a "polo tie" that was admitted into evidence. Expert testimony subsequently showed that it was not a "polo tie," at least not one designed by Ralph Lauren. So the judge granted the injunction against Extra Special, and the next time you see the polo player swinging his mallet you can rest assured that your polo shirt is, in fact, a "polo shirt" after all.

Is it illegal to use your Betamax?

Is it illegal to use your Betamax? That was the question recently decided by a federal district court in California. The case involved a lawsuit by Universal Studios against Sony Corporation, manufacturer of the Betamax, which is one of the many devices now on the market that allow you to record and rerun whatever appears on your TV set. In addition, not only can you record things and cut out commercials, but there are also now a number of places where you can buy prerecorded movies and films of all kinds.

Universal was upset by this for obvious reasons. It claimed that it and a lot of other TV and movie producers were going to be in trouble because of Betamax. It claimed that viewers would watch prerecorded programs, when in pre-Betamax days they would have been watching TV programs, seeing the commercials, and rushing out and buying what was advertised. In addition, Universal claimed that when programs on television were rerun, there would be fewer people watching them because they would have been recorded on the Betamax. Universal said that while there had been no actual harm as yet, the potential for harm was enormous, and the court should stop individuals from using their Betamaxes.

The court reviewed the copyright laws of 1909 and 1976 and noted that both laws failed to deal specifically with this question. Therefore the court had to rely on the fair use doctrine, which is a judge-made exception to the copyright laws. The court said that video recordings for home use fell within the fair use exception. The court said that all the terrible things Universal said were going to happen hadn't happened yet. The court refused to interfere with the private citizen's right to use his or her home recorder on the basis of speculative harm.

Besides, said the court, enforcing the prohibition would be practically impossible and an invasion of the privacy of the Betamax owner, an invasion of privacy that was unwarranted due to the fact that Universal had chosen to beam its programs into private homes to begin with. So sit back, relax, and run your reruns any time you want to.

Out of bounds

If your state line is a river, you can bank on running into a lot of trouble. That's the message of a case recently decided by the U.S. Supreme Court. The case was another chapter in the long battle between the states of Kentucky and Ohio to determine the precise boundary line between them. Surprisingly, the court decided that the boundary line was not in the middle of the river.

Before we tell you just where the boundary is, we should point out that Kentucky and Ohio are not the first states to do battle over a river. In this opinion alone the following states were cited: Nebraska, Mississippi, Arkansas, Illinois, Missouri, Minnesota, Wisconsin, New Jersey, Delaware, Tennessee, Texas, Louisiana, Indiana, New Hampshire, and Maine. In fact, the list of states that have border disputes reads like a recent advertisement for a credit card.

To decide this case, the court cited the case of *Handles Lessee* v. *Anthony,* decided back in 1820. That case held that when a great river is the boundary between nations or states, if the original property is in neither, each holds the middle of the stream. But when one state is the original protector and grants the territory on one side only, it retains the river.

The court reviewed the history of Ohio and Kentucky, going back to when Virginia ceded to the United States "the lands north of the river Ohio." And it was pretty clear to everybody that when Kentucky came along, it included the Ohio River. But the question was whether it now included the low-water mark of the Ohio River back in 1792 when Kentucky was admitted to the Union, or whether it included the much higher low-water mark of today.

It was on this issue that the U.S. Supreme Court came to rule, with four justices deciding that it was the low-water mark back in 1792 and three deciding that it was the low-water mark of today. The majority said its decision was compelled by history; the dissenters said it's impossible to have a state boundary determined by the uncertainty of where a low-water mark was nearly two hundred years ago. But the majority ruled, and you can bet you haven't heard the last of where Kentucky ends and Ohio begins.

Who owns the sea?

For as long as people have sailed the sea, they have argued about who owns it. The earliest known spokesman for freedom of the seas was Hugo Grotius, who in 1609 wrote a treatise taking exception to the generally recognized view that the oceans or parts of them could be appropriated for the exclusive use of a particular nation. He argued that the vast size of the sea made effective occupation and domination impossible, that no borderlines could be established, and that the resources of the sea were virtually inexhaustible. The only exception that Grotius allowed was state control of immediate coastal waters over which there could be complete dominion. This set the stage for the three-mile limit, which was adopted one century later and was based on the fact that an eighteenth-century cannonball could travel just about three miles before it splashed.

On March 1, 1977, the Fishery Conservation and Management Act of 1976 became effective and established a fishery conservation zone two hundred nautical miles offshore. As you might imagine, going from a three-mile limit to a two-hundred-mile limit raises some rather difficult questions, like what happens when Mexico, Canada, and especially Cuba also declare a two-hundred-mile limit? Another question is, what happens to the law when and if the United Nations Conference on the Law of the Sea ever comes up with a treaty?

If history is any indication, enforcement of the two-hundred-mile limit may not be as easy as it was in the first month of the law. In 1952, Chile, Ecuador, and Peru issued the Declaration of

Santiago, setting up a two-hundred-mile limit, and these countries went about enforcing it with great gusto. A celebrated incident occurred when Peru seized an entire whaling fleet in 1954. To get back his boats, Aristotle Onassis had to come up with $3 million.

As for any forthcoming treaty on the law of the sea, the new two-hundred-mile-limit law provides specifically that once ratified, the treaty would govern. We should remember that this year's United Nations Conference on the Law of the Sea was preceded by two international conferences that failed to produce agreement. Interestingly enough, at the 1930 conference it was the United States that argued that the three-mile limit was just right. It looks as if the tide has turned.

Those frightening Liberian freighters

What is a Liberian freighter, anyway? Well, it's a freighter that is one of the nearly twenty-five hundred ships registered under the Liberian flag. Liberia is a small African country about the size of Nebraska, with a population of about a million. You may be wondering why a country this size registers the largest merchant fleet in the world. By way of comparison, the United States has less than six hundred ships registered under its flag. And it is interesting to note that the United States ranks tenth among the fleets of the world, with Japan second after Liberia, followed by the United Kingdom, Norway, Greece, and Panama.

There is relatively little written on the subject of exactly why vessels built in one country and carrying goods between other countries are registered in a place the vessel will probably never see. One article did appear in the *International Labor Review;* it was called "Flags of Convenience and Substandard Vessels" and was rather prophetically named when one considers recent difficulties of Liberian freighters on both coasts of the United States. The article detailed the International Labor Organization's attempts to do something about the flag-of-convenience problem.

The reason the International Labor Organization was interested in the problem in the first place was that one of the motives of transferring registry to a country with which a vessel has no genuine link is that the convenience country may allow labor conditions to exist on ships that simply would not be tolerated by important maritime countries. Other motives deal with tax benefits and safety inspections.

A committee of experts was set up to conduct a survey; the problem was that the only countries that responded to the survey were those that weren't causing the problem. The seafaring members of the committee presented evidence that the crews in flag-of-convenience vessels were exploited, received low wages, worked long hours, and served on ships that were prone to serious accidents involving the safety of life and property at sea and causing ocean pollution, owing to the poor physical conditions of the ships.

While there are several suggestions of what can be done about all this, one thing is certain: The changes probably won't come from the Liberian legislature.

Only one China after all

It looks as if there is only one China after all, and the president can pick which one it is. That's the result of a recent decision of the District of Columbia Court of Appeals. The case started in a federal district court, which held it was illegal for President Carter to have unilaterally terminated the mutual defense treaty with Taiwan. The district court holding was based on the fact that while the Constitution goes into great detail as to how a treaty is entered into, it says nothing about how one is to be ended. The district court held that for a treaty to be terminated, it takes a vote of either two-thirds of the Senate or a majority of both houses and of Congress.

The first question for the Court of Appeals was whether Senator Goldwater, eight other Senators, and sixteen members of the House of Representatives had standing, or the right to bring the suit in the first place. The court said that since the Senators were clearly losing the right to vote on an issue, they did have standing to sue. But on the merits of the case, the Court of Appeals ruled against them and for the President.

The court began its opinion stating that it rejected the district court's holding that because the president cannot enter into a treaty without the consent of the Senate, he must, in all circumstances, seek the same senatorial consent to terminate the treaty. The court cited as an example the fact that while ambassadors who are appointed to serve abroad must be ratified by the Senate, it's never been suggested that the president has to get the Senate's approval before he can fire an ambassador.

The court said further that the Constitution grants specific powers to the president in Article I, but Article II confers on the president broad foreign policy powers that have no limitations. Since the power to terminate a treaty isn't mentioned in Article I, it must then be covered under the broad foreign policy powers in Article II. The court said that the United States considers mainland China to be the legitimate Chinese state. Therefore, in the eyes of the government, Taiwan as a state has ceased to exist, and the president can terminate the treaty on his own.

So when it comes to the termination of treaties, Congress is left standing and watching, and no more.

CHAPTER

10

WHITHER THE LAW:

Do process, and some substance, really matter?

Well, it's been a long journey, and we've looked at a lot of law and a lot of life. As we come to the end, we might ask just where we and the law are going. In case it hasn't always been obvious throughout, I have great respect for the law, that for which it stands, and those who watch over it each day. I also worry about the law, for I see that it spends a great deal of its time mired in delay, and all too often fighting the wrong battles. The stories in this final chapter are about the law itself and provide a window on the process and the substance that make the law work.

Just as it is important to look back, it is important to look ahead; each of us must ask where we are heading, just as the law and those responsible for it must look to see where it is headed. Perhaps it is like sailing—the most important thing is the destination and the goal. For only if we have a goal can we make provisions to reach it. And we should remember always that even if our goal is in sight, we will never reach it if we are sailing into the wind. And if the wind is behind us, we will sail fast and furious, but if we look away for just a moment we may sail right over and past our goal. Even worse, the wind may turn against us with a nasty jibe and dismast us and even sink our ship. So for the law, as for each of us, the way to sail is just off the wind, with a strong hand on the tiller so that when the storm comes up we can fall off just a bit and when it dies down, we can head up. But there's only one problem when you sail just off the wind; you have to tack to your goal, and although it may take a little longer, if we figure our tacks just right, and if we have a sea-worthy boat and a good crew, we will find our harbor, safe and sound, and we will reach our goal.

And so it is with the law—and with life. Nobody said it was going to be easy, but it sure is worthwhile.

From the mouths of babes

We lawyers have a habit of sometimes taking ourselves a little too seriously. That's why it's good to be evaluated by different groups in society. One group that recently took a look at lawyers was a class of nine-year-olds in St. Louis, Missouri. Their teacher, Mr. Ken Wilson, had the results published in a recent edition of *The Barrister,* and I think you'll enjoy hearing what nine-year-olds really think about lawyers.

On the state of the art, the students had the following to say: "A good thing to remember about needing a lawyer is don't." "Lawyers sometimes become judges. Maybe they become attorneys too. I do not know because it takes all my knowing to know that lawyers sometimes become judges."

Other comments were: "A good attorney should keep thinking about his case around the clock—twelve days a week." "The difference between lawyers now and in the past is today they know not to try to do everything but to specialize—like cows give milk, while chickens prefer to lay eggs." One student, when asked, "Will we ever run out of lawyers?" answered, "The chances are 999 out of 100." And last, "Because of computers we won't need lawyers in a few hundred years. Just wait and see."

On the subject of laws themselves, the students had the following to say: "The Justinian Code is a well-known code few people have ever heard of. It was made in 529, but I forget whether it was A.C. or D.C." Another student ran into a problem we lawyers frequently encounter. He wrote, "I looked up what a habeas corpus is twice, but I forgot it three times." Another student said, "Once I had a chance to read a whole stack of law books. Things they say in law books are only to look at, not to understand. They are not really good for anything but being in law books."

On the subject of learning and the law, "Law and order will not be like it should be until it gets like it was when we didn't have any and appreciated all the things law and order could give us." Another student echoed recent remarks by Chief Justice Burger and Attorney General Bell when he wrote, "I am not sure how many lawyers there are in the United States, but trying to find out is one of my constant doings."

One student came up with the reason why lawyers are sometimes called attorneys when he wrote, "By learning that lawyers are sometimes called attorneys, I now know two places in the encyclopedia I can find out about them."

And last, one student summed it all up by saying, "Now that

I've learned all about lawyers, if you ever see me listening to them being talked about as if they were important, you'll notice a twinkle in my eye, and you'll know why."

Disarming the judge

What happens when a legislature decides to disarm judges? That was the question recently decided by the California Supreme Court in one of the first tests of a California law designed to make it impossible for judges to place people who use guns during a robbery on probation. Many judges feel the power to put a person on probation is their inherent right.

Problems have come when legislatures have passed laws designed to remove the probation power. Massachusetts, for example, provides that a person must be jailed one year for possessing an unlicensed firearm, and that sentence cannot be suspended and the person cannot be placed on probation. The California law wasn't drawn quite as precisely, providing instead that "probation shall not be granted for any person who used a firearm during the commission of a robbery."

The first case to test the law involved an off-duty employee of a security company who entered a 7–11 store and pointed an unloaded revolver at the clerk, forcing him to hand over forty dollars. The man admitted he had committed the robbery, but explained he did so in order to convince the owner of the 7–11 store to resubscribe to his security service. He said he had made sure the gun was unloaded and was on his way back to the store to return the money when he was arrested. Based on the fact that he had no previous record and that police and probation officers recommended that he not be sent to prison, the judge decided to strike the charge of use of a firearm, thereby reducing the charges to robbery. The judge then placed the man on probation.

The state appealed, claiming that the judge had no right to place a person on probation who used a gun in the course of a robbery. The California Supreme Court held that the law did not say anything about the right of a judge to strike a charge completely if he chose to do so. Since a judge has always had the right to strike charges, and since there was nothing in the new law that said he couldn't, probation was held to be proper in this case.

So when a legislature decides to disarm judges and, particularly, takes away their right to strike, it had better do so very carefully.

Judge-made jokes aren't funny

What happens when a judge plays a practical joke on a defense lawyer in the middle of a trial? Believe it or not, that was the question recently raised before the Second Circuit Court of Appeals. What happened was that a man was on trial for robbery before the New York Supreme Court. His defense was that he couldn't have been the robber because, he claimed, on the day in question he was in a secure observation ward in Creedmore Psychiatric Hospital. He provided both documentary and testimonial evidence in support of his alibi. The prosecutor asked for time to produce a rebuttal witness, but after a day of trying couldn't locate one and so informed the defense counsel.

The defense attorney, no longer worried about any rebuttal witness, turned to preparation of his closing argument. But just before the jury entered the courtroom, the judge took the prosecutor aside and suggested playing a practical joke on the defense attorney. He said, "Do me a favor; go along with this just for fun. When the defense counsel comes back in here, I want you to tell him that you're going to call rebuttal witnesses after all." The prosecutor replied, "Do you think we ought to do that? I've already told him I wasn't going to call anybody."

But, according to the Court of Appeals, after further coaxing from the judge the prosecutor overcame his reluctance and agreed to participate in the hoax. Even the court stenographer was advised of the joke, and he agreed to pretend to record the remarks since the joke, of course, was to be off the record. The defense attorney walked in, and the prosecutor stood up and announced he was going to call five members of the Creedmore professional staff. The defense attorney immediately jumped up and argued for a long time about the prosecutor's bad faith. After he found it was all a joke, he moved for a mistrial on the grounds of "judicial and prosecutorial misconduct."

The trial judge granted the mistrial. Then the defense attorney moved to bar a second trial on the grounds that in some cases where mistrials have been ordered because of misconduct on the part of the judge or prosecutor, the state has been barred from trying the defendant again. But in this case, said the court, although the trial judge's poor taste was exceeded only by his astonishingly bad judgment, it could not conclude that the judge was motivated by a desire to prejudice or harass the defense attorney and his client.

So there will be another trial, but you can bet that next time even if a funny thing *does* happen on the way to the courtroom, you won't hear about it inside.

Shopping for opinions

What happens when a judge goes shopping for dirty books? That was the question recently raised before the U.S. Supreme Court in a case that stands for the proposition that when a community goes on the warpath against pornography, it had better wage that war with care.

The case got started when an investigator for the New York State Police purchased two reels of film from a so-called adult book store. He watched them, and concluded they violated New York's obscenity laws. He then took the films to a judge so a warrant could be issued for a search of the entire store.

Then things really got interesting, because the investigator asked the judge to come along to determine which things were obscene and which were not. So one morning the judge, the investigator, and nine other police officers paid a visit to the store to see what they could see. They arrested the store clerk, who then cooperated by adjusting the silent film booths so the judge could view the films without depositing any money. The judge viewed 23 films and ordered them seized as obscene. He then viewed 14 other films and ordered them seized also and moved on to the magazine rack. He looked at magazines for between ten seconds and a minute each and seized 397 of them along with 431 other reels of film. This took a whole day, and although three marked police cars were parked outside, customers still came and went; but as the court noted, they didn't stay very long.

The items were then taken to a state police barracks and listed on the warrant, a warrant that had started out as two pages and ended up being sixteen. On the basis of the evidence, the operators of the store were convicted.

The U.S. Supreme Court in a rare unanimous opinion reversed the conviction, saying that what had happened in that store was reminiscent of the general warrant of the eighteenth century which called forth the Fourth Amendment to the Constitution. The Constitution, said the court, requires that warrants be issued by an impartial magistrate in advance of a search. In this case, said the court, the judge became a member and indeed the leader of the search party itself.

So it looks as though the moral of this case is that judges should stay on the bench rather than venturing out into the field.

Coats and ties in Alaska

Yes, you do have to wear a coat and tie in the courtroom, even in Alaska. That's the result of a case recently decided by the Alaska Supreme Court. The case involved a lawyer who was cited for contempt three different times because he refused to wear a coat and tie in the courtroom. The lawyer claimed it was part of his constitutional right to privacy and personal liberty to dress the way he wanted in the courtroom. He also claimed that if he was forced to wear a coat and tie, it would interfere with his representation of his clients because the coat and tie would be viewed by jurors with suspicion. Last, he claimed the rule discriminated against men.

The case finally ended up before the Alaska Supreme Court, which took the opportunity to write what has to be the definitive opinion on the subject of lawyers' dress in the courtroom. The court began by stating that it's clear that a court can adopt minimal standards of dress for attorneys who appear before it, and while the dress code cannot be unduly rigid or dictate matters of taste, the requirement of wearing a coat and tie is reasonable.

The court said it's true that Alaska probably does have fewer coats and ties per capita than any other state in the nation, but it goes too far to claim that a lawyer who has to wear one in court will be viewed with suspicion. If a lawyer is viewed with suspicion, said the court, it's fair to say it's because of something other than what he is wearing.

As for the question of women not having to wear a coat and tie, the court said women are required to wear conservative business attire, and the general standard, therefore, is the same.

One judge dissented, saying the only rule should be that distracting or bizarre attire should not be permitted, but beyond that, judicial interference with the personal liberty of counsel to choose the mode of attire is unconstitutional. But the majority ruled, and although clothes may make the man mad, coats and ties are in the courtroom, and this issue is closed.

Helen Palsgraf's woes

Poor Helen Palsgraf. That's about all one can say when the full story of this woman is finally known. In case you're wondering who Helen Palsgraf was, she's the lady who was the plaintiff in a case that every first-year law student worries about. And in these days of *Paper Chase,* which relives the supposed terror that accompanies the study of law, it'll do us well to remember what happened to Helen Palsgraf.

The case got started on August 25, 1924, when Helen Palsgraf was standing on a railway platform belonging to the Long Island Railway. As she waited on the crowded platform, a train bound for someplace other than Rockaway Beach stopped at the platform, and two men ran forward to catch it. One of the men got on the car without incident, even though the train had started to move away from the platform. The other man, who was carrying a package, jumped aboard the car, but seemed unsteady, as if about to fall. A guard on the car reached out to help him get on, and another guard on the platform pushed him from behind.

With all this pushing and pulling, the package the man was carrying fell to the tracks. What no one knew was that the package contained fireworks, which went off with a tremendous roar. The force of the concussion knocked over a set of scales at the other end of the platform. The falling scales struck Helen, causing injuries for which she brought suit against the Long Island Railroad because of the guard's negligence. The jury found in her favor, awarding six thousand dollars, which in the 1920s was a good deal of money. The case was appealed to the New York Court of Appeals.

On the bench at the time was Justice Benjamin Cardozo, who

wrote the majority opinion overturning the jury award. Justice Cardozo said that the conduct of the railroad guard, if it was a wrong in relation to the holder of the package, was not a wrong in relation to the plaintiff standing far away. The court held that what had happened was simply not foreseeable, and that to hold otherwise would create a duty toward everyone.

The *Harvard Law Record* contacted Lillian Palsgraf, who had been twelve years old at the time and who had left her mother for a moment to buy a newspaper. She saw the package fall and remembered the smoke and the falling scales that hit her mother. She tells us that Helen Palsgraf died twenty years later, upset until her death over her failure to collect from the accident.

So although poor Helen Palsgraf, who was struck by the scales, found no justice—at least in her mind—she has left a legacy that weighs heavily on the minds of all of us, especially first-year law students who meet Helen Palsgraf for the first time.

Flunking out is not unconstitutional

Well, it's finally happened. A law student who flunked out of law school because she failed her constitutional law course has gone to court claiming it was unconstitutional for the school to force her to leave.

After successfully completing two semesters at a state law school, the student received an F in constitutional law and was judged academically deficient at the end of her third semester. She was told she had to leave, but was readmitted for the next academic year on a trial basis. At the end of that year, however, she was again asked to leave, this time because she didn't have a grade average of 2.0. She asked for readmission again, but it was denied. She went to court, claiming that the way the law school figured grade averages violated the due process and equal protection clauses of the Constitution.

The general university rule was that the last grade received in a repeated course completely replaced the prior failing grade. But in the law school, the failing grade was not disregarded, but was added in with the new grade when the total grade average was figured. When the student repeated the course, she got a C. However, because the initial F was figured into her average, she simply didn't make the grade.

The school claimed that it had the right to be tougher on law students than other students because in the particular state involved, Montana, there was no bar exam, and graduation from law school meant being eligible for the immediate practice of law. The student claimed it was arbitrary and unreasonable for the school to include the first grade in figuring her point average; she also claimed that by treating her differently from general university students, the school violated her constitutional rights to due process and equal protection of the law.

But, alas, the student did about as well before the Montana Supreme Court as she did in her constitutional law course. The court held that school authorities must be given absolute discretion in determining whether a student has been academically delinquent and that school authorities are uniquely qualified by training and experience to judge a student's qualifications. As for the equal protection argument, the court held that the study of law is different from the study of other things, and since all law students were treated the same, the equal protection clause was not violated.

Well, at least nobody can say she didn't give it a good try.

Crossing the bar

Please answer the following question: A trailer truck is driving down a narrow road that has a sign posted, "No trucks allowed," and the driver is going sixty miles per hour over a bridge with a thirty-mile-per-hour speed limit. The force of the speeding truck going over the bridge causes a great deal of vibration and rumbling to a series of oil drums, which have been stored in the top of a garage loft in violation of the fire and building codes of the particular village where this drama is unfolding. At the precise moment that the truck is speeding through and the illegally stored oil drums are beginning to roll around the loft, a trespasser is sneaking across the vacant lot located below the loft and is struck on the head by one of the falling drums. What are the rights of the parties?

What I have just read to you was the first question on my bar exam, and questions just like that are answered each year all around the country by about fifty thousand law students who would like nothing more than to become lawyers. According to the statistics, only about 70 percent will pass the exam. Most of them will have spent three years at law schools following another four years of undergraduate school; and the last eight weeks before the exam will have been spent in cram courses.

The stakes are pretty high, for most who already have jobs are going to be rather upset if they have to retake the exam; about the only consolation prize for failing the exam is that most bar-review courses offer a discount if you have to take the test again. And each year there are some who have just refused to give up, with the most recent statistic being a New Yorker who took the exam seven times before he finally passed.

A group of Georgia students decided to go at things a little differently. They sued to declare the whole Georgia bar exam null and void because they said it discriminated against blacks. They lost, but you would think that those who sued would at least be exempted from the exam. By the way, as for the answer to my exam question, I'm sorry, but I could only find the question in my records.

Suing your firm to become a partner

Can you become a partner in a law firm by bringing a lawsuit? Most young lawyers who join a law firm do so with the expectation that some day they will achieve a partnership in the firm. There are many ways to make partner, including staying at the office later than all the other people trying to make partner, bringing in more business, getting along with the people who have already made partner, and the like. But it is doubtful that anyone has ever before selected the route taken by a young man who sought to become a partner in Cravath, Swain and Moore, one of New York's largest and most prestigious law firms.

The law firm had 48 partners and 130 associates, of whom the plaintiff in a case brought in a New York federal court was one.

This young lawyer testified that he joined the firm because he was told that associates would be promoted to partnership based on their efforts and ability. But things apparently didn't go as planned, because the lawyer claimed that he was discriminated against with respect to the type of work he was given, his training, his rotation, and outside opportunities. He said the reason he was discriminated against by the firm was that he was "an Italian and/or Catholic."

The Civil Rights Act makes it unlawful to discriminate against a person with regard to the terms and conditions of his or her employment, or to deprive a person of employment opportunities because of race, color, religion, sex, or national origin. The law firm argued in its defense that the act did not extend to how the partners treated themselves; therefore, how could it apply to the process by which one becomes a partner? It also claimed violation of its partners' constitutional rights of free association and privacy.

But Judge Gagliardi, in writing the decision, said that it didn't matter whether or not the partners themselves were covered by the law. He ruled that the promotion process was employment opportunity, which was clearly covered by the law.

Now that the legal point has been decided, the case of the associate suing his own law firm to become a partner will go back to court for trial. The lesson to be drawn from the case is not clear. Some will see rough justice in a law firm being sued; others will wonder how real a victory will really be. But one thing is clear —equal employment under the law applies to lawyers too.

When can a lawyer fire his client?

We've all heard of cases when clients aren't satisfied with their lawyers, and it is not uncommon to hear clients complain about their attorneys, although sometimes the attorney is just as much a victim of an inefficient system of civil and criminal justice as is the client. But there are situations, as in any profession, where a lawyer has ignored his or her client, has missed a statute of limitations, or in some other way has not properly performed the necessary duties for the client. These situations can lead to termination of the lawyer-client relationship, complaints to the Board of Bar Overseers (or other group that regulates the activities of lawyers) or, in extreme situations, a suit against the lawyer for malpractice.

But what hasn't happened very often is a situation in which the lawyer wants to terminate the relationship with the client, and the client doesn't want to let this happen. A case decided by the New York Civil Court recognized the uniqueness of this question in its opening paragraph, when the court stated, "Common-law attorneys have represented clients at least since the days of Edward I. Yet this [case] raised a question about the attorney-client relation that appears never to have been answered."

The law firm in question began to represent the client on the basis of a retainer, which is a payment made regularly, usually on a monthly basis, to secure the services of a law firm. After several years the retainer was terminated, but a lawyer from the firm continued to represent the client in some pending cases, without charging him a fee, and merely trying to settle the cases. Unfortunately, the cases couldn't be settled, and the lawyer asked the client to get another lawyer. The client refused, and the lawyer went to court, requesting permission to fire his client or, as he put it, seeking leave to withdraw from the cases.

The general rule is that a lawyer can terminate a relationship with a client at any time for a good and sufficient cause and with reasonable notice. Here, however, as the court put it, the lawyer wanted to be relieved solely because he wanted to be relieved. The court finally allowed the lawyer to withdraw; and it looks as if the lawyer can fire his client if he wants to, even though he may have to go to court to do it.

Unpleasant Seat Pleasant, Md.

I'm sure you all have heard of political meetings getting out of hand, but it would be hard to duplicate what happened recently in the town of Seat Pleasant, Maryland. As the court put it, for the mayor chairing the meeting, the seat was anything but pleasant. Things had apparently been rather difficult for the mayor, because the meeting prior to the one that precipitated all the court action had to be adjourned, and the mayor pulled out a gun in the parking lot in the midst of some protesting townspeople.

The next meeting was preceded by the distribution of fliers proclaiming "Seat Pleasant murderers" and making all sorts of claims, including governmental overspending such as full-time pay for a part-time manager. At the meeting a dispute broke out between the manager, who was quite upset at being called a part-time manager, and the mayor. The mayor asked the police

chief to eject the town manager, who preferred not be be ejected
and responded by pulling the police chief's coat over the police
chief's head. The dispute ended abruptly when two other police
officers came to the rescue of their chief and arrested the town
manager for the crime of refusing to leave a public building upon
request.

The town manager was found not guilty, and he then sued the
mayor, the chief of police, and another officer for $3 million for
assault and battery, false arrest, and libel. The lower court judge
entered judgment for $400 for the plaintiff, and the mayor and
the police appealed.

The question for the court was whether town officials, namely
the mayor and the police, were entitled to immunity from suit
because they were public officials. Maryland law, like that of most
states, provides that governmental immunity is extended to all of
the nonmalicious acts of public officials acting in a discretionary
capacity.

The court held that the mayor and the others were clearly
acting in a discretionary capacity, in that the mayor was using his
discretion in insisting upon an orderly recognition of speakers
and in deciding whether or not to call upon the police to maintain
order at an emotionally charged meeting. As for malice, the court
held that the actions of the mayor just didn't measure up to the
definition of malice, which the law defines as the performance of
an act with an evil motive, influenced by hate, the purpose being
to deliberately and willfully injure the plaintiff.

So the judgment for the town manager was reversed, but the
politics of Seat Pleasant left its mark on the common law.

Riot in the courtroom

What happens when there's a riot in the courtroom? That was
the question in a case recently decided by the U.S. District Court
for South Dakota. The incident grew out of a state court criminal
trial of a group of American Indians.

The trial got off to a bad start when spectators in the courtroom, most of whom were Indians, refused to stand when the
judge entered. The judge promptly ordered the spectators carried from the courtroom by court officers. This went on for
several days, and it was clear the judge and the court officers were
getting tired of carrying the Indians out of the courtroom.

One morning they decided to clear it in a different way, using the Sioux Falls police department's tactical squad. This was described as a group of jumpsuited police officers equipped with 4011 riot batons with steel ball ends, gloves with metal knuckles, gas masks, face shields, Mace, heavy boots, handcuffs, and sidearms. The squad entered the courtroom on the run, and as they did so, a woman in the courtroom screamed, "My God, they are going to kill them!" A general melee broke out, and at the end of it a number of Indians were arrested and convicted of the crime of rioting to obstruct justice.

The Indians appealed their conviction to the federal district court, claiming it was unconstitutional. They argued they were found guilty because the jury was not told they had a right of self-defense when attacked in a courtroom by a group of police officers.

The federal district court did set aside the conviction of the Indians on the grounds that the claim of self-defense should have been available and that there was evidence to suggest that the police did use unnecessary and excessive force and were the first to resort to violence when they entered the courtroom. When the trial court refused to instruct the jury on the issue of self-defense, the Indians were in effect deprived of their constitutional right to trial by jury.

So you can be convicted of rioting to obstruct justice, as long as it isn't justice that started the riot.

Briefer briefs

Chief Justice Burger recently issued a call to the bar for briefer briefs, and whether one is a lawyer who has to write them, a judge who has to read them, or a client who has to pay for them, we should all be very glad that the call for briefer briefs has been issued.

The case that elicited the Chief Justice's remarks is one in which a Michigan lawyer had submitted a brief of 216 pages, which was later followed by a 53-page response to the argument made by the other side. The judge said that in this case alone there was a total of more than 600 pages. Since a court hears an average of four cases a day, this would mean that each justice would have to read about 2,400 pages a day, to say nothing of the scores of cases cited in the briefs.

Now it is true that there are law clerks who do a lot of the reading, but we lawyers should have some sympathy for them, for

someone has to read every page of every document that is filed
in court. One might have thought that the very name given to a
brief would have some impact on its length, but, alas, this has
clearly not been the case.

By the way, this piece is only half as long as the others.

Alger Hiss is a lawyer again

On January 25, 1950, Alger Hiss was convicted of two counts
of perjury in his testimony before a federal grand jury, and on
August 1, 1952, his name was struck from the rolls of lawyers
permitted to practice law in the Commonwealth of Massachusetts. Recently he was readmitted to practice. This case shows us
the workings of the system by which lawyers are disciplined.

Hiss was convicted of perjury and served three and one-half
years in the federal prison at Lewisburg, Pennsylvania, and was
subsequently disbarred. All states have some mechanism by
which lawyers can be disciplined or disbarred; some have elaborate mechanisms by which grievances can be presented and dealt
with, others depend on informal mechanisms, usually initiated by
a bar association. This area is extremely difficult, for every lawyer, by the nature of his or her work, has probably at one time
or another made someone rather unhappy; and the line between
errors of judgment, mistakes, or malice and bad faith is sometimes extremely thin and difficult to prove clearly. Most times,
however, conviction of a crime, particularly a crime involving
moral turpitude such as perjury, will lead to disbarment.

As the Supreme Judicial Court of Massachusetts stated in the
Hiss case, "He comes before us now as a convicted perjurer
whose crime is further tainted by the breach of confidence and
trust which underlay his conviction. His conviction and subsequent disbarment are conclusive evidence of his lack of moral
character at the time of his removal from office." Despite this
language, however, the court reinstated Hiss, making it clear that
it did not, in 1975, intend to retry the issue of Hiss's guilt or
innocence; rather it adopted the position that conviction does not
permanently seal the fate of an attorney and that the court will
look instead at present fitness.

The court found that Hiss's life over the decades had been
exemplary—as a scholar, as an assistant to a small manufacturing
company and, most recently, as a salesman for a stationery and
printing-supplies company, the president of which wrote that

he would be glad to engage Hiss as a lawyer if he were read-mitted.

And so, while many would argue that Hiss never should have been convicted to begin with, and others would say he never should practice law again, most lawyers would agree that the reinstatement—after twenty-three years—was a just one.

The privilege of necessity

As we remember the Tall Ships, we might reflect for a moment on a drama that took place when a sailing ship was lost in 1884 —a drama that resulted in one of the most celebrated cases to be tried in the courts of England. The case was that of *Regina* v. *Dudley and Stephens,* and it began in a violent storm that struck a sailing ship when it was sixteen hundred miles from the Cape of Good Hope.

When it appeared that there was no hope for this vessel, Thomas Dudley, Edward Stephens, a Mr. Brooks, and a seven-teen-year-old boy took to an open lifeboat. They had no water, and all they had for food were two one-pound tins of turnips and a small can of turtle soup, which were quickly exhausted. Dudley and Stephens decided that somebody had to be killed and eaten in order to save all the rest. Brooks refused to go along with the scheme, and the boy, who was by this time quite helpless, was not consulted at all as to the plan.

On the next day, Dudley killed the boy and all three survivors remained alive by living off his remains. Four days later, they were picked up by a passing ship. Upon return to England, Dud-ley and Stephens were tried for murder. It was agreed that if they had not killed the boy, they probably would not have lived, and that it was likely that the boy, being in a more weakened condition than the others, would have died before they did.

The defense had a lot of trouble finding any authority to justify this act of cannibalism. It was able to unearth one quote left for posterity by Lord Bacon, who stated that "necessity carrieth a privilege in itself." The court dealt with that principle with the statement that "If Lord Bacon meant to lay down the broad proposition that a man may save his life by killing, if necessary, an innocent and unoffending neighbor, it is certainly not law at the present day."

The court noted that the weakest and most unresisting was the one who was killed, and found both defendants guilty of murder, pronouncing the sentence of death. That sentence was quietly commuted by the queen to six months in prison.

Peanuts in church

Did you know that in Massachusetts it's illegal to eat peanuts in church? Maybe Barbara Seuling knew something we didn't know when she chose that law as the title of her book, *You Can't Eat Peanuts in Church & Other Little-Known Laws.*

Ms. Seuling points out in her introduction that no matter how strange this collection of American laws seems to be, other countries are by no means immune to legislative flights of fancy. In Cambodia, for example, it was once against the law to insult a rice plant. In England during the reign of Henry III, death was the penalty for "Kyllynge, woundynge, or mamynge a fairy." And in the Soviet Union, a train coming upon a person sleeping on the tracks had to stop and wait for the individual to finish the snooze.

Here are a few of Ms. Seuling's choicest tidbits from a book that should be compulsory reading for lawmakers:

In order to discourage little boys from becoming gamblers in Ashland, Wisconsin, a law was placed on the books making it illegal to play marbles for keeps. To take a bath in Boston, you had to have a doctor's written prescription. Spitting against the wind in Sault Saint Marie, Michigan, is unlawful.

In Ziegler, Illinois, there's a law providing that the first four fire fighters to show up at a fire will be paid for their services. Hotel owners in Boston still have to put up and bed down for the night a guest's horse; and in Phoenix, Arizona, every man must wear pants—when he comes to town. In the area of public health, there's an ordinance in Riverside, California, that prohibits kissing on the lips unless both parties first have wiped their lips with carbolized rose water.

Last, a Kentucky statute reads, "No female shall appear in a bathing suit on any highway within this state unless she is escorted by at least two officers or unless she be armed with a club." A subsequent amendment to the original statute reads, "The provisions of this statute shall not apply to females weighing less than ninety pounds nor exceeding two hundred pounds; nor shall it apply to female horses."

Ms. Seuling points out that some of the laws she lists may have been changed. But, she says, "I wouldn't be surprised if someone were mapping out a brand-new freaky law right now."

Getting up to the High Court

"Certiorari denied." With those two words, most of the matters brought to the U.S. Supreme Court are turned away from the court without even a hearing. As the court begins each new term, it is important to realize that very few of the cases brought to it will actually be argued before the justices.

For the 1977–1978 term, the court agreed to hear 33 cases, turning away 799 other litigants who felt that error had been made in the courts below. There is a lot of confusion about just what it means when the Supreme Court denies review and lets a lower court opinion stand. It does mean that whoever won below emerges as the winner, and whoever lost is without any further remedy. But that's about all it means, for the court never says exactly why it doesn't want to review the case. Although people will claim in controversial cases that a refusal to review means something more, it means only that the Supreme Court did not want to hear the case.

So when the court refused to hear the case of *Gaylord* v. *Tacoma School District #10,* it did not mean that the court was adopting a new law that a teacher's homosexuality alone rendered him unfit as a teacher, justifying his dismissal for immorality. What it did mean was that the Tacoma Board #10 won and Mr. Gaylord lost. It did *not* mean that other courts outside the state of Washington were bound to follow that decision, although it could be cited as authority if other courts wanted to go the same way.

Another case the court refused to review was a suit against the publisher of a new book on Ernest Hemingway. In that case, the lower court held that the publisher of a book isn't responsible if an author writes unflattering things about a person he doesn't know.

Other cases turned away involved a person who charged that the police didn't have a right to search his garbage without a warrant, a mother who claimed that her seventeen-year-old son was unconstitutionally shot to death as he fled from a burglary, and a pawnbroker who claimed that laws forcing him to keep records of his transactions were unconstitutional because they violated his customers' right of privacy. For these and more than seven hundred other litigants, the court of last resort is not to be.

Blue Shield for lawyers

What would you think of a Blue Shield card that would pay for a lawyer instead of a doctor? Well, thanks to some recent developments, prepaid legal insurance has moved a lot closer to becoming a reality for millions of people throughout the United States.

The boost came as part of the Tax Reform Act of 1976, a mammoth piece of legislation. One section of that law is being widely hailed by many lawyers and by those who think that people don't use lawyers as much as they should or need to. That section exempts from federal income tax money that is paid by an employer into a prepaid legal plan that will be used to benefit employees. In other words, if you work for a company that decided to contribute money toward a recognized prepaid legal insurance plan, the company could deduct the money paid for such purpose, and you would not be taxed on the value of the legal services you received.

The arguments for prepaid legal insurance are similar to those that are made for prepaid medical insurance: If people pay for legal services by insurance, they will go to see a lawyer early and often, and perhaps avoid getting into a lot of trouble later on. One incoming bar association president recently remarked, "While most people have a family physician, few people have a lasting association with an attorney. This means that people do not use preventive legal advice as they do preventive medicine."

Prepaid legal insurance would pay for almost any legal problem you would be likely to face; wills, divorces, and landlord/tenant problems are usually all covered, and the value of the plan for any given person could run as much as twenty thousand dollars. Serious crimes and automobile accidents (when lawyers are usually paid on the basis of how much they recover for you) are usually not included in the plans. A study of the Shreveport, Louisiana, plan showed that plan members went to lawyers twice as often as before the plan, with lawyers and clients presumably happy with the results.

So Blue Shield for lawyers is coming; hopefully the rate hikes won't be as frequent.

William Kunstler arrives

What happens when a judge gets a nasty letter about a lawyer and turns it over to the newspapers? That was the question recently decided by the U.S. District Court for the Virgin Islands in a case that continues to cloud the sky over the beautiful island of St. Croix.

It all began on the afternoon of September 6, 1972, at the fashionable Mountain Valley Golf Course in St. Croix. Without warning a group of masked men swarmed onto the golf course, shot and killed eight people, and wounded four others. An intensive manhunt was begun, and some days later five men were arrested. All but one of the victims was white, and all the defendants were black. The case immediately took on a high degree of sensationalism with racial overtones.

Then entered attorney William Kunstler who, according to the court, arrived uninvited and took on without pay the defense of one of the defendants. Kunstler's tactics, according to the court, were "scorched earth" all the way. He made four efforts to disqualify Judge Young, who was presiding, and the trial was punctuated by general bedlam.

During the course of the trial Judge Young received a letter from a judge in Baltimore, Maryland. The letter complimented Judge Young on his ability to "withstand" the studied efforts of the defendants and their counsel and went on to describe in not very complimentary terms Mr. Kunstler's defense tactics in a Baltimore trial that involved Black Panthers charged with the murder of a white police officer. After the trial, a photocopy of the letter was turned over to a reporter by the judge, and after it was published in the newspaper, Kunstler sued Judge Young and the *St. Croix Avis* for $4 million.

The court found for Judge Young and the newspaper on two grounds: First, the letter did not charge Kunstler with actual dishonesty or even unprofessional conduct; and, second, the *New York Times* rule applied, which holds that if a public figure has been libeled he or she must prove not only libel, but malice as well.

So the case was dismissed before trial, and the next time Mr. Kunstler goes to the Virgin Islands, it will probably be just for a vacation.

The hearsay rule is sometimes hard of hearing

Let's look at the hearsay rule and why you sometimes can't say what you hear. If you've ever seen or done something that may cause you to have to testify in court, you may run into a rule of evidence that causes more objections and arguments between the lawyers and whispered conferences at the judge's bench than anything else.

It's called the hearsay rule, which is almost better known for its exceptions than for the rule itself. The basis of the hearsay rule is that you often can't testify as to what you heard someone else say. The reasons are obvious: The jury and judge can't be sure that what someone else told you really did happen and was true. So if you see your neighbor run a red light, you can testify about it to your heart's content. But if someone else tells you your neighbor ran the red light, you can't testify because there's no way you can be cross-examined on the question of whether or not he ran the red light, because you simply weren't there.

However, the thing that causes most of the difficulty is not the hearsay rule itself, but the exceptions to it. The two that get the most use are the admission-against-interest exception and the state-of-mind exception. For example, if your neighbor tells you he ran a red light, you can testify to it. The reason is that the law presumes that if anybody makes an admission against his own interest, he would only do that if it were true. So truth of the statement is assumed, and now the only question at issue is whether the statement was said—something a person *can* be cross-examined on.

The second exception is the state-of-mind exception. A current example of this occurred recently during the trial of two Massachusetts state senators charged with extortion. The senators' lawyers sought to keep from the jury statements of another legislator that were allegedly made to the man on the stand, who was a senior official of the company that was allegedly extorted.

The judge allowed the statements in evidence, not for their truth, but to show how they contributed to the state of mind of the witness, who testified that the solicitation of one hundred thousand dollars made him very angry.

How a judge or jury can listen to a statement and not think about whether it's true or not has caused problems for many juries, to say nothing of those on trial. But it looks as if the hearsay rule lets you say what you heard only if the truth of what you said you heard doesn't matter.

Outlawing outlaws

Did you know that until recently, people could still be declared outlaws? A federal district court judge finally outlawed the North Carolina outlaw statute that allowed a person who had been delcared an outlaw to be shot on sight.

The way the law worked was that anyone could file an outlawry proclamation against anybody who committed a felony and fled after the commission of the crime. A judge could then issue a proclamation declaring the person an outlaw; and under the law, "If any person against whom a proclamation has been issued continues to stay out, lurks and conceals himself, any citizen of the state may capture, arrest, and bring him to justice, and in case of resistance, may slay him without accusation of any crime."

In the words of the court, the effect of the proclamation was to license the public to kill an accused felon if he ran after being called on to surrender. The federal court held the law unconstitutional because there was no provision for the outlaw to be heard.

The state argued in support of the law, saying that it should be taken for granted that fleeing felons don't want to be heard anyway. But the court pointed out that if a hearing was offered, the family of the fleeing felon might show up to diminish the risk of death for their relative.

The court also pointed out that between 1943 and 1975 only twenty persons had been declared outlaws and, therefore, all fleeing felons certainly were not treated the same. The court also found that the definition of felon was so broad that a college basketball player who threw a game could be treated the same as a multiple murderer or bank robber or, even worse, the college student could be outlawed while the murderer was not.

But it's over now, and in North Carolina at least, outlaws are outlawed and the memories of the frontier grow a bit dimmer.

When interests conflict

Conflict of interest—what does it really mean? For a long time now, well-meaning people in government and private life have tried to stamp out conflicts of interest. They have tried by state and federal law, regulations, local laws and ordinances, and codes of ethics. Many feel that about all this effort has succeeded in doing is eliminating conflict of interest from people who never had it to begin with and that there has been little or no effect on those in government and industry who do take advantage of their power.

Simply stated, conflict of interest means that your interests are in conflict and that you use your power as a legislator or government official, as a trustee, or as a company director for your own private gain rather than for the benefit of the people you are supposed to be working for. It may be as simple as the legislator who accepts cash to influence an official report, or it may be as subtle as the hospital trustee who votes against hiring the new administrator because he hopes the search committee will get around to interviewing his son-in-law.

The problem is that the opportunity for conflict of interest is everywhere. People who have acquired power usually have high expenses and a lot of friends and have done a lot of favors—and money, favors, and friends are the stock from which conflict of interest is made.

Most statutes in the area of conflict of interest use the criminal law to prohibit state or city employees from receiving money or anything of value from anybody other than the state or city they work for. But the laws haven't ended the conflict, while honest people who have a legitimate service to offer are disqualified from dealing with the government. For example, if a person happens to have the best asphalt paving company in town and wants to help his town by doing the best job at the most reasonable price, but also happens to be a selectman, he will risk jail if his company gets the contract.

Some lawmakers are considering another way. This would be to replace prohibition with the requirement of full disclosure— and careful monitoring by impartial people of any arrangement that could pose a potential conflict. This should allow us to find out what the interests are and make sure that what our officials do is in the *public* interest instead of their own.

The Magna Carta

June 15, 1980, was the 765th anniversary of the signing of the Magna Carta. The Magna Carta, which was brought to Philadelphia for the Bicentennial celebration, is a fascinating document, and perhaps it would do us well to look back to June 15, 1215, when a group of English barons gathered at a meadow called Runnymede. The barons were practical men who had some very specific grievances against King John and who one month earlier had renounced all allegiance to the crown. Now they gathered to present their grievances to King John for his seal. Little did they know that what they won at that meadow for their own self-interest would be won for many generations yet unborn.

The barons were upset over issues that have been duplicated up to the present day. They felt that taxes were simply too high. Since John (unlike his predecessor, Richard the Lion-Hearted) was not an absentee king, the dissatisfaction fell on him personally. In addition to the taxes being too high, John did something else not unknown in our day—he engaged in a very unpopular war, pouring a lot of money into a conflict with Philip Augustus, King of France. During Easter of 1215, the barons presented their demands, prompting King John's comment that may be paraphrased as, why don't they just ask for my whole kingdom? The Magna Carta was organized, somewhat haphazardly, into chapters dealing with the major problems of the day. It was very concerned with the feudal system, by which large sums were exacted from the barons. It also was the first statement of women's rights, with Chapter 8 providing that "no widow shall be compelled to marry so long as she has a mind to live without a husband."

The Magna Carta also had great influence on the administration of justice, providing us with a great deal of what we now take for granted, for instance, that local trials in the criminal law must be tried locally. It also contains the first statement of a trial by jury, with Chapter 39 providing: "No free man shall be taken, imprisoned, disseised, outlawed, banished, or in any way destroyed . . . excepting by the lawful judgment of his peers and by the law of the land."

In 1639 the Magna Carta was brought to America, with the general assembly of Maryland declaring that "the inhabitants of this Province shall have all the rights and liberties according to the great Charter of England." Most of the newly forming states drew upon the language and principles embodied in the document that was signed at Runnymede centuries ago.

Honesty in government

Can you legislate honesty in government? There seems to be an epidemic of exposed conflicts of interest across the nation. In Massachusetts, two state senators were found guilty of extorting money from a New York-based consulting firm as the price of influencing a legislative report. That inspired the Massachusetts legislature to work on a code of ethics. Newspapers in Connecticut reported that the state attorney general traveled frequently on behalf of a private client who was trying to take over the Fontainebleau Hotel. The Connecticut general assembly then prepared legislation to further define conflict of interest. The U.S. Congress was the scene of a major scandal involving a lot of money from Korea that found its way to members of Congress.

The House of Representatives passed a code of ethics limiting members to earning no more than 15 percent over the nearly thirteen-thousand-dollar pay raise that went into effect just before the code of ethics was passed. And a report by the General Accounting Office reported that relatives of at least thirty-four employees of the Federal Communications Commission had financial interests in companies regulated by the FCC. Congress then considered tighter financial disclosure requirements for employees of federal regulatory agencies.

President Carter dealt with the subject very early in his administration, acknowledging that the present federal laws on the subject are inadequate. The president chose to deal with this issue by having high officials of his administration sign a letter of agreement. The official promised to disclose all assets and liabilities as well as sources of income. The official also had to promise that for two years after leaving government service, he or she wouldn't have any business contact with the people or bureaus worked with during his or her government service.

The president himself sold a lot of his stock and put his interest in the family businesses into a trust over which he had no management powers, although he could receive cash distributions of income or principal.

So a lot of people are working very hard to come up with stricter rules of just what is and is not a conflict of interest. Many of the authors of the rules are worried about just how they can be enforced once they are written down. It may be that honesty of the legislator can't be legislated, and that integrity of the regulator can't be regulated—except from within themselves.

A different side of the law

If anything can go wrong, it will. That's the opening line of a book that looks at a different side of the law. The name of the book, by Arthur Block, is *Murphy's Law and Other Reasons Why Things Go Wrong.*

Murphy's Law opens with some lesser-known lawmakers, such as Phenagle. Phenagle's first law is that if an experiment works, something has gone wrong. And Phenagle's third law is that in the correction of data, the figure most obviously correct beyond all need of checking is the mistake. Phenagle's fourth law is that once a job is fouled up, anything done to improve it only makes it worse.

The author then moves on to some rather disturbing laws, including Commoner's second law of ecology, which is, nothing ever goes away. Then comes Howe's law, which says that everyone has a scheme that will not work; and Zmyrge's first law of evolving system dynamics, which says once you open a can of worms the only way to recan them is to use a bigger can. This particular chapter closes with the nonreciprocal law of expectation, which is that negative expectations yield negative results and positive expectations yield negative results.

Then the author examines applied murphology, such as, any wire cut to length will be too short; and a failure will not appear until a unit has passed final inspection; and after the last of sixteen mounting screws has been removed from an access panel, it will be discovered that the wrong access panel has been removed.

Then there's Atwood's fourteenth chronology, which is that no books are lost by lending except those you particularly wanted to keep. But perhaps my favorite is Cole's law, which—you guessed it—is thinly sliced cabbage. And why don't we end with Hartley's first law, which is, you can lead a horse to water, but if you can get him to float on his back, you've really got something.

CASE CITATIONS

Page Source

82   *Schneider v. Coe,* 405 A. 2d 682 (Del. Sup. Ct. 1979)
83   *Russell v. Salem Transp. Co.,* 61 N.J. 502, 295 A. 2d 862 (1972)
86   *People v. Fitzgerald,* 45 N.Y. 2d 574, 384 N.E. 2d 649, 412 N.Y.S. 2d 102
        (1979)
88   *In re Hofbauer,* 65 A.D. 2d 108, 411 N.Y.S. 2d 416 (3d Dept. 1979)
90   *Hart v. Brown,* 29 Conn. Supp. 368, 289 A. 2d 386 (1972)
93   *Miranda v. Arizona,* 384 U.S. 436 (1966)
95   *Dunaway v. New York,* 47 U.S.L.W. 4635 (U.S. June 5, 1979)
96   *Rhode Island v. Innis,* 48 U.S.L.W. 4506 (U.S. May 12, 1980)
97   *People v. Johnson,* 99 Misc. 2d 450, 416 N.Y.S. 2d 495 Sup. Ct N.Y. Co.
        (1979)
98   *Sheppard v. Maxwell,* 384 U.S. 333 (1966)
101   *Mackey v. Montrym,* 47 U.S.L.W. 4798 (U.S. June 25, 1979)
104   *Michigan v. Tyler,* 46 U.S.L.W. 4533 (U.S. May 31, 1978)
105   *Mincey v. Arizona,*   46 U.S.L.W. 4737 (U.S. June 21, 1978)
106   *State v. Gallagher,* 275 N.W. 2d 803 (Minn. Sup. Ct. 1979)
107   *People v. Fugate,* 24 Crim. L. Rep. (BNA) 2513 (Cal. Ct. App. 1979)
109   *Ozuma v. State,* 25 Crim. L. Rep. (BNA) 2099 (Tex. Ct. Crim. App. 1979)
112   *State v. Helfrich,* 48 U.S.L.W. 2308 (Mont. Sup. Ct. Oct. 3, 1979)
113   *Ybarra v. Illinois,* 48 U.S.L.W. 4023 (U.S. Nov. 28, 1979)
118   *State v. Prendergrass,* 24 Crim. L. Rep. (BNA) 2199 (Mont. Sup. Ct. 1979)
119   *United States v. Condolon,* 600 F. 2d 7 (4th Cir. 1979)
120   *United States v. Wright,* 577 F. 2d 378 (6th Cir. 1978)
123   *People v. Blair,* 48 U.S.L.W. 2404 (Cal. Sup. Ct. Nov. 9, 1979)
126   *People v. Rubin,* 96 Cal. App. 3d 968, 158 Cal. Rptr. 488 (1979)
131   *McIntosh v. Washington,* 20 Crim. L. Rep. (BNA) 258 (1977)
132   *Skokie v. National Socialist Party,* 51 Ill. App. 3d 279, 366 N.E. 2d 347
        (1977)
134   *Rosado v. Civiletti,* 48 U.S.L.W. 2731 (2d Cir. Apr. 23, 1980)
134   *Thompson v. County of Almeda,* 88 Cal. App. 3d 936, 152 Cal. Rptr. 226
        (1979)
137   *United States v. Griffin,* 462 F. Supp. 928 (E.D.Ark. 1979)
141   *Holdman v. Olim,* 59 Hawaii 346, 581 P. 2d 1164 (1978)
145   *State v. Major,* 243 Ga. 255, 253 S.E. 2d 724 (1979)
146   *Rummel v. Estelle,* 48 U.S.L.W. 4261 (U.S. Mar. 18, 1980)
147   *M. v. Superior Court of Sonoma County,* 25 Cal. 3d 608, 601 P. 2d 572, 159
        Cal. Rptr. 340 (1979)
148   *Mayberry v. Oklahoma,* 603 P. 2d 1150 (Ct. Crim. App. 1979)
150   *MacLean v. First Northwest Industries, Inc.,* 24 Wash. App. 161, 600 P. 2d
        1027 (1979)
151   *Baxter Springs v. Bryant,* 226 Kan. 383, 598 P. 2d 1051 (1979)
157   FTC Proposed Anendments, 16 C.F.R.
158   *Nik-o-Lok Co. v. Carey,* 85 Misc. 2d 189, 378 N.Y.S. 2d 936 (Sup. Ct.
        Albany Co. 1976)
160   39 C.F.R. §103–529 (1974)
161   *Pacific Legal Foundation v. Department of Transportation,* 47 U.S.L.W. 2520
        (D.C. Cir. Feb. 1, 1979)
166   *National Commission on Egg Nutrition v. FTC,* 570 F. 2d 157 (7th Cir.
        1979)

Page **Source**

167 *Jones v. Rath Packing Co.,* 45 U.S.L.W. 4323 (U.S. Mar. 29, 1977)

169 New York Times, May 27, 1977, § B, at 1, col. 1

174 C.A.B. Reg. 76–158 (1976)

180 *United States v. Philadelphia,* 48 U.S.L.W. 2321 (E.D.Pa. 1979)

181 *Parvi v. Kingston,* 41 N.Y. 2d 553, 362 N.E. 2d 960, 394 N.Y.S. 2d 161 (1977)

182 *Sears, Roebuck & Co. v. San Diego County District Council of Carpenters,* 48 U.S.L.W. 2227 (Cal. Sup. Ct. Sept. 14, 1979)

183 *Richards v. United States Tennis Association,* 93 Misc. 2d 713, 400 N.Y.S. 2d 267 (Sup. Ct. N.Y. Co. 1977)

186 *Greene v. Memphis,* 48 U.S.L.W. 2328 (6th Cir. Nov. 1, 1979)

187 *Smith v. Fussenich* 440 F. Supp. 1077 (D.Conn. 1977)

188 *Personnel Admr. v. Feeney,* 442 U.S. 256 (1979)

193 *Matthews v. State,* 23 Crim. L. Rep. (BNA) 2484 (Fla. Sup. Ct. 1978)

198 *Shea v. Board of Medical Examiners,* 81 Cal. App. 3d 564, 146 Cal. Rptr. 653 (1978)

200 *McGee v. Riekhof,* 442 F. Supp. 1276 (D.Mont. 1978)

201 *Birt v. Saint Mary Mercy Hospital, Inc.,* 370 N.E. 2d 379 (Ind. App. Ct. 1977)

202 *Park v. Chessin,* 60 A.D. 2d 80, 400 N.Y.S. 2d 110 (2d Dept. 1977)

203 *Whalen v. Roe,* 429 U.S. 589 (1977)

207 *Rennie v. Klein,* 47 U.S.L.W. 2353 (D.N.J. Nov. 9, 1978)

208 *Landeros v. Flood,* 17 Cal. 3d 399, 551 P. 2d 389, 131 Cal. Rptr. 69 (1976)

212 *Sparger v. Worley Hospital, Inc.,* 547 S.W. 2d 582 (Tex. Sup. Ct. 1977)

217 *Cathemer v. Hunter,* 27 Ariz. App. 780, 558 P. 2d 975 (1976)

219 *Wilczynski v. Goodman,* 47 U.S.L.W. 2803 (Ill. App. Ct. June 5, 1979)

219 *Johnson v. New York,* 37 N.Y. 2d 378, 334 N.E. 2d 590, 372 N.Y.S. 2d 638 (1975)

221 *In re Quakenbush,* 156 N.J. Super. 282, 383 A. 2d 785 (1978)

229 New York State Bar Committee on Professional Ethics; Opinions, No. 479 (1978)

230 *Morrell v. State,* 46 U.S.L.W. 2506 (Alaska Sup. Ct. Mar. 3, 1978)

231 *Willing v. Mazzocone,* 47 U.S.L.W. 2253 (Pa. Sup. Ct. Oct. 6, 1978)

234 *Schleper v. Ford Motor Co.,* 47 U.S.L.W. 2303 (8th Cir. Oct. 23, 1978)

235 *Maxwell v. Superior Court of Los Angeles County,* 48 U.S.L.W. 2553 (Cal. Ct. App. Feb. 1, 1980)

236 *Cruz v. Beto,* 48 U.S.L.W. 2305 (5th Cir. Oct. 5, 1979)

237 *Reese v. Danforth,* 48 U.S.L.W. 2291 (Pa. Sup. Ct. Oct. 9, 1979)

237 *People v. Felder,* 48 U.S.L.W. 2004 (N.Y. Ct. App. June 7, 1979)

238 *Stahl v. Balsarra,* 60 Hawaii 144, 587 P. 2d 1210 (1978)

239 *Chicago v. Hertz Commercial Leasing Corp.,* 71 Ill. 2d 331, 375 N.E. 2d 1285 (1978)

240 *Kosters v. Seven-Up Co.,* 47 U.S.L.W. 2656 (6th Cir. Mar. 26, 1979)

241 *Turner v. General Motors Corp.,* 47 U.S.L.W. 2656 (Tex. Sup. Ct. Mar. 21, 1979)

242 *Everett v. Buckey Warren, Inc.,* Mass. Adv. Sh. 2424 (1978)

243 *Cardozo v. True,* 342 So. 2d 1053 (Fla. Dist. Ct. App. 1977), *cert. denied,* 353 So. 2d 674 (1977)

Page Source

248   16 C.F.R. § 455 (1976)

249   *Rudisell v. Fifth Third Bank,* 48 U.S.L.W. 2781 (6th Cir. May 20, 1980)

250   *B & M Homes, Inc. v. Hogan,* 376 So. 2d 667 (Ala Sup. Ct. 1979)

251   *People v. Lavender,* 48 U.S.L.W. 2403 (N.Y. Ct. App. Nov. 20, 1979)

252   *Pearlman v. Time,* 4 Media L. Rep. 1529 (Ill. Ct. App. 1978)

253   *Catania v. State Farm Life Insurance Co.,* 48 U.S.L.W. 2177 (Nev. Sup. Ct. Aug. 16, 1979)

259   *Wawszkiewicz v. Treasury Department,* 48 U.S.L.W. 2405 (D.C. Cir. Nov. 20, 1979)

261   *Corso v. Crawford Dog & Cat Hospital, Inc.,* 97 Misc. 2d 530, 415 N.Y.S. 2d 182 (Civ. Ct. Queens Co. 1979)

264   *Equitable Life Assurance Society v. Grosvenor,* 426 F. Supp. 67 (W.D.Tenn. 1976)

265   *Berman & Sons, Inc. v. Jefferson,* Mass. Adv. Sh. 2459 (1979)

267   *Kramarsky v. Stahl Management,* 92 Misc. 2d 1030, 401 N.Y.S. 2d 943 (Sup. Ct. N.Y. Co. 1977)

269   Brandel, *Electronic Funds Transp. Comm. and Const. Law Aspects,* Com. L.J. 78 (1977)

270   *Desselles v. J.C. Penney Co.,* 48 U.S.L.W. 2390 (E.D.La. Nov. 26, 1979)

277   *Causey v. Pan American World Airways, Inc.,* 66 F.R.D. 392 (E.D.Va 1975)

279   *Manfredonia v. American Airlines, Inc.* 47 U.S.L.W. 2745

281   *Taylor v. Superior Court of Los Angeles County,* 48 U.S.L.W. 2196 (Cal. Sup. Ct. Aug. 21, 1979)

282   *Albuquerque v. Redding,* 95 N.M. 757, 605 P. 2d 1156 (1980)

284   Prosser, Law of Torts 378 (4th ed. 1971); *Wolfson v. Chelist,* 284 S.W. 2d 447 (Mo. Sup. Ct. 1955)

285   *Robinson v. Lindsay,* 92 Wash. 2d 410, 598 P. 2d 392 (1979)

287   108 Wash. Daily Rptr. 277 (1980)

289   *Ryder Truck Rental, Inc. v. Korte,* 357 So. 2d 228 (Fla. Dist. Ct. App. 1978)

289   *Black Indus., Inc. v. Emco Helicopters, Inc.,* 19 Wash. App. 697, 577 P. 2d 610 (1978)

290   *Maltman v. Sauer,* 84 Wash. 2d 975, 530 P. 2d 254 (1975)

290   *People v. Thomas,* 46 U.S.L.W. 2238 (N.Y. Sup. Ct. Oct. 28, 1977)

291   *Rieser v. District of Columbia,* 21 Crim. L. Rep. (BNA) 2502 (1977)

294   *Wilson v. Continental Insurance Cos.,* 87 Wis. 2d 310, 274 N.W. 2d 679 (1979)

296   *Uzzell v. Friday,* 47 U.S.L.W. 2505 (4th Cir. Feb. 2, 1979)

297   *DeRonde v. Regents of University of California,* 48 U.S.L.W. 2507 (Cal. Ct. App. Jan. 21, 1980)

299   *Lexington Theological Seminary, Inc. v. Vance,* 47 U.S.L.W. 2788 (Ky. Ct. App. May 18, 1979)

300   *Gomes v. Rhode Island Interscholastic League,* 47 U.S.L.W. 2749 (D.R.I. May 1, 1979)

301   *Blameuser v. Andrews,* 48 U.S.L.W. 2121 (E.D.Wis. Sept. 30, 1979)

302   *Americans United for Separation of Church & State v. Porter,* 48 U.S.L.W. 2543 (W.D.Mich. Jan. 23, 1980)

303   *Mayo v. Satan and His Staff,* 54 F.R.D. 283 (W.D.Pa. 1971)

304   *Bass v. Aetna Insurance Co.,* 370 So. 2d 511 (La. Sup. Ct. 1979)

Page Source

306   *Native American Church v. United States,* 25 Crim L. Rep. (BNA) 2142
       (1979)
307   *International Society for Krishna Consciousness v. Eaves,* 48 U.S.L.W. 2189
       (5th Cir. Aug. 30, 1979)
308   *Frank v. State,* 26 Crim. L. Rep. (BNA) 2439 (Ala. Sup. Ct. 1979)
314   *Doe v. Civil Service Commission,* 48 U.S.L.W. 2541 (S.D.N.Y. Jan. 16,
       1980)
315   *Berg v. Lacrosse Cooler Co.,* 48 U.S.L.W. 2505 (7th Cir. Jan. 8, 1980)
317   *NLRB v. Modern Carpet Indus., Inc.,* 48 U.S.L.W. 2475 (10th Cir. Dec.
       28, 1979)
318   *Ashton v. Civiletti,* 48 U.S.L.W. 2261 (D.C. Cir. Oct. 4, 1979)
321   *Snepp v. United States,* 48 U.S.L.W. 3527 (U.S. Feb. 19, 1980)
322   *Jefferies v. Harris County Community Action Ass'n.,* 48 U.S.L.W. 2733 (5th
       Cir. Apr. 21, 1980)
323   *Avigliano v. Sumitomo Shoji America, Inc.,* 473 F. Supp. 506 (S.D.N.Y.
       1979)
326   *Fireman's Fund Insurance Co. v. Indus. Comm'n. of Arizona,* 119 Ariz. 51,
       579 P. 2d 555 (1978)
328   *Carroll v. Talman Federal Savings & Loan Ass'n,* 604 F. 2d 1028 (7th Cir.
       1979)
329   *Colduvell v. Commonwealth, Unemployment Compensation Board of Review,*
       408 A. 2d 1207 (Pa. Commw. Ct. 1980)
329   *Dependents of Ondler v. Peace Officeers Benefit Fund,* 48 U.S.L.W. 2511
       (Minn. Sup. Ct. Jan. 4, 1980)
331   *Martin v. Platt,* 47 U.S.L.W. 2655 (Ind. Ct. App. Mar. 26, 1979)
332   *Pevsner v. Commissioner,* 48 U.S.L.W. 2200 (T.C. Aug. 13, 1979)
333   *Ford Motor Co. v. NLRB,* 47 U.S.L.W. 4498 (U.S. May 14, 1979)
334   *Davis v. NLRB,* 48 U.S.L.W. 2671 (7th Cir. Mar. 19, 1980)
335   *Hubbard Regional Hospital v. NLRB,* 98 L.R.R.M. 2891
336   *Moore v. Harris,* 49 U.S.L.W. 2008 (4th Cir. June 12, 1980)
339   *Lugosi v. Universal Pictures,* 25 Cal. 3d 813, 603 P. 2d 425, 160 Cal. Rptr,
       323 (1979)
342   *Zamora v. State,* 23 Crim. L. Rep. (BNA) 2491 (Fla. Ct. App. 1978)
345   *FCC v. Midwest Video Corp.,* 47 U.S.L.W. 4335 (U.S. Apr. 2, 1979)
347   *Miller v. Universal City Studios, Inc.,* 460 F. Supp. 984 (S.D.Fla. 1978)
350   *Zweig v. Hearst Corp.,* 594 F. 2d 1261 (9th Cir. 1979)
352   *Wojtowicz v. Delacorte Press,* 58 A.D. 2d 45, 395 N.Y.S. 2d 205, (1st Dept.
       1977)
355   *Conklin v. Sloss,* 86 Cal. App. 3d 241, 150 Cal. Rptr. 121 (1978)
357   *Philadelphia v. Washington Post Co.,* 48 U.S.L.W. 2422 (E.D.Pa. Dec. 5,
       1979)
358   *State Division of Human Rights v. Binghampton Press Co.,* 67 A.D. 2d 231,
       415 N.Y.S. 2d 523 (4th Dept 1979)
361   47 Colorado L. Rev. 422 (1976)
362   *Fountainbleau Hotel Corp. v. Forty-Five Twenty-Five, Inc.,* 114 So. 2d 357
       (Fla. Ct. App. 1959)
363   *British Airways Board v. Port Authority of New York,* 558 F. 2d 75 (2d Cir.
       1977), *on remand,* 437 F. Supp. 804 (S.D.N.Y. 1977), *mod.,* 564 F. 2d
       1002 (2d Cir. 1977)

TABLE OF CASES

INDEX

Finding a Lawyer
to Suit Your Case

A few easy questions
to keep you from having
hard times
with your lawyer later on

- When do I need a lawyer?
- How do I find a lawyer?
- Do I have a case?
- How much will it cost, will it cost more
  than it's worth, and exactly how will I be
  paying?
- How long will it take?
- What's going to happen next?

For the answers to these and other questions for you
and your lawyer, write for Neil Chayet's free brochure.
Send a self-addressed, stamped envelope to:

"Looking at the Law"
Dept. R
WEEI-CBS Radio
4450 Prudential Tower
Boston, MA 02199